W9-ABY-169

Wellesley Studies in Critical Theory,
Literary History, and Culture
(Vol. 8)

AMERICAN WOMEN SHORT STORY WRITERS

GARLAND REFERENCE LIBRARY
OF THE HUMANITIES
(VOL. 1737)

Wellesley Studies in Critical Theory, Literary History, and Culture

General Editor: William E. Cain

MAKING FEMINIST HISTORY
The Literary Scholarship of Sandra M. Gilbert and Susan Gubar
edited by William E. Cain

TEACHING THE CONFLICTS
Gerald Graff, Curricular Reform, and the Culture Wars
edited by William E. Cain

AMERICAN WOMEN SHORT STORY WRITERS
A Collection of Critical Essays
edited by Julie Brown

ALTERNATIVE IDENTITIES
The Self in Literature, History, Theory
Linda Marie Brooks

THE CANON IN THE CLASSROOM
The Pedagogical Implications of Canon Revision in American Literature
edited by John Alberti

GENETIC CODES OF CULTURE?
The Deconstruction of Tradition by Kuhn, Bloom, and Derrida
William Roger Schultz

THE NEW CODES OF CRITICISM AND CONTEMPORARY LITERARY THEORY
Connections and Continuities
edited by William J. Spurlin and Michael Fischer

REGIONALISM RECONSIDERED
New Approaches to the Field
edited by David M. Jordan

REREADING MODERNISM
New Directions in Feminist Criticism
edited by Lisa Rado

AMERICAN WOMEN SHORT STORY WRITERS

A Collection of Critical Essays

Edited by
Julie Brown

GARLAND PUBLISHING, INC.
NEW YORK & LONDON / 1995

Library of Congress Cataloging-in-Publication Data

American women short story writers : a collection of critical essays / edited by Julie Brown.
p. cm. — (Garland reference library of the humanities ; vol. 1737. Wellesley studies in critical theory, literary history, and culture ; vol. 8)
Includes bibliographical references and index.
ISBN 0-8153-1338-1 (alk. paper)
1. Short stories, American—History and criticism. I. Brown, Julie, 1961– . II. Series: Garland reference library of the humanities ; vol. 1737. III. Series: Garland reference library of the humanities. Wellesley studies in critical theory, literary history, and culture ; vol. 8.
PS374.S5A3968 1995
813'.0109—dc20 94-8739

Printed on acid-free, 250-year-life paper
Manufactured in the United States of America

For Bobby

Contents

General Editor's Introduction

The volumes in this series, Wellesley Studies in Critical Theory, Literary History, and Culture, are designed to reflect, develop, and extend important trends and tendencies in contemporary criticism. The careful scrutiny of literary texts in their own right of course remains a crucial part of the work that critics and teachers perform: this traditional task has not been devalued or neglected. But other types of interdisciplinary and contextual work are now being done, in large measure as a result of the emphasis on "theory" that began in the late 1960s and early 1970s and that has accelerated since that time. Critics and teachers now examine texts of all sorts—literary and non-literary alike—and, more generally, have taken the entire complex, multi-faceted field of culture as the object for their analytical attention. The discipline of literary studies has radically changed, and the scale and scope of this series is intended to illustrate this challenging fact.

Theory has signified many things, but one of the most crucial has been the insistent questioning of familiar categories and distinctions. As theory has grown in its scope and intensified in importance, it has reoriented the idea of the literary canon: There is no longer a single canon, but many canons. It has also opened up and complicated the meanings of history, and the materials and forms that constitute it. Literary history continues to be vigorously written, but now as a kind of history that intersects with other histories that involve politics, economics, race relations, the role of women in society, and many more. And the breadth of this historical inquiry has impelled many in literary studies to view themselves more as cultural critics and general intellectuals than as literary scholars.

Theory, history, culture: these are the formidable terms around which the volumes in this series have been organized. A number of these volumes will be the product of a single author or editor. But perhaps even more of them will be collaborative ventures, emerging from the joint enterprise of editors, essayists, and respondents or commentators. In each volume, and as a whole, the series will aim to highlight both distinctive contributions to knowledge and a process of exchange, discussion, and debate. It will make available new kinds of work, as well as fresh approaches to criticism's traditional tasks, and indicate new ways through which such work can be done.

William E. Cain
Wellesley College

Acknowledgments

Special thanks to Amy Shoenberger for research and typing. Thanks to Teresa Hirt for her professional editing assistance. Thanks to Youngstown State University for giving me time off to work on this project and for financial support to hire student aides. Thanks also to my editor, William Cain, for his encouragement and help through a difficult time.

Introduction

Julie Brown

I write short stories. I read short stories by American women. I teach short stories by American women. For a long time, I believed there was little literary criticism or theory available on American women's short stories—over the years I have pieced together information found in genre studies, women's studies, and American studies, compiling files for myself and readers for my students. Until I read Alicia Ostriker's wonderful *Stealing the Language: The Emergence of Women's Poetry in America* (1986) and Sandra Gilbert and Susan Gubar's comprehensive *The Madwoman in the Attic: The Woman Writer and the Nineteenth-Century Literary Imagination* (1984), I hadn't realized that, alongside these books outlining the histories of women's poetry and women's novels (respectively), a book outlining the history of women's short stories was needed.

In her introduction, Ostriker discusses her reasons for launching an in-depth study of women's poetry. Looking back over her literary education, she laments,

> My opinions on poetry were . . . formed predominantly by reading male poets and by the dicta of professors and critics who eloquently and reverently represented what Matthew Arnold called "the best that has been thought and said" in western culture. That their eloquence veiled gender bias, and that what they believed to be "universal" was only partial, did not occur to me. (2)

A poet herself, Ostriker must have found it difficult to value her own work when the work of others like her had been systematically ignored and discounted for so long. She eventually came to realize that "we cannot measure the work of women poets, past or present, without a thorough—and if possible demystified—awareness of the critical context in which they have composed and continue to compose their work" (2).

Gilbert and Gubar set out to write a historical study of (British) women's novels for similar reasons. As they note in their preface, "We realized that, like many other feminists, we were trying to recover not only a major (and neglected) female literature but a whole (neglected) female history" (xii). Their monumental study not only outlines the history of women's novels but also gives important information about the biographies of the women who wrote them, their thematic and stylistic concerns, the economic climates in which they published, and the public's reactions to their works.

Why has no one written such a comprehensive study of American women's short stories?

Short story genre critics often preface their studies by stating how neglected the short story genre is; then they proceed to offer a study that adds to the body of story criticism that probably began with Poe's review of Hawthorne's *Twice Told Tales* (1842) and continues through such works as Clare Hanson's *Re-reading the Short Story* (1989). Hanson's question is typical: "Why has the short story been neglected, in both academic and non-academic critical circles? It is a form, after all, which is immensely popular with readers, and perhaps more importantly, with writers" (1). What Hanson and her peers fail to notice, however, is that the short story in general (read: male short story) has indeed received a great deal of attention over the past 150 years but that the female short story in particular has received very little.

Short story criticism has reached us in two waves. The first wave began, perhaps, with Poe's review of Hawthorne's *Twice Told Tales* (1842), continued through Brander Matthews's *The Philosophy of the Short Story* (1901), and culminated in studies by Robert Wilson Neal (1918), Fred Lewis Pattee (1923), Roger Cuff (1953), and Frank O'Connor (1963). Predictably, these critics focus on the lives, texts, and theories of white male practitioners of the short story form. Most of these "first wave" critics do not even mention women authors, although an exception to this group is Pattee. Unfortunately, Pattee mentions women authors only to disparage their efforts (more on this follows).

When I examined second wave criticism, beginning with Charles May's *Short Story Theories* (1976), I was surprised to find the same thing: building on the criticism that preceded them (always a quotation from Poe, a nod to Matthews, an acknowledgment of O'Connor), these critics also focus mainly on male authors and their stories, nearly ignoring the contributions that women and other minorities have made to the genre. May's book does include 7 essays (out of 24) by female critics, but beyond a few brief references, there are no essays about women authors or their stories.

Susan Lohafer's *Coming to Terms with the Short Story* (1983) does not focus on women writers either, except for a few pages on Joyce Carol Oates and Kate Chopin. Valerie Shaw's *The Short Story* (1983) is dominated by references to male-authored texts and theories as well. In her bibliography of story writers, for example, she lists 40 male authors and only 12 female.

Finally, Clare Hanson's *Re-reading the Short Story* does contain one essay called "Gender and Genre" by Mary Eagleton (there are also two essays about Doris Lessing's stories, but these are not discussed in terms of gender). "Gender and Genre" begins with two odd disclaimers. Eagleton says, "Firstly, I am not speaking as an expert on the short story. . . . I am speaking from my interest in feminist literary criticism, but here lies my second disclaimer, for feminist criticism which has had so much to say about women writers . . . has had much less to say about genre" (55). She then goes on to discuss the general aims of feminist literary criticism but says very little about short stories by women, ending with the suggestion that we apply everything she says about novels to short stories.

Both waves of short story genre criticism have focused on five areas. Each of these areas is so slanted toward male authors that one would almost think that women have hardly written short stories at all, when in fact, I would estimate that one-third to one-half of all stories written between 1820 and 1900 were by women (see Gilbert and Gubar 5).

The first task of the short story genre critic is usually to define the short story, beginning with Poe's definition that a story be read in "one sitting" and produce a "unified effect." H.G. Wells provides a particularly phallic description of the short story. As quoted by Shaw, Wells said that "in order to produce its 'one single vivid effect,' the short story must 'seize the attention at the outset, and never relaxing, gather it together more and more until the climax is reached.' . . . [It must] 'explode and finish before interruption occurs or fatigue sets in'" (48). It should be noted that, while definitions of the form differ, most critics feel compelled to *define* the genre, often using masculine terms.

The second task has been to pinpoint the origins of the short story. It is usually traced back to Washington Irving, or further back to Boccaccio's *The Decameron* (1351–1353) or Chaucer's *The Canturbury Tales* (1387–1400). But Somerset Maugham has gone even further back than this, to an origin of which contemporary American author Robert Bly would certainly approve. "It is natural," Maugham says, "for men to tell tales, and I suppose the short story was created in the night of time when the hunter, to beguile the leisure of his fellows when they had eaten and drunk their fill, narrated by the cavern fire some fantastic incident he had heard of" (Shaw 83). Obviously, the identification of this origin makes it clear that the short story was a product of the male imagination and that, since females presumably never left the cave to hunt, they never had stories to tell.

Thirdly, once the critic has established the short story origins, the writer moves on to trace the *history* of the genre. In American literature this often follows the chain of Irving/Melville/ Hawthorne/Poe to Harte/Twain/Fitzgerald/ Hemingway to Barth/Coover/Barthelme/Carver. Women, especially lesbians and women of color, are almost always excluded from this lineup, to differing degrees. Nina Baym explains this phenomenon by telling us that "the critic does not like the idea of women as writers, does not believe that women can be writers, and hence does not see them even when they are right before his eyes" (64). One exception to this is Pattee's *The Development of the American Short Story*, which does mention numerous women authors, a few of them in a positive light. This work is important because he preserves the names of many women writers whose works have gone out of print since he wrote his study in 1923. Unfortunately, most of his remarks about their stories are ambivalent at best, derogatory at worst. Of Elizabeth Stuart Phelps's story "'Tenty Scran," for example, he notes that "even a sophomore might point out its inherent weakness of structure" (179). Of Rose Terry Cooke, he notes, "That the short story differed from the novel save alone in the attribute of length she never seems to have discovered" (176). Pattee devotes an entire chapter to "The Rise of the Lady's Book," where he examines periodicals such as *Godey's* that published numerous women authors. His thesis seems to be that women "ruined" the genre with their "sentimental" stories, and it is with a sigh of relief that he explains how gentlemen's magazines and literary magazines rescued the genre from "feminized fiction" (169). This sentiment is echoed 40 years later by William Peden, who reassuringly informs us that *Esquire* and *Playboy* have been "major forces" (13) in contemporary short fiction. Apparently, he never read *Redbook* or *Cosmopolitan*. Furthermore, with the rise of *The New Yorker* story, Harold Ross (an early *New Yorker* editor) notes that fiction is no longer written for the "little old lady in Dubuque" (Peden 11).

In the fourth task, once the history is established, each critic then identifies the *masters* of the genre. Most of these pronouncements are articulated in words similar to A.E. Coppard, when he says (as quoted by O'Connor) that "if he ever edited an anthology of short stories he would have an easy job because half the book would be by Chekhov, and the other half by Maupassant" (62). A woman writer might be identified as the best local colorist or the best teller of the ghost story, or even as the best woman writer, but never the best writer, and certainly never the master (mistress) of the genre.

Finally, the fifth task of the short story genre critic is *theorizing* the short story. After history has answered the *who, when,* and *where* questions, theory begins to ask *how* and *why.* Short story critics mainly offer theories explaining how short stories are written (or should be written) and how short stories are read (or should be read). These theories usually begin with the words of Poe and Brander Matthews, and if we are lucky, they might look in the direction of Virginia Woolf or Eudora Welty. These theories then end in agreement with male theorists such as Tzvetan Todorov, Jean-François Lyotard, or Wolfgang Iser. A sad recurrence is the development of theory that denigrates stories by women rather than considering the possibility that women might write differently from men. Somerset Maugham, for example, offered a theory that the best short stories are "well made" and "strongly plotted" and then accused Katherine Mansfield of writing plotless stories "using atmosphere to 'decorate a story so thin' that it could not exist without its 'trimmings'" (Shaw 16). (A feminist critic, such as Shaw, would recognize the lyrical nature of Mansfield's work that deliberately "dislodge[s] the narrative element" [Shaw 16]). This is the same phenomenon that has also been used to criticize the brilliance and originality of women's poetry: "Originality in a woman poet is censured by the commentator or is invisible to him because it does not resemble masculine originalities with which he is already familiar" (Ostriker 6).

I believe Clare Hanson comes closest to identifying the direction in which short story theorists should move in the future. In her excellent introduction, she ponders the fact that "the short story has offered itself to losers and loners, exiles, women, blacks—writers who for one reason or another have not been part of the ruling 'narrative' or epistemological/ experiential framework of their society" (2). Ironically, stories by these marginalized groups have been excluded from academic study at the same time the academics were pleading that the genre itself was excluded. Hanson takes the first step toward a feminist critique of the genre when she posits that "the short story has been from its inception a particularly appropriate vehicle for the expression of the ex-centric, alienated vision of women" (3). How sad it is, then, in light of this observation, that Hanson included in her collection only one essay that could have discussed women's contributions to the short story genre (Mary Eagleton's "Gender and Genre") but didn't.

Feminist critics have produced essays, articles, and books that perform the delightful and important tasks of rescuing, identifying, analyzing, and celebrating works by women writers. Feminist criticism has devoted itself to helping us understand the poems and novels that women have written, but curiously little scholarship has been written about the woman's short story, and what scholarship does exist is scattered. Individual stories are sometimes singled out, especially Charlotte Perkins Gilman's "The Yellow Wallpaper." Individual authors, such as Eudora Welty or Flannery O'Connor, are often studied. The short story is used to illustrate such literary trends as local color, female gothic, or modernism. Recently, feminist scholars have been reevaluating the work of female magazine editors such as Sarah Hale. But, to my knowledge, there has not yet been a systematic book-length evaluation of the contributions that American women have made to the short story genre. And to begin such a study, we must begin with questions.

Will we use the same *definition* for women's short stories that have been used to describe male stories? Will we define the genre anew? Will we decide that such definitions are limiting and abandon them altogether? Edith Wharton (as quoted by Barraca) reminds us that "general rules in art are useful chiefly as a lamp in a mine, or a handrail down a black stairway; they are necessary for the sake of the guidance they give, but it is a mistake, once they are formulated, to be too much in awe of them" (8). Thus, it may be that feminist critics will refuse to define the short story, for definitions limit, exclude, and deaden our capacity for surprise. Eudora Welty says that "a short story writer can try anything . . . because the power and stirring of the mind never rests. It is what the power will try that will most pertinently define the short story. Not rules, not aesthetics, not problems and their solution" (Shaw 1).

Will it be necessary for us to pinpoint the *origin* of the woman's short story? It might be difficult to name the first female short story author in America, since many women published either using masculine pen names or anonymously. Susan Koppelman has noted that Catherine Maria Sedgewick (1789–1867) and Lydia Maria Child (1802–1880) were among the earliest women to publish their stories, both publishing in the mid-1820s ("Interim" 2). Koppelman maintains, furthermore, that it is pointless to argue about who wrote the first story anyway, since "along with Irving and a few other early colleagues, this *group* of writers invented that fluid, undefinable but recognizable genre we know as the American short story. The creation of a literary genre is not the work of a single individual; it is an antiphonal and collaborative work" ("Interim" 2; emphasis added). Therefore, we may view American women's short stories as springing not from the pen of one isolated woman but from the pens of a community of women who shared and read each other's works.

If we look further back, we will of course find that storytelling is indeed a very female art form (complete with "legitimate" mythological origins), beginning perhaps with Scheherazade (*The Arabian Nights' Entertainment*) or Penelope (Homer's *Odyssey*), who told stories for their survival. The very alphabets with which stories are written were given to us by female deities: Carmenta created a Latin alphabet, Medusa gave the alphabet to Hercules, Isis gave the alphabet to the Egyptians, and Kali invented the Sanskrit alphabet (Kramarae and Teichler 41). Recognizing that the short story in America has been written by people other than white males, we should also look at other origins of the short story, including Chinese talk/story (which must have influenced Maxine Hong Kingston and Amy Tan), Native American oral histories and chants (to better understand works by Leslie Marmon Silko and Louise Erdrich), and African American folk tales and slave narratives (see Zora Neale Hurston's short stories). It is also likely, in spite of Maugham's "caveman hunter" scenario, that the very earliest women's stories were fairy tales women told to their children at twilight, old wives' tales women passed on to preserve knowledge, or love stories women whispered to each other with a wink while the men were away. Why not? "[M]any of the stories we heard as children were told to us by women. We heard those words in a female voice; thus, we associate our earliest stories with women" (Barreca 2).

The names of many of the first women storytellers/writers may have been forgotten, but "women writers have their own rich and important tradition. A shared fund of secrets, silences, surprises, and truths belong to those who have experienced growing up female in a world where the experience is erased, written over, or devalued" (Barreca 2). No one asks, "who made the first wheel?" or "who wove the first cloth?"; therefore, we might also view the short story as the by-product of communal living, a craft developed and practiced by people who had something important to say to each other.

What is the *history* of the female storytelling tradition? What will we gain when we have reclaimed our history? How much of it has been lost? Why is it lost? Can we write a history of the woman's short story that will be inclusive of all the kinds of women who write stories? Or should women instead write the histories of their stories? Where should we begin?

Over the past few years, numerous women editors have gathered anthologies of American women's short stories. This is surely a very important first step toward learning and rediscovering the history. Judith Fetterley's excellent *Provisions: A Reader from 19th-Century American Women* (1985), for example, gathers important short stories from the nineteenth century, a period that is often underrepresented in American women's literary history. As she notes in her useful and interesting introduction, "Without access to the primary texts, there could be no community of readers, and without such a community there could be, as I saw it, no finally intelligent criticism. Clearly, then, the first task of the reader-critic committed to this material was to get it into print" (2).

Others, including Irene Zahava, Susan Cahill, and Stephanie Spinner, agree with Fetterley and have also compiled collections. Susan Koppelman has been especially industrious in editing anthologies by women writers (see the bibliography for titles of her works). Koppelman edits books thematically and historically (mother/daughter stories, Christmas stories, "The Other Woman" stories), showing the different ways women have written about the same themes throughout history. In her recent essay "About Anthologists," she defines her task as an anthologist:

> An anthologist is a teacher making a syllabus public and permanent by putting its contents between the covers of a book. An anthologist is a Florenz Ziegfeld, producing a variety show in which each act has to keep the audience engaged and has to prepare them for the next act. An

> anthologist is a midwife assisting artists in delivering their work to the world. An anthologist is a cultural anthropologist putting together the artifacts of a people in such a way that the shared culture becomes visible. (2)

Koppelman is also currently compiling a book-length bibliography of women's short stories from 1820 to the present. Such a list will surely be an invaluable tool for studies. (See, at the end of this book, the bibliographies compiled by Susan Koppelman [story collections and anthologies by women] and Amy Shoenberger [critical studies about women's stories]).

Many anthologists, including Regina Barreca and Susan Cahill, have worked to show the diversity of women's experiences in their anthologies. Wendy Martin (1990) is notable for her efforts to gather contemporary short stories by women of very diverse ethnicities, religions, and ages. Her introduction notes that "from its earliest beginnings, North American culture has been multi-ethnic and multi-racial, but only recently has there been a concerted effort to acknowledge this fact" (3), and then explains how she wants to reflect women's cultural diversity in her anthology. This philosophy of anthologizing echoes that of Laura Holloway, who edited one of the first anthologies of women's stories in 1889 (*The Women's Story as Told by Twenty American Women*). In her introduction, Holloway writes that "the differences in population, the varieties of classes, and the broad distinctions in local coloring are vividly exhibited in the annals of American fiction, the largest contributors to which are women" (Barreca, 12).

Although Terry McMillan's *Breaking Ice: An Anthology of Contemporary African American Fiction* (1990) contains stories by African American men as well as women, it gathers together many important stories by women of color for the first time. McMillan explains in her introduction that rage was one of the primary motivations for her to edit the collection. She noticed that few, if any, black writers appeared in collections like *Best American Short Stories*, and wrote, "I was appalled as I snatched every last one of these anthologies off my bookshelf, and could literally count on one hand the number of African-American writers who were in the table of contents. I sat at my desk and fumed. My heart pounded with anger. How dare they!" (xviii).

She compiled an anthology that was arranged alphabetically, rather than hierarchically, and included not only published authors, but also "emerging" and unpublished authors as well (McMillan, xxii). This book was compiled, in part, so that others would not live with the same lack of self-knowledge that she had earlier had: "As a child," she says, "I didn't know that African-American people wrote books" (xv). Another important anthology is Asha Kanwar's *The Unforgetting Heart: An Anthology of Short Stories by African American Women (1859–1992)*, which includes even more short stories by black women and covers a broader period.

Lesbian authors, too, are finally being recognized for their short stories. Several magazines, including *Common Lives/Lesbian Lives* and *Sinister Wisdom*, now actively publish short stories by and about lesbians. Lee Fleming's anthology *Tide Lines: Stories of Change by Lesbians* (1991) gathers together 27 short stories that focus on the theme of change. The publisher notes, "*All* human beings experience change, but in this anthology, change occurs because we are *lesbians*" (back cover). Fleming's goal in editing this anthology echoes the goals of other women anthologists, celebrating the shared experiences of women within the lesbian community, while at the same time celebrating the differences.

As more and more anthologies of women's stories are compiled, we may want to look at the larger picture—at how the short story form has been used by women from 1820 to the present. We might ask more questions. What is the history of women who wrote stories? What is the publishing history of women's stories? What is the history of women's writing education? What is the history of women as short story readers? We must think carefully about ways of reporting this information. Rather than one single narrative, the grand picture might be conceived of spatially, like a sky filled with stars, some of which form groupings, some of which fly alone. Like the stars, the vast number of stories written by women are "largely unread and unexplored" (Koppelman, "Interim" 1).

Unlike patriarchal critics of the short story form, feminist critics will undoubtedly be uninterested in the question of "who is the best." Wendy Martin explains the subtitle of her collection by noting, "This book calls them 'the best' of their era because they are clearly *among* the best, not because they are superior to the many fine stories which could not be included: literature by its very nature makes such pat rankings meaningless" (7). Women readers, I believe, are more eager to discuss their favorite stories, to share them with each other, and to continually add to and change the list of favorites, recognizing that because one story is in current favor it is not necessarily better than any other story.

What questions will best help us to reach a theory of the women's short story? To begin, we should ask how women's histories, cultures, and physiologies affect the way women write stories. For an examination of how the "short story cycle" is connected to theories of women's sociology, see Margot Kelley's "Gender and Genre: The Case of the Novel-in-Stories" in this collection.

We should ask what political gains were made by women through their short stories. In this volume, see Bruce Mills's essay "Literary Excellence and Social Reform" for a study of how Lydia Maria Child sought to combine aesthetic and political goals, and Sherry Lee Linkon's essay on Rose Terry Cooke for a study of how female "anti-feminists" used the short story to further their peculiar political goals.

We should ask how women's use of language (*écriture feminine*) affects the way our stories are narrated. In this volume, for a study of the female use of "epiphany," see Mary Burgan's essay. See Ken Johnson's essay on Dorothy Parker for a look at how she used repetition and lack of closure to tell her stories in a "modern" voice. Timothy Morris's essay examines the stories of Elizabeth Stoddard as a stepping-stone between "sentimental" and "modern" fiction.

We should ask how women have used and altered the short story form to suit women's purposes. Barreca observes that "women writers challenge even the most traditional patterns for the short story, subverting the basic prescriptions" (6). In this volume, for examinations of subgenres and their uses, see Gail Smith's study of Louisa May Alcott's "Confidence Stories," Stephanie Branson's study of fantastic stories by women, and Barbara Patrick's essay about the female ghost story in America.

We should ask what topics women short story writers choose to write about. Barreca writes, "[Women's short stories] often depict the lives of women who would be considered perfectly ordinary because they have gone through much of their lives not calling attention to themselves; however, they are actually extraordinary women whose dreams, ambitions, desires, and rages have been suppressed" (7). Perhaps the short story is the perfect form to document what Woolf called "the accumulation of unrecorded life" (93). Or, in Carolyn Kizer's words, women writers are "the custodians of the world's best kept secret:/ Merely the private lives of one-half of humanity" (Ostriker 6).

We should ask about the factors that influence public reception of women's short stories. In this volume, Lillian Faderman's essay, for example, shows how the portrayal of lesbianism in women's magazine fiction changed drastically as the public's "knowledge" of sexual issues changed. Ellen Gruber Garvey's essay shows how stories that depicted women as authors varied from magazine to magazine according to the class of the readers.

We should ask how race and ethnicity have influenced women's short stories. In this volume, see especially the essays by Susan Koppelman, Barbara Shollar, Linda Karell, A. LaVonne Brown Ruoff, Bill Mullen, Dolan Hubbard, and Douglas Anderson.

We should ask how women writers have influenced or have been influenced by male authors. In this volume, see Margaret Rozga's fascinating essay of how Joyce Carol Oates "re-imagined" stories by James Joyce and Anton Chekhov. Ken Johnson suggests in his essay how Dorothy Parker's innovations may have influenced the work of her male contemporaries, Hemingway and Fitzgerald.

We should ask how women have been taught to write, and how they best learn. My own essay, "The Great Ventriloquist Act," examines the ways that contemporary patriarchal culture and the creative writing pedagogy derived from it have "squelched" the female voice in beginning writers.

We should ask why women write stories. Edna Ferber notes, "I wrote short stories for the same reason that a child has who begins to walk after he has learned to stand up and to balance himself. It was for me the next natural step following newspaper reporting" (ix). Alice Walker writes because she wants to gather "the historical and psychological threads of the life of my ancestors" (Barreca 12). A character in Nora Ephron's *Heartburn* says telling stories is important "because if I tell the story, I control the version. Because if I tell the story, I can make you laugh, and I would rather have you laugh than feel sorry for me. Because if I tell the story, it doesn't hurt as much. Because if I tell the story, I can get on with it."

We should ask why women's stories have been ignored for so long. It is toward answers to these and other questions that this book has been written.

I would like to mention briefly here a curious phenomenon that occurred after I issued calls for essays on the topic of American women short story writers. In addition to many wonderful proposals on my stated topic, I received dozens of proposals about women novelists and dozens about male authors of the short story. This further reinforced my belief that a collective blind spot exists at the juncture between the concepts *women* and *short story* and further strengthened my resolve to see this project through to the end. It is my hope that the research gathered in this collection will inspire others to continue work in this field. This work has already begun: Since writing the essay on female epiphany, Mary Burgan has begun work on a book-length study of short stories by southern white women. After writing the essay on black women writers, Bill Mullen has compiled an anthology of their works. And Susan Koppelman's bibliography, begun at my request for a "list of women short story authors," has already exploded to nearly 100 pages!

WORKS CITED

Barreca, Regina, ed. Introduction, *Women of the Century: Thirty Modern Short Stories.* New York: St. Martin's, 1993, pp. 1–16.

Baym, Nina. "Melodramas of Beset Manhood: How Theories of American Fiction Exclude Women." *The New Feminist Criticism: Essays on Women, Literature, and Theory*. Ed. Elaine Showalter. New York: Pantheon, 1985, pp. 63–80.

Cuff, Roger Penn, ed. *An American Short Story Survey*. Harrisburg, PA: Stackpole, 1953.

Eagleton, Mary. "Gender and Genre." *Re-reading the Short Story*. Ed. Clare Hanson. New York: St. Martin's, 1989, pp. 55–68.

Ferber, Edna. *One Basket.* Chicago: People's Book Club, 1947.

Fetterley, Judith, ed. Introduction, *Provisions: A Reader from 19th-Century American Women.* Bloomington: Indiana University Press, 1985, pp. 1–40.

Fleming, Lee. *Tide Lines: Stories of Change by Lesbians*. Charlottetown, Prince Edward Island (Canada): Gynergy Books, 1991.

Gilbert, Sandra M., and Susan Gubar. *The Madwoman in the Attic: The Woman Writer and the Nineteenth-Century Literary Imagination.* New Haven, CT: Yale University Press, 1984.

Hanson, Clare, ed. *Re-reading the Short Story.* New York: St. Martin's, 1989.

Kanwar, Asha, ed. *The Unforgetting Heart: An Anthology of Short Stories by African American Women (1859–1992).* San Francisco: Aunt Lute Books, 1993.

Koppelman, Susan. "About Anthologists," unpublished, 1993.

———. "An Interim Attempt to Sketch a History of U.S. Women's Short Stories," unpublished.

Kramarae, Cheris, and Paula A. Treichler. *A Feminist Dictionary.* London: Pandora Press, 1985.

Lohafer, Susan. *Coming to Terms with the Short Story.* Baton Rouge: Louisiana State University Press, 1983.

McMillan, Terry, ed. Introduction, *Breaking Ice: An Anthology of Contemporary African American Fiction.* New York: Penguin, 1990, pp. xv–xxiv.

Martin, Wendy, ed. Introduction, *We Are the Stories We Tell: The Best Short Stories by North American Women Since 1945.* New York: Pantheon, 1990, pp. 3–7.

Matthews, Brander. *The Philosophy of the Short Story*. New York: Peter Smith, 1931.

May, Charles E., ed. *Short Story Theories.* Athens: Ohio University Press, 1976.

Neal, Robert Wilson. *Today's Short Stories Analyzed.* New York: Oxford University Press, 1918.

O'Connor, Frank. *The Lonely Voice: A Study of the Short Story*. New York: World, 1963.

Ostriker, Alicia Suskin. *Stealing the Language: The Emergence of Women's Poetry in America*. Boston: Beacon, 1986.

Pattee, Fred Lewis. *The Development of the American Short Story.* New York: Harper & Brothers, 1923; New York: Biblo and Tannen, 1970.

Peden, William. *The American Short Story: Continuity and Change, 1940–1975.* Boston: Houghton Mifflin, 1975.

Poe, Edgar Allan. "Review of *Twice Told Tales*," in *Graham's Magazine*, May 1842. Rpt. in Charles May, ed., pp. 45–51.

Shaw, Valerie. *The Short Story: A Critical Introduction*. London: Longman, 1983.

Showalter, Elaine, ed. *The New Feminist Criticism: Essays on Women, Literature, and Theory.* New York: Pantheon, 1985.

Woolf, Virginia. *A Room of One's Own.* New York: Harcourt Brace Jovanovich, 1957.

American Women Short Story Writers

Literary Excellence and Social Reform: Lydia Maria Child's Ultraisms for the 1840s

Bruce Mills

Fifteen months after retiring from a tumultuous two-year editorship of the *National Anti-Slavery Standard*, Lydia Maria Child voiced astonishment over the literary success of *Letters from New York* (1845), a collection of journalistic transcendental essays first printed in the pages of her abolitionist newspaper. "The great popularity of [*Letters*] surprises me," she wrote, "for it is full of ultraisms." Encouraged by this success, Child announced that she meant "to devote the remainder of [her] life to the attainment of literary excellence" (*Selected Letters* 209). Between January 1845 and May 1848, her devotion to her art took the form of 24 stories and sketches published in the *Columbian Lady's and Gentleman's Magazine* and the *Union Magazine of Literature and Art*. To twentieth-century scholars, her efforts to craft an artistic vision consistent with both her literary and reformist views raise intriguing questions: What does her magazine fiction reveal about her (and her era's) notion of what makes an "artful" prose tale? And, significantly, why did she turn to this genre in order to pursue literary success as well as reform? Apparently, Child felt that her short fiction offered the best form in which to create cultural parables merging literary and political concerns.

Child's magazine fiction provides us with such an interesting and revealing case study because it reflects her unique position within key antebellum literary and reform communities. In 1824, she secured her reputation within the Boston area by publishing *Hobomok*, a historical novel that answered the call for a national literature. While suffering some rebuke for depicting an interracial marriage between Hobomok, a Pequot Indian, and Mary Conant, a white Puritan woman, the book still received strong support from such prominent figures as Harvard professor George Ticknor and Unitarian minister, historian, and Harvard president Jared Sparks. While editor of the *North American Review*, Sparks reviewed *Hobomok* along with nine other American novels, writing that Child's book was not of "the same ephemeral class, with some others of our American novels," and that it "will stand the test of repeated readings, and it will obtain them" (95). Child entered the ranks of the New England literati, then, with strong recommendations.

Having written for an audience whose values were instituted through Harvard College, the Unitarian church, and the *North American Review*, Child had cause to study the fiction and nonfiction of Boston letters. When she published the ground-breaking *An Appeal in Favor of That Class of Americans Called Africans* (1833), then, she would have known what would potentially reach and outrage her readers. The text, one of the first book-length calls for the immediate emancipation of slaves, sought a more moderate rhetoric than that of her friend William Lloyd Garrison. However, the book also marked a shift in Child's affinities. No longer could she depend upon the support of George Ticknor, a key figure who had not only helped revive *Hobomok* but also gained for Child access to the rich scholarly resources in the Boston Athenaeum. Because of her involvement in the abolitionist movement, her writing increasingly reflected the tension between finding the right form for her audience and arguing for reform principles.

These particular affiliations tell us much about the tensions of the period. And, importantly, they paint in bold strokes the unique contribution Child would make to her era's fiction. Child's connection to leading transcendentalists, however, further colors this collage of influences. Her brother, Convers Francis, a Unitarian minister, was an original member of the Transcendentalist Club, which first met on September 19, 1836.

Because of her close relationship with Convers and her own literary reputation, Child became acquainted with such figures as Ralph Waldo Emerson and Margaret Fuller. She attended Emerson's lectures in the mid-1830s (Boston) and early 1840s (New York) and Fuller's conversations in the late 1830s (Boston).

Clearly, Child's intersecting relationships with prominent Boston Unitarians, abolitionists, and transcendentalists suggest that she had ample opportunity to reflect upon the best ways to harmonize "good" stories with the public good. But beyond this suggestive though brief sketch of her place within the literary and political landscape, her works themselves—especially *Letters from New York*—give further evidence of the evolution of her literary views. Continuously embroiled in antislavery infighting, she sought the literary essay and short fiction as a way to keep hold of core truths, truths that were increasingly hidden in the day-to-day bustle of worldly affairs, or, in Child's specific situation, in the managing of an abolitionist newspaper.

Child speaks of the debilitating effects of the "outward" in her initial "letter" from New York (originally published on August 19, 1841 in the *National Anti-Slavery Standard*). Troubled by the filth and finery of the city, she seems as if she is overcome by the noisy discord of money-making. Her lament, however, is short-lived. "But now," she acknowledges, "I have lost the power of looking merely on the surface. Every thing seems to me to come from the Infinite, to be filled with the Infinite, to be tending toward the Infinite" (*Letters from New York* 14). Child ends the essay with a pronouncement that would guide her until her last "letter" in late 1844:

> Therefore blame me not, if I turn wearily aside from the dusty road of reforming duty, to gather flowers in sheltered nooks, or play with gems in hidden grottoes. The Practical has striven hard to suffocate the Ideal within me; but it is immortal, and cannot die. It needs but a glance of Beauty from earth or sky, and it starts into blooming life, like the aloe touched by fairy wand. (17)

Child is being a bit disingenuous here, for, rather than turning from her "reforming duty," she is embracing it. The duty, however, leads her to metaphor and symbol; that is, it urges her toward fiction. Veiled in this apparent shirking of her abolitionist mission is an assertion of the artist's role in reform. It takes a "fairy wand" to illuminate "Beauty," and it is this wand that promises to evoke the most fruitful changes. As Child later wrote in an April 1843 contribution to the *Dial*, beauty is the "union, and perfect proportion" of "LOVE and WISDOM" (490).

In the middle years of the 1840s, Child sought consistently to offer glimpses of beauty in fictional form. For an editor deadlined by the weekly columns of statistical and anecdotal horrors of slavery and given to a transcendental epistemology, the attempts to give linguistic shape to beauty as well as truth satisfied both a personal and cultural need. The problem became how to articulate this ideal in ways that could be understood, that is, in ways that might lead to an intuitive recognition of higher truths and thus to a harmonizing of the material and spiritual. Child knew the power of story and myth to shape affections. And, in her mind, a change in the affections must precede any lasting reform—individual or national. Writing to Convers on July 27, 1834, she argues that "it is more safe and useful to dwell upon the necessity of keeping the heart pure, than of enlightening the understanding. An educated man can more safely trust to his conscience than to his understanding" (*Letters of Lydia Maria Child* 15). In her own characterization of transcendentalism published a decade later, she describes a more essential "faculty" of understanding. Detailing the philosophical roots of transcendentalism, she writes that, contrary to the philosophy of Locke, not "*all* knowledge is received through the senses" and that "the highest, and therefore most universal, truths are revealed within the soul, to a faculty *transcending* the understanding." She continues:

> This faculty they call pure Reason; it being peculiar to them to use that word in contradistinction to the Understanding. To this pure Reason, which some of their writers call "The God Within," they believe that all perceptions of the Good, the True, and the Beautiful, are revealed, in its unconscious quietude; and that the province of the Understanding, with its five handmaids, the Senses, is confined merely to external things, such as facts, scientific laws, &c. (*Letters, Second Series* 125–126)

Clearly, Child's decision to turn from the essay to short fiction suggests that she felt the short prose tale enabled her to attend to this "faculty" and thus to foster reform through the truths revealed in "unconscious quietude." Her private confession to friends that her New York "letters" are "full of ultraisms" acknowledges her own deliberate attempt to speak to a sense that lies beyond cold reasoning and shows her anxiety that readers might not understand the higher truth.

Highly suggestive in Child's "ultraist" short fiction of the 1840s is the way she utilizes "sibling" relationships to explore a more spiritualized or harmonizing love. Perhaps the most peculiar and telling manifestation of this plotting—and one that invites further analysis because of its incestuous overtones—is "The Children of Mt. Ida." Published in the April 1845 issue of the *Columbian Lady's and Gentleman's Magazine,* the story traces the lives of Corythus and Oenone, two orphans who are raised as brother and sister and later live as husband and wife. Corythus is first found on the Phrygian hills by the shepherd and shepherdess Mygdomus and Arisba. Unable to discover who has abandoned the infant boy, they adopt him. Three years later, during the festival of Bacchus, they take in another child who had been left on Mt. Ida and found by a village woman. "They were like unrecorded wild flowers," Child writes of their early years. "Their foster-parents spoke of them to strangers as the forest-found, and the river-child" (146).

This connection to the natural world eases the discomfort of the seemingly unnatural relationship that they later form. ("Placed in outward circumstances so harmonious with nature, they were drawn toward each other by an attraction as pure and unconscious as the flowers" [147].) Rather than view their marriage as a violation of some social taboo, Child encourages readers to see it as emblematic. Through the union, we witness the outflowing of some higher truth; the outward and the inward are in unison. Interestingly, the harmony that Child depicts is not simply a pastoral affinity with the land. Instead, she imagines it as an accord between those attributes that have conventionally differentiated and often separated male and female characters.

The period of greatest literal and emblematic significance emerges when Corythus and Oenone confront the growing dissonance of their own distinct genders. While first imaging them like the numerous magazine illustrations of idealized children ("But the most beautiful sight was to see them kneeling hand in hand before the altar of Cybele, in the grove, with wreaths about their heads and garlands in their hands, while the setting sun sprinkled gold among the shadow-foliage on the pure white marble" [146]), Child goes on to distinguish the particular ways both mature. That is, she uses the gender differentiation between the two characters to exemplify distinctions between spiritual and physical beauty. Oenone's whole self, Child writes, "was vivacious and impressible in the extreme; and so transparent were her senses, that the separation between earthly and spiritual existence seemed to be of the thinnest and clearest crystal" (146). While physically attractive, then, Oenone's spirituality is her definitive characteristic. Corythus, on the other hand, is distinguished by outward traits: He has "[a] figure slender but vigorous; a free, proud carriage of the head, glowing complexion; sparkling eyes, voluptuous mouth, and a pervading expression of self-satisfaction and joy in his own existence" (147).

Child makes it quite clear that both characters represent qualities that must be joined, that the beauty of their lives derives from a union of complementary traits and sensibilities. Interestingly, however, Child initially seems to view Corythus as the stronger of the two, his physical strength being the primary criterion:

> A nature thus strong and ardent of course exercised a powerful influence over her higher but more ethereal and susceptible life. Then, too, the constant communion of glances and sounds, and the subtle influence of atmosphere and scenery, had so intertwined their souls, that emotions in the stronger were felt by the weaker, in vibrations audible as a voice. (147)

Yet, even here this apparent strength is qualified by its dependence upon the communion with Oenone's "subtle influence." In fact, she is said to make Corythus "half afraid" by her power to divine his thoughts.

Not surprisingly, such a beginning signals a tragic ending. Frightened one evening by the cymbals, drums, and pipes of pilgrims on the way to the temple of Cybele, Oenone swoons and, in a sleep, tells Corythus that he will marry "the most beautiful princess in the world" (149). Tempted first by this prediction and then after by the praise and finery of princes who have ventured to Mt. Ida, Corythus does in fact abandon Oenone to pursue an honor and fame that make his shepherd life seem "unmanly and dull" (147) but that eventually lead to his own death. It is an outcome that we expect, and, significantly, it is one that Oenone herself has also prophesied. As predicted, he only returns to her to die; then, immediately after his death, she also dies.

The end of this narrative is also worth noting, for it reveals how Child sought to recontextualize and reconfigure the myth of Oenone and Corythus for a wider audience. Corythus, as many of Child's readers might have known, was the famed Paris of Homer's *Iliad*. He had been left on Mt. Ida because soothsayers had predicted he would cause the destruction of Troy. In the Greek story, however, the goddesses (Hera, Queen of Heaven; Pallas, Goddess of Wisdom; and Aphrodite, Goddess of Love) extend Paris more choices than simply Oenone and Helen. To an audience well versed in Homer, Child's idyllic depiction of the early relationship between Corythus and Oenone and the sympathetic portrayal of Oenone's position following the desertion would have invited another reading of the "Judgement of Paris" and the *Iliad*.

If the *Iliad* taught in secular terms the far-reaching danger of pride and wrath, then Child's prelude to the epic cultivated a new understanding: The deeper cause of pride resides in rejecting a spiritual wholeness, a wholeness best understood through images predominantly associated with women. The lesson Corythus learns is an old one. In becoming enamored of the voluptuousness of Helen, he loses sight of a redemptive truth exemplified in Oenone's "innocent spiritual beauty" (150). For Child, however, this old truth emerges in increasing calls for new unions—unions that stories of "marriage" embodied. It is no wonder that in the contemporaneous "Woman in the Nineteenth Century" Margaret Fuller also sought to imagine a new relationship between men and women, a relationship where male and female "are perpetually passing into one another" (310). Not surprisingly, Child met with Fuller during the period in which both were working in New York, and wrote a supportive review of "Woman in the Nineteenth Century" for the *Boston Courier* of February 12, 1845 (*Selected Letters* 217).

In this alienation between the sexes, then, can be discerned a profound feeling of estrangement that embodied more (and could be used for more) than simply a conventional plot line. At least for some, this estrangement captured a deeply felt disenchantment with the practical, with the way quiet lives could come to foster a desperate and divided self as easily as it separated home and work. While "The Children of Mt. Ida" employs a common plotting, it also represents in Child's magazine fiction (and other writings of the period) what seems to be a story that the culture had reason to tell itself in many ways and in many forms: the tale of women whose sufferings result from traits or qualities conventionally associated with masculinity (physical strength, logical reasoning, ambition). In slightly different terms, it is the tale of women and men who seek relationships that could engender both private and public change. If the sentiment at the core of these fictions is that of alienation—for surely readers were meant to feel a tragic estrangement in the division between Oenone and Corythus—then Child invokes more than a simple plot line in feminizing and spiritualizing the way this alienation manifests itself. She encourages readers to reevaluate those masculine values that mistake worldly beauty for higher truths.

Whereas in "The Children of Mt. Ida" Child sacrifices both protagonists, she chooses not to do so in "Thot and Freia: A Romance of the Spirit Land," the story that perhaps best represents her renewed pursuit of literary excellence. Making this story her first contribution to the *Columbian* suggests her own sense of its literary significance. Child had published the piece at least twice before, first in the *National Anti-Slavery Standard* and later in *Letters from New York, Second Series* (1845). The fact that the story was the lead for the January 1846 issue verifies Child's popularity after *Letters from New York* and further implies the special importance of this thrice-told tale.

In "Thot and Freia," Child uses the gods of northern European myth to introduce the role of the feminine in achieving a spiritual wholeness. An opening footnote sets up the contrast that directs the plot: "In the Mythology of the North, Freia is the Goddess of Love, or Feeling; likewise of the Spring. She is passionately enamored of Music. Thot is synonymous with Art, Science, or Skill" (1). As in "The Children of Mt. Ida," Child goes on to describe the masculine character as one who fails to recognize a higher spiritual reality. Thot, a mythic spirit "not good enough for heaven, or bad enough for hell," is "strong and sinewy, like a man of iron, with an eye that looked as if he thought creation was his anvil, on which he could fashion all things" (1). In his striving to create his own beautiful world lies both Thot's tragic flaw and his redeeming virtue. Having heard Freia's song in the Vale of Ida, he has vaguely imagined a world of true beauty:

> From her harp, I heard the tones to which the trees grow, and the blossoms unfold; and with the tones came to me the primeval words whispered into the heart of each tree, and blossom, and gem, at the moment of its creation; the word which gave them being, and which they must forever obey. I burned with intense desire to press farther into the inmost heart of all being, and learn the one primeval tone, in the one primeval word, from which flowed the universe. Then I was exiled from the glorious valley, and giants now guard its rainbow bridge, that I cannot again pass over. (2)

In this striving for the primeval tone, Thot mirrors the redeeming quality of such romantic protagonists as Goethe's Faust. That Child sees this striving as redemptive is made clear by the fact that Freia does in fact answer his sincere appeal and again plays her inspiring music.

Unfortunately, Thot succumbs to the demons of his own limitations and thus misinterprets the meaning of Freia's song. Misunderstanding that beauty resides as much in the heart as in the outward appearance of trees, blossoms, and gems, he mistakes the visible (the real or practical) for the ideal and seeks to engineer his vision:

> Then came over him again the wish to compel all things; to create a world by his own almighty skill. "If I only knew the primeval word of *her* life," thought he, "if I could make *her* my slave, then could I easily create a fitting dwelling for myself, and chase those proud deities from their valley of golden forests, to the cold dark fogs of Nilfheim." (2)

Driven now by pride instead of a genuine desire for beauty, he commands the goddess to reappear and, when he sees her shadowy form slowly rise, he exclaims, "She came, though reluctantly, at the command of my will. Is Will then the central life?—the primeval word, from which electricity had being?" (2). Thot becomes convinced of his power to enslave Freia, and after much mathematical pondering (2), he mutters a spell that seeks to "bring Freia into his power, and extort from her the primeval word of her being" (3). The figure who appears, however, is a false Freia. The fact that she is but a northern poetess sent by the gods to mock Thot remains hidden from both Thot and the reader. Not until he has failed to give nature life within his glittering cave in "the New World across the ocean" (3) and this manufactured sterility has caused the poetess's death (5) is it revealed that the gods had tricked him.

If the story had ended here, Child would have mirrored in many ways the tale of Corythus and Oenone. With death literally at Thot's feet, we are left pondering the tragic futility of his unchecked will. Instead of such a denouement, however, she chooses to imagine a new relationship between the true Freia and Thot, a relationship that produces a "mountain-child" purged of the pride and will that confused Thot and further magnified the pain of his exile. Only after he has tenderly carried the body of the poetess to her tomb and tearfully mourned her death does Freia again return—this time with a message that Thot is now willing to hear: "Thou and I, dear Thot, are one from all eternity. Thou has made this mournful separation, by reversing the divine laws of our being. Thou has thought to create the outward, and then compel the inward to give it life. But the inward forms the outward, and thus only can the outward live" (6). Freia's message echoes the verse from Goethe that serves as the tale's epigraph: "There is nought within, and nought without;/ For whatever is in, will out./ Haste thou then to learn in season/ This plain-published mystic reason" (1). When Child uttered surprise at readers' apparent willingness to embrace "ultraisms," or distilled truths, no doubt she had such a moral from "Thot and Freia" in mind.

If Child's efforts to achieve literary excellence were read without some knowledge of the literary and reform principles that guided her, readers might be inclined to see a shallow sentiment in her stories, a sentiment that seems to evoke a superficial emotionalism instead of a deeply rooted cultural anxiety. In fact, one current survey of the period's literary magazines considers the *Columbian*'s tales insubstantial and indistinguishable. They read, writes Arthur Wrobel (1986), with "numbing uniformity." In grouping "Thot and Freia" with those tales that explore the "purely imaginative" (108), he further implies that the fiction can be understood *en masse* and thus that it has little literary currency. Wrobel concludes:

> [At] best, the chief value of its contents lies in providing historians studying the popular mind of the period with source materials. The literature it published probably nudged Poe into the contemplation of writing free from a confining didacticism and provided Henry James with the impetus later in the century to formulate an art of fiction. (111)

Perhaps, however, it is important to recall that Poe's reflection upon truth in his review of Hawthorne's *Twice-Told Tales*—the section, that is, which follows his discussion of the importance of the single effect—reveals that he has not been nudged too far from the popular tales he so widely reviewed. "But Truth is often," Poe argued, "and in very great degree, the aim of the tale. Some of the finest tales are tales of ratiocination. Thus the field of this species of composition, if not in so elevated a region on the mountain of Mind, is a table-land of far vaster extent than the domain of the mere poem. Its products are never so rich, but infinitely more numerous, and more appreciable by the mass of mankind" (109). Rather than canonize and then characterize Poe as aloof from a widely read body of fiction, it is perhaps as useful to see the popular short fiction he read and reviewed as central to his conception of the prose tale itself. That Child and Poe share a preoccupation with how definitions of beauty and truth apply to short fiction reflects the broader attempt to understand the role of the genre in literature and life.

The implication that popular tales like "The Children of Mt. Ida" and "Thot and Freia" served only as a kind of disposable reading for Poe and James arises from a conception of literary history as genealogy. But, it seems to me, different questions must be asked in order to beget a different lineage—or to move beyond the notion of lineage altogether. Does not Child's writing, after all, represent her own attempt to "formulate an art of fiction"? And, we might ask, if there is a uniformity in the tales, then is it not possible that these stories embody something worth telling—a deep cultural division, in fact, that demands of writers more than a superficial understanding of their art? At least, given the cursory quality of Wrobel's own judgment, it might be valuable to consider this other possibility.

As I have argued, in Child's case evidence suggests that, while she wrote her share of didactic tales and knew the financial rewards gained by writing for a popular audience, she also demonstrated a studied commitment to her art and understood the reforming power of the imagination. To be purely imaginative neither separated the fiction from pressing cultural issues nor pandered to lowbrow tastes. "The Children of Mt. Ida," then, is not conventional; it uses the era's conventions to enter the public discourse. Child's letters during the late 1830s and early 1840s reflect the growing dissatisfaction with "'Change" (Exchange), that is, with the power of economic interests to direct moral concerns. Those conditions and beliefs that fostered and/or accepted such wrongs as slavery called for another "change," for a reform of the heart.

Child's fiction shows that striving for literary excellence led her to examine even more closely the form of the short story. That in tales tracing romantic relationships lies the stuff of art. That, in fact, the period of estrangement within such relationships could be fictionalized in ways that moved readers toward a fuller understanding of higher truths.

It is not the scope of this exploration to work out thoroughly the many ways Child's fiction resonates with the writings of other transcendentalists. It is worth noting, however, that Child apparently intended her stories to revise some of the ways her peers imagined a higher reality. In questioning the role of will, for instance, she enters the dialogue taken up by Emerson. To Emerson, "[T]he materialist insists on facts, on history, on the force of circumstances and the animal wants of man; the idealist on the power of Thought and Will, on inspiration, on miracle, on individual culture" ("The Transcendentalist" 193). The contrast Emerson sets up represents only a small part of his thinking. Set beside "Thot and Freia," however, we begin to sense that his imagination turns toward different terms and images. In Emerson's world of self-reliant, "representative" men, will, it seems, would connect man to the world of action. In a sense, will compelled others. Apparently, while having heard and been inspired by Emerson's New York lectures, this masculine rendering of transcendental truths troubled Child. Along with Fuller, she sought to redefine old stories and myths, to plot a central place for a feminized spirituality, and thus to turn transcendental "ultraisms" into tales that changed the way people could imagine and act.

WORKS CITED

Child, Lydia Maria. "The Children of Mt. Ida." *Columbian Lady's and Gentleman's Magazine* (April 1845): 145–154.

———. *Letters from New York*. New York: C.S. Francis, 1845. Rpt. Freeport, NY: Books for Libraries, 1970.

———. *Letters from New York, Second Series*. New York: C.S. Francis, 1845.

———. *Letters of Lydia Maria Child, with a Biographical Introduction by John G. Whittier and an Appendix by Wendell Phillips*. Boston: Houghton Mifflin, 1882.

———. *Lydia Maria Child: Selected Letters, 1817–1880*. Ed. Milton Meltzer, Patricia G. Holland, and Francine Krasno. Amherst: University of Massachusetts Press, 1982.

———. "Thot and Freia: A Romance of the Spirit Land." *Columbian Lady's and Gentleman's Magazine* (January 1845): 1–7.

———. "What Is Beauty." *Dial* (April 1843): 490–492.

Emerson, Ralph Waldo. "The Transcendentalist." *Selections from Ralph Waldo Emerson*. Ed. Stephen E. Whicher. Boston: Houghton Mifflin, 1957, pp. 192–207.

Fuller, Margaret. "Woman in the Nineteenth Century." *The Essential Margaret Fuller*. Ed. Jeffrey Steele. New Brunswick, NJ: Rutgers University Press, 1992, pp. 243–378.

Poe, Edgar Allan. "Review of *Twice-Told Tales*, by Nathaniel Hawthorne." *The Complete Works of Edgar Allan Poe, Volume XI*. Ed. James A. Harrison. New York: AMS, 1965, pp. 104–113.

Sparks, Jared. "Recent American Novels." *North American Review* (July 1825): 86–95.

Wrobel, Arthur. "The Columbian Lady's and Gentleman's Magazine." *American Literary Magazines: The 18th and 19th Centuries*. Ed. Edward E. Chielens. New York: Greenwood, 1986, pp. 107–112.

Fiction as Political Discourse: Rose Terry Cooke's Antisuffrage Short Stories

Sherry Lee Linkon

In an 1857 story for *Harper's,* Rose Terry Cooke presented the first of her many arguments against women's rights, beginning a critique of her "strong-minded sisters" that would continue throughout her life. In a long digression from the plot of "Rachel's Refusal," Cooke's heroine explains to her suitor the foolishness of the women's rights movement:

> [Strong-minded women] attempt to be reasonable that they may insure a hearing from men, who always call loudly for reasons; and women, having no more rational answer to give than their own instinctive nature affords, go seeking after some more common and better-appreciated truth—rake up from the dust of years all their inequalities in the social scale for a special pretext, and then illogically go on to wrangle for power, hoping thereby to compel peace. Do you suppose any woman would care a straw for her own property or individual prerogative if her husband loved her well and truly enough to make her feel her self lost and gained in him? (798)

Rachel goes on to suggest that the true solution to women's problems lies in changing men's behavior toward women:

> When the right and lawful authority of man is so love-tempered that a woman's due obedience is sweet and glad, . . . [t]hen women will have no wrongs, nor any rights, nor any self. . . .

> Men will respect their goodness, love their loveliness, be too proud not to protect their dependence, and too "tender and true" to be unkind, even in thought, to the sensitive and timid heart that beats only with and for their own. (799)

As this passage suggests, Cooke believed that women would not need the vote if men and women would both fulfill their intended roles.

Cooke followed this story with many others illustrating the power of good womanhood and the evils of male selfishness, as well as several essays specifically criticizing the women's rights movement. Her short stories, together with fiction and essays by other individual antisuffragists, offer important historical data on women's opposition to woman suffrage, especially for the period between 1850 and 1890.[1] Like other women writers on both sides of the suffrage debate, she used fiction more often than essays to engage in political discourse. Indeed, for Cooke as for other women of her time, the short story offered a proper, discreet, and powerful political tool, even though her stories often advocated women's silence.

Born in Hartford, Connecticut, in 1827, Rose Terry came from a prominent family of lawyers, doctors, and politicians, although her father worked as a landscape gardener. She attended the Hartford Female Seminary, taught school for a few years, and spent a number of years tending to her invalid parents. She did not marry until she was age 47, and she had no children of her own. Her husband, Rollin Cooke, was only 30 when they wed, a widower with two children. In the early 1880s, he invested and lost her $20,000 inheritance; thus her writing was essential to the family's economy for the last decade of her life.

She wrote primarily short stories and poems, though she also published a number of essays and several novels. Short stories were the staple of Cooke's economic life, and they allowed her to reach large and varied audiences. Like other prominent writers of her day, she published in both "literary" magazines and the better religious weeklies, such as the *Independent*, as well as in children's magazines. One of her stories, "Sally Parson's Duty," was the lead story in the premiere issue of the *Atlantic Monthly*, the most influential and important magazine of the mid-nineteenth century, and her stories appeared there regularly. She was both popular with readers and respected by her peers. The success of her career suggests that she combined fiction with political commentary effectively, appealing to readers and editors because of both her writing style and her ideology.

The few historians who have written about the "Anti" supporters have ignored Cooke. She wrote most of her stories before the antisuffrage movement formed official organizations in the 1890s. The first antisuffrage meeting did not occur until 1882 (Camhi 138), and the first official organization, the Massachusetts Association Opposed to the Further Extension of Suffrage to Women, did not form until 1895, three years after Cooke's death. While she could not have joined an antisuffrage organization, Cooke's writings reflect the ideas that later "Anti" organizations would espouse. Like them, she supported improvements in women's status, worried about the effects of suffrage on women and on society, feared the political influence of blacks and immigrants, and offered a strong critique of American culture, especially the individualism and commercialism she saw in men's behavior.

The short story was Cooke's most important tool in the fight against women's rights. Stories allowed her to illustrate both the power of good womanhood and the problems women faced because of their own weakness, something she could not accomplish as dramatically in essays or poetry. Nearly 30 of the almost 200 stories Cooke published during her career dealt specifically with "The Woman Question," and many others focused on women's experiences.

The most interesting aspect of Cooke's political use of the short story is her combination of idealized portraits of good womanhood with complex and contradictory visions of the conditions of women's lives. Previous scholarship has emphasized Cooke's critique of women's oppression during the nineteenth century, and she is best known for her grim portraits of abused wives and lonely spinsters.[2] These have gained Cooke a place in literary history as one of the first realists and led one critic to identify her work as "among the earliest and best feminist contributions to American fiction" (Toth 151). But these stories represent only part of Cooke's body of fiction. The majority of Cooke's work has been ignored, brushed aside as "exercises in didacticism" and "potboilers" (Downey 62, 65). When we read both the more well known realist tales and her "sentimental" works in light of her antisuffrage essays and her most overtly political stories, such as "Rachel's Refusal," the complexity and contradictions of Cooke's political ideology become clear. While she presents a fairly consistent critique of male values, Cooke's ideas about women's virtue and weakness are harder to reconcile, and they reflect one of the central problems in "Anti" rhetoric.

Tension between women's power and women's weakness pervades Cooke's fiction. While she consistently portrays men's greed and selfishness as causes of social and personal problems and shows how good women can influence such evil men to change their ways, she also suggests that women may bring suffering on themselves through their own weakness. In addition, Cooke's fiction reveals a tension between the value of good womanhood and the costs it entails. In some of her stories, the effort to maintain virtue and influence others leads women to emotional breakdowns, ill health, and even death. Thus, Cooke's stories show that both women's weakness and their goodness may cause them suffering. And yet she clung steadfastly to her faith in the power of good womanhood.

Cooke's stories often revolve around a direct conflict between women's moral virtue and men's evil. Cooke's good women repeatedly convert others, both women and men, through four qualities: domesticity, piety-in-action, motherliness, and selflessness, all of which often require individual suffering. Cooke calls some of these women "female saints," a term that implies both martyrdom and the ability to perform miracles. Her most ideal heroines use self-sacrifice, occasionally to the point of severe illness or even death, to inspire seemingly miraculous transformations in those around them. Moreover, these stories consistently suggest that Christian faith inspires good women. In Cooke's eyes, the good woman and the true Christian woman were identical.

In "Two Saints" (1885), Cooke describes two women who suffer through great personal troubles and not only survive but also transform those around them. "Saint the First," Serena, transforms her gruff, unappreciative husband and his five dirty, unruly sons through her hard work as a wife and mother. Despite the family's poverty and rudeness, she creates a pleasant, peaceful home. Her faith and goodness so inspire her stepsons that they become Christians. Serena has, Cooke explains, done her duty, rather than worrying or complaining about the harshness of her lot, and she dies unaware of her own goodness.

"Saint the Second," Nancy Pratt, gives up her happy, independent solitude to care for her stepfather, a cranky man she has long resented and who needs constant care. Like many Cooke old maids,[3] Nancy is known for her sharp tongue and unrequested advice. The chore of caring for a crotchety old man does not appeal to her, but in caring for him, she finds that she can set aside her own sharpness and treat even an unwelcome housemate kindly. In the act of nursing the dependent old man, Nancy's true feminine nature emerges, and, both mellowed by their experience, she and her stepfather learn to love one another. Serena and Nancy work hard, and neither enters her difficult situation without resignation and trepidation, but both persevere and both succeed. As the label "Saint" implies, these women exemplify Cooke's ideals of feminine and Christian virtues.

Cooke combines her vision of good womanhood with a strong critique of male behavior and values. She portrays men's evil as exactly the opposite of women's goodness: disregard for home and community, selfishness, greed, and false piety. In a number of Cooke stories, selfish men seek to marry in order to avoid paying housekeepers, thus denigrating the sentimental ideal of marriage and the home. In "Mrs. Flint's Married Experience" (1880), for example, Deacon Flint marries the widow Sarepta Gold to gain an unpaid housekeeper and then isolates and starves her to death, proclaiming his own piety all the while. When she leaves him late in the story, he tells the town minister that "Mis' Flint is a miser'ble histericky female, a dreadful weak vessel, and noways inclined to foller Scripter" (408), implying that he is the better Christian in the family.

In other stories, men's greed combines with false piety and cruelty in dramatic portraits of evil. In "The Ring Fetter" (1859), for example, Abner Dimock marries Mehitable Hyde because she has money and property. He then abuses her physically and emotionally, eventually driving her to commit suicide in order to escape him. In other tales, men steal money from orphans, neglect their wives, use religion to justify cheating their neighbors, and engage in that most troublesome of nineteenth-century vices, drinking. This pattern in Cooke's short stories suggests that she saw individual male evil as the primary challenge to good womanhood. Her stories imply that the central problem in nineteenth-century women's lives was not their lack of political power, their economic dependence, or their limited access to education, but the potential for male evil that surrounded them. The solution was not to change women's position in society but to change individual men, a task that burdened most of Cooke's heroines.

Thus, many of Cooke's stories show good women successfully transforming evil men. Her temperance tales offer her most hopeful, if melodramatic, vision of the power of women's influence as the agent of social reform. In "One of Them" (1879), for example, Sarah resists the temptation to divorce her drunkard husband and nurses him after he is injured while drunk. When he begs her for a drink, her reply and his response demonstrate the effectiveness of women's love and faith:

> "James, it is better to die than live a drunkard; but you will not die. The Lord will answer my prayers first."
>
> Her face shone with the light of faith as she spoke and awed the man into silence, for he knew she prayed, night and noon and morning, as one who will not be denied, and prayed for him. Not in vain either, for when at last James crept up to his feet, lame for life and weak as a man can be, he had learned to cling to the only sure help as his Helper, and on far mightier strength than his own rested his weak heart and dismayed head. (5)

This passage, embroidered with the language of prayer, is Cooke's most idealistic vision of good womanhood as a direct solution to the problems of men's behavior, but the idea it represents appears in many of her stories.

The path to such reform is not always smooth, however, and as Cooke noted in several of her antisuffrage articles and illustrated in her short stories, most women were not nearly as good as Sarah. While Cooke's portraits of successful good women and greedy, selfish men illustrate clearly the main points of her social critique, her less successful women draw our attention to the conflicts within Cooke's own position. They show us where her idealism failed, as well as the ideological boundaries she would not cross.

In several stories, Cooke suggests that women fail to influence others because they are not strong enough, physically or morally. Worn down by the hard work of rural farm life, they succumb to the power of evil men. Weakened by the same selfish desires so many of Cooke's men face, they place their own interests over the needs of others and thus participate in their own downfall. Some of Cooke's heroines are worn down by the daily struggle of homemaking, being moral and spiritual guides, and setting aside their own needs for those of others. Unlike Cooke's saints, such women do not often successfully influence those around them. They are simply not saintly enough to rise above their difficult situations.

Good womanhood does not always triumph in Cooke's fiction, but often, women's weakness is as much to blame as men's evil. Cooke judges moral weakness more harshly than physical weakness, though she does express some sympathy for both. Sarepta Gold, the heroine of "Mrs. Flint's Married Experience," is a morally weak woman who accepts the tainted marriage proposal of an evil man. While he sees her as a cheap replacement for his current housekeeper, she is impressed by his social prominence, fooled by his false piety, and worried about her own economic and social security as she approaches old age. She marries Flint out of selfishness, not out of a true desire to fulfill her feminine duty or to do him any good. Although Cooke describes Sarepta's position sympathetically, pointing out the reasonable attractiveness of "the idea of a home" to "a woman who is no longer young" (377), she explicitly calls her a weak woman. Because of this weakness, Sarepta is not good enough to have any influence over Flint. She is only moderately religious, domestically capable but not a household miracle worker, and unable to nurture a man who offers and accepts no affection. Deacon Flint will not allow her to gain any moral ground because he claims it himself. He blocks all opportunities for Sarepta to express feminine virtue, and she does not have the physical or moral strength to overcome such obstacles. Sarepta is not an evil woman; she is simply weak, in spirit and body.

Cooke sees problems in women's physical weakness as well as their moral weakness. While "Antis" insisted that women were morally and intellectually equal or even superior to men, they often cited women's physical weakness as a key reason to keep women from voting. They were not strong enough to fight in wars or physically enforce the law, so they should not vote, "Antis" argued. Cooke highlights this point in "Miss Lucinda" (1861). The story revolves around a very capable old maid who relies on the assistance of a hired hand to complete her chores. The narrator comments wryly that "one might as well try to live without one's bread and butter as without the aid of the dominant sex." She continues, saying that "[w]hen I see women split wood, unload coal-carts, move wash-tubs, and roll barrels of flour and apples handily down cellar-ways or up into carts, then I shall believe in the sublime theories of the strong-minded sisters" (159).

If women's physical weakness made the equality of men and women impossible in Cooke's eyes, it also sometimes made good womanhood impossible. Cooke writes of many women whose energies were exhausted by the physical labor of rural life. Moral and spiritual strength were too much to ask of a woman worn down by an endless round of chores. In "Freedom Wheeler's Controversy with Providence" (1877), Cooke describes the daily chores of Freedom's overworked (and, like many Cooke characters, aptly named) wife, Lowly:

> Lowly went on, with the addition of a big naughty baby to take care of, waking before light to get her "chores" out of the way, prepare breakfast, skim cream, strain new milk and set it, scald pans, churn, work and put down butter,

> feed pigs and hens, bake, wash, iron, scrub, mend, make, nurse baby, fetch wood from the shed, and water from the well. (330)

While Lowly's hard work establishes her good intentions and her "selfless" acceptance of her husband's authority, it also reveals quite grimly the hard, heavy labor of rural New England housekeeping. Not surprisingly, Lowly's work, combined with frequent childbirth and her husband's rough ways, weakens and eventually kills her. Her death, however, begins the process of transforming Freedom from a selfish, unsympathetic man into a good husband and true Christian, a process that is completed by a stronger second wife.

Lowly's story highlights one of the key problems of Cooke's representation of women's weakness. Cooke presents feminine sainthood as a goal for good women, but her stories also show that it entails significant and even life-threatening costs. Thus, she seems both to advocate and to warn against her own idealized vision of femininity. "Our Slave" (1888) explores the problem dramatically when the title character's efforts to fulfill the goals of good womanhood almost kill her. As second wife and stepmother, her position is similar to Serena's in "Two Saints," although her husband is not as poor and her stepchildren are even more unfriendly than Serena's. In her effort to be a good wife and mother, she works hard in the home, making and selling lace to maintain the family's middle-class status when her husband's business hits hard times. Her selfless refusal to let her stepchildren know how hard she is working, combined with their unfriendliness, weakens her physically until she becomes ill with typhoid fever and almost dies. In what comes close to being the ultimate feminine self-sacrifice, her severe illness alerts her teenage stepdaughters to her selflessness, and they learn a strong lesson in feminine virtue from her example. In the end, she does not die. Her newly enlightened stepdaughters take care of her, demonstrating their transformation into good women.

While the story focuses on the stepdaughters' experiences as they learn the values of good womanhood, it also reveals the potential dangers of selflessness. A woman may risk her own life by devoting herself too strongly to the ideals of good womanhood. However, such severe selflessness does, in the end, allow a woman to influence those around her. Is the risk worth taking? Does good womanhood require the sacrifice of a woman's very life in the name of moral influence? In "Our Slave" the answer seems to be "yes." The drama is not about the risks of good womanhood; it is about the successful transformation of several selfish young women into selfless, nurturing, Christian women. Nonetheless, the problems and dangers of good womanhood cannot be completely erased by the daughters' conversions.

Cooke's heroines often influence others through their own physical and emotional weakness. Their failing health forces others around them to notice and appreciate their good womanhood. No Cooke heroine ever points out to her family her own hard work or selflessness. Such self-attention would undercut a woman's position as moral guide and martyr. Physical or mental illness is acceptable, however, perhaps even expected of a good woman. After all, women were supposed to be weaker than men and more susceptible to both physical illness and "hysteria." Such problems draw attention to women that they cannot draw to themselves, and they provide more overt persuasion for ungrateful friends and relatives than a good woman can supply on her own.

Cooke's short stories leave the reader with overt messages of the power of good womanhood but do not resolve underlying doubts about the cost and potential failure of that power. In particular, Cooke's fiction highlights the problem of women's silence. Had "Our Slave" been willing to call attention to herself and her hard work, she might have been able to effect change without risking her life. But the conservative definition of good womanhood does not allow such selfishness or self-attention. Thus Cooke consistently presents silence as a positive feminine trait, and her stories usually show women's silence earning them rewards.

Even when women's silence is more dangerous, Cooke herself remains almost entirely mute. In "Bell's Trouble" (1886), Cooke tells of a young wife who endures her stepmother's criticisms and whose efforts to work hard enough and maintain her silence drive her to insanity. Cooke places Bell's silence at the center of the story, describing her thoughts but rarely allowing her to speak. The conflict between the ideals of good womanhood and the dangers its silence poses for women becomes clear. Despite this grim vision of the dangers of feminine silence, Cooke explains approvingly that Bell's "wifely devotion and her unselfish nature" give her the "strength to conceal her trouble entirely from her husband" (26).

Indeed, although her stories often show the dangers of pursuing feminine virtue, Cooke consistently backs away from any overt critique of the ideal of good womanhood. Instead, like many antisuffragists, she blames women for not achieving it. Rather than acknowledging that women's influence might not have great power, she blames the failure of good womanhood on women's weakness and attempts to show that the costs of feminine virtue, even the death or severe illness of a good woman, are worthwhile if they lead to the conversion of those around her.

How can we account for this conflicted vision? What we know of Cooke's life offers little help here, in part because most of her personal papers were destroyed by a family member after her death. We cannot, for example, compare Cooke's own marriage with those she describes in her stories because we have almost no information on her relationship with her husband. Her portraits of false marriages begin with "The Ring Fetter" in 1859, 14 years before she married, and continue throughout her career. "Rachel's Refusal" in 1857 starts her argument against suffrage, but other stories and essays continue the argument until 1892, the year Cooke died. She created both strong and weak women throughout her career. Indeed, the publication dates of Cooke's stories suggest little change in her ideas over time. She did not become more conservative during her lifetime, nor did her ideas about women's roles seem to change as her own roles changed.

We might attribute the contradictions in Cooke's fiction to the differences between realism and sentimentalism. Certainly, some of her more "sentimental" tales, such as "Two Saints," seem to be the least conflicted of her fiction, while the most problematic stories, like "Mrs. Flint's Married Experience," have been celebrated as models of realist fiction. As Alfred Habegger argues in *Gender, Fantasy and Realism in American Literature*, one of the central characteristics of realist fiction was its challenge to idealized gender roles. Josephine Donovan notes in her study of *New England Local Color Literature* that one of the central traits of the tradition she claims Cooke helped found was "a critique of inauthentic female characters" in opposition to "sentimental romance" (3). Based on these studies, we might read Cooke's contradictions as evidence of a struggle between her literary and political ideas. That is, the contradictions may stem, in part, from her efforts to negotiate her position in the literary world. She sought not only to sell her work but also to position herself within either the circle of realists or the New England women local colorists "school" that Donovan identifies. To maintain her place in either literary circle, Cooke's stories would have to contain a realistic instead of an idealistic view of good womanhood. As realism gained prominence, religious periodicals like the *Independent*, which sought to compete with the *Atlantic Monthly* as a literary magazine, may also have demanded more complex images of women's lives. Yet, as her stories show, Cooke could never fully reconcile her literary and her political ideas about the representation of gender.

The primary source of Cooke's contradictions lies in the ideology of the "Anti" movement. She could not suggest that good womanhood sometimes failed; that would undermine her antisuffrage argument that women's influence was an effective alternative to political activity. If good womanhood could fail, then women might not have the power the "Antis" claimed for them, and their program would not work. The "Antis" further complicated their argument by suggesting that women might not always be good enough. If women were not strong enough to fulfill their mission as moral guides, how could they be trusted to vote? Thus, antisuffragists argued that women both had sufficient power without the vote and, at the same time, were emotionally, morally, and physically unfit to vote. This double-edged view of women lay at the heart of women's arguments against suffrage, and it was the central problem of the "Antis."

Cooke's stories illustrate this problematic ideology quite clearly. With her conservative faith in the power of individual influence, she could never directly criticize the ideal of good womanhood, even though its problems haunt her fiction. She was too much of a realist to deny that feminine virtue could fail to reform or convert others, even in a woman's immediate family. Nor could she ignore the difficulties she knew women experienced in their efforts to meet the ideal image of the good woman. She attempted to persuade readers that their suffering would yield positive results, but her insistence that women could create change through individual influence does not erase the flaws she reveals in the ideal. Rather than consider the possibility that women's traditional role might itself be problematic and should be changed to guarantee women access to political power and more open roles, Cooke and other "Antis" offered an alternative but often contradictory analysis.

NOTES

1. See, for example, the works of Rebecca Harding Davis and Gail Hamilton.

2. See, for example, Elizabeth Ammons's introduction to the Rutgers American Women Writers collection of Cooke's stories, *"How Celia Changed Her Mind" and Selected Stories,* as well as Downey's and Toth's dissertations and Josephine Donovan's chapter on Cooke in *New England Local Color Literature.*

3. Cooke used the term "old maid" deliberately, I believe, to suggest both the potential stigma of failing to secure a husband and her single characters' defiant attitudes toward their situations. Cooke's single women are often quirky, plain-spoken nonconformists, and her admiration and sympathy for them is quite clear. She comments in "Miss Lucinda" that she had "a reverence for poor old maids as great as for the nine Muses" (31). I use the term because Cooke insisted upon it in her own writing.

WORKS CITED

Ammons, Elizabeth. Introduction, *"How Celia Changed Her Mind" and Selected Stories*. Ed. Elizabeth Ammons. New Brunswick, NJ: Rutgers University Press, 1986, pp. ix–xxxv.

Camhi, Jane Jerome. "Women Against Women: American Antisuffragism, 1880–1920." Diss. Tufts University, 1973.

Cooke, Rose Terry. "Bell's Trouble." *Independent* (Feb. 1886): 218–220.

———. "Freedom Wheeler's Controversy with Providence." *Atlantic Monthly* (July 1877): 65–84; Rpt. in *Somebody's Neighbors*. 1881, New York: Irvington, 1972, pp. 320–367.

———. *"How Celia Changed Her Mind" and Selected Stories.* Ed. Elizabeth Ammons. New Brunswick, NJ: Rutgers University Press, 1986.

———. "Miss Lucinda." *Atlantic Monthly* (Aug. 1861): 141–159; Rpt. in *"How Celia Changed Her Mind" and Selected Stories.* Ed. Elizabeth Ammons. New Brunswick, NJ: Rutgers University Press, 1986, pp. 151–181.

———. "Mrs. Flint's Married Experience." *Harper's* (Dec. 1880): 79–101, Rpt. in *Somebody's Neighbors.* 1881. New York: Irvington, 1972.

———. "One of Them." *Independent* (Nov. 20, 1879): 3–5.

———. "Our Slave." *Independent* (Nov. 8, 1888): 1450–1451.

———. "Rachel's Refusal." *Harper's* (Nov. 1857): 797–803.

———. "The Ring Fetter." *Atlantic Monthly* (Aug. 1859): 154–170; Rpt. in *"How Celia Changed Her Mind" and Selected Stories.* Ed. Elizabeth Ammons. New Brunswick, NJ: Rutgers University Press, 1986, pp. 32–58.

———. *Somebody's Neighbors.* 1881. New York: Irvington, 1972.

———. "Two Saints." *Root-Bound and Other Sketches.* Boston: Congregational Sunday School and Publishing Society, 1885, pp. 83–107.

Donovan, Josephine. *New England Local Color Literature: A Woman's Tradition.* New York: Ungar, 1983.

Downey, Jean. "A Biographical and Critical Study of Rose Terry Cooke." Diss. University of Ottawa, 1956.

Habegger, Alfred. *Gender, Fantasy and Realism in American Literature.* New York: Columbia University Press, 1982.

Toth, Susan E.A. "More Than Local Color: A Reappraisal of Rose Terry Cooke, Mary Wilkins Freeman, and Alice Brown." Diss. University of Minnesota, 1969.

Elizabeth Stoddard: An Examination of Her Work as Pivot Between Exploratory Fiction and the Modern Short Story[1]

Timothy Morris

American fiction of the mid-nineteenth century is famous for its openings. Narrators identify themselves: "My name is Arthur Gordon Pym." "Call me Ishmael." "I am a rather elderly man." Or settings are described in detail: "Late in the afternoon of a chilly day in February, two gentlemen were sitting alone over their wine, in a well-furnished dining parlor, in the town of P____, in Kentucky." "Four individuals, in whose fortunes we should be glad to interest the reader, happened to be standing in one of the saloons of the sculpture gallery in the capitol at Rome."[2]

There are murky depths beneath every one of these limpid openings, but at least when we start, we know where we are and with whom we are dealing. Readers of the May 1860 issue of the *Atlantic Monthly*, then, might have been bemused by a story that opened like this:

> "What have I got that you would like to have? Your letters are tied up and directed to you. Mother will give them to you, when she finds them in my desk. I could execute my last will myself, if it were not for giving her additional pain. I will leave everything for her to do except this: take these letters, and when I am dead, give them to Frank. There is not a reproach in them, and they are full of wit;

> but he won't laugh, when he reads them again. Choose now, what will you have of mine?"
>
> "Well," I said, "give me the gold pen-holder that Redmond sent you after he went away."
>
> Laura rose up in her bed, and seized me by my shoulder, and shook me, crying between her teeth, "You love him! you love him!" Then she fell back on her pillow. (526)

These are the opening paragraphs of Elizabeth Stoddard's "My Own Story." They are remarkable for their indirection, and they become less clear after one has read the entire story. A reader trying to piece together the network of relationships from the opening paragraphs might infer that Frank loves Laura, who loves Redmond, and the narrator also loves Redmond, who may love Laura. That would be hard enough to follow; but actually, Frank is engaged to Laura, who loves Harry Lothrop, who will in the future court the narrator, Margaret, who loves Redmond, who is engaged to marry yet another woman, but loves Margaret. This tangle of asymmetrical triangles fails to account for the intense emotion with which Laura greets Margaret's request for Redmond's gift. Laura's conduct has no motive and her language is ambiguous, especially her statement, "I could execute my last will myself, if it were not for giving her additional pain." Laura's mother does not figure at all in the rest of the story, and one is left wondering whether Laura wants to cause her mother pain or spare her mother pain, or whether "pain" is meant in the sense of busy effort that will dispel grief or in the sense of emotional trauma.

"My Own Story" was Stoddard's first published fiction. She was 37 years old. A New Englander, she had been married for eight years to the rising New York man of letters Richard Henry Stoddard and had already published poetry and journalism. When James Russell Lowell accepted "My Own Story" for the *Atlantic Monthly*, he was fostering the start of a long career in fiction; Stoddard went on to write three novels and dozens of short stories before her death in 1902 (Zagarell). It was a literary career not unlike that of Rebecca Harding Davis, who would debut in the *Atlantic Monthly* in 1861 with "Life in the Iron-Mills" and marry the Philadelphia man of letters Clarke Davis. But where Davis's interests would take her into social concerns that foreshadowed realism and naturalism, Stoddard's introspective and personal concerns have left her with a tenuous position in literary history.

In fact, the publication of "My Own Story" in 1860 can serve as a pivotal point in an as yet largely unwritten literary history of the development of American modernism. Marianne DeKoven has shown in her study *Rich and Strange: Gender, History, Modernism* that modernism and gender are more complexly related than received literary histories would acknowledge. The common wisdom views modernist writing as an elitist, male, aestheticist genre. DeKoven argues instead that women writers like Kate Chopin and Charlotte Perkins Gilman broke new ground in the 1890s with their feminist formal experiments. Such "gendered" early modernism employs "an unresolved contradiction or unsynthesized dialectic . . . that enacts in the realm of form an alternative to culture's hegemonic dualisms, roots of those structures of inequity that socialism and feminism proposed to eradicate" (DeKoven 4). In DeKoven's analysis, one might say that the whole range of Victorian fiction from sentimental to naturalist accepts the assumptions of patriarchy and capitalism, encoding them in the explicitly managed narratives whose openings open this essay, and in the clinical analyses of realistic fiction. But however politically liberal the rhetoric of Victorian fiction, it only realizes a truly liberating potential when it breaks out of managed narrative constraints, as in *The Awakening* or "The Yellow Wallpaper."

DeKoven's insights help establish Chopin and Gilman as precursors of "high" modernism, but it is important to realize in turn that 1890s women modernists had precursors. The structures of hegemony that modernist form confronted in the 1890s were in place in the 1850s. But the typical form that women writers used to confront cultural hegemony in the 1850s could not be described as modernist, because it draws so heavily on the culture's hegemonic structures to confront those structures themselves—in particular, drawing on feminized evangelical Christianity and the "separate spheres" ideology to confront slavery, women's economic and political powerlessness, the oppression of Native Americans, and (sometimes) capitalism. This is the form that Susan K. Harris calls "exploratory," the form of Susan Warner's *The Wide, Wide World*, E.D.E.N. Southworth's *The Deserted Wife,* Augusta Jane Evans's *St. Elmo*, and perhaps most saliently, the fiction of Harriet Beecher Stowe. These works explore the contradictions in American culture, presenting the same unresolved issues as later modernist works, but in a multivoiced narrative that presents contradictions without speaking *through* them or ascribing authority to the voices of the "unsynthesized dialectic." In fact, the fiction of Warner, Evans, and Stowe typically subordinates its multivocal portrait of American culture to a synthetic argument that explicitly resolves its tensions.

Harris notes that the tendency of exploratory fiction toward resolution weakens, but does not erase, the explorations conducted in the course of those works. The unequivocal narrative voices heard at the start of this essay can be seen as one way of managing these narrative resolutions. Sometimes the managing narrator is a withdrawn third person, speaking from a foundation of doctrine so unshakable that the narrator never needs to intervene to put a "spin" on unruly narrative developments. This withdrawn narrator is best presented in the works of Warner or Evans. More often, the narrator in exploratory fiction is a first person who constantly intervenes to manage the reader's perceptions—the phenomenon of narrative "intrusion" so disliked by readers who have grown up with the literature and cinema of direct presentation.

The managing narrator is in turn a reflection of the social contexts of mid-nineteenth-century storytelling, the "parlor literature" described by Joan Hedrick. Hedrick's research brings out a fascinating analogue to the position of the woman writer: the position of the woman storyteller, in a mixed-sex group, needing to demonstrate an appropriate sense of her own gender role while composing a story that could interest the varied concerns and fantasies of the audience. The self-conscious narrators of Stowe's fiction are the product of this audience situation. They are politically radical, competently domestic, threateningly apocalyptic, and reassuringly maternal all at the same time. They must stir women to power within a sphere of action explicitly limited to the sphere of domestic persuasion in order to demonstrate their femininity to their audience.

Above all, the narrator of "parlor literature" must strive to bracket or to balance potentially disturbing narrative elements. For every vengeful Cassy, there must be an Uncle Tom to take the morally higher ground of self-sacrifice. For every Bacchanalian Dred of the swamps, there must be a long-suffering Millie whose rhetoric of forgiveness implausibly defeats his. Passions are evoked and given dialogic play, only to be subsumed into an overall philosophy of quietism. Without narrative management, such passions would carry a dangerously autonomous weight in the final narrative mix.[3]

Narrative management is precisely what the short stories of Elizabeth Stoddard lack. In striking contrast to the majority of women's fiction of the 1850s and 1860s, her stories typically are narrated from within by their central characters. When a first-person narrator is present in the fiction of Stowe, she is typically external to the story, relaying events she has witnessed (or even, as in *The Minister's Wooing*, that she has self-admittedly created for a didactic purpose). But the narrator of Stoddard's "My Own Story" (1860), "Lemorne *Versus* Huell" (1863), "The Prescription" (1864), and "The Visit" (1868) is in each case the central woman in the story. In each case, the narrator is a passionate woman who does not transcend her interested perspective or manage the events of her experienced narrative. (The same narrative situation occurs in Stoddard's best-known work, her first novel, *The Morgesons* (1862), which is told by its central character, Cassandra Morgeson.) Several of Stoddard's other stories from the 1860s are told from the limited perspective of a central female reflector-character: "The Chimneys" (1865) and "Lucy Tavish's Journey" (1867); others are told in direct presentation ("A Partie Carée," 1862) or even with a quasi-dramatic framework that heightens the sense of unmediated experience ("Tuberoses," 1863).[4]

"The Prescription" is perhaps the most vivid example of the potential of Stoddard's narrative technique for complicating the exploratory possibilities of the short story. "The Prescription" begins with a sentence that (apparently) elaborates its title, but does little else in the way of exposition: "The Doctor said that change of air would do me good, and that the farther I went from home the better" (2616). The plot line moves outward from this sentence in an oscillating direction, first backtracking, then going forward, then further back than before, then further forward. It is a plot of marital estrangement and reconciliation narrated by the wife, Caroline Fuller. The doctor's prescription of a "change of air" is given in response to that estrangement, a situation not explained directly but presented by means of an emblematic object, "a torn Zouave jacket of white Marseilles" (2616), which her husband, Gérard, has forcibly cut off Caroline's body just before the doctor's entrance. Caroline is silent throughout the jacket-cutting incident and indeed throughout the entire opening conversation between the doctor and her husband, except for a parting comment on the doctor's orders that might be a metacommentary on her own narratives: "You had better make them more explicit" (2617).

The narrative kernel of "The Prescription" is ultimately explicit enough: The actual "prescription" that the Doctor hands Caroline in a sealed envelope, as she departs for her stay in the fishing village of Marlow, is "Comprehend yourself" (2621), and the result of her efforts at self-comprehension, catalyzed by the Bowmans, the elderly couple she stays with there, is that she and Gérard are brought back together again, presumably to be happy ever after. But the process of reconciliation is incomprehensible, consisting merely of Gérard spending a night sitting up outside his wife's room. Their estrangement, too, has been unmotivated, or motivated by forces that lie beneath the narrator's consciousness. After a period of eventless existence at the Bowmans's, Caroline takes stock of her relationship with Gérard in the one passage that qualifies as exposition, halfway through the story. She begins with "two facts. I lived with grandmother, and married Gérard Fuller" (2622). But just as in the opening scene, sequential narrative and explanation are foregone in favor of a metonymic incident: Gérard's destroying the arrangement of her hair after a male friend has admired it (2622).

In the process of comprehending herself, Caroline admits, "I have been living and not thinking; 19 years of unconscious doing what I have been directed to do" (2622). But "The Prescription" is far from being a story of the development of its narrator's discursive sense of self-knowledge. Even as she begins "thinking," Caroline thinks in the images and memories of doing and is literally unable to narratize those images into an analytical framework. She begins a diary in order to write out her self-analysis, but her writing is immediately interrupted by external events and by a sense that writing is itself inadequate: "I long to say something that is really important, and should never be seen by human eye" (2624). The internal contradictions of the situation of the Victorian woman narrator are dramatically displayed here: In order to fully express herself, the narrator must hide her writing forever, particularly from her husband (who, predictably, later discovers the diary and disparages her effort). Caroline's admission of the inadequacy of writing to her situation calls into question the larger adequacy of "The Prescription" to deal with the issue of her marriage, or (again by metonymy) of any fiction to deal with any marriage. That Stoddard's own marriage was marked by cycles of doubt and intense reconciliation, as well as a certain professional rivalry, shows the potential interest of this passage from "The Prescription" to her biography (Zagarell).

The fictional husband and wife are finally reunited not by any analysis—still less by putting Gérard in therapy for incipient domestic violence—but by the fact that her attempts at analysis keep being eclipsed by the vague "images . . . of a plain man and woman named Gérard and Caroline" (2624). After an attempt at dialogue breaks down, Gérard spends his night in the hallway. A few days later they embrace each other in terms so clichéd and devoid of original thought that Mr. Bowman cannot help critiquing their performance:

> "Caroline!"
> "Gérard!"
> "Now isn't this enough to make me down sick?" cried the old man. (2627)

The story closes with the narrator telling her husband that he has become her "ideal man," providing a neat closure to a failure to live up to marital ideals. But it is an ending that is less a true resolution than a silent abandonment of the problem. A managed resolution would demand some sort of reformation on Gérard's part; here, he exhibits none. The reader does not know whether the power struggle that has characterized their marriage has been resolved equitably, by a reimposition of Gérard's authority, by some mutual subordination to the will of God, by family intervention, or by any other mechanism than the resumption of the silence that prevailed before the narrative began. With such an ending, "The Prescription" becomes a commentary on the arbitrary nature of narrative management, and how that management artificially channels the expression of women's experience. Caroline realizes that there is still no public rhetoric in which to express a critique of Victorian marriage; but all the same Stoddard is unwilling to avail herself of the many public rhetorics that are an apology for Victorian marriage: motherhood, separate spheres, feminized Christianity, duty, progress. Choosing not to have recourse to an available voice may be the first step toward the development of an alternative voice.

Still, "The Prescription" ends with a reconciliation, however reticent it may be about its motivations. It does *not* end with the immersion in madness or suicide that would characterize later modernists like Gilman or Chopin. Stoddard's short stories uniformly end with apparent marital happiness—excepting only "Lemorne *Versus* Huell," which ends with its narrator realizing in a dream that her husband is a scoundrel. Probably because of the modernity of its ending, "Lemorne *Versus* Huell" has been the first of Stoddard's stories to become widely anthologized. But Stoddard's other stories resist their own happy endings by violating narrative conventions. The more that narration itself is revealed as a managing fiction, the more closure of narrative tends to be revealed as arbitrary. The happy-marriage ending can then be read as politically tendentious rather than biologically predestined.

"My Own Story," in fact, offers, at the start of Stoddard's career in fiction, an epitome of her reaction to conventional narrative devices. Women's fiction across the entire period employs as a favorite motif a death scene of one of the heroine's female friends. When Jane's friend Helen Burns dies in Charlotte Brontë's *Jane Eyre*, or Ellen Montgomery's friend Alice Humphreys dies in *The Wide, Wide World*, or, still later, the narrator's aunt dies in Elizabeth Stuart Phelps's *The Gate's Ajar* (1869), each heroine loses a spiritual mentor, while at the same time having the independence of her own faith confirmed. "My

Own Story" opens in the middle of such a death scene, but it is anything but an example of spiritual instruction. The dying Laura, convulsed by unresolved passions, is the first to acknowledge that she isn't being a good moribund role model: "'It is strange,' she said, 'when I know that I must die, that I should be so moved by earthly passions and so interested in earthly speculations'" (526). Recognizing the indecorousness of her own behavior, Laura concludes her interview with Margaret in appropriate fashion: "'Margaret'—she spoke like a little child,—'I am going to heaven'" (527). But she does not die at this point. She dismisses Margaret, who goes home and deliberately never returns, learning of her friend's death only when she sees that "the blinds had been thrown back and the windows opened" (527).

Margaret gives Frank his letters and gets her own letters and those of the man she knows Laura was in love with, Harry Lothrop, with her penholder. Then, she writes impulsively to Harry to let him know that Laura is dead and that she has his letters—an act that touches off Harry's courtship of her. "Another lover," she muses, "and Redmond's friend, and Laura's. But it all belongs to the comedy we play" (529). Of course, Margaret has instigated this "comedy" herself. With Laura dead and Redmond engaged to be married, she throws herself into a love affair to exasperate her dead friend (who has assured her while dying that "the doctrine of compensation extends beyond this world" [526]) and punish her living lover for his fidelity to his fiancée. But she has already warned her readers that she will not practice the self-abnegation they might expect from a Victorian heroine:

> I can afford to confess that I possessed beauty; for half my faults and miseries arose from the fact of my being beautiful. I was not vain, but as conscious of my beauty as I was of that of a flower, and sometimes it intoxicated me. For, in spite of the comforting novels of the Jane Eyre school, it is hardly possible to set an undue value upon beauty; it defies ennui. (528)

If we expected a narrator out of Charlotte Brontë, we have gotten one who unsettlingly foreshadows Oscar Wilde.

"My Own Story" proceeds backward from this character note to fill in the development of the tangle of relationships that arose the summer before Laura's death, and then moves far forward to Margaret's rejection of Harry's proposal in favor of the newly widowed Redmond. The narrative spans many years in its 20 pages and is arbitrarily constructed, introducing two key characters—Margaret's brother and his wife—only three-quarters of the way through. Yet this would come to be Stoddard's typical narrative style. "Lucy Tavish's Journey" introduces John Tavish—Lucy's cousin and eventual husband—only when it is almost over, and identifies him only at the very end. The artist Bassett, who "squares" a romantic triangle in "A Partie Carée," is introduced late, and his full identity is not revealed till the end (his motives and tactics in sorting out the relationships in the party of four lovers are open to doubt even at the story's end). Margaret herself voices the aesthetic principle behind this narrative asymmetry when she says, "Dramatic unities are never preserved in life; if they were, how poetical would all these things be! But Time whirls us round, showing us our many-sided feelings as carelessly as a child rattles the bits of glass in his kaleidoscope" (546). The kaleidoscope as a metaphor for narrative technique, however appropriate to Laurence Sterne before or Gertrude Stein afterward, is as alien to nineteenth-century fiction as any trope could be. And central to Margaret's (and Stoddard's) use of the kaleidoscope metaphor is the sense that the individual speaking subject, the narrator herself, is nothing but a temporal and unrepeatable sequence of kaleidoscopic images. For such a narrator to manage the telling even of "her own story" would be to break faith with the essential contingency of all historically situated lives.

Stoddard's short fiction has never been collected in book form, though a few stories were reprinted in collections during her lifetime (1823–1902): "Osgood's Predicament" (1863), a more humorous variation of the themes of "The Prescription," appeared in the Scribner collection of *Stories by American Authors*; "My Own Story," in Constance Cary Harrison's *Short Stories* in 1893. Today, only "Lemorne *Versus* Huell," "The Prescription," and "Collected by a Valetudinarian" (1870) are widely available; in addition, "The Chimneys" was reprinted in *Legacy* in 1990.

Her influence, therefore, seems to have been limited. In a sense, her immediate followers, like A.D.T. Whitney, Elizabeth Stuart Phelps, and Mary Hallock Foote, and her more distant descendants Gilman, Chopin, and Stein, had to "rediscover" some of the same narrative solutions to the contradictions of their situations that Stoddard had developed in the 1860s. But the existence of such a remarkable series of stories in that decade calls for further study—much as an equally brilliant set of narratives, also largely published in *Harper's*, helped to reestablish the canonical place of Herman Melville when they were rediscovered decades ago.

NOTES

1. I thank Sandra Zagarell for encouraging me to write this essay, and I thank the students in English 5326 at the University of Texas at Arlington for providing the research community in which it was written.

2. The works whose opening sentences are given here are these, of course: Edgar Allan Poe's *The Narrative of Arthur Gordon Pym of Nantucket* (1838); Herman Melville's *Moby-Dick* (1851) and "Bartleby, the Scrivener" (1853); Harriet Beecher Stowe's *Uncle Tom's Cabin* (1852); and Nathaniel Hawthorne's *The Marble Faun* (1860).

3. The fact that many works that exhibit narratorial "intrusion" are by men and have male narrators is a complicating factor beyond the scope of this essay or volume. Aside from Stowe, the most egregiously self-reflexive Victorian author/narrator is Anthony Trollope, quite possibly for reasons of class and audience very different from the dynamic in American women writers.

4. For each of Stoddard's stories I have quoted from the most easily available edition; in the "Works Cited" list below I have given both that edition and the citation for the original printing.

Works Cited

DeKoven, Marianne. *Rich and Strange: Gender, History, Modernism.* Princeton, NJ: Princeton University Press, 1991.

Harris, Susan K. *19th-Century American Women's Novels: Interpretive Strategies.* New York: Cambridge University Press, 1990.

Hedrick, Joan D. "Parlor Literature: Harriet Beecher Stowe and the Question of 'Great Women Artists'." *Signs* 17 (Winter 1992): 275–303.

Stoddard, Elizabeth D.B. "The Chimneys." *Harper's* (November 1865): 726–732. Rpt. in *Legacy* 7.2 (1990): 27–37.

———. "Collected by a Valetudinarian." *Harper's* (December 1870): 96–105. Rpt. in *The Morgesons and Other Writings, Published and Unpublished*. Eds. Lawrence Buell and Sandra A. Zagarelli. Philadelphia: University of Pennsylvania Press, 1984, pp. 285–308.

———. "Lemorne *Versus* Huell." *Harper's* (March 1863): 537–543; Rpt. in *The Morgesons and Other Writings, Published and Unpublished.* Philadelphia: University of Pennsylvania Press, 1984.

———. "Lucy Tavish's Journey." *Harper's* (October 1867): 656–663.

———. "My Own Story." *Atlantic Monthly* (May 1860): 526–547; Rpt. in *Short Stories*. Ed. Constance Cary Harrison. New York: Ayer, 1893, pp. 1–73.

———. "Osgood's Predicament." *Harper's* (June 1863): 52–61. Rpt. in *Stories by American Authors.* Vol. 8. Eds. Charles Scribner's Sons Staff. New York: Scribner's, 1884, pp. 170–206.

———. "A Partie Carée." *Harper's* (Sept. 1862): 466–479.

———. "The Prescription." *Harper's* (May 1864): 794–800. Rpt. in *The Heath Anthology of American Literature.* Vol. 1. Eds. Paul Lauter et al. Lexington, MA: Heath, 1990, pp. 2616–2628.

———. "Tuberoses." *Harper's* (January 1863): 191–197.

———. "The Visit." *Harper's* (November 1868): 802–809.

Zagarell, Sandra A. "*Legacy* Profile: Elizabeth Drew Barstow Stoddard (1823–1902)." *Legacy* 8.1 (1991): 39–49.

Who Was That Masked Woman? Gender and Form in Louisa May Alcott's Confidence Stories

Gail K. Smith

> I intend to illuminate the Ledger with a blood & thunder tale as they are easy to "compoze" & are better paid than moral & elaborate works of Shakespeare so dont be shocked if I send you a paper containing a picture of Indians, pirates, wolves, bears & distressed damsels in a grand tableau over a title like this "The Maniac Bride" or "The Bath of Blood: A Thrilling Tale of Passion."

On June 22, 1862, a budding young author from Concord, Massachusetts, wrote these lines to her friend Alf Whitman. From 1862 to 1868, she would pen numerous "blood & thunder tales," with thrilling titles like "Pauline's Passion and Punishment" or "The Mysterious Key and What It Opened." Printed in sensational illustrated weeklies like *Frank Leslie's Illustrated Newspaper* and *The Flag of Our Union,* they brought much-needed cash to the writer and thrills, spills, and chills to thousands of readers. But virtually no one knew that the author, "A.M. Barnard," was none other than "The Children's Friend," the author of *Flower Fables* and—in 1868–1869—*Little Women.* "A.M. Barnard" was Louisa May Alcott.

At the suggestion of Alcott collector Carroll Atwood Wilson, Leona Rostenberg, an antiquarian bookseller, set out in the early 1940s to find Alcott's pseudonymous and anonymous "blood and thunder" stories. While Ednah D. Cheney had mentioned the stories in passing in her 1889 biography of Alcott (105–107), both the titles and Alcott's pseudonym were as yet unknown. No manuscripts existed, and it was uncertain where Alcott had published the stories. Rostenberg, along with business partner Madeleine B. Stern, found at the Houghton Library several letters between Alcott and James R. Elliott of Elliott, Thomes, and Talbott, publishers of *The Flag of Our Union*. Here were the titles and locations of several Alcott thrillers, in addition to the revelation that Alcott was writing as "A.M. Barnard." Comparing cryptic references in Alcott's journals to the crumbling pages of "A.M. Barnard" in the cheap weeklies yielded story after story by Alcott. Rostenberg announced her discovery in the *Papers of the Bibliographical Society of America* in 1943, and after years of continued sleuthing she and Stern published three landmark collections under Stern's editorship: *Behind a Mask: The Unknown Thrillers of Louisa May Alcott* (1975), *Plots and Counterplots: More Unknown Thrillers of Louisa May Alcott* (1976), and *A Double Life: Newly Discovered Thrillers of Louisa May Alcott* (1988). The American public discovered, to their amazement, that like Jo March in *Little Women*, Alcott began her career as a writer of lurid stories she was reluctant to own as hers.

Initially the reception of these stories has focused on the hitherto-unknown "side" of Alcott herself. Critics have mainly assumed that these tales reveal the "real" Alcott, who later retires behind a mask of domesticity to write the *Little Women* series. Accompanying this interpretation of Alcott's life are parallel readings of her sensational heroines as angry women who must screen their passion with the mask of conventional womanhood. Studies by Ann Douglas, Judith Fetterley, and Martha Saxton, along with Madeleine Stern's introductions to all three thriller collections, draw on the mask image to explain how Alcott—amateur actress and pseudonymous writer as she was—expressed her real self both "behind the mask" of "A.M. Barnard" and through her actress/trickster characters. But while there is a good deal of evidence from letters and journal entries that Alcott found release in writing her "blood and thunder" tales, the image of the mask, which recurs in these stories and in the criticism about them, is more complex in Alcott's hands than a simple distinction between reality and assumed identity. Examining Alcott's play with masks, acting, and deception reveals that these stories consciously manipulate fictional conventions about identity, character, and the task of the author.

A number of the rediscovered "blood and thunder" stories feature a female protagonist who uses trickery and theatrical ability to hoodwink her audience, usually male. The stories, in fact, are more than "obliquely feminist" (Stern, Introduction, *Behind a Mask* xxviii). Alcott, an outspoken supporter of women's rights and the first woman to vote in a Concord (Massachusetts) election, might be expected to depart from the typical gender roles of the Gothic cliffhanger or the sensational romance—the sinister male mastermind, for instance, or the melting, virtuous heroine. Nowhere is Alcott's skillful reworking of gender and identity more apparent than in her stories of women who gain the trust and devotion of their willing victims in order to outwit them and gain what they desire. Stories like "V.V., Or, Plots and Counterplots," *Behind a Mask, Or, A Woman's Power*, and "Pauline's Passion and Punishment" revise the male tradition of the confidence story. In fact, Alcott writes story after story featuring what we might call a "confidence woman." To understand the significance of that act, we must first examine the tradition of the confidence man in American fiction.

The term "confidence man" was apparently coined to describe an American criminal, William Thompson, arrested in 1849 for playing on the gullibility of strangers whom he asked to leave their watches with him (Lindberg 6). As John G. Blair and Gary Lindberg point out, the figure of the confidence man is related to but distinct from both the mythic trickster figure (Odysseus, Hermes, or Esu the Signifying Monkey, for example) and the picaro (Blair 22–23; Gates 237). The confidence man, unlike the nearly universal trickster figure, "inhabits a modern, highly differentiated, literate society" (Lindberg 8); unlike the picaro, the confidence man "has usually lost his sense of the ludicrous. Game-playing . . . is the source of his being. Hence such figures commonly evoke a moral seriousness rare among picaresque rogues" (Blair 23). And, as Blair notes, the confidence man owes his success to the willing complicity of his victims (17).

From early American works onward, the confidence man has played his part. Preceding the American confidence story were the orally influenced tales of the early nineteenth century, now known as "Southwestern humor," which gave the related genres of the trickster tale and the picaresque an especially crude, violent, aggressive, and intensely masculine—often misogynistic—flavor. Johnson Jones Hopper's gambler character, Simon Suggs, sets the theme for the nascent confidence-man tradition with his maxim, "It is good to be shifty in a new country." Subsequent writers would represent again and again the shifty character that America seemed to breed. Edgar Allan Poe's slippery confidence men and his own authorial deceptions owe much to the precursor genre of the Southwestern trickster tale or picaresque. Herman Melville's *The Confidence-Man: His Masquerade* (1857) pulls a joke on the reader attempting to identify the confidence man's avatars, and satirizes both his characters and the America they represent.

Studies by Gary Lindberg, John G. Blair, and Victor Myers Hoar, Jr., have considered the confidence man in American and European literature, commenting on its moral qualities and its appropriateness to America. These critics, however, have based their conclusions on a literary canon made up solely of men who created male confidence artists. It has long been assumed that the confidence artist in American literature is necessarily masculine because the confidence man was a stock figure in the supposedly "man's world" of the frontier (Cohen and Dillingham xxvii). There were, however, actual "confidence women" succeeding at matrimonial swindles in young America (Nash 133–146), as well as women writers who explored the confidence theme and created female tricksters in their fiction. And the female trickster figure was hardly new; writers could draw on a long tradition of the *femme fatale* (often called a witch or sorceress)—Circe, Jezebel, Morgan le Fay—and the female spinner of plots—Athena, Penelope, Scheherezade.

Concerns with female deceivers were common in American politics and literature up to Alcott's time. In early America, the Puritans exhibited a particular fear of women who were "shifty characters" in their extremely "new country." Anne Hutchinson was accused of sorcery and banished from the Bay

Colony when her lay prayer meetings were perceived as a challenge to the primacy of the male clergy. Cotton Mather executed many women deemed witches; often, they were midwives or others who in some way crossed traditional gender boundaries (in the case of the midwives, women were infiltrating the male world of medicine). The figure of the confidence artist became prevalent in the literature of Jacksonian America, along with concerns about unheard-of social mobility and the rule of the formerly disenfranchised. Several American women writers from the 1830s onward were rethinking both the supposed masculinity of confidence games and the male condemnation of female tricksters. Caroline Kirkland's *A New Home, Who'll Follow* (1839) satirized the gullibility of male pioneers whose greed and delusions of grandeur make them susceptible to the land speculator's confidence schemes. The fugitive slave in Harriet Jacobs's autobiographical novel, *Incidents in the Life of a Slave Girl* (1860), described her clever machinations from her attic hiding place, where she arranges to have letters from herself posted from faraway cities to her old master, so he will never suspect she is living within sight of his house. Far from being a "sorceress," Jacobs is a highly moral trickster who manages to hoodwink her depraved master in order to save herself and her family.

By the time of Alcott's productive years, as Susan P. Casteras has noted, images of "female sages and sorceresses" were particularly prevalent in British Victorian art. Casteras speculates that these images express the anxieties of male artists—especially the Pre-Raphaelites—toward the "New Woman" of intellect and achievement, who was gaining political, social, and legal power (142–144). Across the Atlantic, Louisa May Alcott was delving into the same concerns through the vehicle of the confidence woman and the confidence story.

It is interesting to note that literary confidence games seem to fit best in the tale or short story. Lindberg points out that "the confidence man belongs in an episodic plot because he possesses no ground of continuity on the basis of which to perpetuate 'himself.' . . . A story centered around a con man must share his impermanence" (24). Even *The Confidence-Man*, sometimes called a novel, is organized in discrete encounters. The short, self-contained narrative, with a setup, a period of deception, and a discovery (on the part of the characters, or the reader, or both), is the norm in a confidence story. In fact, the short story is admirably suited to the subject. In a "con," in literature as in life, timing is all-important. The quickness—or at least the sudden turns—needed for a "trick" to be successful before it is found out dictates the length of the event and hence the length of the narrative.

Alcott's confidence women clearly partake of elements of the confidence-man tradition, as well as the tales of a mythical female trickster or *femme fatale*. The victims are in some way willing participants in the deception they undergo, and the stories proceed with the usual periods of the setup, the successful deception, and the final discovery. Yet unlike Poe, Alcott does not always wish to leave us with a clear picture of what is real and what is false. The "discovery," for instance, is in some stories rather ambiguous. In addition, unlike Poe and Melville, Alcott is highly conscious of traditional gender roles in this genre. Her confidence women cross gender boundaries, acting in traditionally masculine ways and forcing men into "feminized" roles of subservience, ignorance, passivity, and powerlessness. In exploring the machinations of a confidence woman, Alcott complexifies both the conventions of gender roles and the conventions of the confidence story.

As in other confidence stories, timing is of the utmost importance in Alcott's stories. In fact, Alcott's confidence women frequently comment on their careful attention to timing as they weave their plots and cast their scenes—as do Alcott's narrators. Using the language of the dramatic director and the author, they encourage the reader to consider the ways in which the stories they enact reflect the form they take. Alcott's confidence women consciously manipulate their victims' access to knowledge, their emotions, their gendered perceptions, and their assumptions about gender in others; in doing so these heroines "write" the confidence tale we read. At the same time, Alcott herself, we realize, shapes her story to manipulate our access to knowledge, our emotions, and our assumptions about gender—and, finally, our assumptions about the relation between author and reader.

In two of Alcott's most interesting confidence stories, the narrative "con" takes place both within the story—as the heroines hoodwink the other characters—and outside the story—as Alcott misleads and dupes the reader. In "Pauline's Passion and Punishment" (1863) and *Behind a Mask, Or, A Woman's Power* (1866), self-conscious artificers and confidence women, become figures for Alcott, the amateur actress and struggling author. By virtue of the work they do, dictated by an instinct for self-preservation and by passionate emotion, both Alcott and her heroines cross boundaries traditionally drawn between the sexes. And in the working-out of the narrative "con," Alcott's confidence women dupe their audience just as Alcott, it turns out, dupes her readers. Like Melville, Alcott plays a confidence game with her audience. By making her confidence artists women, and the confidence game specifically about gender, especially about womanhood, Alcott gives a fascinating twist to the traditions of her male predecessors. The success of her own confidence game rests on her skillful play with her audience's assumptions about gender and form.

Behind a Mask is more properly considered a novella, and is therefore beyond the scope of this study. But much can be learned from Alcott's first confidence story, "Pauline's Passion and Punishment," which won a $100 prize from *Frank Leslie's Illustrated Newspaper* in 1862 (Stern, Introduction, *Behind a Mask* xx). "Pauline's Passion and Punishment" blurs gender boundaries at the same time that it explores the traditional gendering of the story it tells.

Pauline Valary—strong, beautiful, and penniless—has waited six months for her lover, Gilbert Redmond, to return and take her away from the Cuban plantation where she serves as a personal companion. But as the story opens, Pauline reads a letter from Gilbert explaining that he has been obliged to marry an heiress back in America. Vowing revenge, Pauline manipulates the love-smitten young Cuban heir, Manuel, into marrying her. Together they set out to wreak vengeance on Gilbert and his bride.

From the first scene onward, Alcott plays with the ideas of identity and gender. At first, Pauline's "real" self seems readily definable. When we first read of her, she has apparently just undergone a metamorphosis from a happy, hopeful woman to a woman who resembles a "wild creature in its cage" (107). Since Pauline is in this first scene alone and unobserved by any character, we assume that this passionate and masterful woman is the new, true Pauline—yet in doing so we are already positing the existence of an earlier, different Pauline whom we have never met. Already we are making assumptions based on what we think a woman is "naturally" like before a devastating change makes her "unnatural" and "unwomanly." Her own words to her friend Manuel seem to confirm that this second self is now the real Pauline: "See me as I am, not the gay girl you have known, but a revengeful woman" (114). Much of the story supports the hypothesis that the "real" Pauline is the cold, vengeful, inexorable mastermind, whose only warm spot is her "real regard for her husband, for though sisterly, it was sincere" (124). Yet in the subsequent imagery of the mask the idea of Pauline's real self becomes less and less fixed as the tale progresses.

From the beginning, Pauline comments on the inversions of gender expectations that characterize the story. Pauline herself is no "little woman"; she is "ardent, dominant, and subtle," one who will "dare to act where feebler souls would only dare desire" (109). The pecking order in her relationships is immediately established: Manuel, "eager yet timid," enters the opening scene answering Pauline's "Come!" with the submissiveness of his dog (109–110). He tells Pauline, "I swear to obey you in all things; make me what you will, for soul and body I am wholly yours henceforth" (116). Pauline then takes the male role by proposing to Manuel, who accepts humbly with grateful tears, his lips ("sensitive as any woman's") trembling with love (113). Her plan, she tells him, is to "play" the happy bride who lives only for her husband, while the feminine Manuel must "enact the man" (119). Adorned with wealth and splendor, Pauline will fascinate Gilbert again, so that she can experience the pleasure of spurning him.

As she thinks out her plot, Pauline comments on the form her narrative will take. Gilbert's fateful letter closes with the plea: "leave my punishment to remorse and time." In a fascinating response, however, Pauline rewrites this ending. She tells Manuel, "Leave Gilbert to remorse—and me" (110). Eliminating two letters of Gilbert's closing word, Pauline effectively rewrites Gilbert's version of their love story. And replacing "time" with "me" suggests what the story will bear out—that Pauline's chief weapon and the chief difference between men and women in the story will be timing. The emphasis on reversed endings continues, fittingly, at the end of the first chapter, when Pauline "said low to herself, 'This is an old, old story, but it shall have a new ending'" (116).

Throughout the story, Pauline attempts to keep rigid control both of time—the pace of the story she plots—and of gender. For Pauline, they are inextricably intertwined. After reading Gilbert's letter, she tells Manuel, "There are fates more terrible than death; weapons more keen than poniards, more noiseless than pistols. Women use such, and work out a subtler vengeance than men can conceive" (110). Manuel finds Pauline's feminine timing distastefully slow. He suggests killing Gilbert outright. But to Pauline, male revenge is "brief and paltry" (110). A woman's pace, a woman's timing, will direct the plot Pauline creates. It was Gilbert who paced their six-month separation; once Pauline discovers his deception, she claims control of time and of plot. After searching for Gilbert and his new wife, Pauline and her new husband Manuel find them in a fashionable resort. "Our three weeks' search is ended, and the real interest of the plot begins," Pauline tells Manuel (118).

When Pauline and Manuel attend a ball at which Gilbert and his wife are present, the real Pauline and her mask are at first still distinguishable. We interpret the honeymooning love she shows Manuel in the presence of Gilbert as merely an act to cause Gilbert pain, and we assume that her coldness to Gilbert is real, since she has told Manuel that she feels only contempt for Gilbert. Her masking, however, receives a new twist in an intriguing scene at the ball. Gilbert and Pauline are left alone, and her fixed gaze prompts him to ask her to "take off your mask as I do mine—we are alone now, and may see each other as we are." Pauline "swept her hand across her face as if obeying him, yet no change followed, as she said with a cold smile, 'It is off; what next?'" (123). We might at first read this as indicating that Pauline's coldness to Gilbert is no mask, but reality. Another possible reading, however, is that Pauline is still wearing her "mask"; the narrator tells us that she only acts "as if" she obeys Gilbert's request. Pauline herself says she has removed the mask, but we know she may be acting in Gilbert's presence. Is Pauline now pretending not to be acting, or is she being her real self? To complicate the matter further, the narrator tells us in this scene that Pauline still feels some passion for Gilbert, and has only been suppressing it (126). This calls into question our earlier assumption that her coldness toward Gilbert reflected her real self; we are now told that it is a mask she has assumed in front of both Gilbert and Manuel. Has Pauline removed one mask of coldness only to reveal another? Alcott structures the scene in such a way that questions about Pauline's "true" feelings cannot be answered. As Pauline plays with the assumptions of her men, the narrator plays equally fast and loose with the reader's assumptions about masks and the woman's self. In reading the tale, we begin to realize that the assumptions we are drawing on to interpret Pauline owe much to stereotypes about gender and about the form of the confidence tale.

In fact, what we have is a double confidence tale. As the story winds to its close, notable parallels between Gilbert and Pauline increase. Both are "masked" in some sense, and it becomes evident that each is plotting against the other. In an intriguing balcony scene, Pauline urges Manuel to use her lorgnette to spy on Gilbert, who is spying on them with a telescope from a room across the courtyard (134–135). Each watching the other, each deceiving the other, Pauline and Gilbert are both plotters, both seeking to direct the play in which they are living. Each tries to double cross the other: While Pauline schemes with Manuel to get Gilbert's wife fascinated with Manuel and Gilbert fascinated with Pauline, Gilbert is cheating at cards and forging checks to gain money to repay the gambling debts he owes Manuel, debts which place him in Pauline's power. Both Pauline and Gilbert, then, are artists in the confidence game—Gilbert first won Pauline's "confidence" as a lover, then spurned her; Pauline seeks to make Gilbert believe in her, then reveals to him he has been duped. The fascinating situation Alcott sets up is a conflict between a confidence man and a confidence woman, each of whom very consciously uses gendered roles to try to gain control of the plot. Their game of confidence is a microcosm of the conflict between men and women.

At the story's end, Pauline's narrative reaches its climax. When at last Gilbert and Pauline stand alone at the top of a waterfall, waiting for Manuel and Gilbert's wife to join them, Pauline senses with a writer's thrill that the denouement is at hand. Gilbert begs her to run away with him, and "Pauline felt that the time had come, and in the drawing of a breath was ready for it, with every sense alert, every power under full control. . . . [T]he sudden advent of the instant which must end her work sent an unwonted color to her cheek" (147).

At the same time, Pauline seems to become more traditionally feminine. She succeeds in obtaining an impassioned avowal of love from Gilbert, and as he pleads with her, Pauline's response is a warm and loving look, which the narrator calls "a glow of womanly emotion too genuine to be feigned." Pacing her response with stunning effect, Pauline tells Gilbert,

> Yes, I love; not as of old, with a girl's blind infatuation, but with the warmth and wisdom of heart, mind, and soul. . . . I have been once deceived, but faith still endures, and I believe that I may yet earn this crowning gift of a woman's life for the man who shall make my happiness as I make his. . . . And that beloved is—my husband. (149–150)

By the end of her speech her drawn-out, conscious manipulation of Gilbert's (and the reader's) expectations is apparent. At the same time, the carefully crafted ambiguity of her speech, and the time she takes to say it, raise questions on several levels about the "genuineness" of this "womanly emotion." Before she reaches the words "my husband," the emotion does seem directed to Gilbert; does this mean that her buried passion for him has surfaced, or that her "genuineness" in this scene is only a mask worn to hurt him? When Pauline "reveals" that her emotion is directed toward Manuel, the matter is still far from simple; since Pauline is evidently trying to hurt Gilbert, how can we know whether she genuinely feels love for the husband she has looked on as merely a friend? Confusion only increases when Gilbert asks imploringly, "Pauline, this is a jest?" and Pauline answers, "To me it is; to you—a bitter earnest" (150). We are left wondering how much of the scene has been a jest; might even her "genuine womanly emotion" for Manuel be false, merely part of the jest she is playing on Gilbert? In a sense, Alcott has arranged this tale to jest with the reader in the same ways that Pauline jests with Gilbert.

Finally, Pauline begins to lose control of the timing of her plot and the ending of her narrative. Once she spurns Gilbert, he seems to acknowledge that she is still the "author" in charge of their story; "as if his fate lay in her hands," he asks her, "How will it end? how will it end?" "As it began—in sorrow, shame, and loss," Pauline replies. She then ends their story, telling him "the dark history of the wrong and the atonement wrung from him with such pitiless patience" and pronounces "the final word of doom" (150). Gilbert, however, suddenly turns the narrative around. He inserts a second ending, which nullifies the effect of the first. "[H]e waited till she ended, then used the one retaliation she had left him," challenging the approaching Manuel to defend himself. "I swear I will end this jest of yours in a more bitter earnest than you prophesied," he exclaims. Taking up the masculine, swift method of violent revenge that Pauline had earlier scorned, Gilbert proceeds to sweep the luckless Manuel off the cliff to a watery death (152).

Pauline has received her punishment. If Pauline's "womanly emotion" for Manuel at the end is genuine, as the narrator suggests, then her pathetic fate is that she has finally become the loving wife she had intended merely to act out. Admitting that her happiness, like that of a traditional wife, now depends on her husband, she promptly loses him forever. Gilbert's rewriting of Pauline's intended ending forces traditional gender roles to snap back into place. As he enacts male vengeance, she is forced to watch in impotent passivity while feeling true, "womanly" emotions for her dead husband. The male plotter replaces the female; masculine timing prevails over feminine timing; and Pauline is left standing "impotent" at cliff's edge with the character who has, in effect, taken the pen out of her hand. Pauline's "design" as a confidence woman has led only to her sorrowful "impotence" as a "true woman," her loss of the husband she has, it seems, grown to love, and her subjection to the potent and violent confidence man.

In the novella *Behind a Mask, Or, A Woman's Power* (1866), Alcott explores the problems she raises in "Pauline's Passion and Punishment," but with a different result. If Pauline's "con" of Gilbert is, in a sense, too successful, Jean's is just successful enough that she emerges the clear winner in a world where, as Ann Douglas has noted, "a woman's power" is synonymous with her powers of deception ("Mysteries" 236). Jean's "little woman" act wins her a wealthy, titled husband. If deception is a "woman's power," the stories suggest further that in fact deception is the essence of womanhood. Unlike the men in these stories, who have coherent selves behind their masks, Alcott's confidence women can be seen as wearing masks that may only cover other masks beneath. The masked "self" of the successful confidence woman escapes definition, because self and mask are ultimately indistinguishable.

Alcott's other confidence stories, "V.V., Or, Plots and Counterplots" (1865) and "The Mysterious Key and What It Opened" (1867), are quite different. "V.V." again features a *femme fatale*, Virginie Varens, who manipulates men's passions until her treacheries blast her hopes for union with the only man she really loves. Yet Virginie's evil, as Martha Saxton has observed, appears to be without immediate motive; her wiles are merely the result of caprice (*Louisa May* 273). In "The Mysterious Key," Alcott experiments with a male confidence artist, a young Italian revolutionary in disguise as a gardener at an English estate. Perhaps because the confidence man figure challenges no elements of the confidence story genre, Alcott does not explore the connections between gender and form in this story. "The Mysterious Key" is an interesting and atypical recasting of Alcott's confidence-women stories; the conflict this time is not between the sexes but between the lower and upper classes.

But Alcott's greatest contribution to the short story is her regendering of the confidence story. Alcott's confidence woman bends both gender and form while she manipulates conventions of character and identity. With the creation of the confidence woman, Alcott takes her place as one of the innovators of the American short story. Her experimentation with "blood & thunder" accomplished, perhaps, more than she knew.

WORKS CITED

Alcott, Louisa May. *The Journals of Louisa May Alcott*. Eds. Joel Myerson et al. Boston: Little, Brown, 1989.

———. "Pauline's Passion and Punishment." *Behind a Mask: The Unknown Thrillers of Louisa May Alcott*. Ed. Madeleine B. Stern. New York: Quill, 1984, pp. 105–152.

Blair, John G. *The Confidence Man in Modern Fiction: A Rogue's Gallery with Six Portraits*. New York: Barnes & Noble, 1979.

Casteras, Susan P. "Malleus Malificarum or The Witches' Hammer: Victorian Visions of Female Sages and Sorceresses." *Victorian Sages and Cultural Discourse: Renegotiating Gender and Power*. Ed. Thaïs E. Morgan. New Brunswick, NJ: Rutgers University Press, 1990.

Cheney, Ednah D., ed. *Louisa May Alcott: Her Life, Letters, and Journals*. 1889. Boston: Roberts Brothers, 1890.

Cohen, Hennig, and William B. Dillingham, eds. *Humor of the Old Southwest*. 2nd ed. Athens: University of Georgia Press, 1975.

Douglas, Ann. Introduction, *Little Women*, by Louisa May Alcott. New York: Signet, 1983, pp. xviii–xix.

———. "Mysteries of Louisa May Alcott." *Critical Essays on Louisa May Alcott*. Ed. Madeleine B. Stern. Boston: G.K. Hall, 1984, pp. 231–240.

Fetterley, Judith. "Impersonating 'Little Women': The Radicalism of Alcott's *Behind a Mask*." *Women's Studies: An Interdisciplinary Journal* 10 (1983): 1–14.

———. "*Little Women*: Alcott's Civil War." *Feminist Studies* 5 (1979): 369–383.

Gates, Henry Louis, Jr. *Figures in Black: Words, Signs, and the "Racial" Self*. New York: Oxford University Press, 1987.

Hoar, Victor Myers, Jr. "The Confidence Man in American Literature." Thesis. University of Illinois Press, 1965.

Lindberg, Gary. *The Confidence Man in American Literature*. New York: Oxford University Press, 1982.

Nash, Jay Robert. *Hustlers and Con Men: An Anecdotal History of the Con Man and His Games*. New York: M. Evans & Co., 1976.

Rostenberg, Leona. "Some Anonymous and Pseudonymous Thrillers of Louisa May Alcott." *Papers of the Bibliographical Society of America* 37 (1943): 131–140.

Saxton, Martha. *Louisa May: A Modern Biography of Louisa May Alcott*. Boston: Houghton Mifflin, 1977.

———. "The Secret Imaginings of Louisa Alcott." *Critical Essays on Louisa May Alcott*. Ed. Madeleine B. Stern. Boston: G.K. Hall, 1984, pp. 256–260.

Shealy, Daniel, ed. *Louisa May Alcott: Selected Fiction*. Boston: Little, Brown, 1990.

Stern, Madeleine B. *Louisa May Alcott*. Norman: University of Oklahoma Press, 1950.

Stern, Madeleine B, ed. *Behind a Mask: The Unknown Thrillers of Louisa May Alcott*. New York: Quill, 1984.

———. *Plots and Counterplots: More Unknown Thrillers of Louisa May Alcott*. New York: Morrow, 1976.

Stern, Madeleine B., et al., eds. *A Double Life: Newly Discovered Thrillers of Louisa May Alcott*. Boston: Little, Brown, 1988.

Ripe Fruit: Fantastic Elements in the Short Fiction of Ellen Glasgow, Edith Wharton, and Eudora Welty

Stephanie Branson

Ellen Glasgow (1873–1945) published her first short story, called "A Woman of Tomorrow," in *Short Stories* when she was only 22. Throughout her long career, Glasgow continued to write short stories, despite her own feeling that she was a novelist by nature, and against the specific advice of editors such as Walter Hines Page who suggested that she should not waste her time on such a "minor genre."

In spite of Edith Wharton's (1862–1937) "depressing discovery" that the faculty for enjoying ghost stories had "almost become atrophied in modern man," and even though she felt that the two conditions required for the appearance of ghosts, "silence and continuity," were "abhorrent to the modern mind" (Preface, *Ghost Stories* 2–3), the author of *The House of Mirth* and *The Age of Innocence* produced enough tales of the supernatural over the course of her career to fill a good-sized volume.

Eudora Welty (1909–) values mystery above all other qualities in fiction. She states in an essay on the short story that "the first thing we see about a story is its mystery" ("Reading and Writing" 164). For Welty, "beauty springs from deviation" (176), and the many short stories she has written and published describe the indescribable—love, loss, and longing—in a broadly Gothic manner. Welty has published fine novels, but her favored form of fiction has been the short story; even *The Optimist's*

Daughter, for which she won the Pulitzer Prize, is an expansion of the short story by that name that appeared in *The New Yorker*. At least one critic has argued that the story of Laura Hand is better told in the original form.

Glasgow, Wharton, and Welty share an interest in and a practice of writing what was considered at the time to be "minor" fiction, generically and philosophically. Each wrote fantastic short stories from the turn of the century onward, over decades dominated by realistic and modernistic novels. Eudora Welty's stories are most often evaluated as realistic fiction, while Glasgow's and Wharton's ghost stories have been virtually ignored by literary critics.

The fantastic stories of these three women writers deserve serious attention because they represent a special form of social commentary, a parallel discourse running contrary to what can be seen as the dominant discourses of masculine realistic and modernistic fiction. Eudora Welty criticizes the dominant discourse:

> [O]urs is the century of unreason, the stamp of our behavior is violence or isolation; non-meaning is looked upon with some solemnity; and for the purpose of writing novels, most human behavior is looked at through the frame, or the knothole, of alienation. (*The Eye of the Story* 10)

In Glasgow's, Wharton's, and Welty's stories, women as well as men can act against convention, and there is an implied obligation to find imaginative solutions to human problems such as misogyny in dream, vision, and myth.

The generic affinity that I propose exists between certain fantastic short stories by these writers that can be explored through recurrent elements that I identify within those stories: Supernatural *mise-en-scènes* propose a communion of character and setting; in the operation of *weird* or supernaturally guided action, individual impulse collaborates with external fatefulness; and supernatural characterization links life to death.

Three representative stories will be the subject of this analysis: Glasgow's "Whispering Leaves," Wharton's "Bewitched," and Welty's "Moon Lake." These stories are visionary: they suggest new modes of perceiving reality for solving the problems of human existence, and they reflect a more organic and progressive *weltanschauung* (or world view) than that found in most realistic fiction.

Before I proceed to delineate how these fantastic elements operate in the three stories to be studied, a definition of the concept of "fantasy" is in order. In *Fantasy and Mimesis*, Kathryn Hume defines fantasy as "any departure from consensus reality" (21). For Hume, fantasy implies a desire to "change givens and alter reality" (20). Hume's subtitle, *Responses to Reality in Western Literature*, expresses her contention that both fantasy and mimesis (or, the essential structure of realistic literature) are *responses* to reality, rather than direct representations of it. She contends that most works of Western literature contain both mimetic and fantastic elements, but sees academics as "curiously blind" to the presence of fantasy "because our traditional approaches to literature are based on mimetic assumptions" (3). Ann Swinfen indicates that the "major difference" between fantastic and realistic fiction is that fantastic literature "takes account of areas of experience—imaginative, subconscious, visionary—which free the human spirit to range beyond the limits of empirical world reality" (231). Glasgow, Wharton, and Welty use fantasy to question the limitations imposed, especially on women, by empirically defined existence.

As Alastair Fowler points out in *Kinds of Literature*, *mise-en-scène*, or setting, is "a highly developed feature with romance, science fiction, the Gothic short story, and the psychological novel" (68). This is due in part to the fact that fantastic writers often vivify their characters' environs; that is, the setting becomes a "living character" of the story. Edith Wharton stresses in *The Writing of Fiction* the importance of "situation" in the short story in particular (48). In verisimilar works of all kinds, a multiplicity of straightforward detail is sufficient to the purpose of setting the fictional scene: In fantastic fiction supernatural detail is introduced in concert with realistic detail, and mood, or in Fowler's terms "emotional coloration" (67) has heightened importance.

In Glasgow's "Whispering Leaves," a supernatural scene is set early in the story when Uncle Moab, the carriage driver of the estate from which the story takes its name, tells the narrator,

Miss Effie, that all of the black servants have left Whispering Leaves out of fear (*Collected Stories* 141). Glasgow delays the explanation of what might be fearful at the estate until a little later in the story. In the same conversation between driver and guest, Uncle Moab describes an unusual phenomenon at Whispering Leaves: it is simply overrun with birds (142). The naive narrator, as yet unacquainted with Mammy Rhody, a ghost who haunts the estate, says in response, "If there were nothing more dangerous than birds at Whispering Leaves, I could be happy there" (142).

Soon thereafter, the narrator does meet the ghost who haunts Whispering Leaves and whose mission it is to save the strange boy Pell from threatened destruction (144). As in other Glasgow stories, such as "The Shadowy Third," supernatural agents collaborate with living agents to protect those at risk—women and children—from a violent, uncaring world. The unnaturally abundant birds, who at Whispering Leaves never cease their chattering (not at night, or even in winter, as Uncle Moab relates [143]), become an external, "natural" reflection of the inward, human tribulation in the house itself. The owner of the estate, Cousin Pelham, is a "vain, spoiled, selfish" man who cares for no one, not even his son Pell (152). Because Pell's dead mother has now been replaced in the household by an insensitive stepmother, Mammy Rhody (the child's deceased nanny) and the narrator are summoned to balance the inhumanity of the current inhabitants of the estate and to save the life of the little boy.

Thus, Glasgow uses the pathetic fallacy, or "the attribution of feeling to things" (Miles 1), to illustrate a connection between the characters (living and dead) and their environment. A similar spirit of place, or *genius loci*, is present in Edith Wharton's "Bewitched." The story is set in the dead of winter, in and around a desolate area called Lonetop. Isolated and bleak, the Rutledge and Brand farms inhabited by the central characters of "Bewitched" have a history of violence and witchcraft. This history destines Saul Rutledge and Sylvester Brand to sorrow and bewitchment, qualities reflected in both the weather they experience and the landscape they inhabit.

The specific site of supernatural activity in "Bewitched" is a "tumble-down shack" built by a "queer hermit fellow" in a hollow by a pond wherein "the air was as soundless and empty as an unswung bell" (161). It is here that the ghost of Ora Brand waits for Saul Rutledge, who was once her intended. She "draws" him to the shack at sunset, and the strain of this bewitchment threatens his life, as well as his current marriage.

The supernatural setting, or *mise-en-scène*, in Wharton's "Bewitched"—Hemlock County, scene of massacre and witch trials—suggests that a desolate winter landscape can parallel the desolation of the human spirit. Sylvester Brand had refused to allow his daughter Ora to marry Saul Rutledge, and this thwarting of romance indirectly leads to her death. Saul develops an "ague of the mind" as a result of Ora's attempt to reunite with him after her death. As Deacon Hibben puts it, "Something's sucking the life clean out of him" (160). That "something" is Ora's "spell" on the one hand, or the power of her thwarted love for her victim on the other. Sylvester Brand shoots his already-dead daughter, Ora, and loses his second daughter to disease. The bewitchment that Ora visits upon Saul Rutledge reflects a heritage of bewitchment in the Brand family.

Eudora Welty states in *Place in Fiction* that "the spirit of things is what is sought" (15). As in Glasgow's "Whispering Leaves" and in Wharton's "Bewitched," the lake in the story "Moon Lake" harbors a *genius loci* of supernatural dimension:

> Luminous of course but hidden from them, Moon Lake streamed out in the night. By moonlight sometimes it seemed to run like a river. Beyond the cry of the frogs there were the sounds of a boat moored somewhere, of its vague, clumsy reaching at the shore, those sounds that are recognized as being made by something sightless. When did boats have eyes—once? . . . Beyond lay the deep part, some bottomless parts, said Moody. Here and there was the quicksand that stirred your footprint and kissed your heel. All snakes, harmless and harmful, were freely playing now; they put a trailing, moony division between weed and weed—bright, turning, bright and turning. (361)

Later in the story, Easter, Welty's diminutive female Christ figure, falls into the lake and apparently drowns. Another "lake," the lifeguard Loch Morrison, brings her back to life, but not before she is transformed by the regenerative power of the magical lake into which she has fallen. Easter merges with the lake, and her companions fear lest "Her secret voice, if soundless then possibly visible, might work out of her terrible mouth like a vine, preening and sprung with flowers. Or a snake would come out" (369–370). Welty weds the orphan girl and the magical lake through this parallel imagery, infusing her character with the spirit of place.

In animating normally inanimate elements of a character's environment, Glasgow, Wharton, and Welty implicitly prescribe an organic and comprehensively vital universe. Guiding their characters supernaturally to participate in personal and collective destiny is a second method used by these writers to empower them through fantasy. This pattern of change involves the ancient mystical concept of *weird*. *Weird* was common as a noun, adjective, or verb in Old English, with all of its usages tied to fate. It is useful to recall its former meaning here in order to designate the definition of fate found in the short stories I am discussing. This use is distinct in several important ways from both classical and modern (i.e., naturalistic) conceptions of fate. Fate in the classical tradition engenders a spirit of helplessness in characters such as Oedipus. Modern writers like Hemingway equate the human condition with imprisonment, and fate with doom or death. Glasgow, Wharton, and Welty delineate instead a universe in which supernatural forces within and without the characters potentially guide them to fulfillment, provided the characters participate in their *weird*.

In Glasgow's "Whispering Leaves," for example, the narrator, Miss Effie, asks permission to visit the house in which her mother and grandmother were born (140). As she is initiated into the atmosphere of Whispering Leaves, she becomes aware of the fact that her cousin Pell is in danger, and that somehow she has been called to the estate for his sake. After her first encounter with the ghost of Mammy Rhody, she feels that the old woman recognizes her (although she had never met her in her lifetime) and that "she possessed some secret which she wished to confide" (147). Throughout the story, Glasgow emphasizes a matrilineal tie that binds Miss Effie to the now-dead women of her family and also to Mammy Rhody. Her *weird* involves collaborating with Mammy Rhody to protect her little cousin, a promise that the nanny made to Pell's mother as Pell's mother was dying.

In Wharton's "Bewitched," most of the action is supernaturally motivated. Saul Rutledge's *weird* was to marry Ora Brand, but because he marries someone else instead, thus thwarting his destiny and hers, supernatural forces conspire to kill him, much as they do Heathcliff in Emily Brontë's *Wuthering Heights*. Saul Rutledge is "bewitched"; he relates the story of his encounters with Ora "in a low automatic tone, as if some invisible agent were dictating his words, or even uttering them for him" (154). The other characters in the story—Prudence Rutledge, Deacon Hibben, Sylvester Brand, and Orrin Bosworth—are inextricably drawn to a shack, the site of supernatural visitation, to witness the unwholesome result of a father interfering inappropriately in the life of his daughter.

In Welty's "Moon Lake," it is Easter's fate to "drown" in the lake, so that her spirit might be strengthened. She is a natural leader: "Easter was dominant among the orphans. It was not that she was so bad. . . . It was wonderful to have with them someone dangerous but not, so far, or provenly, bad" (346–347). The danger or courage that the other orphans recognize in Easter takes on a spiritual dimension once she has experienced death and resurrection. This quality is related through another character, Nina, who envies Easter her triumph over death:

> In that passionate instant, when they reached Easter and took her up, many feelings returned to Nina, some joining and some conflicting. At least what had happened to Easter was out in the world. . . . There it remained—mystery, if only for being hard and cruel and, by something Nina felt inside her body, murderous. (372)

Easter involuntarily fulfills her *weird* by plunging into the lake of death and by reemerging from it.

The final fantastic element I wish to discuss is supernatural characterization. Mammy Rhody in Glasgow's "Whispering Leaves," Ora Brand in Wharton's "Bewitched," and Easter in Welty's "Moon Lake" can all be seen as ghosts who return from the dead to fulfill a specific purpose in the world. Glasgow,

Wharton, and Welty use supernatural characterization to suggest an immaterial dimension that transcends death. The fact that not all of the characters in these stories recognize or "see" these ghosts suggests that not all of the characters are equally imaginative. In the three stories analyzed here, the authors leave the question open as to whether or not ghosts are present; they suggest that it is a privilege to see ghosts but that it requires effort to participate in the numinous aspects of existence.

In Glasgow's "Whispering Leaves," for example, the most sensitive characters in the story—Miss Effie, Pell, and all of the black servants—see Mammy Rhody's ghost. The others do not. The story ends with an illustration of this contrast in perception:

> The next instant my heart melted with joy, for I saw that she was bringing the child in her arms. . . . Even the unperceiving eyes about me, though they could see only material things, knew that Pell had come unharmed out of the fire. To them it was merely a shadow, a veil of smoke, which surrounded him. I alone saw the dark arms that enfolded him. (163)

Miss Effie can perceive nonmaterial as well as material things, and this provides her with a richer experience of life. Because she is the narrator, her mode of perception is privileged, and the ghost is also "seen" by the reader.

A number of critics reading Wharton's "Bewitched" interpret the death of Ora's sister Venny with which the story ends to mean that Saul Rutledge was not being drawn to the shack by Ora, but rather that he was meeting Venny disguised as Ora. Thus when Sylvester Brand shoots the apparition of his daughter, he is really shooting Venny. This would then turn a ghost story revolving around bewitchment into a psychological study of superstition. But Wharton refrains from solving the mystery entirely, by offering a different cause for Venny's death, pneumonia, and by providing supernatural detail that cannot be easily dismissed. For example, Deacon Hibben and Orrin Bosworth see light, bare footprints in the snow that they feel can only have been made by a ghost (163). In addition, while Saul Rutledge may be wasting away because he *believes* he is bewitched, without supernatural power to draw him to the shack, Venny could not have drawn him from afar or against his will. Finally, Prudence Rutledge has seen Ora and her husband together, and since it is unlikely that as she has known Venny all of her life, she would not recognize her even in disguise. The wish to believe in ghosts is not strong in Prudence Rutledge, which is conveyed by her cold, practical manner (and by her name).

In Welty's "Moon Lake," Easter is not exactly a ghost. However, she is assigned many ghostlike qualities even before her mishap in the lake—she seldom speaks, she is aloof from all of the other girls, and she appears to have secret knowledge of life and death. Nina remarks that "the night knew about Easter" and that "the night loved some more than others, served some more than others"; in this scene, it is Easter whom "he" serves (361–362). Easter, who, because she cannot swim, "had no intention of going in the lake," nevertheless falls from the diving board on the last day of summer camp (364). For a full 9 pages of the 32-page story, Easter is unconscious and presumed dead. Loch repeatedly works her inert body, until the lifesaver is the only one who believes she might still be alive. Welty convinces her reader that Easter is dead, and this sense is confirmed by her friend Nina's musing that Easter is "beyond dying and beyond being remembered about" (370).

Easter comes back from near death because it is not yet time for her to die and because she will grow up to be a leader of men and women. Mammy Rhody returns from death to save Pell from dying prematurely in the fire and to fulfill the vow she made to his dying mother. Ora Brand returns from the grave, as she had promised Saul Rutledge that she would, in order to be with him in death, since that privilege was denied to her in life. Thus, supernatural characterization in these stories interweaves with supernaturally guided action, or *weird*.

Having identified fantastic elements in the three stories, I will conclude by briefly examining the connection between feminism and fantasy in "Whispering Leaves," "Bewitched," and "Moon Lake." Glasgow wrote that the "chief end . . . of all literature is to increase our understanding of life and heighten our consciousness" (*A Certain Measure* 30). This goal accords well with what Cheri Register calls a "common task" of feminism: "The illumination of 'female experience,' which will help us to decide *how* to transform the world" (268). For Edith Wharton, a well-written story would offer "a natural unembellished fragment of experience, detached like a ripe fruit from the tree" (*The Writing of Fiction* 49). The "fruit" produced by these writers encourages spiritual as well as practical evolution. The stories propose a new way of seeing that will break what Ann Weick calls "a perception monopoly": she claims that "the dominant Western paradigm [i.e., Cartesian science] is based on an incomplete and therefore erroneous definition of the nature of reality" ("Other Ways of Seeing" 187). Weick calls for a "recentering" of our perception of reality, to include personal visions such as those offered in the stories of Glasgow, Wharton, and Welty.

Both feminism as a sociopolitical project and fantasy as a literary mode require imaginative departures from conventional interpretations of society and reality. The fantastic short stories of my study deserve reevaluation because they portray important aspects of women's lives in an imaginative way and suggest the possibility for change in an organic universe.

Works Cited

Fowler, Alastair. *Kinds of Literature: An Introduction to the Theory of Genres and Modes.* Cambridge, MA: Harvard University Press, 1982.

Glasgow, Ellen. *A Certain Measure: An Interpretation of Prose Fiction.* New York: Harcourt Brace Jovanovich, 1943.

———. *The Collected Stories of Ellen Glasgow*. Ed. Richard K. Meeker. Baton Rouge: Louisiana State University Press, 1963.

———. "Whispering Leaves." *The Collected Stories of Ellen Glasgow*. Ed. Richard K. Meeker. Baton Rouge: Louisiana State University Press, 1963, pp. 140–164.

———. "A Woman of Tomorrow." *Short Stories* XIX (1895): 415–427.

Hume, Kathryn. *Fantasy and Mimesis: Responses to Reality in Western Literature.* New York: Methuen, 1984.

Miles, Josephine. *Pathetic Fallacy in the Nineteenth Century: A Study of a Changing Relation Between Object and Emotion.* New York: Octagon, 1976.

Register, Cheri. "Review Essay: Literary Criticism." *Signs* (Winter 1980): 268–282.

Swinfen, Ann. *In Defense of Fantasy: A Study of the Genre in English and American Literature Since 1945.* London: Routledge, 1984.

Weick, Ann. "Other Ways of Seeing: The Female Vision." *Seeing Female: Social Roles and Personal Lives.* Ed. Sharon S. Brehm. New York: Greenwood, 1988, pp. 185–194.

Welty, Eudora. *The Collected Stories of Eudora Welty*. Ed. Peggy W. Prenshaw. Jackson: University Press of Mississippi, 1984.

———. *The Eye of the Story: Selected Essays and Reviews.* New York: Random House, 1978.

———. "Moon Lake." *The Collected Stories of Eudora Welty*. Ed. Peggy W. Prenshaw. New York: Harcourt Brace Jovanovich, 1980, pp. 342–374.

———. *Place in Fiction*. New York: House of Books, 1957.

———. "The Reading and Writing of Short Stories." *Short Story Theories.* Ed. Charles E. May. Athens: Ohio University Press, 1976, pp. 156–177.

Wharton, Edith. "Bewitched." *The Ghost Stories of Edith Wharton*. New York: Scribner's, 1973, pp. 145–168.

———. *The Ghost Stories of Edith Wharton.* New York: Scribner's, 1973.

———. *The Writing of Fiction*. New York: Octagon, 1966.

Lady Terrorists: Nineteenth-Century American Women Writers and the Ghost Story

Barbara Patrick

Supernatural fiction has always been a significant part of the American literary tradition, with many of our first and most eminent writers among its adherents—Charles Brockden Brown, Washington Irving, Nathaniel Hawthorne, Edgar Allan Poe, and Henry James, to name the most prominent. Historically, writers have adopted the Gothic mode in order to explore evil and the causes of evil. In America, Gothicists have been preoccupied by the problems of perception and imperfect knowledge: the existence of the alleged specter, as well as the perceptions of the characters and the tale-teller, are in question.

Just as James Fenimore Cooper, Brown, and Irving purported to create a distinctly *American* Gothic mode, American women created a distinctly *feminine* Gothic mode, in which Gothic vehicles could express women's concerns. A great many nineteenth-century American women writers, best known for their work in other genres, experimented with the ghost story; among them, Louisa May Alcott, Gertrude Atherton, Alice Brown, Rebecca Harding Davis, Mary Wilkins Freeman, Charlotte Perkins Gilman, Georgia Wood Pangborn, Elizabeth Stuart Phelps, Harriet Spofford, Harriet Beecher Stowe, Edith Wharton, Ellen Glasgow, and Willa Cather all at least tried their hand at ghostly fiction.

These women's works differ from their male counterparts' in that the women's tales are not so much about what we cannot know (epistemological doubt) or the fact that people frighten themselves with chimeras (psychodrama): Their supernatural tales address a world in which things *are* frightening—not least of which are the silencing and marginalization of women. In women's supernatural fiction, the misapprehension of reality exposes the true horror of reality, that is, the reality of a world wherein a woman could not "experience passion or wield power without violating societal mandates or transgressing moral boundaries" (Bendixen xxxiv). Traditionally, Gothic literature has explored evil; in the hands of American women the evils explored are social evils, systematically perpetrated against women. Again and again, women writers found in the supernatural tale metaphors for the unredressed wrongs women have suffered, for the invisibility of women's work, and for women's emotional, social, and political oppression. Just as ghosts speak from a world beyond to the world we know, these writers speak from the world of the text to the world of the reader.

Critics of American literature—the formers and reformers of the canon, Gothicists and feminists alike—have slighted women's tales of terror. In the words of Lynnette Carpenter and Wendy Kolmar, ghost story writers "remain invisible to many critics" (12). Donald Ringe, for instance, in his otherwise definitive work, *American Gothic*, published in 1982, does not include in his discussion a single female author and concludes that the American Gothic ended with the Civil War. Yet with women writers and women readers, the ghost story remained extremely popular well into the twentieth century.

The feminine Gothic tradition cannot be ignored nor dismissed as second rate. Perhaps the ghost story underwent revision in form and changes of purpose in the latter half of the nineteenth century, but it continued to be a popular and highly artful literary form, one particularly satisfying to women authors and prevalent in women's magazines, perhaps because female authors were able to use the conventions of the ghost story to veil messages otherwise unacceptable in their day. The nineteenth century's sudden upsurge in the number of magazines published and in the size of the reading population ensured a demand for short fiction; an increase of leisure time for women of the upper and middle classes fed this demand and perhaps accounts for the burgeoning of literature by, for, and about women.

The premise of the ghost story—that ghosts return from the grave—undermines a fundamental assumption about reality. Having unseated one assumption about the way things "must be," the ghost story frees authors and readers to question other constructs that they may previously have considered inviolate, among them the role of women in American culture. Subverting the ghost story to their own purposes, nineteenth-century female Gothicists went beyond their male counterparts' preoccupation with epistemology to address the (im)morality of the treatment of women in America, questioning what Ann Douglas and other historians have come to call the "Doctrine of the Two Spheres" and the "Cult of True Womanhood." Behind the veil of the supernatural, the feminist Gothicists protested the narrowness of women's roles and limitations on women's influence.

Unlike Hawthorne, Irving, and Poe, who drew on a distant past and used exotic, explicitly Gothic settings, American women writing ghost stories placed their narratives in contemporary, realistic settings. It is particularly striking that these writers would choose to include a ghost—a most antirealistic device—in what are otherwise scrupulously realistic stories. Perhaps it is because these stories defy the categories invented by literary historians that these stories have largely been ignored.

Especially significant in women's ghost stories is their depiction of the home. Far from being a safe haven, the home is a place of stultification, exhaustion, treachery, and terror. In ghost stories, women Gothicists portrayed a range of horrors attendant upon women's confinement to domestic pursuits. In such stories the presence of the supernatural is an obvious source of terror, but the true menace arises from the oppression of and violence against women, as well as the withholding of knowledge and power from women.

Three of the best tales using the conventions of the ghost story to veil feminist concerns are Mary Wilkins Freeman's

"Luella Miller," Elizabeth Stuart Phelps's "No News," and Harriet Beecher Stowe's "The Ghost in the Cap'n Brown House." These stories illustrate the three possible options available to the writer of ghostly fiction: (1) the ghost exists, (2) the ghost does not exist and is perceived as a result of a mistake or mental aberration, or (3) the ghost perhaps exists.

Mary Wilkins Freeman, placing her narratives in the ambiguous realm that Hawthorne described in *The Scarlet Letter* as "neutral territory . . . where the Actual and the Imaginary may meet" (38) questioned assumptions regarding a "woman's place" in her society. Few writers have managed (or tried) to document the debilitating effects of work in the home, but in her story "Luella Miller" (1903) Freeman depicts the mortifying effects of women's domestication. Freeman begins her narrative with a long description of a home that has become a source of terror. Luella, an uncommonly beautiful woman, is "a slight, pliant sort of creature, as ready with a strong yielding to fate and as unbreakable as a willow" (40). That is to say, her strength comes from an inveterate passivity. We see Luella in contrast with Lydia Anderson, the stout, unbending, no-nonsense spinster who narrates Luella's story. The story's force depends on the cumulative effect of the deaths of those who help the supposedly frail Luella Miller. Luella, appointed as schoolmistress despite her lack of education, gets help from one of the older students, who "used to do all the teachin' for her, while [Luella] sat back and did embroidery work" (41). The student dies mysteriously. Later, Luella's husband performs all the housework, since Luella is allegedly too frail for such work. He dies of exhaustion the year after their marriage. When Luella's sister-in-law comes to keep house for her, the sister-in-law dies. Luella gets help from her Aunt Abby. Aunt Abby dies. A neighbor neglects her own home to wash, cook, and clean for the supposedly helpless Luella. The neighbor dies.

Throughout this account, Lydia Anderson, the narrator, makes clear that she believes Luella is no more helpless than anyone else and should do her own work. Yet Lydia paints a picture of a truly disabled Luella; having been petted and pampered all her life Luella cannot make it on her own. She dies. The story climaxes with Lydia's glimpse of Luella's ghost being helped along through the air by the ghosts (or angels) of her husband and neighbors.

Susan Allen Toth, in "Defiant Light: A Positive View of Mary Wilkins Freeman," has suggested that critics of Freeman—Perry Westbrook, Jay Martin, and Austin Warren, for example—have read her work as "morbid cultural documentation" (82), emphasizing the often warped, highly individual wills of Freeman's characters in conflict with their communities. According to Toth, the critics' resulting focus on gloom, misery, decay, and extinction has obscured the real dramatic conflict at the heart of Freeman's best short stories—Freeman's "modern and complex sense of the constant mutual adjustment necessary between individual and community" (83).

Toth's essay does not address Freeman's ghost stories, but her analysis holds true for them as well. If we focus on the individual will, that is, on Luella's apparent selfishness, as most critics have, we miss the real drama, or the interplay between a character's willfulness at odds with community values. Freeman in "Luella Miller" depicts persons whose wills are very much (perhaps too much) the products of community values. She portrays a world that allows women few alternatives for self-definition. The women of this world "find themselves" either by throwing themselves into the work allowed them (the keeping of the house) or falling into the other role allowed them (that of the beautiful but helpless female). Luella typifies the latter, in the process exploiting the former. Lydia, the narrator, stands apart to criticize the folly of both types.

Freeman thus depicts a world that divides its women into two groups—those who do for themselves and those who have things done for them. Once we understand this, it becomes obvious that Freeman does not blame Luella Miller; instead, she attends to the forces that have molded her, documenting the need for change both in the individual and in the societal forces that have shaped her. Freeman presents Luella, Lydia, and the women of this community as women with few choices open to them.

Luella exemplifies a type common to mid-nineteenth-century America, the invalidated woman—that is, the woman who, regarded as an invalid, becomes invalid. Luella seeks power in the world through manipulative behavior, the best means available to her. Her power over others derives from her remaining weak. Luella does no work because she is not trained for it, nor is it in her interest to work. Having been successful at getting others to do for her, Luella is incapable of supporting herself. That she victimizes others highlights the fact that she is a victim as well. Her community allows her special treatment as a substitute for power, not an acknowledgment of it.

In contrast to Luella are all the other stonily silent women of the village. Capable women, they care for Luella in addition to their own household responsibilities, but in every case their selflessness proves their undoing. Those who help Luella in small ways become sick. Those who do more die mysteriously.

By having Lydia narrate the tale, Freeman presents her audience with an instructive contrast. Lydia's presence is more than mere fictional convenience. Her life and her attitudes contrast both to Luella's and to those of the self-sacrificing women who fall prey to Luella's vampirism. Freeman presents Lydia as Luella's opposite. Unlike Luella, Lydia is a woman of genuine strength. Unmarried, she is able to express herself frankly and lead the life she chooses. Quite rightly, she refuses to grant Luella the privileges others deem Luella is due. Lydia thus represents the possibility of transcending the stereotypical roles provided women by the community. In opposing Lydia to Luella on the one hand, and to the self-sacrificing neighbor women on the other, Freeman suggests a way out of the traps set for women by this society. Lydia differs from Luella, who, rewarded for frailty, becomes frail. Likewise, Lydia differs from the many women who surrender their lives to undeserving and ungrateful recipients.

In opposing her characters thus, Freeman suggests that as long as women's choices are binary, no change is possible. The deaths and ghostly resurrections of the main characters underscore the fact that only Lydia survives to witness their eerie return. Freeman seems to suggest that without a change in the community's understanding of women's roles, Luella and women like her will never find the lively strength latent within them, nor will uncritically self-sacrificing women learn to defy deathly exploitation.

While Freeman makes no attempt in this story to explain her ghosts' existence, her contemporary Elizabeth Stuart Phelps does so in another ghost story, "No News" (1869), a situation in which the ghost is illusory. Here, a woman driven to exhaustion by the tasks of motherhood looks like a ghost and is thus mistaken for one. In this story, surprisingly modern in tone, Phelps pleads the case of the young mother run ragged and exposes men's indifference to women's work in the home.

Phelps's narrator, now past the age of childbearing, describes the lives of her friend Harrie (Harriet) Sharpe and Harrie's husband, known only as Dr. Sharpe. She notes that the couple got along well till the first baby came, noting that though Dr. Sharpe was a noted physician and "knew about babies and illness," the fact that "his own baby would lie and scream till two o'clock in the morning was a source of perpetual astonishment to him" (10). Phelps, through her narrator, notes that it is Harrie Sharpe who assumes sole charge of caring for the newborn and its subsequent siblings, though it is Dr. Sharpe who considers himself inconvenienced by their arrival.

When Harrie's friend Pauline comes to visit, Harrie's exhaustion becomes evident. In contrast to Pauline—beautiful, intellectual, cosmopolitan—Harrie is haggard, *harried*, and wan. While Pauline amuses Harrie's husband with her wit, Harrie, having stayed up all night with the baby, struggles to stay awake. While Harrie tends the house, Harrie's husband takes Pauline driving and sailing. Harrie begins to doubt herself as her husband pays her less and less attention; she sadly concludes, "When you have three babies to look after, it is too late to make yourself over" (21).

Depressed over her husband's attraction to Pauline, and exhausted by her maternal duties, Harrie goes boating in a cold rain intending to drown herself. When Dr. Sharpe and Pauline come home from an outing to find Harrie missing, they discern what has happened in their absence and presume Harrie to have drowned. Finally, in a melodramatic turn of events, the narrator and Pauline see what they believe to be Harrie's ghost staggering into the house.

As it turns out, it is not Harrie's ghost but Harrie herself, who in a final exertion of will has repudiated death to find her way back to her husband and children. The story ends happily, with Dr. Sharpe at least somewhat contrite over his inattention to his wife's work and worth; nevertheless, Phelps's tale makes painfully clear the physical and emotional burdens of child-rearing. Moreover, Phelps emphasizes the "invisibility" of the work that Harrie performs; the work that has rendered her a wraith. It takes Harrie's supposed death—and the supposed appearance of her ghost—to make her husband see her as a living being with needs of her own.

In "The Ghost in the Cap'n Brown House" (1872), Harriet Beecher Stowe went beyond describing the vulnerability, loneliness, and inanition that home-bound women suffer to describe the systematic discounting of women by an androcentric culture. At issue in this tale are women's lack of credibility, their powerlessness, and their potential for victimization in a society that conspires against their empowerment. Though Stowe's other ghost stories are not noticeably feminist, "The Ghost in the Cap'n Brown House" focuses on the lives of women in a society pledged to preserving men's power. She describes a time when being a woman and being a ghost were markedly similar conditions. Stowe's depiction of powerlessness and radical uncertainty could unsettle even the most imperturbable of readers, though Stowe couches her feminist message within a comic narrative frame.

The tale begins when a seamstress goes to mend the wardrobe of the wealthy, retired seafarer Captain Brown. Staying at his house, she thinks she sees an elusive, ethereal figure (a woman) whose existence she cannot verify. Soon the woman's (or ghost's) existence or nonexistence becomes the talk of the town, though no one dares confront the powerful Captain Brown to settle the matter. Interestingly, Stowe never resolves the ambiguity regarding the ghostly woman's existence; the ambiguity itself becomes the story's theme.

On the one hand, if what the seamstress sees is a ghost—or if she imagines it altogether—the story is comic, like Stowe's other regional realist tales narrated by the shiftless but good-hearted Sam Lawson (whose narrative voice unites all of Stowe's *Oldtown Fireside Stories*). In fact, the story reads like a comedy, as when Sam shrewdly but gently mocks women's "inability" to keep a secret. Stowe maintains the story's comic effect by allowing leeway for believing that the seamstress builds her story out of a simple dream. But if the figure whom the seamstress sees is in fact a woman, the story is not a comedy, but a horror story. Who is the woman? Why is she there? Why is she kept sequestered, then whisked away in a carriage at three o'clock in the morning? And why is the face that seamstress saw so very mournful?

The women of the community are the first to suspect that something is amiss in the captain's household. But they soon find that without the cooperation of the men of the community, it is impossible to verify their suspicions. The men are loathe to interfere on behalf of anything so indefinite as a ghost-woman; the captain's power and respectability go unquestioned. Seemingly the town fathers' sense of propriety overshadows any other concern, including, potentially, a woman's well-being. *If* the woman exists, she must live in complete isolation, with no legal rights and no hope of human aid. Which is to say, she might as well be a ghost.

By thus equating a woman with a ghost, Stowe incisively describes the condition of women in nineteenth-century American. A ghost, unacknowledged by the laws of reason, might as well not exist. Not recognized by law, a nineteenth-century woman's existence was similarly dependent on men's willingness to acknowledge her. Neither the ghost of the story's title nor the putative woman have legal rights; neither have choice or the power of self-direction; each is supposed to be unseen and unheard; neither is deemed worthy of protection.

In the situation that Stowe contrives, the community discounts women's perceptions and limits their power. The women of Stowe's fictional community suspect that something is amiss in the captain's household, but they soon find that without the cooperation of the men, it is impossible to verify their suspicions. The ghost, if she exists, exists behind closed doors. The woman, if she is a woman, remains silent and unknown. That the town's women are powerless to effect their wishes drives home Stowe's point that women are powerless in a society constructed to safeguard men's power and status.

No doubt this was a radical message for Stowe's audience. Certainly she couches her message carefully: one can read this story attending only to its comic elements. The narrative frame softens and even obscures the feminist message. But there is nothing comic about the hidden woman's plight—if there is a woman. And even if there is not, there is nothing funny about the way in which the town leaders discount the womenfolk's perceptions and concerns.

Significantly, Stowe's tale defies the conventions of linear narrative. The story concludes without a resolution to the puzzle of the ghost-woman's existence. Stowe's refusal to resolve the tale's ambiguity unsettles the reader, who has no way out of the radical uncertainty into which Stowe thrusts her. Not only is Stowe's technique unsettling, but her near-complete identification of a woman and a ghost calls attention to the fact that under the doctrine of the two spheres, a ghostly invisibility and a lack of material power characterized women's experience.

For Freeman, Phelps, and Stowe, as for many other American women writers, the ghost story was an ideal vehicle for revealing the social ills present in American culture. Whether real, imagined, or ambiguous, the presence of a ghost in an otherwise "realistic" tale drew attention to the horrors of living in patriarchal culture, particularly the oppression of women through domestication, the withholding of power and knowledge from women, and the discounting of women and women's perceptions.

Toril Moi in *Sexual/Textual Politics* calls attention to the erroneous idea that feminists must be angry all the time. She goes on to praise the way in which Mikhail Bakhtin shows that laughter, as well as anger, is a revolutionary vehicle, subversive of the prevailing power structure. Perhaps what is true of laughter is also true of horror, which likewise subverts our understanding of what is or must be real. Moi writes, "[T]he ironist is extremely hard to assail, precisely because it is virtually impossible to fix her or his text convincingly" (40). The same might be said of the writer of tales of terror, the literary terrorist, if you will, who dodges the question of what must be real by exploring what might be real if we have the courage to suspend habitual modes of thought and action.

In Moi's words, women have "produced literary works that are in some sense palimpsestic, works whose surface designs conceal or obscure deeper, less accessible (and less socially acceptable) levels of meaning" (73). Moi's assessment is especially apt where the woman writer has elected to practice the conventions of the ghost story, in whose gaps and absences, apparitions, and horrors, we feel not only the anger but also the irony, the courage, and the creativity of women.

WORKS CITED

Bendixen, Alfred, ed. *Haunted Women: The Best Supernatural Tales by American Women Writers.* New York: Ungar, 1985.

Carpenter, Lynette, and Wendy Kolmar, eds. Introduction, *Haunting the House of Fiction: Feminist Perspectives on Ghost Stories by American Women*. Nashville: University of Tennessee Press, 1991.

Degler, Carl. *At Odds: Women and the Family in America from the Revolution to the Present.* New York: Oxford University Press, 1980.

Douglas, Ann. *The Feminization of American Culture.* New York: Anchor Press, 1988.

Freeman, Mary E. Wilkins. "Luella Miller." *The Wind in the Rose Bush and Other Stories of the Supernatural*. New York: Doubleday, 1903. Rpt. in *Collected Ghost Stories of Mary Wilkins Freeman*. Ed. Edward Wagenknecht. Sauk City, WI: Arkham House, 1974, pp. 39–53.

Hawthorne, Nathaniel. *The Scarlet Letter.* Ed. Harry Levin. Boston: Houghton Mifflin, 1960.

Moi, Toril. *Sexual/Textual Politics: Feminist Literary Theory.* London: Methuen, 1985.

Phelps (Ward), Elizabeth Stuart. "No News." *Men, Women, and Ghosts*. Boston: Fields, Osgood, 1869, pp. 1–31.

Ringe, Donald. *American Gothic: Imagination and Reason in Nineteenth-Century Fiction.* Lexington: University Press of Kentucky, 1982.

Stowe, Harriet Beecher. "The Ghost in the Cap'n Brown House." *Sam Lawson's Oldtown Fireside Stories*. Vol. 2. Boston: Osgood, 1872, pp. 329–341.

Toth, Susan Allen. "Defiant Light: A Positive View of Mary Wilkins Freeman." *New England Quarterly* 46 (March 1973): 82–93.

Representations of Female Authorship in Turn-of-the-Century American Magazine Fiction

Ellen Gruber Garvey

> "It's hard work to write steadily, but I can, and yet all this trouble would be saved if I married Philip Astor."
>
> "You do not like him; you would not be happy with him," her better self reasoned. (Ashton 15)

> Foolish women . . . would as soon pet and stroke a Remington typewriter as a stubborn, refractory husband or lover. (Barr 4)

In the 1890s period of magazine proliferation and new mass readerships, female authorship as a topic was treated differently in magazines addressed to different classes. This essay examines this division as it appears in magazines published for poorer women and magazines published for middle-class women. Periodicals that reached a largely poorer and rural readership, such as *Ladies' World*, presented authorship along with other approved methods that provided women—particularly married women—a way to add to household income. Additionally, these magazines provided forums for these women to publish their work. On the other hand, middle-class magazines such as *Munsey's* and *Ladies' Home Journal*, cast female authorship, with other forms of female entrepreneurship, in a more ambivalent light. In the middle-class magazine stories marriage displaces or forecloses authorship, and women characters find authorship incompatible with marriage. Moreover, the middle-class magazine stories were more likely to insist on a strict division between amateur and professional writing in their own editorial selections.

Advertising in Magazines for Middle-Class and Poorer Women

Broadly stated, the representation of female authorship in both types of magazines correlates with their increasing dependence on advertising rather than subscription fees for their revenues, and with the editors' and publishers' assumptions about their readers' sources of money for advertised goods. By the mid-1890s, both types of magazines followed a strategy of dropping their cover prices, increasing their circulations, and relying on ads for revenues. In essence, these publishers no longer sold the magazine to the reader, but sold the reader to the advertiser, and represented the interests of the advertisers. Reading the magazine in its entirety as a text, not simply as an envelope for literature, can therefore tell us something about what shaped trends in fiction publishing. The stories and the advertising project must be considered together.

Magazines acted in the interests of the advertisers as a whole by encouraging consumption. This encouragement took different forms according to the presumed class of the reader. Stories addressed to poorer women suggested ways to earn money that could be spent on advertised goods, and writing was presented as an almost emblematic way to earn money. Stories addressed to women who were presumed to be middle-class shoppers discouraged such work in favor of life as a married consumer.

The Theme of Earning in Mail-Order Magazines

Inexpensive magazines addressed to rural and poorer women preceded the middle-class magazines in the low cover price/high-circulation strategy of relying on advertising for revenues.

Monthlies such as *Ladies' World* and *Comfort* were called mail-order magazines because they ran ads that solicited mail orders and sometimes offered mail-order goods themselves, rather than mainly advertising the nationally distributed goods that predominated in middle-class magazines. Readers were likely to make, rather than purchase, more goods than middle-class women. Even as late as the 1890s, *Ladies' World* columns reflected this orientation with recipes for making such items as skin lotions and beef extract at home—items already commercially produced and heavily advertised in the middle-class magazines.

Advertisers faced a special problem in addressing the reader of such periodicals: She was likely not to have cash. Cash brought in through such traditional women's market activities such as egg and poultry sales and butter making might already be allocated for ongoing expenses so were not available to buy the new advertised goods. Individual advertisers recognized the readers' situation, advertising poultry incubators, and often offering such goods as china as premiums for purchasing staples like coffee. Many ads offered entrepreneurial opportunities; often an ad both touted a product such as flower seeds for sale and sought agents to sell it.

While both articles and stories in these magazines showed readers ways to earn money, the stories played out the social consequences of earning and spending. The low-priced tabloid monthly *Ladies' World*, edited in the 1890s by Frances E. Fryatt, provides some examples of this strategy.

Ladies' World stories repeatedly suggested that women could earn money by starting a business or by taking on some new task or variant of a task they already did, and that doing so would not only enable but also legitimate consumption. The similar plots of several stories reflect a suspicion of the source of goods and concern with how commodities arrived in a household. "One Woman's Way," by Velma Caldwell-Melville (1890), begins with the narrator visiting "John's wife," while John's mother vehemently disapproves of the extravagance of purchasing a $35 bedroom set. After the mother-in-law leaves, the wife explains that she earned all the money for the set. The narrator is surprised: she knows how busy a farm woman must be caring for a husband, two babies, and two hired men, and seeing to the milk, butter, and poultry, the money from which is already earmarked for necessities. The bedroom set? John let her use land to grow berries on, her father gave her plants, and she bartered her sewing for a neighbor's labor, and used the money from each year's berry sales to make the home—her workplace—more comfortable, by buying furniture, for example.

Her economic orientation is contrasted with her mother-in-law's outmoded one: "John's mother boasts that she has neither earned nor wasted a cent since she was married" (15). To neither earn nor waste, however, is no longer a virtue: the stories suggest that by contrast, one might not only have nice things, but may achieve greater efficiency and even economy. In the 1904 *Ladies' World* serial "The Rebellion of Reuel's Wife" by Adella F. Veazie, Mazie's hatred of housework actually leads her family to greater ease. She begins by planting a flowerbed for her own pleasure, starts a flower seed business, and soon branches out into landscaping, bringing in enough money to support the family when her husband is disabled. Mazie's mother-in-law objects even to the first flowerbed. She counters Mazie's defense of it as a rest from housekeeping by championing old-fashioned household production:

> "If I got any chance to set down an' rest, I always had my knittin' work handy so as to keep busy at something *useful*. Why, I've always knit every stockin' an' mitten that Nathan ever wore since I married him, and all my own . . ."
>
> Mazie gave a little gasp of dismay. "Why surely you wouldn't expect me to knit stockings now, when they can be bought for less than the yarn would cost," she exclaimed. (March 1904, 4)

Mazie's understanding of new economic possibilities allows her to see that earning extra cash lets her replace her own inefficient labor with manufactured goods: the more she earns, the more she is entitled to take advantage of such replacements. The same idea appears in M. Vaughn's 1891 story "John's Wife," which elaborates the pattern of the other John's wife of the berry story in "One Woman's Way." Here again, a woman seems to violate propriety, to act out of bounds. Writing is her means for earning.

In "John's Wife," Jerusha and her mother believe cousin John's wife, Claribel, spends beyond his means. Not only does Claribel have hanging lamps and china dishes, but, in a farm woman's vision of luxury, she puts out her washing and ironing, hires someone to clean and bake, and has "all their best clothes made, to say nothin' of *buyin'* them" (3). She also indulges in charity, spending money to help the town's poor and invalids, and buys children's books to increase Sunday school attendance.

Jerusha and her mother righteously confront John and Claribel. Claribel explains that she had once been a correspondent to a few magazines and had planned to give it up when she married:

> But loving the work and being impressed by the poverty in and about the village, also the lack of interest on the part of the children in school, Sunday-school, or in fact, anything good, she had resolved to again take up her pen, and *by careful management she could put out a part of her work and make much more than she could save by trying to do it all herself* [emphasis added]. (3)

She avoided telling them about her writing because she believes they'd think her "silly to suppose I could write anything worth publishing; what I wrote seemed so insignificant to me that I did not want anyone I knew to read the wretched 'yarns' I spun" (3).

Although the narrator assures us that Claribel does not go on to be a great writer, her story has taught others. From it, Jerusha "learned not to be curious, not to be suspicious, not to be envious, and not to 'jump at conclusions' when they were based only on circumstantial evidence, and above all not to whisper words that might cause any to be misjudged" (3).

Women's authorship here is strictly a money-making proposition—in line with raising berries or flowers. Not only is Claribel's writing said not to be artistic, but her moral effect also does not come through her writing. Rather, it comes through her power as a consumer as she does good through her gifts to the town from the proceeds. Her use of money to hire people to do her housework is finally sanctioned because she has taken up the moral housekeeping of the community.

The link that *Ladies' World* stories thematized between working inside the home at money-making enterprises, authorship, and purchasing power, and between writing and shopping, continued into a strategy to attract advertisers: In 1904, the magazine offered cash prizes in a contest inviting readers to write stories made up from the advertisements. Writing in the contest both offered a means to earn cash to buy advertised products and brought the reader into more intimate contact with the advertising.

Ladies' World presented writing as both a way to earn money and a source of self-reliance and independence. In Bertha Ashton's 1892 children's story, "Aunt Crawford's Wise Will; Or Perseverance Conquers All Things," Aunt Desire Crawford threatens to cut her 22-year-old namesake niece out of her will for her indolence, but will leave the money on the condition that "ten years from now you have made a name for yourself" (15). As a child, young Desire wrote "short but bright stories," but expecting the inheritance, she has grown lazy. Angry at the condition set by her aunt, she turns to the alternative:

> "It's hard work to write steadily, but I can, and yet all this trouble would be saved if I married Philip Astor."
>
> "You do not like him; you would not be happy with him," her better self reasoned. "But his money, think of that. Work is irksome. An easy time you would have as his wife," something else whispered to her. (15)

Her better self wins the argument, and she resolves "to please her aunt and be a better woman" by embarking on a career as a writer of juvenile stories. She achieves fame for her writing, "calculated to make the children happier and more contented with their lot," while she "never forgot to instill in her stories the wish to be independent" (15). The story supplies detailed encouragement for becoming a published writer, showing young Desire persisting in her writing past the first few rejections.

Over and over, *Ladies' World* stories proclaimed that earning money gave women a necessary measure of power and control over their own workplace, the house. If married women earned money, they were entitled to spend it on services and the type of goods advertised in the magazine that would ease their work or substitute for it. Moreover, earning money was probably the only way these readers could obtain such goods. In order to escape drudgery in the home, in other words, they would have to take up some better-paid form of productive labor; writing was just one type of such labor.

Women Authors as Characters in Middle-Class Magazines

> Lately there has been a great deal of fretful, impatient, womanly writing, about the degrading, depressing influence of household work; and it has been urged that it is better for wives and mothers to write or sew, or do any kind of mental work, in order to make money to relieve themselves of the duties of cooking and nursing. Women who have this idea ought never to have become wives, and they ought never, never, never to have become mothers. For if there is any loftier work than making homes lovely, and sweet, and restful, or any holier work than nursing and training her own little children, no woman will find it in writing, or sewing, or preaching, or lecturing, or in any craft of hand or head known to mortals. (Barr 4)

Unlike the poorer rural woman, the middle-class urban married woman of the 1890s had money to spend on shopping. She was increasingly less engaged in an economy of production. While that shift was of course a new one, in this period what replaced home production of goods, and what replaced the generic items that had already replaced some goods, was nationally advertised, branded merchandise. The middle-class woman not only no longer made skin lotion and beef extract at home, but part of her job had become reading ads and selecting the right brand of nationally advertised skin lotion or beef extract. The elaboration of such tasks as shopping wisely for the family and "managing" the family became the focus of a new cult of the home.

Stories about female authorship in middle-class magazines allegorized the surrender of independent work and autonomy at marriage. Marriage was often specifically linked with consumption within this emerging cult of the home. Unlike the *Ladies' World* stories where paid work continued after marriage and where unmarried independence was esteemed, in middle-class magazine stories, authorship offered women the possibility of finding only incomplete satisfaction and fulfillment as productive workers, and only *outside* of marriage. The plots, however, foreclosed this possibility, and suggested that having money to spend and spending it were ultimately superior pleasures.

On the most basic level, assuming an intact family with a middle-class breadwinning husband, earning money was simply a distraction from the wife's chief task of purchasing goods for the household. A middle-class husband's income was a far more plausible resource than what most women could bring in through her own work. So it is perhaps not surprising that stories in middle-class magazines that depended on advertising goods that only middle-class households were likely to afford generally disapproved of or through their plots subverted women's earning attempts.

When women writers appear in courtship stories, marriage makes writing redundant. Marriage to the right man would supply a woman's material needs, including the need for goods advertised in the magazine. This trade-off is explicit in Adelaide Rouse's "The Story of a Story," in *Munsey's*, in which a woman wants to sell her stories to earn money to buy herself a bicycle. Her work is rejected, and her ambition to write is traded for engagement to the assistant editor who rejected her story—and his purchase of a tandem bicycle to be ridden with him. So the woman's writing is a poor strategy for consumption. Writing, then, is displaced by marriage to a man who can provide material goods even if the independence and mobility that were part of her original desire are no longer included. Both her riding and her writing are now under editorial control.

Although the young woman in Rouse's story writes badly, an unmarried woman's good writing can lead to marriage. In another *Munsey's* story, "The Unhonored Profession" by Marguerite Tracy, writing and marriage are virtually interchangeable. The nameless narrator is a writer courted by Wolfe Hamilton, a doctor with whom she has a comradely friendship but has refused to marry. Visiting her, he asks whether she thinks he might interest another woman, Leila, in story writing.

Believing Leila is in love with him, Wolfe thinks Leila should take up writing to take her mind off her presumed love for him, since, Wolfe explains to the narrator, "you always tell me, when I ask you to marry me, that you would love me if you weren't too much interested in your writing to think of loving anybody" (941). A few days later Leila, who does not in fact love Wolfe, advises the narrator to marry him:

> Anybody can write stories—at least there are always plenty of 'em written. You never saw a magazine published empty because they didn't have any stories to put in. But everyone can't look after that ridiculous Wolfe Hamilton, and with his money and position that's worth an intelligent woman's while. (942)

Story writing here is something anyone can do, not in the sense that it is as accessible to all as raising berries might be, but in that too many people are doing it already. Marriage to a successful man like Wolfe Hamilton, on the other hand, with its duties of emotional caretaking, takes exceptional talent and will be well remunerated. Marriage and writing are not only interchangeable but evidently mutually exclusive.

To the extent that marriage and writing were set in opposition in *Ladies' World*, as we saw in "Aunt Crawford's Wise Will," writing was clearly the better alternative. But the world of "The Unhonored Profession" in *Munsey's* is very different from that of *Ladies' World* stories where writing can continue after marriage and is one of a variety of means by which married women can earn money. One reason for the contrast may be found in the expected duties of a farm wife—providing for the physical needs of the household, whether by producing goods herself or by earning the money to buy them. The work of the middle-class urban wife, however, was not only becoming harder to pin down, but it centrally included the ill-defined, never-ending labor of providing emotional succor. The narrator of Tracy's story must choose between continuing to make her psychic investment in her fictional characters and devoting her emotional and psychological energies to "look after" Wolfe. She chooses between creating her own characters and building Wolfe's character.

Writing is not only displaced by marriage but, as we have seen, can directly lead to it. The fact that a woman once *did* write becomes, once it is safely displaced, one of her attractions; it gives her better knowledge of her husband's needs. An 1896 story in *Ladies' Home Journal*, a magazine overtly and paternalistically opposed to women's writing, follows this pattern. "The Woman's Edition" by Bessie Chandler uses the general incompetence of women writers as a foil for the competence of the main woman character. But her competence pales beside that of an able and competent man. Marriage to him becomes the logical action to take.

In Chandler's story, a group of women inexperienced in publishing put out their town's newspaper for a one-day women's edition benefiting a temperance cause. Because she has no husband and children to take care of, Grace Waters, a young college graduate, is chosen editor-in-chief, against her wishes, because she wants to avoid Mr. Terance, the paper's regular editor, who is in love with her.

As an educated woman tied to the standards of the "regular" edition and the world of commerce, she becomes a touchstone of reasonableness and a means for making fun of the bad writing and naiveté of the other women on the paper. Grace nonetheless finds pathos in the large quantities of bad poetry submitted and the unbusinesslike way in which the women bring it in:

> When I think of all these little springs of poetry that these good, hard-working domestic women have been concealing all these years, I could just weep. I'm going to write something about the "Submerged Sentiment" of middle-aged women. (5)

Finally the paper is assembled, but Grace breaks down when she discovers that the first page is full of drastic mistakes. Mr. Terance heroically stops the presses and fixes everything while she cries. As all is remedied, and as newsgirls gaily sell the paper in the background, she agrees to marry him. The editor of the women's edition finds her match in the real editor. The woman's edition is clearly the inferior version; it appears for only a single day and is produced for charity rather than pay. Work on it, however, leads to marriage, once Grace learns to appreciate Mr. Terance. She now understands enough about the professional life of her future husband to follow his talk and understand his interests.

"The Woman's Edition" raises questions about literary professionalism and the status of the woman amateur. Chandler, as the writer of this story, attempts to draw a definitive line between herself and such amateurs. Her stereotyped foolish women writers turn out ridiculous poetry, even while she asserts that the stereotype does not apply to her heroine or, presumably, to herself. The amateur is not a speaking subject who can describe her own situation or experience. Nor is she either a forebear to the professional writer or someone who could potentially become such a writer: The amateurs in the story instead seem frozen in positions of permanent naiveté and incompetence, forever available as topics for the essay Grace might write and the short story Chandler has written. But Grace will perhaps not write the essay after all. Given that she held the editorship specifically because she did not have a husband, we can assume that she will abandon that line of work once married, and that once she becomes a "good, hard-working domestic" woman *she* at least will know better than to gush forth with springs of poetry.

Opportunities for Writers

Up to this point I have talked about women's writing as a topic *within* stories. As such stories by women as Adelaide Rouse's "Story of a Story" in *Munsey's* and Bessie Chandler's "Woman's Edition" in *Ladies' Home Journal* imply, disapproval of women's writing and defining it within stories as suspect are separate from a magazine's practice of printing work by women. Although the *Journal*'s contempt for women's writing did not keep it from printing a good deal of work by women, in other structural ways the *Journal* impeded the more fluid movement between amateur and professional writing allowed by other women's magazines of the period.

The approach in the Chandler story, dividing foolish amateurs and real professionals, exemplifies the strict distinction

Journal editor Edward Bok promulgated between publishing the work of professional women writers and suggesting that readers might become writers. Bok's columns fulminated against women writing, and especially against the notion that his readers might make money from their writing or editorial projects. Bok ridiculed readers for thinking they could earn money by compiling literary extracts or bits from scrapbooks or by selling their poems. While his mockery could have been understood as an endorsement of a higher level of professionalism for women writers, it mystified the process, denied links between tentative and more ambitious writing projects, and eliminated a layer of apprenticeship. (Bok's antipathy toward such literary and quasi-literary apprenticeship for women sharply contrasts with his celebration of his own youthful entrepreneurship in his autobiography, where he shows himself converting small writing tasks into cash and parlaying them into larger writing projects [Garvey 422–424].)

In contrast with *Ladies' World*, where writing was not so different from raising berries, the *Journal* suggested that writing is not something anyone can do. One element missing from the *Journal* was the type of forum for casual writing available in some publications addressed to poorer women. Contemporaneous periodicals for poorer women such as *Comfort*, *The Household*, and *Housekeeper's Weekly* consistently published letters from readers that constituted a lively portion of the copy. Letters slid into articles as editors of such periodicals actively asked "aspiring authors" to send in material; for example, Henry Ferris, the editor of the five-cent *Housekeeper's Weekly: Woman's Own Paper*, explained in 1890 that the paper "is mostly written by its readers. . . . I assume that my readers are intelligent women, competent to distinguish themselves between good and bad literature; . . . I *want* every reader to be a contributor" (7). Contributors were paid. Though *Housekeeper's Weekly* printed few if any short stories per se, articles often included exemplary anecdotes and stories written using the conventions of fiction—pieces that might be thought of as stepping-stones to story writing. Moreover, the paucity of information on many of the short story writers in *Ladies' World*, which published much fiction, suggests that *Ladies' World* too was open to publishing unknown amateur writers.

At the same time that *Ladies' Home Journal* was so busily telling women how unprofessional their writing was, and how foolish they were for thinking they could earn money from it, the *Journal* in fact filled its pages with unpaid reader-generated material. In some issues, perhaps a quarter of the magazine's editorial matter was made up of columns of answers to readers' letters on child-rearing, etiquette, religious activities, and appearance. The fact that the letters themselves rarely appeared in the *Journal* reinforced the sense that women's voices should not be heard in public. The writer became simply a consumer of advice. The real work of the middle-class *Journal* reader was shopping, not writing or earning money.

Conclusion

All the magazines discussed here published stories by women, as did magazines at the turn of the century in general. When stories in these magazines incorporated a woman writer as a character, however, differences emerged in their treatment. As we have seen, these differences in treatment of women's authorship as a topic within stories corresponded to differences in the class addressed by the magazines, and these differences were, in turn, conditioned by all of these periodicals' dependence on advertising. In magazine stories for poorer and rural women, authorship was both a valued source of independence and a way for women to augment the family income—and thus have money to spend on advertised goods. Magazines of this type in fact provided forums in which writers might exercise their developing abilities, inviting them into a community of writers. In the middle-class magazines discussed here, on the other hand, female literary work was posed as an inferior alternative to marriage, one that would be naturally and logically displaced by marriage. Writing, like other professional work for women most notably attacked in *Ladies' Home Journal*, would take time and attention away from a wife's more important duties as housekeeper—duties that were of particular significance to advertisers selling household goods.

Works Cited

Ashton, Bertha. "Aunt Crawford's Wise Will; Or Perseverance Conquers All Things." *Ladies' World* (March 1892): 15.

Barr, Amelia. "Have Women Found New Weapons?" *Ladies' Home Journal* (June 1894): 4.

Caldwell-Melville, Velma. "One Woman's Way." *Ladies' World* (August 1890): 15.

Chandler, Bessie. "The Woman's Edition." *Ladies' Home Journal* (May 1896): 5,6.

Ferris, Henry. Note from the Editor. *Housekeeper's Weekly* (May 17, 1890): 7.

Garvey, Ellen. "Commercial Fiction: Advertising and Fiction in American Magazines, 1880s to 1910s." Diss. University of Pennsylvania, 1992.

Leach, Anna. "In the Fifth Flat." *Munsey's* (February 1894): 507–510.

Mott, Frank Luther. *A History of American Magazines, 1885–1905*. Vol. 4. Five vols., 1741–1930. Cambridge, MA: Harvard University Press, 1957.

Rouse, Adelaide. "The Story of a Story." *Munsey's* (October 1896): 47.

Tracy, Marguerite. "The Unhonored Profession." *Munsey's* (March 1901): 941.

Vaughn, M. "John's Wife." *Ladies' World* (October 1891): 3.

Veazie, Adella F. "The Rebellion of Reuel's Wife." *Ladies' World* (March 1904–May 1904): 4+.

Lesbian Magazine Fiction in the Early Twentieth Century*

Lillian Faderman

To Carol

My love has a forehead broad and fair,
And the breeze-blown curls of her chestnut hair
Fall over it softly, the gold and the red
A shining aureole round her head.
Her clear eyes gleam with an amber light
For sunbeams dance in them swift and bright!
And over those eyes so golden brown,
Long, shadowy lashes droop gently down . . .
Oh, pale with envy the rose doth grow
That my lady lifts to her cheeks' warm glow! . . .
But for joy its blushes would come again
If my lady to kiss the rose should deign.

Jean Lennox (Dubois)

If the above poem had been written by one female character to another in magazine fiction after 1920, the poetess of the story would no doubt have been rushed off to a psychoanalyst to undergo treatment for her mental malady, or she would have ended her fictional existence broken in half by a tree, justly punished by nature (with a little help from a right-thinking heterosexual) for her transgression. Much more likely, such a poem would not have been written by a fictional female to another after the first two decades of the twentieth century, because most popular magazines by that time considered the explicit discussion of same-sex love taboo. In the early twentieth century, however, and throughout the nineteenth century, popular stories often treated the subject totally without self-consciousness and without awareness that such relationships were "unhealthy" or "immoral."[1]

I am not suggesting that before our era women were permitted rampant sexual expression with each other, but rather that homoaffectional expression between women was far less restricted in the past, that permissible behavior included caressing, holding, exchanges of endearments, and expressions of intense emotional commitment to each other. While it is unlikely that many of these relationships would have included genital contact, it was barely more likely that a love relationship between a man and a woman before marriage would have included genital contact either. And just as the male-female relationship is nevertheless characterized as heterosexual, the female-female relationship of similar intensity may be characterized as homosexual.

Such homosexual relationships were not considered threatening in previous centuries for two reasons. First of all, it was clearly understood that a woman would give up her female love with the advent of a suitable male who could (a) support her, in an era when almost no work opportunities were available for women outside of the lower class, (b) provide her with status in the community—which was generally closer-knit and more dictatorial with regard to lifestyles than it is today, and (c) provide her with a family, the *sine qua non* of her existence in the days before the contemporary women's movement and concerns of overpopulation. This tacit understanding is suggested by novelists such as Henry Wadsworth Longfellow and Oliver Wendell Holmes who were reflecting their society's calm acknowledgment of homoaffectional ties and the confidence that those ties would not be destructive to the fabric of society when they characterized love relationships between women as a "rehearsal in girlhood of the great drama of woman's life" (Longfellow) and observed that "the friendships of young girls prefigure the closer relations which will one day come in and dissolve their earlier intimacies" (Holmes).

Second, "lesbian" as a sexual category was until recently virtually nonexistent. One might in fact say that lesbianism and the familiar contemporary attitudes toward female homosexuality are for the most part an invention of our times. It was, in fact, not until the 1880s and the work of scientists such as Richard von Krafft-Ebing, Magnus Hirschfeld, and Havelock Ellis that lesbianism became a "medical problem." As late as 1894 Dr. Allan Hamilton wrote in *The American Journal of Insanity*, a professional journal for alienists and neurologists, that "until within a comparatively recent period the mere insinuation that there could be anything improper in the intimate relations of two women would have drawn upon the head of the maker of such a suggestion a degree of censure of the most pronounced and enduring character." He attributes recognition by his contemporaries of the existence of such variance to "romances from the pens of French and German writers" of the last 30 years, such as Theophile Gautier's *Mademoiselle de Maupin*. But apparently recognition was not particularly widespread, since Hamilton speaks in the same article of a "case" of lesbianism that had come to his attention a few years earlier: "at that time her mental perversion was not of a recognized kind" (Hamilton).

Legal prosecution of homosexuality seems to have focused almost exclusively on males in pretwentieth-century America and England. In his collection of historical documents titled *Gay American History: Lesbians and Gay Men in the U.S.A.*, Jonathan Katz includes evidence of a half-dozen executions and other forms of punishment of gay men in America. But suggestions that women were similarly prosecuted are scant.[2] Even once the medical profession and the law became aware—whether through French and German novels or the writings of Krafft-Ebing, Ellis, Hirschfeld, and others—that female homosexuality existed, most same-sex relationships would have been permitted to continue undisturbed because it was believed that "true" lesbians were rare and were readily identifiable. According to Havelock Ellis, writing in an American medical journal in 1895, sexual inversion in women was generally accompanied by exhaustion, hysteria, and epilepsy (Katz 139).[3] According to Allan Hamilton, the female homosexual "was usually of a masculine type, or if she presented none of the 'characteristics' of the male, was a subject of pelvic disorders, with scanty menstruation, and was more or less hysterical or insane"

(Hamilton). Thus if a woman appeared reasonably feminine and in good health, by definition she was not an invert and her love for another woman was not suspect.

In short, before the 1920s women were permitted a broader spectrum of expressions of love for their own sex,[4] primarily for two reasons: (1) love relationships between women were not threatening, since it was understood that women would marry if they could, for economic and social reasons, despite such affectional ties; (2) it was generally believed that women, being for the most part nonsexual outside of procreative activity, were entirely unlikely to engage in "improper . . . intimate relations" with other females, and that those few who did transgress were easily identifiable through external characteristics. Although, as Hamilton points out, by the mid-nineteenth century there were a number of French and German novels that dealt with love between women in a manner that suggested decadence and corruption, those novels—and even the late nineteenth-century "discoveries" of medical men—were familiar to the mass of the population. Thus it was that popular magazine fiction, well into the twentieth century, could depict female-female love relationships with an openness that later became, as I shall discuss, impossible.

Early twentieth-century "lesbian"[5] fiction appeared in England and America in magazines such as *Ladies' Home Journal, Century, Harper's, Strand*, and even magazines for children such as *St. Nicholas*. Frequently the setting is a girls' school or a women's college, and the love relationship centers around a freshman and an older student or, just as often, a younger woman and an older woman who serves as her mentor, whether inside an academic situation or out. It was possible that these two types of relationships became the focus of so many homoaffectional stories after the popularity of Josephine Dodge Daskam's *Smith College Stories* (which was first published in 1900 and reissued a number of times in the following decades) and Mary MacLane's *The Story of Mary MacLane,* an autobiographic confessional (which was published in 1902 and was followed by two sequels and a number of reprints). At least two of Daskam's stories, "A Case of Interference" and "The Evolutions of Evangeline," seem to reflect the ordinariness of emotional involvements between women. In the latter story, for example, the older girls invite the younger girls to dances and customarily ask, "What color is your gown? I should like to send you some flowers." When one older girl, Biscuits, is obliged to invite Evangeline, who is not attractive to her, "visions of the pretty little freshman she had in mind on filling out her [dance] programme flashed before her with irritating clearness." When another freshman is disappointed in her hope of being escorted to the dance by her favorite sophomore, the narrator observes, "[T]he little freshman cried herself to sleep, for she had dreamed for nights of going with Suzanne, whom she admired to stupefaction."

The Story of Mary MacLane is particularly straightforward about the narrator's love for a former teacher, Fannie Corbin (whom she affectionately calls the anemone lady), who is 12 or 13 years older than Mary. Mary speaks of her passion for Fannie "burn[ing] with a vivid fire of its own." Fannie is "my first love—my only dear one," and "the thought of her fills me with a multitude of feelings, passionate yet wonderfully tender." With her, Mary experiences "a convulsion and a melting within." Mary believes that if she could live with Fanny "in some little out-of-the-world place high up on the side of a mountain for the rest of my life—what more would I desire?" Lest the reader think that platonic love alone is being described here, Mary says, "I feel in the anemone lady a strange attraction of sex. . . . Do you think a man is the only creature with whom one may fall in love?"

Modern critics have been wont to explain such statements by attributing the description of what seems to be same-sex love to the rhetoric and sentimentality of the age,[6] and thus denying the validity of the speaker's feeling. But such criticism skirts the issue. If a female character is conceived to have cried all night over her disappointment about not being taken to a dance by another female, or if she claims that all her desire would be fulfilled if she could live with her beloved for the rest of her life, surely that author intended the reader to believe that the character feels a certain powerful emotion (which her age has permitted her to express and which another age might force her to deny). Whether that emotion is described in extravagant terms and phrases such as "stupefaction" or "a convulsion and melting with" is irrelevant in this respect. What is relevant is that it has been communicated to the reader that the female character was emotionally touched by another female.

The language in Jeanette Lee's "The Cat and the King," which appeared in *Ladies' Home Journal* in October 1919, is similarly extravagant. The characters here, too, are students at a women's college. When the freshman Flora sees her idol, the senior Annette, the narrator observes: "To the freshman gazing from her walk, it was as if a goddess, high-enshrined and touched by the rising sun, stood revealed. She gave a gasp of pleasure." Perhaps it is easy to dismiss such a description as rhetoric and sentimentality of the age. But it is less easy to dismiss the *fact* of the character's emotion and the *action* of the story: Flora has a crush on Annette, a senior and the captain of the college ball team. When Annette hurts her ankle and is hospitalized in the school infirmary, Flora decides the best way to meet her idol is to feign a strange illness and to be hospitalized too. But on Flora's first day in the infirmary, Annette is released. A kindly woman doctor discerns what has been happening and helpfully devises two ways to get the girls together: she employs Flora in her lab where Annette also works, and she has Flora placed on the ball team. The doctor exits from the story, telling Flora happily, "You are to report at once to the captain—in her room."

It is inconceivable that such a story would have been printed in a magazine such as *Ladies' Home Journal* a decade or even a few years later. In a more psychoanalytically sophisticated society, the rapture that Flora expresses over her beloved would generally be considered appropriate only if that beloved were of the opposite sex. When Flora's roommate assures her, "You can live if you don't make the team [and thus lose the opportunity to be near Annette]." "Other folks do," Flora responds, "*I can't!*" When, in the infirmary, the doctor says, as she is taking Flora's pulse, that Flora will have a bed near Annette, the pulse speeds up so that the doctor "started and glanced sharply down at the wrist under her fingers." When Flora is in Annette's presence she is described as looking at Annette "adoringly," watching her "with devoted happy eyes" and gazing "at the beloved face." When Annette is released from the infirmary sooner than Flora expected, Flora "subsided, a bundle of sobs, under the tumbled clothes."

Even more inconceivable today is a story of this nature in a children's magazine. "The Lass of the Silver Sword," which was published serially in *St. Nicholas: A Magazine for Young People* during 1908–1909, opens at a girls' boarding school in the midst of a basketball game. As in "The Cat and the King," the older girl, Carol Armstrong, age 18, is loved by the younger Jean Lennox: the narrator states that "Jean had fallen in love with [Carol] at first sight." Again, the description of her involvement is one that the reader might expect to find in contemporary popular magazines only if the subjects were male and female:

> Alas! the course of true love never did run smooth! Jean had not dared to confess her admiration to anyone but Cecily Brook, whom she had pledged to keep her secret. Now and then she made offerings of candy and flowers anonymously, leaving them on Carol's desk, and so far all Carol's attempts to play detective had failed, and it looked as if her admired would remain forever unknown.

But, as a prank, two other girls steal Jean's notebook, which contains "poems and stories, and *odes*" to Carol, and having discovered that "she's dead in love with her," they send the notebook to Carol. Carol is delighted by the discovery, and she tells Jean: "To think I might have gone on to the end of school, and never found you out, you dear!"

Although there is some vague suggestion of heterosexual interests in the story, the real emotional center is the relationship between Jean and Carol; frequently when it seems to have shifted slightly, in fact it has remained the same. For example, Jean has written a novel in which Carol is the protagonist. A scene from the work is cited in which Carol is happily awaiting the approach of a handsome young man with the knightly name of Arthur de Lancy. But just previous to the discussion of this fantasy, Jean has talked about forming with her other school friends an order of knights, The Silver Sword, of which she is to become the leader. Thus it is likely that the author is suggesting that Jean fantasizes herself as a King Arthur or a Lancelot and that she herself is Carol's love interest in her apparently heterosexual fictions.

The physical affection that Jean and Carol exchange is totally without the self-consciousness that would be inevitable in a post-Freudian era. For example, at one point in the story, "Carol came in, caught Jean, whirled her around, pulled her down on a cot, and gave her a warm kiss." At a later point Carol pulled Jean "in to her lap and hugged her tight. 'You precious little Jeanie Queen! I never saw anything so dear as you in all my life.'" Most significantly, there is nothing covert in their relationship. All the other characters understand that these two are devoted to each other, and their popularity does not suffer: Jan is elected to head the Order of the Silver Sword, and Jan and Carol together organize a girls' camp, which their classmates are eager to attend.

It must be emphasized at this point that most of these stories do *not* deal with prepubescent friendships or the kinds of relationships Freudians such as Helene Deutsch and Clara Thompson have described as being necessary to a young girl's psychosexual development but dangerous if they are permitted to continue into adolescence or postadolescence. The characters generally are young adults and sometimes even mature women. For example, O. Henry's short story "The Last Leaf," which was first published in *Strand* in 1906, concerns two women, Sue from Maine and Joanna from California, who met in New York and now live together and support themselves as artists. They are liberated women even to the extent that they have dropped their feminine names: Joanna is called Johnsy and Sue is called Sudie.

Johnsy is severely ill with pneumonia. The doctor informs Sue that her friend's chances of recovery are one in ten and that she will live only if she has a stronger desire to fight for her life. In the dialogue that follows between Sue and the doctor, O. Henry seems to validate the women's independent life-style, and even their relationship. The doctor comes off as being pompous and insensitive. He tells Sue:

> "Your little lady has made up her mind that she's not going to get well. Has she anything on her mind?"
>
> "She—she wanted to paint the Bay of Naples some day," said Sue.

> "Paint?—bosh! Has she anything on her mind worth thinking about twice—a man, for instance?"
>
> "A man?" said Sue, with a jew's-harp twang in her voice. "Is a man worth—but, no, doctor, there is nothing of the kind."

O. Henry suggests not only that, for these women, men are not of amorous interest but also that the two are almost everything to each other. And when Sudie fears that Johnsy is dying, she implores her, "Dear, dear! . . . Think of me if you won't think of yourself. What would I do?" The only other area of importance in their lives is their art. When Johnsy recovers she tells her mate with serious conviction, "Sudie, some day I hope to paint the Bay of Naples." There is no hint in this early twentieth-century piece of popular magazine fiction that the two women will be distracted from their interest in each other and their profession by what in the doctor's unimaginative terms is something "worth thinking about twice—a man, for instance."

Perhaps a popular writer such as O. Henry could afford to be so sympathetic in his view of these characters because women had not achieved independence in significant numbers by 1906: it was not yet socially threatening if occasional independent women—those who, for example, could eke out a living as artists and were bohemian enough to ignore convention—chose to devote themselves to one another. Most women still had no means of becoming independent; they must and would marry, regardless of their youthful emotional ties.

The general inevitability of marriage for those ordinary women who had no extraordinary calling is suggested in a story that appeared in *Harper's* in 1912, "The Beautiful House" by Catherine Wells. The author is apparently very sympathetic to the extraordinary character, Mary Hastings, who remains unmarried, and to her love for Sylvia Brunton (who leaves her for a man); but the lack of permanence in such relationships is emphasized not only in the action of the story but even in the somewhat heavy-handed symbolism. Sylvia and Mary find a beautiful house, which they both love and hope to inhabit together. The caretaker explains that the house is called "Love o' Women" because "it won't last long." And, in fact, the house burns to the ground as Mary loses Sylvia to her handsome male cousin, Evan Hardi.

Mary, a 35-year-old woman, is consistently described in positive terms: she is "handsome" and has a "dignity of carriage that went beyond her years." She suffers from none of the characteristics that popular literature has so often attributed to the "old maid":

> Spinsterhood suited her temperament and had not faded her vitality in the slightest degree; indeed, her independence and the passage of time had marked her only with a finer gravity of bearing. Her occupation gave her abiding content, she was an able and even distinguished landscape painter, and her sufficient income was increased by the sale of her sketches that she liked least. Her best work she either kept or gave away.

Like the two women in O. Henry's story, she is a committed artist. Sylvia, on the other hand, is not committed to her art; and, as far as the reader can see, she is not economically independent. She is described as "one of the time-markers," who thinks she wants to be an artist because she has an

> overpowering sense of the responsibility of life that comes to the serious young [we are told that she is between age 20 and 30], a trust of years and opportunity which must be met, it seemed to her, and met instantly, and which she had all too hastily supposed was an obligation to paint pictures.

Sylvia attended an art school where "Mary Hastings saw her, and in a manner fell in love with her." On her own level, Sylvia seems to return the affection, and they continue for a while in perfect intimacy; "and then to intensify their communion they found the House, which gathered together the threads of their love, and held it as a body should its soul." At this point Sylvia seems as involved in the relationship as Mary. It is she who convinces Mary that they must have the "beautiful house":

> "We could come here together," Sylvia went on. "Just whenever we wanted to. Just you and I, Mary beloved," she almost whispered, "wouldn't you like it?" Her slender hands lay out along the table, palms turned up. Mary

> gathered them in her own hands and kissed them. "I should like it!" she said, whimsically insistent on the moderate word.

But despite her "adoration" of Mary, and her insistence that she "can't possibly do without seeing" Mary frequently, Sylvia is after all only a "time-marker" who seems to be waiting to pass on to something else, while Mary, "although she did not perceive it," soon permits herself to "picture their relationship to each other . . . crystalized and enduring."

The relationship is not without an erotic element, at least in Mary's mind: for example, as Sylvia admires an old bust in the garden of the beautiful house, "Mary thought of nothing else but how adorable Sylvia looked there, with the transparent pink of her skin against the old gray stone head." Mary's love is certainly what would be called "homosexual" in more recent times, but since having come from a less sophisticated time, the author did not avail herself of terms that would have suggested "perversity" or "abnormality"—Mary is the most sympathetic character, while Sylvia appears to be a flibbertigibbet, and Evan is silly and insensitive. He looks at the beautiful old ivy in the garden, for example: "he stopped and became serious. 'If you were to strip down that ivy,' he said with animation, 'you could have a fives-court here.'"

Sylvia goes off with him in perfect contentment, with "the happy security of a bird that drops upon its nest," while Mary mourns. However, the author's point is clearly not that all women need and want a heterosexual relationship, but rather that most women do not have Mary's resources: her strength, her commitment to her art, and, not the least of these, her ability to support herself. Because women such as Mary are rare, it is likely that the "love o' women" will be impermanent—not because it is inherently flawed, but because most women require the "happy security" of a "nest," i.e., marriage and family.

In Helen Hull's "The Fire," which appeared in *Century* in 1917, the older character, Miss Egert, is again a self-supporting artist, an unmarried woman who is perfectly happy with her lot, despite the fact that she must battle her brother's "attempts to make [her] see reason" and the community's suspicion of her independence. The author is completely sympathetic to her and makes us admire her strength, her gentleness, and her joy in beautiful things.

Cynthia Bates, her young art student, loves her. Cynthia's mother becomes suspicious of the relationship, believing that it causes Cynthia to "drift away from us, your head full of silly notions," and she forbids Cynthia to continue her art lessons and even her visits to Miss Egert. Her opposition is complex: she fears that Cynthia will develop under Miss Egert's influence values that will make her unsatisfied with the unimaginative, staid, routine-ridden lives of her parents, and that she will lose hold over Cynthia, who begins to worship art and beauty, which are alien to Mrs. Bates. But by 1917, toward the close of World War I, which was largely responsible for the beginning of women's changing status in our society, late nineteenth-century theories such as those of Hirschfeld and Ellis (which had long been confined to medical journals and books for professional men) were gradually filtering down into popular consciousness. Perhaps by this time affection between women was becoming slightly suspect. There are hints in Hull's story that Mrs. Bates fears not only Miss Egert's artistic influence on her daughter but the possibility of an erotic relationship between them as well. "What were you doing when I found you?" she yells at her daughter. "Holding hands! Is that the right thing for you? She's turning your head." When Cynthia protests that they were talking about beauty, her mother is outraged:

> Beauty? You disobey your mother, hurt her, to talk about beauty at night with an old maid! . . . Pretending to be an artist . . . to get young girls who are foolish enough to listen to her sentimentalizing. . . . I've always trusted you, depended on you; now I can't even trust you.

And there does in fact seen to be an erotic element that is here inextricably mixed with the women's roles as mentor of beauty and courage and devoted pupil, as their farewell scene suggests:

> Cynthia's fingers unclasped, and one hand closed desperately around Miss Egert's. Her heart fluttered in her temples, her throat, her breast. She clung to the fingers, pulling herself slowly up from an inarticulate abyss. "Miss Egert,"—she stumbled into words,—"I can't bear it, not

> coming here! Nobody else cares except you about sensible things. You do, beautiful, wonderful things."
>
> "You'd have to find them for yourself, Cynthia." Miss Egert's fingers moved under the girl's grasp. Then she bent towards Cynthia and kissed her with soft, pale lips that trembled against the girl's mouth. "Cynthia, don't let anyone stop you! Keep searching!" She drew back, poised for a moment in the shadow before she rose. Through Cynthia ran the swift feet of white ecstasy. She was pledging herself to some tremendous mystery, which trembled all about her.

And although Cynthia bows to her mother's pressure to the extent that she gives up Miss Egert, it is made clear that she will not give up Miss Egert's influence, which is seen as being entirely positive and constructive in contrast to the pathetically narrow ideals that Cynthia's parents try to impose on their daughter.

However, such distinctly positive views of same-sex relationships seem to have disappeared from popular literature shortly after this point. The change in attitude came about primarily for the reasons I have hinted at above. First of all, women on a large scale were gaining a modicum of economic freedom, their helping roles in World War I having liberated them from traditional stereotypes and given them some semblance of independence. This meant that, perhaps for the first time in history, love relationships between women could conceivably be permanent, and need not be only a "rehearsal in girlhood of the great drama of woman's life." Not only could women support themselves, but they were also mobile; they could move out of the community in which they were raised and thereby free themselves of the social dictates that would have demanded that they eventually form a heterosexual relationship and dissolve their earlier intimacies. A society that could not yet come to terms with women as sexual beings outside of their procreative functions, and that had no concerns of the veils of overpopulation, would find such female liberation truly threatening. In addition to these circumstances, the change in attitude toward female-female relationships may also be attributed to the popularization of psychology and particularly Freudianism, as evinced by mass circulation magazine articles that appeared about this time with titles such as "How It Feels to Be Psychoanalyzed," "Freud and Our Frailties," and "A New Diagnosis for Hidden Mental Taint." Everyone who read now became "wise" about the existence of "perversion," and relationships that could have been carried on without self-consciousness earlier would from this point on be scrutinized for "taint." Labels were now available, and to thus label would categorize a same-sex relationship, limit and define it, and emphasize the erotic (viz., homo*sexual*), even if that were a minor or incidental aspect of the love relationship.

Popular magazines such as *Ladies' Home Journal* and *St. Nicholas* no longer printed fiction that dealt with same-sex love. Magazines with a more sophisticated readership, such as *Harper's*, *Dial*, and *Vanity Fair*, did occasionally print such stories, but only if they presented same-sex love in a fairly negative light or if the treatment of the subject was so veiled that it was barely discernible. So-called "art" magazines alone were likely to publish occasional stories in which same-sex love was treated openly and with some sympathy.

One indication of the rapidly changing attitudes toward love between women after World War I is suggested by a comparison of "The Beautiful House," which was published in *Harper's* in 1912, and a serialized novel, *Julie Cane*, by Harvey O'Higgins, which appeared in the same magazine 12 years later. The widespread Freudian consciousness that had overtaken the pages of popular magazines at this time is suggested by a poem by Elias Lieberman, which (only incidentally) immediately preceded the first installment of *Julie Cane* in the February 1924 issue: "Our lives would not be so complex / Without suppressed desires and sex" (422). *Julie Cane* is rife with suppressed desires and sex. Here too, as in the stories discussed above, there is a relationship between an older woman, Martha, and a younger, Julie Cane; but in contrast to the earlier stories, the "spinster" is unhappy and neurotic rather than productive, content, and dignified. She develops her "fixation" on Julie (who is somewhat tomboyish because of her odd upbringing) as a manifestation of a neurosis that has grown and gotten out of hand—and this fixation is a desperate, pathetic thing to witness:

> "Do you love me?" she would whisper. Julie, blushing and awkward would answer "Yes" in an abrupt, strained voice, like a boy. And Martha would murmur tearfully, "You're so sweet." (235)

As her "sickness" progresses she "puts herself to sleep at night imagining Julie [is] in her arms." She is obsessive about seeing Julie every day. In the evening she locks herself in the sewing room to sew clothes for the girl: "She kissed the undergarments that were to touch the beloved young body, and when she had made a dress for Julie she caressed it with her hands and hugged it to her breast so that it might, by proxy, be her arms around Julie whenever Julie wore it" (236). When she has the opportunity actually to try clothes on her beloved, "her hands shook, her heart suffocated, and she turned Julie away from her and wept." After the girl leaves the room, Martha "sat with her face in her hands, her cheeks burning against her cold fingers, her mouth aching, seeing still the dimples in Julie's shoulders, kissing them in her imagination and crying weakly, starved." When she thinks that Julie is leaving her to go away to college, she finally has a "nervous breakdown" (243).

Unlike the noble artist in "The Fire," who teaches her pupil about beauty and courage, the woman here is fatuous. "She was determined to make Julie over in her own image, not only externally but in the inward graces," and she foists on her unwilling pupil Victorian philosophies and attitudes that the Roaring Twenties would have found laughable. "She endeavored to convert her pupil to the gospel of young ladyhood according to Ruskin and Tennyson, giving Julie copies of *Sesame and Lilies* and Tennyson's *Princess* as a Sunday-school teacher might give a prize Bible." While the older woman in the earlier story is completely admirable, poor Martha is simply pitiable. At best, she becomes a reconciled old maid once she accepts Julie's forthcoming marriage. She then has a complete recovery from her "invalidism."

Thus, in the few magazine stories dealing with the subject that were published in the 1920s, love between women was generally treated as a morbidity—a stage of illness that must be gotten over if one was to be wholesome again. D.H. Lawrence's *The Fox*, which was serialized in *Dial* magazine in 1922, presents, as later observers have pointed out, a "clinical" study of this "morbidity": Edmund Bergler, for example, in his essay "D.H. Lawrence's *The Fox* and the Psychoanalytic Theory of Lesbianism," believes that "the effectiveness of *The Fox* derives from Lawrence's predominantly correct . . . observations of a series of clinically verifiable facts on Lesbianism" (Moore 49–55).[7] Commentators such as Bergler neglect to see beyond their own Freudian assumptions to the fearful concerns of the novelist with regard to the growing independence of women in the second decade of the twentieth century.[8] *The Fox* is less a "clinically correct" study of lesbianism[9] than a study of Lawrence's worry that women have taken their pursuit for independence too far.

The Fox is set on a farm in the year 1918, right after the war, which taught English women that they could fend for themselves in the world if need be, and even do the world some good, that they need not be stuck in petticoats and tight corsets, and that there was a world outside of their insulated communities to which they could even travel alone if they liked. The two women of *The Fox* decide to live on a farm together and work it by themselves. One learns carpentry and joinery and goes about in breeches and puttees, belted coat, and loose cap. To a reactionary such as Lawrence, their notions—which were characteristic of many of the English and American feminists of his day—were certainly disturbing.

By comparing Lawrence's first version of "The Fox"[10] with the novel length version that was published four years later in *Dial* (1922), one sees something of his mounting hostility, which appears to be a response to his worry that men are more and more losing hold over women, who are becoming "self-important." In the first version, Henry and March marry, "although to Banford it seemed utterly impossible," and Banford is permitted to live. In the *Dial* version, Henry kills her. As her body quivers with little convulsions, he knows that she is really dead, or will be soon: "He knew it, that it was so. He knew it in his soul and his blood. The inner necessity of his life was fulfilling itself, it was he who was to live. The thorn was drawn out of his bowels." This mounting hostility is also evident in passages such as those in which Henry decides to make March his wife. Lawrence added to the *Dial* version a long description in which Henry's pursuit of March is likened to a hunter stalking a deer: "It is a subtle, profound battle of wills, which takes place in the invisible. And it is a battle never finished till your bullet goes home." Lawrence concludes this description with Henry's realization that "it was as a young hunter that he wanted to bring down March as his quarry."

That two women could be a great deal to each other while they awaited men to lead them to marriage and the real business of life is negligible; that they could believe that the real business of life is in their being a great deal to each other and that men are only incidental to their lives—as women could now, for the first time in history, believe—is, of course, frightening to a society that prefers to conserve old social patterns. It is probably for this reason that a magazine of the 1920s would publish a story such as *The Fox*, which teaches that lesbians must either be killed or captured, and not stories such as those of the earlier period, which focused on woman's love for another woman and her personal growth through that love. There were very few lesbian stories published in magazines after World War I that did not carry a moral such as Lawrence's: women could not find satisfaction with each other, and some terrible disaster would befall those who tested this truth.

The few lesbian stories that did not emphasize this moral appeared only in "art" magazines such as *The Little Review* (which was, in fact, run by two lesbians, Margaret Anderson and Jane Heap), or their subject matter was disguised in what amounted to a code language. As an example of the latter is Gertrude Stein's "Miss Furr and Miss Skeene," which appeared in *Vanity Fair* in 1922. The story is a play on the word "gay," which was not yet widely understood to mean homosexual; however, those who had become a part of what was by this time a flourishing lesbian subculture would have discerned what Stein meant by her description of Georgine Skeene and Helen Furr:

> They were regular in being gay, they learned little things that are things in being gay, they learned many little things that are things in being gay, they were gay every day, they were regular, they were gay, they were gay the

> same length of time every day, they were gay, they were quite regularly gay.

Those *Vanity Fair* readers who were not familiar with the language of the subculture would no doubt have thought this a story in the notorious, wacky Stein style about two happy women.

The lesbian stories which appeared in *The Little Review* never suggested that two women could live together happily ever after, but they are noteworthy because, unlike the stories of the 1920s that appeared in magazines such as *Harper's* and *Dial*, they presented in a sympathetic manner lesbian characters who were not sick. For example, Os-Anders's story "Karen: A Novel," which appeared in *The Little Review* in spring 1922,[11] is concerned with a middle-aged Norwegian immigrant woman, Karen, who loves from a distance Dorothea, a woman of her age but not of her class: "She wished she had the courage to go to her, to die for her" (23). When she sees Dorothea she cannot "take her eyes away" (23); her love for Dorothea is to Karen one of the most important things in her life: "Each person has only one or two thoughts—one of hers had been Dorothea" (25). When Dorothea dies her husband Andreas asks Karen to marry him because he cannot run the farm by himself. She accepts only because she wants to be near what will remind her of Dorothea, and the marriage is apparently never consummated. With Andreas's death one of Dorothea's daughters is anxious to claim the farm for herself and threatens Karen: "I will go to the church and tell them why you were never my father's wife" (27), referring, of course, to Karen's lesbian love for Dorothea. But it is the daughter here who, in her cruelty and pettiness, is seen as being sick, not the lesbian character. The story ends with Karen bedridden after an accident. The author pointedly attempts to maintain the reader's sympathy for Karen through the conclusion:

> She was helpless now. She could not be going any more in the night, as she had gone in all the years since Dorothea died, with bucket and soap to wash Dorothea's tombstone: to keep it white. Walking the long miles to the graveyard, in the night, to do this for Dorothea. She was old and helpless now—there was nothing—nothing. (28)

It is illuminating to compare this story particularly to *Julie Cane*, which was published in *Harper's* about the same time (i.e., early 1920s). The *Harper's* story, intended of course for a wider reading audience, insists on the morbidity of Martha, a middle-aged woman who falls in love with another female, and her attachment is laughable. Karen's love for Dorothea in the *The Little Review* story is sad because it is never satisfied, but it is seen as being neither morbid nor laughable. The author of "Karen" and the editors of *The Little Review* seem to have been so concerned with not reflecting the societal fears toward same-sex love of the 1920s that they reached for another extreme in a totally noble and selfless character who would claim all of the reader's sympathy.

However, outside of "art" magazine fiction and stories in code such as Stein's "Miss Furr and Miss Skeene," lesbianism, by this time, was seldom dealt with in magazines, and where it was treated the author invariably showed lesbian love to be sick. Only in the last few years has the image begun to change in periodicals other than those devoted to an exclusively lesbian readership. The feminist movement, with its interest in viewing same-sex relationships in a new and positive way, accounts for much of this change, as is reflected in popular feminist periodicals such as *Ms*. But magazines such as *Ladies' Home Journal* and contemporary equivalents of *St. Nicholas*, which are tuned in to the fears of the most conservative elements of the population, still do not publish stories that sympathetically portray same-sex love as did *Ladies' Home Journal*'s "The Cat and the King" and *St. Nicholas*'s "The Lass of the Silver Sword" in the early decades of the twentieth century.

Same-sex relationships, although the nature of the emotions involved may not have changed over the last 60 or 70 years, are no longer seen in the same light: In our sex-conscious era readers are not likely to believe in the possibility of an intense sentimental love between two women that is entirely devoid of an erotic component. But, more pertinently, because of the growth of women's social and economic independence, it may no longer be assumed that love between women is merely transitional to heterosexuality, and because of the popularization of "medical" views (from Krafft-Ebing to Freud and his disciples), such relationships have been defined by labels that suggest they are morbid, perverse, and generally unpleasant.

NOTES

*Originally published in the *Journal of Popular Culture* 11 (Spring 1978): 800–817. Reprinted with permission.

1. See, for example, nineteenth-century novels such as Henry Wadsworth Longfellow's *Kavanagh* (1849) and Oliver Wendell Holmes's *A Mortal Antipathy* (1885). In both of these novels, the central female characters form powerful love attachments to other female characters.

2. In 1638, for example, John Cotton proposed that the Massachusetts Bay Colony penal code place sexual relations between women on a par with those between men for legal purposes. His proposal was rejected. While there is abundant evidence of the persecution of male homosexuals in the eighteenth century, American historians have been able to find no information relevant to the legal or even social persecution of female-female relations. There is also no record of significant persecution of lesbian women throughout most of the nineteenth century, until the last two decades of that century.

3. It is revealing to note that, while Ellis maintained that such ailments were typical of the lesbian, the subjects of several of his case histories were free of them.

4. See Carroll Smith-Rosenberg's, "The Female World of Love and Ritual: Relations Between Women in Nineteenth Century America," in *Signs: Journal of Women in Culture and Society* 1.1 (Autumn 1975): 1–24. See also William Taylor and Christopher Lasch's "Two Kindred Spirits: Sorority and Family in New England, 1839–1846," in *New England Quarterly* 36.1 (March 1963): 23–41. Both articles study the correspondence between nineteenth-century women and conclude that intense female-female love relationships were entirely common in the nineteenth century.

5. The word "lesbian" would not, of course, have been used in such fiction or, for that matter, anywhere outside of a few medical texts. The 1903 edition of the *O.E.D.* defines "lesbian" only as meaning "of or pertaining to the Land of Lesbos, in the northern part of the Grecian archipelago."

6. See, for example, two reviews attacking a study which suggests that Emily Dickinson had homoaffectional attachments: John Ciardi, *New England Quarterly* 25 (1952): 93–98, and Grace B. Sherrer, *American Literature* 24 (1952): 255–258.

7. Bergler enumerates, in a scientific tone, six observations about Lawrence's supposedly accurate "knowledge" of "these sick women."

8. As Frank Kermode notes in *D.H. Lawrence* (New York: Viking, 1973), in the years following World War I, Lawrence seems to have reached a sort of apogee, perhaps because it was becoming shockingly clear to him that women were moving in the direction of freedom—a direction opposite to what he saw as necessary if the world was to right itself—more rapidly than ever at this time. His letters of this period suggest his hostility to "self-important" and "bullying" females, both in his own life and in the world in general.

9. See contemporary discussions of lesbianism that very effectively take issue with Freudian biases: for example, Bettie Wysor's *The Lesbian Myth* (New York: Random House, 1974); Jane Rule's *Lesbian Images* (Garden City, New York: Doubleday, 1975); Martha Shelley's "Notes of a Radical Lesbian," in *Sisterhood Is Powerful*. Ed. Robin Morgan (New York: Vintage, 1970); and Shere Hite's *The Hite Report* (New York: Dell, 1976).

10. In Moore's *D.H. Lawrence: A Critical Survey*, pp. 28–48.

11. I have been unable to ascertain definitely the identity of Os-Anders, but I believe the name to have been a pseudonym for Margaret Anderson, who infrequently wrote fiction. It is likely that Anderson would have used some pseudonym if "Karen" is her story, not only because of the subject matter but also because she would have been sensitive to accusations of vanity she might have received for publishing her own fiction.

Works Cited

Bergler, Edmund. "D.H. Lawrence's *The Fox* and the Psychoanalytic Theory of Lesbianism." *D.H. Lawrence: A Critical Survey*. Ed. Harry T. Moore. London: Forum House, 1969, pp. 49–55.

Daskam, Josephine Dodge. *Smith College Stories.* 1900. New York: Scribner's, 1921.

Dubois, Margaret (Mary) Constance. "The Lass of the Silver Sword." *St. Nicholas* (Dec. 1908–Oct. 1909).

Hamilton, Allan McLane. "The Civil Responsibility of Sexual Perverts." *The American Journal of Insanity* 52.4 (April 1896): 503–509.

Henry, O. (pseud. Sydney Porter). "The Last Leaf." *Strand* (1906).

Holmes, Oliver Wendell. *A Mortal Antipathy: First Opening of the New Portfolio.* New York: Houghton Mifflin, 1885.

Hull, Helen. "The Fire." *Century* 95 (Nov. 1917): 105–114.

Katz, Jonathan. *Gay American History: Lesbians and Gay Men in the U.S.A.* New York: Thomas Y. Crowell, 1976.

Kermode, Frank. *D.H. Lawrence.* New York: Viking, 1973.

Lee, Jeanette. "The Cat and the King." *Ladies' Home Journal* (October 1919): 10+.

Leiberman, Elias. "Fiction Formulas." *Harper's* 148 (Feb. 1924): 421–422.

Longfellow, Henry Wadsworth. *Kavanagh*. Boston: Ticknor, 1849.

MacLane, Mary. *The Story of Mary MacLane.* Chicago: Herbert Stone, 1902.

Moore, Harry T., ed. *D.H. Lawrence: A Critical Survey.* London: Forum House, 1969.

O'Higgins, Harvey. *Julie Cane. Harper's* 148 (serialized beginning March 1924): 425+.

Os-Anders. "Karen: A Novel." *The Little Review* (Spring 1922): 23–28.

Stein, Gertrude. "Miss Furr and Miss Skeene." *Vanity Fair* (1922).

Wells, Catherine. "The Beautiful House." *Harper's* 124 (1912): 503–511.

Martha Wolfenstein's *Idyls of the Gass* and the Dilemma of Ethnic Self-Representation

Barbara Shollar

In a period of extraordinary (literary) ferment when immigrant and working-class characters were entering our fiction in works by ethnic writers, Martha Wolfenstein (1869–1906) became the first Jewish American woman to utilize the short story as a form through which to explore Jewish American identity. Wolfenstein, born in Insterburg, Prussia, to Dr. Samuel Wolfenstein and Bertha Brieger, was educated in Cleveland public schools, where her father, an eminent Reform rabbi, became the superintendent of the Jewish Orphan Asylum. Little else of her life is known save that it was cut short by tuberculosis at age 36. A number of her tales were published in *Lippincott's Magazine*, but the collections were brought out by the Jewish Publication Society. Nonetheless, they were reviewed by mainstream-culture journals and newspapers as well as by the Jewish press. The public reception to Wolfenstein's work is in itself worthy of analysis and will be discussed later in the essay.

I would like first to introduce aspects of Wolfenstein's *oeuvre*, suggest its relationship to the local-color tradition—especially that of other women writers of the period—and, finally, mark the difference ethnicity makes in the deployment of its strategies. Focusing primarily on the first of Wolfenstein's two collections, I claim that her writing was a strategy for (re)locating the Jew in America and insuring that she was "at home" here.

A few definitions may be in order. The term "ethnic" is used to delineate the category of social and cultural characteristics that deviate from the norms established by the hegemonic culture; ethnicity then becomes the basis on which the subordinate group self-consciously fashions itself as a political minority, in order to negotiate with the dominant culture. Such definitions are not meant to render the dominant—in this case, American Protestant, white—culture ethnically neutral, but rather to underscore the political origins of cultural definitions and their historical relativity. While I use "ethnic" instead of the more specific term "Jewish," because the point I wish to make pertains not only to that specific group but to all those groups that are so marked, my discussion relies on the example of Jewish American representation. Local-color literature constituted ethnicity through its representation. Allegorically, then, the genre participated in and created the reality of modern American life.

In two collections of short stories, *Idyls of the Gass* (1901) and *A Renegade and Other Tales* (1905), Wolfenstein appropriated an earlier regional model, using the techniques of local color, to re-create the goings-on of the village of Moritz in the Austrian Empire, most particularly the activities of those dwellers in the *Judengasse*, or the Jewish street of the town, in the period roughly from 1840 through the 1860s. In addition to the American literary tradition, however, she also relied on the romantic tradition in German literature that turned to the common folk and regional landscape for the sources of a new realism. (Thus it is not surprising that her stories found a German audience when they were translated and published in the Viennese newspaper *Die Zeit*.) Glenda Hobbes's definition helps us to understand this fusion:

> While local color usually describes a nineteenth-century American literary movement, it can refer to any work whose author points out decorative regional details to add interest to the narrative. "Regional" works may include descriptions of landscape and customs, but they are intrinsic and crucial to an understanding of plot and character. (83)

Wolfenstein, in her first collection, is at pains to emphasize the mundane arena of her work, "a poor and ordinary sort of place at the best," in which the economy, amusements, and food are of the simplest, and people have "many problems, but all of the bread and butter order" (*Idyls of the Gass* 14, 15). Like other American female local colorists, she self-consciously spurns romance and other more fantastic genres, as well as the extraordinary nature of their protagonists:

> I might, if I chose, tell you the fairy-like tale of the wealth of the Rothschilds, or the fascinating story of the Jew who rose to the papal throne of Rome; I might take you to the romantic old ghettos of Spain or the ancient one at Rome . . . , but I prefer to come to the old Jews' street of Moritz and tell its homely tales. (*Idyls of the Gass,* 27)

In choosing this humble subject matter, Wolfenstein sets out to ethnicize "American" regionalism (albeit she chooses foreign territory as the terrain—a point to which I shall return later in the essay. Suffice it to say here that her text provides a history for the Jew in America). Consequently, the customs and traditions that she emphasizes are not merely those pertaining to a rural way of life, but those defining the traditional Jewish community in western Europe. For example, her characters live according to the dietary rules of *kashrut*, which prevent them from dining with their Gentile neighbors (unless they find means—sometimes ingenious, sometimes droll—of circumventing the rules) or accepting nonkosher bread that may stave off starvation or eating a sweet meat to reward an errand. Wolfenstein also ethnicizes regionalism by narrating how people's lives are shaped, restricted and distorted, by laws that limit their right to own the land they farm and to ply their tannery craft with new leather. She shows how the edicts of the Austrian Empire and the Gentile culture at various times prohibit them from selling their goods at town fairs or gaining entrance to the university or teaching there. Wolfenstein's stories also expose the prejudices that make the Jews subject to the daily insults of petty anti-Semitism, the still harsher charges of and trials for ritual murder, and the severest consequences of pogroms. Still more, Wolfenstein delineates a historicized psychology. That is, she conveys some of the patterns of thought that derive from such traditional ways of living and their relationship to circumstance. In stories, comic and serious, she records and defines the (religious/traditional) Jewish sensibility and its impact, much as other local-color writers captured what we think of as the Puritan identity or the American/Southern world view that seemed rooted in the soil of their respective regions.

Wolfenstein's writings bear much in common with that of other female writers who dominate the local-color tradition. I would like here to analyze those commonalities, particularly as they contribute to the structural unity of her work. Wolfenstein, like Alice Brown in *Meadow-Grass* (1895) and *Tiverton Tales* (1899) and Sarah Orne Jewett in *The Country of the Pointed Firs* (1896) and other Dunnet Landing stories, produced a text that is not simply a collection of discrete short stories but a complexly organized whole correlative of the universe it inscribes. By beginning *in medias res* and then filling in the history of their characters at appropriate points in the narrative, and by using linking devices and allusions to knit together the individual stories, local-color writers create the illusion of development and depth within the compass of the short tale, while taking advantage of the tale's ability to hone in on intimate relations and imbue ordinary encounters with dignity. Moreover, while such writers do not necessarily focus on the evolution of character per se, they do depict various events that frequently shed light on the collective status of the community, creating the effect of extending the story beyond its own borders.

Wolfenstein does not only appropriate the techniques of these writers that raise the genre to a new level of aesthetic sophistication and endow it with new power; like other female local colorists, she also reshapes the tale from a female perspective. As Susan Allen Toth and others have argued, female local colorists create a new woman in their fiction, one characterized by strength, often severely tested by circumstances and triumphing over them (17). In many female local-color portraits, the single women characters eschew marriage and "find other sources of emotional fulfillment," especially in mother-daughter bonds and in love between women (Toth 19–20; see also Donovan; Fetterley and Pryse). From a structural point of view, the centrality of this female figure and the bonding relationship also becomes the basis for unifying individual stories. The relationship between the narrator and Mrs. Todd in Jewett's *Country of the Pointed Firs* is exemplary in embodying the structural and thematic aspects of this gendered perspective. Moreover, Fetterley and Pryse, seeking to distinguish the distinctive quality of the female narrative point of view, have suggested that women writers seek not to hold the characters and their values up to ridicule "but rather to present regional experience from within, so as to engage the reader's sympathy and identification" (xii). Donovan, in particular, has stressed the anti-Calvinist, social gospel origins of this perspective, along with the matriarchal values of the community (57, 59, 78). All concur with Elaine Sargent Apthorp that this empathetic style was gradually secularized in the local-color genre to express the notion of a common humanity (7).

In sum, all these strategies contribute to create a whole that is greater than the sum of its parts and to express a distinctively female voice. Their variant uses in Wolfenstein also point to the ways in which an American-Jewish ethnic subjectivity reshapes hegemonic female concerns.

Idyls of the Gass focuses on the town baker, Maryam, and her grandson Shimmelè, who has come from the family farm to live with her. The early stories alternate between Maryam's good deeds and Shimmelè's sometimes mischievous exploits, in the process conveying the growing trust and confidence between the two characters and their deepening relationship. As in stories by hegemonic female writers, Wolfenstein makes a matriarch the central figure and uses the bonding relationship between two characters to unify the discrete stories. But the primary relationship with a male child, rather than the solitary female figure or female dyad, signals an important shift that is intended to specify the centrality of this family-centered pattern to Jewish self-definition and distinguish it from that of the dominant (female) culture. From the traditional Jewish point of view, the male had the major responsibility for carrying on the religious tradition; leaders of the Jewish American community frequently idealized the mother-son family bond as the basis of religious and spiritual life in its representations both to counter the

Gentile culture and the strain of asceticism found in Christian theology and to oppose the threat of the women's movement and its valorization of the single life, especially for women. Indirectly, it was also a means of underscoring the private domestic nature of the community's religious commitment in order to avoid any charge of national disloyalty. It implicitly stressed the Jews' permanent settlement in this country, by serving to distinguish the Jews from other immigrant groups, which tended to be characterized by single males, and, consequently, greater mobility and rates of return to the old country (see, for example, Hirsch; Kohut).

As the baker, Maryam is in daily touch with all the villagers when they come to buy bread from her and to bring their *shalet,* or ironware pots, to heat the sabbath meal in her oven. Their special orders signal occasions for festivity or mourning and, just as often, initiate tales that describe their origins. And though the flour paste that seals the lid keeps the contents of the sabbath pot hidden from her, Maryam in her wisdom has learned to ascertain the state of her neighbors' affairs by lifting the pot to deduce the substance and its capacity to meet the family's needs. Maryam sometimes "mistakenly" trades pots and thus redistributes the wealth, such as it is, of the *gass* (street), at the same time meting out justice to those lacking in proper humility ("Maryam Administers Justice" *Idyls* 143–158); other times she foists a "superfluous" *shalet* intended for beggar-guests who never arrive upon other, needier households ("The Backstub" *Idyls* 107–122). Other stories provide still more occasions for acts of invisible charity. The trope of food is in part a marker of ethnicity—food as necessary sustenance and food as a source of nurture. But food as the central means of symbolic exchange also structures and unifies the stories.

Maryam's workplace and home in the *backstub* (alleyway), as much as Maryam herself, is the pivot of the village, much like the village store of New England and southern local-color fame, from which a variety of tales extend like lines radiating outward from a central web. As the source of the community's daily bread, it is a metonym for the largely self-sustaining quasi-feudal economy focused primarily on survival. As the community's bakery, by definition kosher, it manifests the Jewish community's coherence and unity, and potentially also expresses the community's ghettolike character.

Wolfenstein threads the narrative of Maryam and Shimmelè's family fortunes (including those of her two sons) through this web, weaving back and forth in time to account for current circumstances and to establish links with other families and their tales. The story of "The Kiddush Cup" (*Idyls* 162–182), however, adds a new dimension to the communal life. Related by Maryam every sabbath, when the silver cup is filled with wine for the Friday evening prayer, the tale commemorates the ruse by which Shimmelè's grandfather saved the lives of six Austrian soldiers, at risk to his own life, during the Napoleonic Wars. Thematically, the story within the story introduces the problem of Jewish-Gentile relations. Symbolically, it signifies the apex of those relations, for the cup is not merely a gift of wealth but a token of the Gentile's appreciation and acceptance of the Jew as a Jew, as signified by the cup's function in religious ritual. Maryam asserts, "It must always remain in the family . . . and go from father to son, to be a sign and a hope in dark days that the Jew shall some day have justice" (*Idyls* 180). Structurally, the story represents the turning point of the book. From this, the ninth chapter, the mood gradually darkens: stories dwell on personal misfortune and communal famine, which render life in the *gass* increasingly exiguous.

This mood culminates in a series of events that drastically alter the community. Once again, Jewish-Gentile relations are the focus. The growing anti-Semitism that makes Shimmelè the butt of a gang of rowdies as he returns home from an errand is recounted in "Tears" (*Idyls* 241–260). In "The Source of Tears" (*Idyls* 261–278), Maryam initially evokes an earlier time, when Jewish-Gentile relations were generally friendly, symbolized by the story of the butcher Michal Katzev and his wife, who, in gratitude for their own daughter's recovery from illness, take in a Christian beggar girl. Having received the permission of the parish priest to raise her, they send her to school to insure that she learns to read and write, buy her a crucifix and prayer book and drag her unwillingly to church to secure her faith, and pay her wages when she is old enough to work to enable her to marry. When, in the present time, Julsa disappears with her 40 gulden, only to be found dead in a ravine several weeks later, Katzev and his wife are arrested for ritual murder. They are ultimately acquitted—not because they have sworn alibis or the so-called witnesses are shown to be perjurers, nor because there is a recognition that such action is at total odds with the actual relations of the foster parents and the young woman or the ethics of their religious commitment—but because of insufficient evidence. And the acquittal only serves as fuel to hatemongers, who incite an already embittered, besotted, and famished peasantry and send the Jews into hiding. In the watch that ends the night, the mob storms Maryam's house, and espying the Kiddush cup, wreak their havoc in search of greater wealth, killing Maryam and the blind son who has leapt to her defense. When Shimmelè's cries are met with silence, he must walk out to a world of devastation and ruin, empty of those he loves ("Shimmelè Prays" *Idyls* 279–295).

This final story parallels "The Kiddush Cup," inverting the tale and nullifying its promise. By this means, Wolfenstein structures the whole with a climax and denouement and endows it with a cumulative power that is usually reserved for the novel. Moreover, the depiction of a vanished world characteristically conceived as nostalgia here becomes something quite otherwise. What is normally bathed in a lambent atmosphere has tragic plangency—there is no home to which the Jews can return. The text that places America on the farthest verge—beyond the margin, as it were—nonetheless constitutes Jews at once as an inevitable presence and as "outsiders" within its borders.

Wolfenstein's project to ethnicize regionalism represents a major dilemma, raising the question of how to represent the Jew's distinct identity without making the Jew "too Jewish," that is, without rendering the Jew as the "other" and invoking the prejudices of the dominant culture. That the burden fell to the ethnic writer, who needed to accommodate her material to that culture without pandering to it, is still another way of characterizing the dilemma. The issue is evident from the nature of the reviews that greeted the book's publication, particularly if we analyze those that originated in the mainstream press of the dominant culture versus those that appeared in the Jewish press. To begin with the former, *Outlook* judged Wolfenstein's work favorably, finding it "full of local color," but it designated the details, utilizing the Spencerian-influenced terminology of the time, as "*race* [emphasis added] peculiarities treated with knowledge and skill and withal broad human sympathy and delicate humor" (Review of *Renegade, Outlook* 1087). The reviewer is positively inclined toward the representation; nonetheless, his use of the term "race" signals a view of character as genetically rather than culturally determined, and is, therefore, potentially racist, because it renders difference, and the outsider's status becomes immutable. The comment of the *New York Times* reviewer indirectly points to a more tendentious view of the work: "The prevailing atmospheric effect is gray, a dull sad gray, and there is always a sense of what may be called the joy of suffering, a sort of reveling in the luxury of woe" (Review of *Renegade* 113).

Before elaborating on this description, I would like to note that this emphasis is in sharp contrast to the comments of Jewish reviewers, who underlined Wolfenstein's "delicate humor" and "fine sentiment" (while not denying her "intense seriousness") and distinguished her work from the gloomy ghetto tales of the Russian Jewish writer of the Old World and the New (Review of *Renegade, Jewish Comment* 3). Emma Wolf, a novelist who had written on Jewish themes as well, also noted that Wolfenstein "has . . . chosen to pass by, all that is ugly and sordid" (4). Another critic anonymously summed up Wolfenstein's achievement, indicating that "her point of view [was] unclouded by a bizarre and erratic outlook upon the world. . . . In spite of the darkness that is bound to creep over portrayal[s] of Jewish life, her tales are full of sunshine and display a people not altogether free and secure, but still happy and hopeful" ("Martha Wolfenstein" *Jewish Comment* 1).

What, then, lies behind the *Times* pronouncement, beyond perhaps the peevish, ill-humored projection of its writer? The subtext is the stereotype of the Jew obsessed by her fate in the Diaspora, wallowing in self-pity. The Jew was self-indulgent, presumably exaggerating the incidents that befell her, too quick to take offense, too willing to cast herself in the role of victim. Behind the stereotypical notion of the melancholic Jew—and the Gentile's vague repugnance—lies an older romantic conception of the Jew's sadness as deriving from her refusal to accept Christ. Willfully cut off from the possibility of grace, the Jew must be forever isolated from Christian humankind, of which her grief is a token (Anderson n.p.). The subtext clarifies the dilemma—and danger—of representing a specifically Jewish identity rooted in traditional values to a predominantly Gentile audience, an issue to which other Jewish critics were sensitive.

One anonymous commentator, reviewing a text by two other Jewish authors, thus argued that a depiction of the Jew was best avoided on two grounds:

> The Jew is, in the main, not altogether unlike his fellow-men, and there should hence be no need of emphasizing certain exotic peculiarities. . . . [In addition,] the Jew must seek to become as long as he lives here an integral factor in the body politic, not a stranger whom certain potent charms may sway. ("Review of Ghetto" *Jewish Comment* 6)

The first argument is philosophical, based on Enlightenment notions of a universal humanity, while the second is political, based on expediency and notions of enlightened self-interest. Their implicit contradiction, I would argue, has much to do with the Jew's self-definition during the period of the books' publications and her position in this country at that time. Before moving to a consideration of Wolfenstein's effort to resolve the conflict in her own project, therefore, I would like to suggest the relevant social context that makes her text exemplary.

Briefly, Wolfenstein's point of view, based on her national and socioeconomic origins and period of immigration as well as the internal evidence of her texts, seems consistent with that of Reform Judaism. The movement was initiated in the early nineteenth century in Germany, and by the 1890s, its doctrine and social practices constituted the hegemonic discourse of (as opposed to within) the subordinate culture vis-à-vis the dominant culture in America. Characterized by some of its critics and historians as the Protestant form of Judaism, the Reform movement was the most thoroughgoing effort to rethink/restructure Judaism in accordance with the demands—intellectual, socioeconomic, and political—of modern life. Though it eventually moderated its stance, the movement began by eliminating all forms of traditional ritual observance (see Meyer; Sachar).

The Jews' position in the United States during the period of Wolfenstein's coming of age and the publication of her works was generally favorable: The Jews were for the most part granted full civic equality and political participation. Beginning in the late 1880s, however, they were increasingly subjected to various forms of social discrimination, including restricted housing and quotas in hiring and education, and were consistently excluded from (Protestant) elite institutions and establishments. German Jews, who constituted the primary immigrants from 1848 through the late 1860s and were generally economically secure, found themselves experiencing a cultural and status anxiety in this country that was new to them. In part, that anxiety was the product of their new visibility, the result of the greater wave of Russian Jewish immigrants arriving from the 1880s onward, and their sometimes reluctant identification with them (see Goren 571–598; Howe 137).

It is in these contexts that Wolfenstein's local-color fiction and its strategies are exemplary, as Amy Kaplan puts it, in "imagining and managing the threats of social change" (10). Foremost of these strategies is the one frequently utilized by other local colorists as well—that of setting her stories in the past. For traditional critics of American literary history, this strategy is retrograde. Brian Lee, to take but one instance, declares that regionalism constitutes "some form of temporal and spatial escape." Disparagingly, he notes that the writers of such fiction "were forever looking backwards in the vain hope of resurrecting a vanishing ideal that could somehow be equated with contemporary America" (58). How irrelevant a criticism this is to Wolfenstein's work is all too apparent. One might argue that Wolfenstein's resurrection of the past is a nostalgic tribute to the German Jewish community, at a time when its ascendancy within American culture was already foreclosed by the numerical superiority of Russian Jews. But the very substance, structure, and thrust of her work is designed to make us aware that the world she describes is, willy-nilly, gone forever. The pogrom that destroys the community renders associations with such a world painful indeed. The implicit result is, as I have suggested earlier, a (re)location of the Jew onto American soil. Rather than constituting a form of escapism, Wolfenstein's work affirms the inevitable presence of the Jew, and must be understood as an effort to define the Jew in the present American circumstance.

Ironically, setting the stories not only in the past but in a foreign country, the spatial equivalent of that vanished past, suits this purpose. The containment effected by spatial displacement, as practiced by the ethnic regionalist, psychically distances both the Jewish American writer and the American reader from the European protagonist. The ethnic regionalist thus reassures the dominant culture of the essential Americanness of the American Jew. That is, the literary tradition simultaneously incorporates difference and neutralizes the threat posed to the hegemonic culture by that difference. From the perspective of the subordinate culture, the strategy, at the least, gives muted expression to profound differences in Christian and Jewish socialization and experience that may serve to explain differences in points of view and concerns. And at its most extreme, it counters "the despair of deracination" with "the hope of restoring attachment to remnant places" by a dialogue with the dead (Lutwack 184, 145. Lutwack makes these comments in a discussion of the quest narrative).

Much depends on perspective. And nowhere is this more evident than in Wolfenstein's appropriation of the female local colorist's empathetic style, which is, like the story's time and setting, inevitably complicated by the dilemma of ethnic regionalism. Wolfenstein is concerned to present her characters sympathetically, but the particular manifestations of Jewish subjectivity are somewhat at odds with the presumption of a common humanity on which such sympathy rests. She resolves this dilemma by the strategic and radical transfiguration of the central heroine Maryam and, especially, of the male protagonist Shimmelè.

Astute in her capacity to distinguish between true piety and superstition, Maryam is, if not a totally secularized figure of virtue, characterized essentially by a spiritual goodness, whose religious observance is defined more by her charitable acts than by a (disagreeable) concern with religious ritual, that is, those observances that have traditionally set Jews apart and that might prove embarrassing to their Americanized counterparts.

Maryam's acts of charity, and the persistent emphasis on the poverty-stricken villagers' reluctance to acknowledge their need, moreover, serve a double purpose, since they imply long-standing and proud traditions of self-help and thus tacitly allay anxieties of the hegemonic culture and its Protestant elite that the immigrant hordes would tax their resources and burden the state.

Shimmelè, too, is represented as a boy with a "head of iron" (an intellect) whose love of learning is valorized and, most important, impels his desire to debunk superstition. In two stories, "How Shimmelè Became a Sceptic" and "And a Scoffer," the child is shown growing in knowledge and experience that enables him to throw off what are viewed as the excrescences of true belief. In the first, the boy, having been taught to regard a *Cohen* (descendant of the high priests in the Holy Temple at Jerusalem) with awe, is dismayed to confront one in the flesh. He is put off by the *schnorrer's* (beggar's) unclean appearance, and, when, into the bargain, the man prays "directly under his mother's cheeseboard" and surreptitiously reaches for the food during the service, Shimmelè responds indignantly: "The Spirit of God is stealing the cheeses" (*Idyls* 64, 65).

If the boy's unwitting (?) exposure of the beggar is the product of his childhood innocence in the former story, the latter story reveals his acting out of a calculated empiricism. Having been told that one must knock at the *shul* (house of study and prayer) before entering, because the spirits of the dead have gone there to pray during the night and will strike anyone living dumb at the first sight, blind at the second sight, and dead on the third, Shimmelè determines to test this proposition. When he confesses his infraction to his grandmother, rather than expressing anger, Maryam discovers in this action proof of his intelligence and an adumbration of his one day becoming chief rabbi. Moreover, "From that day he was man in the house, Maryam's helper and confidant" (*Idyls* 82). Under this dispensation, Maryam makes a pact with Shimmelè to keep his discovery secret from the rest of the village. What makes him truly spiritual in the eyes of the intended audience is what makes him, from the traditional point of view, a nonbeliever. Maryam's approval makes sense only if we understand the text configuring the Jew's assenting to a nonparticularistic divinity. The coded text thus assures the Gentile reader that the Jew who is to arrive on her shores is a person much like herself, whose coming of age metonymically signals that the Jew has reached a level of civilization equal to her own. The common core of humanity that the reader shares with the subjects is granted only by acceding to the mores of the dominant culture. Thus is the dilemma of ethnic regionalism resolved, and the threat posed to the dominant culture neutralized.

Apthorp, seeking to analyze the difference between the realism of male and female writers, distinguishes between the naturalism of plotting and theme and what she calls the sentimental perspective of the narrative point of view. She goes on to discuss the different kinds of irony available to each of these literary traditions: the (male) naturalist aims at "the breakdown of the reader's illusions about human nature," while the (female) sentimentalist aims at "the reform of her conscience and behavior toward other people" (9). Wolfenstein, too, achieved a tonality that overall tended to the reform of the Gentile conscience and behavior toward the Jews, to revise Apthorp's dictum. But she did so in ways that manifested the contradictions inherent in inscribing and constructing what Woodrow Wilson and Theodore Roosevelt were pleased to call "hyphenated Americans."

WORKS CITED

Anderson, George K. *The Legend of the Wandering Jew.* Hanover, NH: University Press of New England, 1991.

Apthorp, Elaine Sargent. "Sentiment, Naturalism, and the Female Regionalist." *Legacy* 7.1: 3–22.

Brown, Charlotte, Paula Hyman, and Sonya Michel. *The Jewish Woman in America.* New York: New American Library, 1977.

Donovan, Josephine. *New England Local Color Literature: A Women's Tradition.* New York: Ungar, 1983.

Fetterley, Judith, and Marjorie Pryse. Introduction. *American Women Regionalists, 1850–1930.* Eds. Judith Fetterley and Marjorie Pryse. New York: Norton, 1992, pp. xi–xx.

Goren, Arthur A. "Jews." *Harvard Encyclopedia of American Ethnic Groups.* Eds. Stephan Thernstrom et al. Cambridge, MA: Harvard University Press, 1980, pp. 571–598.

Hirsch, Emil. "My Religion and the Crucifixion Viewed from a Jewish Standpoint." *The Jewish People: History, Religion, Literature.* Eds. Jacob B. Agus et al. New York: Arno Press, 1973.

Hobbes, Glenda. "Harriet Arnow's Kentucky Novels: Beyond Local Color." *Regionalism and the Female Imagination: A Collection of Essays.* Ed. Emily Toth. New York: Human Sciences, 1985, pp. 83–92.

Howe, Irving. *World of Our Fathers: The Journey of the East European Jews to America and the Life They Found and Made.* New York: Harcourt Brace Jovanovich, 1976.

Kaplan, Amy. *The Social Construction of American Realism.* Chicago: University of Chicago Press, 1988.

Kohut, Rebekah. *My Portion (an Autobiography).* Introduction by Henrietta Szold. New York: Seltzer, 1925.

Koppelman, Susan. Personal communication (via Julie Brown). August 13, 1993.

Lee, Brian. *American Fiction, 1865–1940.* Longman Literature in English Series. New York: Longman, 1987.

Lutwack, Leonard. *The Role of Place in Literature.* Syracuse, NY: Syracuse University Press, 1984.

"Martha Wolfenstein." Obituary. *The American Hebrew* (March 23, 1906): 539–541.

"Martha Wolfenstein." Obituary. *The American Israelite* (March 22, 1906): 6.

"Martha Wolfenstein." Obituary. *Jewish Comment* (March 23, 1906): 1.

Meyer, Michael A. "Response to Modernity: A History of the Reform Movement in Judaism." *Studies in Jewish History.* Ed. Jehuda Reinharz. New York: Oxford University Press, 1988.

Review of *Ghetto Silhouettes*, by David Warfield and Marguerita A. Hamm. *Jewish Comment* (Sept. 6, 1902): 6.

Review of "A Monk from the Ghetto," by Martha Wolfenstein. *Jewish Comment* (July 20, 1900): 1.

Review of *A Renegade and Other Tales*, by Martha Wolfenstein. *Jewish Comment* (Dec. 22, 1905): 3.

Review of *A Renegade and Other Tales*, by Martha Wolfenstein. *New York Times* (Feb. 24, 1906): 113.

Review of *A Renegade and Other Tales*, by Martha Wolfenstein. *Outlook* (Dec. 30, 1905): 1087.

Sachar, Howard Morley. *The Course of Modern Jewish History*. New York: Dell, 1977.

Singer, Isidore, ed. "Martha Wolfenstein." *Jewish Encyclopedia*. Vol. 12. New York: Ktav Publishing House, n.d., p. 550.

Toth, Susan Allen. "'The Rarest and Most Peculiar Grape': Versions of the New England Woman in Nineteenth-Century Local Color Literature." *Regionalism and the Female Imagination: A Collection of Essays*. Ed. Emily Toth. New York: Human Sciences, 1985, pp. 15–28.

Wolf, Emma. Review of *Idyls of the Gass*, by Martha Wolfenstein. *Jewish Comment* (Dec. 6, 1901): 2, 4.

Wolfenstein, Martha. *Idyls of the Gass*. Short Story Index Reprint Series. Vol. 1. Freeport, NY: Books for Libraries, 1969.

———. *A Renegade and Other Tales*. Philadelphia: The Jewish Publication Society of America, 1905.

Fannie Hurst's Short Stories of Working Women—"Oats for the Woman," "Sob Sister," and Contemporary Reader Responses: A Meditation

Susan Koppelman

My area of scholarly specialization is U.S. women's short stories. I used to think of myself as an inter- and multidisciplinary generalist. Then about 10 years ago, people began asking me what I do, and in trying to answer that question, I realized that I had become a specialist, but one who brings to that specialty the inclinations, the instincts, and the training of a generalist.

I have been doing research on short stories written between 1826 and the present by women in the United States since my first book, *Images of Women in Fiction: Feminist Perspectives*, was published in 1972. Nine years ago I began to publish the results of that research in a series of thematic and historical anthologies of short stories. In the third of these volumes, *Between Mothers and Daughters: Stories Across a Generation*, I included Fannie Hurst's 1917 story, "Oats for the Woman," the first Hurst story to have been reprinted in more than 40 years (bibliographical information on Hurst's stories mentioned in this essay appear as a checklist following).

Author, social activist, and media personality, Fannie Hurst (1885–1968) provided her readers—who seem to have been mostly women, since she published most of her stories in women's magazines—with a means of examining and reflecting on their own lives. She published 17 novels—among them

Lummox (1923), *Back Street* (1931), *Imitation of Life* (1933), and *Lonely Parade* (1942)—and more than 300 short stories during her career. Of these, only 63 stories were collected from their original periodical publications and reprinted in 8 books. Of these 63, about one-third of them portray lower-class and lower middle-class urban working women.

In these stories, Hurst created images of working women in five major trades or professions. She wrote about women in the garment industry, especially models. "Oats for the Woman" is one of the most poignant of these. She wrote about department store clerks at a time when the number of women earning their living in that kind of work was enormous and ever-growing. We might think of these women as the "Lowell Mill Girls" of the early part of this century. One of the most popular of these stories is "The Nth Commandment," originally published in the 1914 Christmas issue of the *Saturday Evening Post*. I have since reprinted this story in *"May Your Days Be Merry and Bright": Christmas Stories by Women* and have been delighted by the enthusiastic letters from readers. Hurst wrote about women who earned their living at one place or another on the continuum of domestic labor—from charwomen to housewives to boardinghouse landladies. The most famous of her boardinghouse stories, an important mother-daughter story, is "Ice Water Pl—!" included in Edward J. O'Brien's *Best American Short Stories of 1919*. She wrote about the unglamorous and hard work lives of women in the performing arts—from sideshow fat ladies ("Even as You and I"), to road show repertory theater company character actors ("The Character Woman"), to chorus girls ("The Wrong Pew"), to stage and screen stars ("Breakers Ahead!"), to classical musicians ("Humoresque"), and opera prima donnas. Hurst sees all work in the arts as true work,[1] work that, as much as any other, ought to be fairly compensated, ought not to be performed in unhealthy, unsafe circumstances, and ought not to expose women engaged in it to sexual harassment. And she wrote about women who earned their livings by selling sex—ranging from high-class mistresses of wealthy and powerful men ("Back Pay"), to street hookers ("A Petal on the Current"), to hoods' molls ("Sob Sister"). Her kept women stories combine the work of women in domestic labor and women in the performing arts. In these stories, she seems to be fulfilling the role of Virginia Woolf's hypothetical "new woman" novelist, Mary Carmichael:

> Mary Carmichael will go without kindness or condescension, but in the spirit of fellowship into those small, scented rooms where sit the courtesan, the harlot and the lady with the pug dog. There they still sit in the rough and ready-made clothes that the male writer has had perforce to clap upon their shoulders. But Mary Carmichael will have out her scissors and fit them close to every hollow and angle. It will be a curious sight, when it comes, to see those women as they are, but we must wait a little, for Mary Carmichael will still be encumbered with that self-consciousness in the presence of "sin" which is the legacy of our sexual barbarity. She will still wear the shoddy old fetters of class on her feet. (Woolf 92)[2]

It was one of Hurst's stories about such a woman whose story's title became the epithet used to discount Fannie Hurst as an artist. Immediately after the publication of "Sob Sister," Hurst was hailed by critics for the power of her portrayal:

> I remember very well an April day some six years ago, when I was coming slowly home from the village post office with the morning's mail in my pocket and an open magazine in my hand. The world was ringing with shouts for battle, on every corner men were gesticulating and arguing. The United States had at last been stung to action—we were going to war.
>
> But I was utterly indifferent. The interest aroused in me by the black, four-inch type headline in the morning paper had evaporated; for the moment it mattered not to me whether the French capitulated, the Germans triumphed, or the United States entered the fray. I was reading "Sob Sister," by Fannie Hurst. I was absorbed, thrilled, fascinated by this living, breathing, throbbing glimpse of an older war—the war that is as old as Eve's oldest daughter.
>
> The position of Fannie Hurst in the world of letters cannot be properly estimated without taking into account this truly remarkable short story. It is as daring a literary achievement as we have in the language; perfect portraiture, a superb example of the art of writing and the conquest of a field almost untouched by English and

> American authors. That it came from the hand of a woman, and an extremely young woman, makes it all the more astonishing; but "Sob Sister" is an astonishing story on all counts. (Farrar 268)

In later years, Fannie Hurst began to be sneered at as the "sob sister" of American literature. In fact, it was not until I began writing this essay that I began to think of that term being applied to Fannie Hurst in a new way. I had always assumed it had been used to represent the accusation of "sentimentality." And indeed it has come, in our present time, to be thought of that way. Those critics who dismiss her by repeating the second-hand charge of "literary sob sister" are generally unfamiliar with the story whose title the phrase is.

But I am beginning to wonder if the use of that term to disparage Hurst was not originally intended to have overtones of sexual accusation. I wonder if this is not another example of the *ad feminum* argument made against literary women since the days of Aphra Behn, also accused, both blatantly and indirectly, of sexual irregularity.

As I first read Hurst's once-famous and later opprobrious story "Sob Sister," I kept being reminded of Dorothy Parker's (1893–1967) famous, frequently reprinted, and critically acclaimed short story "Big Blonde" (1929). I am sure Parker knew the Hurst stories. Parker could not possibly have helped knowing Hurst's stories unless she worked full-time at being ignorant of the writer all America loved and read and talked about, a writer who shared the celebrity gossip columns with her in their mutually adopted hometown, New York.

And from what scholars of nineteenth-century feminism have been telling us lately about why Hawthorne and his ilk disliked "the damned scribbling women," we know how much economic jealousy could motivate writers[3]—just like the rest of the population. And if not jealousy, certainly there must have been curiosity about Hurst and her enormous success. And if not jealousy or curiosity, then the clever acerb's need for intimacy with the object of mockery. For any and all and more reasons, I feel certain that Dorothy Parker knew Fannie Hurst's work.

For years I have been saying that it is clear to me from my examination of the tables of contents of a couple hundred short story anthologies that the white boys seem to have been practicing quota systems and tokenism all along. There is usually a trinity of three white Gentile women writers who appear in their anthologies. (And now we see the same token/quota system has developed in the work of white feminist anthologists—there is a trinity of black women writers and no room for more black women—unless you expand the number of genres—and the number of black women is usually decreased by the addition of other women of color.)

I have also said that the white boys choose a male member from each minority group they have been frightened or lobbied or jolted into noticing and including in their anthologies. The male representative they choose is the one who seems to most closely embrace their particular patriarchal biases and values. And that pseudo-white boy is given the power to decide which members of his minority group will be chosen as the tokens to be rewarded with inclusion, acknowledgment, and at least a meager living.

These pseudo-white boy minority patriarchs do their best to suppress the writings of the women in their community, to turn the women against each other (usually by praising or granting them privileges in contrast to each other), and to allow favored women to be hatchet women who destroy the careers of competing women who are less favored (for whatever reason) by the boys.

So in 1929 Tess Slesinger (1905–1945) wrote a vicious review of *Procession*, a collection of Fannie Hurst's stories (9M).

But there are things in Slesinger's work that remind me of Hurst's work. In her recently newly famous story, "Missus Flinders," which is the last chapter in her 1934 novel *The Unpossessed* (reprinted by The Feminist Press, 1984), she tells a devastating abortion story that might have been written by Fannie Hurst, as might her "Mother to Dinner" (from her 1935 collection of stories *Time: The Present*, reprinted in Koppelman's *Between Mothers and Daughters*), a painful story of a woman torn between her love for and loyalty to her mother and her husband and is similar to Hurst's "Solitary Reaper."

I have been thinking all along that Slesinger and Hurst did different kinds of writing. But now that I think about it again I realize that for the most part they did not. The quality of women's emotional pain in the work of both writers is the same. Slesinger's characters are not ethnics, as are Hurst's. But the issues are often the same.

When Hurst writes about supposedly non-Jewish characters who seem to me to be Jewish and she has them refer to early church affiliations, what she describes as their memories are memories of the practices of Reform Judaism and the organizational habits of Reform temples. In the same way that their non-Jewishness is inauthentic when she attempts to pin it down with details, so is there something inauthentic about the absence of ethnicity in the characters of Tess Slesinger.

The point of all of this is that because of reading Fannie Hurst's "Sob Sister," for the first time, I saw Parker as a Jewish woman writer. And because of what I have discovered about the various quota systems in literature, I see Parker, Hurst, and Edna Ferber, women of the same generation, as having been in competition with each other for the coveted token spot for a Jewish woman writer in some hierarchical niche in the contemporary canon. And I see Slesinger as the woman of the succeeding generation, fighting for her place, which can only come to her by *re*-placing the Jewish women of the previous generation.

There were many other Jewish women writing early in the twentieth century, but they do not seem to have been in competition with these three insofar as there was not an overlap of subject matter. To mention a few, there were Anzia Yezierska, Mary Antin, Thyra Samter Winslow, and Viola Brothers Shore.[4]

As we gather the evidence and investigate these matters more closely, I believe we will discover that the white Protestant women were more likely to befriend and support each other than were the women writers of minority groups. Minority women writers undoubtedly had female support systems, because I do not think women writers could survive without them. Furthermore, my research has revealed the extensive support system in Mary Antin's (1881–1949) life—but I don't think they were other like writers, the way I think, for instance, that the Cary sisters (Alice and Phoebe) had each other and Mary Clemmer Ames and Mrs. Crowley and other women writers, and Annie Adams Fields made it possible for all those wonderful New England women writers to be friends, acquaintances, and supporters of one another.

At any rate, five classes of working women figure most prominently and most frequently in the short stories of Fannie Hurst. Her portrayal of these working women in the popular magazines available to mass audiences encouraged their real-life models to take pride in the heroism of their daily working lives. She helped working women recognize that the problems of sexual harassment, unhealthy and unsafe working conditions, inadequate benefits, age discrimination, and unequal pay were problems of all working women. Fannie Hurst cared about working women; she clearly meant to be their advocate, as her involvement with a variety of organizations designed to improve the lot of working women demonstrates. But her most important means of advocacy was through her fiction.

Anatomy of Me, Hurst's 1958 autobiography, includes her memories of Willie, the black woman domestic who labored in the Hurst household during Fannie's youth. As a child, Hurst remembers that she had an acute and uncomfortable awareness of the fact that Willie worked too hard, was treated unfairly by Fannie's mother, and worked under oppressive and unhealthy conditions—too many hours, too little mitigation of uncomfortable climatic conditions, too little reward, and too little respect. Hurst seems to have wanted her readers to connect this awareness in the child to socially conscious fiction and to social action in the adult. (However, her autobiography is filled with evasions and misinformation: for example, her memory of having lived on Cates Avenue, where Willie lived in a room on the third floor is, according to St. Louis city directories for the years 1885 through 1909, incorrect; her family did not move to the Cates Avenue address until Fannie was in college). Whatever her personal and/or psychological reasons for including this account of Willie, it is clear that she had an affinity for working-class women.

Hurst's first contact with Eleanor Roosevelt and her subsequent involvement with the women of the New Deal came, as Hurst remembers in her autobiography, when the two women came independently to the cause of domestic workers.

Hurst did not just "do good" and write about what she saw in her temporary jobs in factories, department stores, and restaurants and in her endless wandering through the streets of New York City, her attendance at sessions of night court, and her visits to all sorts of social agencies. She also studied the history and conditions of working women. While an undergraduate at Washington University, Hurst studied history and economics. Especially pertinent was a course called "Labor" described as follows: "the theory of wages, the condition of wage-earners in Europe and America, labor legislation, labor organizations and other plans for the benefit of wage-earners" (*Washington University Record* 1905). Additionally, I have examined that portion of her personal library housed at Washington University and the records housed in the Brandeis University library of her complete personal library at the time of her death and found books related to the subject of labor history. It is clear from the publication dates of some of these books that her interest in labor issues continued throughout her life.

I tell all of this about Hurst to preface the story of how her story "Oats for the Woman" has been received by contemporary readers.

I am told by colleagues who have used *Between Mothers and Daughters* as a text in a variety of courses on college campuses that "Oats for the Woman" evokes strong emotional responses from students, often making them cry and even more often making them furious. Students of all ages—the traditional eighteen to twenty-two year old, the returning older student, part- and full-time workers trying to upgrade employment status, taking the course because it is the only one available when they are free to take a class or because it fulfills a requirement, retired people coming to school to fulfill a lifetime ambition or just as a diversion, an entertainment—all these different kinds of students, I have been told, are moved by "Oats for the Woman."

"Oats for the Woman" is a story about a working woman, Hattie Becker, who earned a living as a model in New York for nine years and then became a domestic worker. (Female garment industry workers were one of the groups that Hurst portrayed repeatedly in her fiction, and models especially seem to have been major figures in her panorama of working women.) At age 34 it was becoming increasingly difficult for Hattie to keep the slender figure and youthful appearance necessary to continue working in her trade. She had had an affair with her employer, Leon Kessler, who courted her "with the most devilish kind of promises there are. The kind you was too smart to put in words or—or in writing. You—you only looked 'em" (91). She had trusted him "to make it all right for her," but he abandoned her after three years. He then, for "old times' sake," kept her in his employ "out of the goodness of his heart," although he more than got his money's worth out of her as a saleswoman. When he began to harass yet another, younger model, Hattie begged him to "let up" on Cissie. Kessler threatens to fire her, making it clear that she is not in any position to intervene on behalf of a "good girl" because she is not one herself. He claims that "you knew what you were doing!" Sadly she agrees that "I guess I knew what I was doing, all right, or if I didn't, I ought to have. I was rotten—or I couldn't have done it, I guess. Only, deep inside of me I was waiting and banking on you" (91).

Hattie knows she has few options, all of them more difficult than the situation she is already in. On the periphery of her consciousness are constant frightening examples of women older than she who have gone from similar situations to unemployment, poverty, humiliation, and self-destruction.

When I.W. Goldstone, a wealthy department store owner from St. Louis and a widower 18 years older than she, proposes to her, she accepts his offer of the new "job"—being his wife and a mother to Effie, his pubescent daughter—with gratitude and relief so immense that it feels like love. She worries that Kessler will tell her suitor that she is not a "pure" woman. She must beg the man who seduced and abandoned her not to betray her again. He agrees and feels magnanimous.

She moves into a big house, close enough to a park to smell "the lilacs and the gasoline" in spring, and takes off her corsets forever. She is very good at her new job. She loves her work, and she loves the people with whom she works. She is safe. She has a home.

Then, three years later, Kessler, as he has half-promised, half-threatened, reenters the picture. He travels to visit his

Midwest trade, and I.W. brings him home. He is completely enchanted by the innocent, lovely, ready-for-marriage daughter Effie. He falls in love and wants to marry her.

But Hattie has come to love Effie as her own and cannot allow the seducer to become the son-in-law of the woman he has seduced, to allow the cad to marry the daughter of his victim.

Hattie opposes the relationship between Effie and Kessler on logical grounds—he is twice her age, their backgrounds are incompatibile, Effie is too young. I.W. shrugs off all her objections, claiming always that there are no differences between Kessler and himself when he was a young man.

Hattie insists that I.W. not allow their daughter to be tied to this man, and when he demands to know why she is so unreasonably resistent that she tells him—without telling him. That is, she tells him "[Kessler] ain't good enough," he has a terrible reputation among the women who work for him, he has been a loose man, but her husband is only amused:

> "I'm surprised, Hattie, you should hold so against a man his wild oats."
>
> "Then why ain't oats for the man oats for the woman? It's the men that sow the wild oats and the women—us women that's got to reap them!"
>
> "Say, life is life. Do you want to put your head up against a brick wall?"
>
> "A wall that men built!"
>
> "It's always hard, Hattie, for good women like you . . . to understand. It's better you don't. You shouldn't even think about it. . . . If I didn't know Leon Kessler was no worse than ninety-nine good husbands in a hundred, you think I would let him lay a finger on the apple of my eye? . . . Maybe he wasn't a Sunday-school boy in his day—but say, show me one that was." (109–110)

I.W. continues to dismiss Hattie's concern, but "her voice was rising now in hysteria, slipping up frequently beyond her control." Finally, he realizes that her growing hysteria reflects something more than concern for their daughter, for *his* daughter. He begins to suspect that she is talking about herself, and so he accuses her.

> "Don't make me say it!" she pleads. "It don't make me worse than it makes him," she insists.
>
> She was pounding the floor with her bare palms, her face so distorted that the mouth drawn tight over the teeth was as wide and empty as a mask's, and sobs caught and hiccoughed in her throat.
>
> "I didn't know, I.W.! Don't kill me for what I didn't know."

And with that, his suspicions are confirmed. His fury is frightening. He threatens to kill her. He orders her out of his house, out of his life, to protect them both from the consequences of what he thinks of as his justifiable outrage, to protect them both from her murder.

And with that, she loses her live-in job and all its benefits. She loses her old-age pension, her health insurance, her income. She is literally turned out of the house, in the middle of the night, wearing only her night clothes, with nowhere to go, no one to go to. Her future is left to our horrified imaginations.

What is it about this story that makes contemporary readers cry and rage at Hattie's fate? When I included the story in my collection, I worried whether modern readers would find such rigid, outdated morality more amusing than worthy of sympathy.

But what readers tell me, or tell their teachers on essay exams, which are often sent on to me, is that Hattie's predicament is one they identify with, one they are frightened by. It doesn't matter that some of the rules, in some parts of the world, have changed. What matters is that there are still rules, made by men, made by bosses, and enforced on women, on workers. What matters is that the vulnerability is still there. What matters is that Hattie—and perhaps they themselves—are being set up to lose.

In 1989, I taught a course on mothers and daughters, using *Between Mothers and Daughters* in the OASIS (Older Adult Service and Information System) program in St. Louis, which is sponsored by the May Department Stores. The seven women in the class ranged in age from 62 to 79 years old. Two of them were cancer survivors. All were mothers of daughters. They were articulate, good storytellers, wonderfully supportive of each other, intelligent, interested in the most radical things I had to say, and lots of fun. They were *so* smart—the kind of smart that people have when they are "natural experts" about the subject matter. Confident, knowledgeable, able to make daring intellectual leaps, comfortable enough with the depths of their knowledge and experience that they could be funny too. And they were eager: eager to read, eager to share the decisions about what we would do with our time together, eager to tell their own stories, and equally eager to listen to each other.

None of them had had any direct contact or experience with contemporary feminism, but none of them flinched when I talked about heteropatriarchy, about women's oppression, about the setup to fail as mothers in this system where women have all the responsibility and none of the power. None of them took exception with my explanation of the connections between the officially perceived value of a psychological theory (in this case, Freudianism) and its usefulness for the manipulation of the "people" into seeking the goals, making the sacrifices, and sharing the values of those in power.

When the class during which we were scheduled to discuss "Oats for the Woman" came, one of the women had not finished the story. So two of the other women took turns retelling the story. And then another, one with a New York accent and a flair for dramatic reading, read the last two pages aloud, the pages in which Hattie and I.W. have their final confrontation about Leon and the issue of "wild oats" and I.W. chases Hattie from the house. We were all stunned by the power of the reading and speechless for a few minutes after she finished reading. I cried.

Then we began to talk about the ending. I had always assumed that at the end of the story, I.W. Goldstone really did kick Hattie out into the street. When I tried to imagine what Hattie's life might have been after that night, my mind always switched to *Lummox*, Hurst's novel about a woman who earned her living doing domestic work. I imagined Hattie ending her days scrubbing floors on her hands and knees, late at night in empty office buildings.

Ah, but the women in my class! They imagined differently. And so much better than I. They all agreed that I.W. did *not* kick her out. "Remember," they insisted, "the talk about how people had gossiped and laughed at him when he brought Hattie, a New York model, a *young* woman, home as his wife? Remember how he said that his daughter's marriage to Kessler would be good for the business? Well, kicking Hattie out into the street would not only make him a laughing stock, but it would be bad for business. It would be clear that he had made a bad bargain. And his daughter's reputation would be tainted because her father had brought *that* sort of a woman into their home. I.W. wouldn't *dare* kick Hattie out!"

They all agreed. I.W. would have kept Hattie right where she was, in that big comfortable house. He would keep her there for his sake, not for hers, keep her to protect his pride, not to save her life, keep her there not out of compassion and understanding, but out of egotism.

And they all also agreed that he would not have allowed Effie to marry Kessler. There was no final agreement among the women about what would happen with the daughter, or about what exactly she would be told was the reason for her father forbidding the marriage. Perhaps I.W. would fake an illness and claim his need for his daughter's company on an extended European voyage for the sake of his health. But whatever it was, they agreed that he would never tell his daughter what her "mommy" had "done" and why Kessler was *persona non grata*.

One of the women ventured the opinion that although I.W. wouldn't kick Hattie out, he would make her life miserable. As another of the women put it, "Yes, he will keep her in the house and humiliate her daily; he will make her pay and pay and pay—as long as they both live." Much bitter laughter of agreement greeted that remark.

And then another woman said, "But he won't live long enough to do any *real* damage. They've been together three years when this happens; he was fifty-two to her thirty-four when they got married. So he's fifty-five by now. And she's not the only one who's put on weight during those three years. He's a lot older and he's been eating a lot more cholesterol than she has. He's going to die and leave her a very rich widow. And anticipating his death will keep her sane."

Everyone was pleased with this final reading beyond the ending. They all loved the story. They asked me how old Hurst was when she wrote it, and I told them that she was age 31 when it was published. They smiled at each other and me, and one of them explained to me that although it was a wonderful story, neither Hurst at that age, nor I at mine, could understand yet how such a story would really end. But they knew that after the curtain comes down on a Greek tragedy, all the corpses on stage get up and take a picnic to the seashore. They *knew* absolutely that Hattie Becker Goldstone would survive, would become wealthy, would get as fat as she liked, and would retain the affection and companionship of her adopted daughter Effie.

NOTES

1. This idea came from Glynis Carr in her essay "I am the Grape Fermenting" forthcoming in *Fanny Hurst: The Woman and Her Work.* Ed. Susan Koppelman, University of Illinois Press.

2. This passage was brought to my attention by Joanna Russ after she read the copy of "Sob Sister" I gave her.

3. See especially Mary Kelley's *Private Woman, Public Stage: Literary Domesticity in Nineteenth-Century America* (New York: Oxford, 1984) and Gaye Tuchman and Nina E. Fortin's *Edging Women Out: Victorian Novelists, Publishers, and Social Change* (New Haven, CT: Yale University Press, 1989).

4. I discuss support systems of female writers extensively in the article "Mary Antin (1881–1949)." *Dictionary of Literary Biography, Yearbook: 1984.* Detroit: Gale Research Company, 1985, pp. 225–231.

WORKS CITED

Cornillon, Susan Koppelman, ed. *Images of Women in Fiction: Feminist Perspectives.* Bowling Green, OH: Bowling Green University Popular Press, 1972.

Farrar, John C. *The Literary Spotlight.* New York: Ayer, 1924.

Hurst, Fannie. *Anatomy of Me: A Wanderer in Search of Herself*. Garden City, NY: Doubleday, 1958.

Koppelman, Susan. "Mary Antin (1881–1949)." *Dictionary of Literary Biography, Yearbook 1984.* Detroit: Gale Research Company, 1985, pp. 225–231.

———, ed. *Between Mothers and Daughters: Stories Across a Generation.* Old Westbury, NY: The Feminist Press, 1985.

———. *"May Your Days Be Merry and Bright": Christmas Stories by Women.* New York: Mentor, 1991.

Slesinger, Tess. Review of *Procession*, by Fannie Hurst. *New York Evening Post* (Jan. 19, 1929): 9M.

Washington University Record, 1905. St. Louis, MO.

Woolf, Virginia. *A Room of One's Own.* New York: Harcourt, Brace, and World, 1957.

CHECKLIST OF FANNIE HURST'S STORIES

"Back Pay." *Cosmopolitan* (Nov. 1919). Rpt. *The Vertical City.* New York: Harper, 1922; *The Stories Editors Buy and Why.* Comp. Jean Wick. New York: Small, 1921; *Famous Story Magazine* (Feb. 1926).

"Breakers Ahead." *Cosmopolitan* (June 1914). Rpt. *Just Around the Corner; Romance En Casserole*. New York: Harper, 1914.

"The Character Woman." *Saturday Evening Post* (Sept. 12, 1914): 11+.

"Even as You and I." *Cosmopolitan* (April 1919). Rpt. *Famous Story Magazine* (Feb. 1927).

"Humoresque." *Cosmopolitan* (March 1919). Rpt. *Humoresque: A Laugh on Life with a Tear Behind It*. New York: Harper, 1919; *O. Henry*

Memorial Award Prize Stories for Class Reading. Ed. Ralph P. Boas and Barbara M. Hahn. New York: Holt, 1925; *Best American Short Stories, 1919–1924.* Ed. Blanche Colton Williams. New York: Doubleday, 1926.

"Ice Water Pl—!" *Collier's Weekly* (Oct. 21, 1916). Rpt. *Best Short Stories of 1916.* Ed. Edward J. O'Brien. Boston: Houghton Mifflin, 1917; *Gaslight Sonatas.* New York: Harper, 1918; *Short Stories.* Ed. H.C. Schweikert. New York: Harcourt Brace Jovanovich, 1925.

"The Nth Commandment." *Saturday Evening Post* (Dec. 5, 1914): 12+. Rpt. *Every Soul Hath Its Song.* New York: Harper, 1916; *"May Your Days Be Merry and Bright": Christmas Stories by Women.* New York: Mentor, 1991.

"Oats for the Woman." *Cosmopolitan* (June 1917). Rpt. *Humoresque: A Laugh on Life with a Tear Behind It.* New York: Harper, 1919; *Between Mothers and Daughters: Stories Across a Generation*. Ed. Susan Koppelman. Old Westbury, NY: The Feminist Press, 1985, pp. 83–112.

"Petal on a Currant." *Cosmopolitan* (June 1918). Rpt. *Humoresque: A Laugh on Life with a Tear Behind It.* New York: Harper, 1919; *Famous Story Magazine* (Jan. 1927).

"Sob Sister." *Metropolitan* (Feb. 1916). Rpt. *Every Soul Hath Its Song.* New York: Harper, 1916; *Famous Story* (Oct. 1925).

"Solitary Reaper." *Cosmopolitan* (May 1917).

"The Wrong Pew." *Saturday Evening Post* (Jan. 6, 1917): 5+.

Lost Borders and Blurred Boundaries: Mary Austin as Storyteller

Linda K. Karell

> Out there where the borders of conscience break down, where there is no convention, and behavior is of little account except as it gets you your desire, almost anything might happen; does happen, in fact, though I shall have trouble making you believe it.
>
> Mary Austin, *Lost Borders*

In her 1932 autobiography, *Earth Horizon*, Mary Austin records an experience from her childhood that sets the tone for her writing as an adult. Austin writes that her creative storytelling angered her mother, who interpreted her young daughter's "storying" as a "wicked" insistence on relating imagined events as if they had actually happened: "Mother said she supposed she'd have to punish you or you would grow up a storyteller. Well, you *did* see them. If you got punished for it, you'd simply have to stand it" (42, 43). Austin's textual reconstruction—her story—of her resistance emphasizes that storytelling capable of challenging rigid definitions of truth may evoke punishment, particularly for women whose speech may be interpreted as lies and whose resistance is measured by their ability to endure. Austin locates another form of resistance in the act of writing the autobiography itself. In some places, as in the above passage, Austin erodes the distinction between author, subject, and reader by aligning reader with subject through her use of the second-person pronoun "you." Elsewhere in *Earth Horizon*, she frequently splits the autobiographical subject into the first-person "I" and the third-person "she." In each case, Austin prevents the stable opposition of subject to object that is a prerequisite to relationships of dominance and submission. In *Lost Borders* (1909), as its title suggests, storytelling performs similar acts of boundary blurring, thus revealing the debilitating conventions of domination that the enforcement of stable boundaries helps to construct and maintain.

Austin was born Mary Hunter in 1868 in Carlinville, Illinois. After her graduation from college, she traveled to southern California with her mother and brothers in order to homestead. Like her fictive narrator in *Lost Borders*, Austin interacted with the region's diverse populations. She visited Native Americans and was politically active to help secure fair legal treatment for the Native and Hispanic cultures she valued. In California, Austin met and married Wallace Austin, embarked upon a teaching career, and encountered the landscape and cultures that would dominate her thinking and writing throughout her life. Although she left the desert in 1906 (and was later divorced from Wallace Austin), her time there had a formative influence on her writing and helped to encourage her independence as a feminist and an activist.

Austin wrote and published in almost every conceivable literary genre and was widely known and respected as a literary artist at her death in 1934. However, Austin's work has received little sustained critical attention, and today it is generally excluded from the American literary canon. At best, a small selection of Austin's early fiction, including *Lost Borders*, is granted moderate respect as "local-color" writing. In both her fiction and nonfiction, Austin crafted an authorial voice that tended toward both the confidently transcendent and the feminist. She explicitly described herself as a storyteller, a mystic, a prophet, and a maverick, and with the determination of the female child who elected punishment over silencing, she repeatedly challenged cultural expectations about what a woman should write. To assist her in this challenge, she claimed the literary authority of an essential female spirituality that was dramatically influenced by her understanding of Native American spiritual beliefs and oral storytelling traditions.

Austin's acknowledgment of Native American influence in her writing, her typically brash confidence, and her articulate self-presentation have resulted in her writing often being read through the related critical lenses of Western Christian assumptions and disappointed gender expectations. For example, distinctions between the author and her characters are often elided entirely in the criticism, subjecting Austin to parody during her lifetime and to personal insult and condescension since then. References to her weight, physical appearance, and unconventional spiritual beliefs regularly intrude into assessments of her writing. Even sympathetic readings that attempt to reexamine Austin's contributions to literature and feminism tend to be "marred by the war between affection and exasperation, respect and dismissal, that appears to overtake many who try to write about Austin" (Porter 307). Alternating affection and exasperation may be reasonable responses to Austin's work. Particularly in *Lost Borders*, Austin's graceful poeticism edges into a mystical obliqueness, while her biting wit occasionally lashes out to reassert cultural stereotypes of female incapacity. However, dismissing Austin because she can be essentialistic and even contradictory is a self-defeating gesture of academic protectionism that ignores the contributions Austin's writing makes to contemporary feminist debate. By drawing on Native American spiritual beliefs in *Lost Borders*, Austin challenges the ethno- and intellectual centrisim that construct the boundaries of much contemporary feminist theorizing that cleaves feminists into what appear to be two opposed camps: essentialists and everyone else. Throughout *Lost Borders*, Austin's claims to essentialism prove valuable as a form of identity politics, as a strategy to obtain legitimate and necessary cultural power, and as an aspect of her understanding of the relationship between female subjectivity and spirituality. At the same time, Austin displays a consistent awareness that identity is constructed and fragile.

In *Lost Borders*, a collection of 14 short stories set in the desert region of California, Austin explores a series of oppositions rigidly enforced in Western culture: male/female, self/other, sacred/secular, and oral/written literature. In my examination of a selection of stories from *Lost Borders*, I argue that Austin attempts to claim a spiritually authorized power for marginalized characters by employing borders and boundaries as recurring metaphors of resistance toward the dominant white culture's definitions of femininity, literature, and cultural superiority. Central to my reading of this collection is my belief that Austin's claim is grounded in her conviction that storytelling is itself a spiritual act capable of radical reconceptions of gender and identity. I argue that *Lost Borders* embodies Austin's insistence that spirituality is an *essential* component of female subjectivity, an insistence that authorizes female agency by privileging the female storyteller who narrates and unifies the collection. Paradoxically, however, Austin's essentialism reintroduces the troubling conflation of femininity, spirituality, and nature that has historically authorized attempts to master the female.

In the closing passage of "The Land," the first story in *Lost Borders*, Austin describes the California desert as the site of an essential femininity:

> If the desert were a woman, I know well what like she would be: deep-breasted, broad in the hips, tawny, with tawny hair, great masses of it lying smooth along her perfect curves, full-lipped like a sphinx, but not heavy-lidded like one, eyes sane and steady as the polished jewel of her skies, such a countenance as should make men serve without desiring her, such a largeness to her mind as should make their sins of no account, passionate, but not necessitous, patient—and you could not move her, no, not if you had all the earth to give, so much as one tawny hair's-breadth beyond her own desires. (160)

Austin simultaneously represents the desert landscape of *Lost Borders*, the physical site of the stories her narrator tells, as a sexualized, desirous, female body and as a figure of mystical spirituality. Austin explicitly rejects the patriarchal construction of feminine "otherness" based on the oppositions between sexual and spiritual that was so intensely a focus of her midwestern Methodist childhood. Instead, her image of the desert emphasizes their integration; borders between sexuality and spirituality are fluid. Throughout *Lost Borders*, Austin represents the desert landscape as an active and central character whose power derives from her spiritual authority.

Before examining more fully the ways in which Austin grants her *Lost Borders* characters agency through spiritual authority, I want first to explore the basis of her spiritual understanding. Her autobiography gives us insights into the ways in which Native American spirituality influenced Austin's adult understanding of spirituality and helps to clarify its relationship to authorial production. In *Earth Horizon*, Austin describes visiting a Paiute medicine man, and subsequently defines her experience of spirituality as involving a reciprocal relationship with a responsive power that she designates as the Friend-of-the-Soul-of-Man:

> The Paiutes were basket-makers; the finest of their sort. What Mary drew from them was their naked craft, the subtle sympathies of twig and root and bark; she consorted with them; she laid herself open to the influences of the wild, the thing done, accomplished. She entered into their lives, the life of the campody, the strange secret life of the tribe, the struggle of Whiteness with Darkness, the struggle of the individual soul with the Friend-of-the-Soul-of-Man. She learned what it meant; how to prevail; how to measure her strength against it. Learning that, she learned to write. (289)

The passage is simultaneously a metaphor for the writing process and a description of a spiritual initiation Austin credited with teaching her to write. In the Paiute culture Austin describes, as in Native American cultures generally, the valorized distinction in Western culture between secular and spiritual disappears. As Austin's description suggests, tasks of everyday artistry such as basket-weaving are both functional and spiritual. In this context, storytelling must likewise be understood as both a functional and a spiritual act. As Leslie Silko insists when she writes, "You don't have anything / if you don't have the stories," Native Americans understand the power to shape the world that inheres in stories (2). Until the emergence of deconstruction, Western understandings of language insisted on word/meaning stability, while in traditional Native beliefs, the question is not one of the putative stability or instability of meaning but of the effect of language in the world. Words have spiritual power; they are living entities that have a manifest effect on the world. Storytellers may be healers; certainly they are historians and culture-bearers.

Austin, then, like the narrator of *Lost Borders*, grounds her authority to speak in a spiritual understanding that is dramatically influenced by Native American spiritual and literary traditions. James Ruppert has shown that "Austin hoped to give the writers of her day guidance in their struggle to revitalize their art" by returning to a consideration of the interdependent effects of the land and spirit evident in Native American literary forms (Mary Austin's "Landscape" 389). By crediting the Paiutes with her growing talent as a writer, Austin both attempts to legitimate an ancient literary heritage largely unrecognized within Western culture's valuation of written literature and to assert that her own authority as a storyteller implicitly derives from the spiritual potency of the literary models she follows. Nonetheless, her representations of Native Americans in the above passage from her autobiography are marred by stereotyping and insistent gestures of appropriation and colonization. Austin reinforces oppositions between tame/wild and whiteness/darkness, producing a primitive "other" in service to a white culture. Her allusion to a "strange secret life" encountered with Native Americans recapitulates the stereotype of an alien and exotic race whose mysterious knowledge is harnessed to revitalize white culture.

Austin's reliance on essentialistic conceptions of gender and racial identity here and in her representations of the desert landscape is troubling. However, it is important to consider the complexities of Austin's Native American influence before pejoratively branding her "essentialist." In *The Sacred Hoop*, Paula Gunn Allen writes, "We are the land. To the best of my understanding, that is the fundamental idea that permeates American Indian life; the land (Mother) and the people (mothers) are the same[;] . . . the earth *is* being as all creatures are also being: aware, palpable, intelligent, alive" (119). The stories in *Lost Borders* consistently present the desert as just such an active being. In "The Hoodoo of the Minnietta," for example, we read that "the desert had [McKenna], cat-like, between her paws"

(164); in "The Return of Mr. Wills," the desert's "insatiable spirit . . . will reach out and take Mr. Wills again" (187); and in "The Ploughed Lands," Gavin is lost in the desert "in the grip of another mistress who might or might not loose his bonds" (177). While Gavin becomes "his own man" only after he leaves the desert behind for "white people, towns, farms" (179), other white male characters never escape the desert's power: "Out there beyond the towns the long Wilderness lies brooding, imperturbable; she puts out to adventurous minds glittering fragments of fortune or romance, like the lures men use to catch antelopes—clip! then she has them" (182). Conceiving and representing the land as feminine is a central aspect of Native American spiritual belief. Unlike inscriptions of a feminine landscape common to American literature produced by whites, however, Native American conceptions of a feminine landscape work to prevent the exploitation of the land and its inhabitants by positing an ongoing relationship among them. Austin's essentialism is grounded in her awareness of this difference in spiritual understanding and results in representations of a female desert who is dangerous mainly to those men who attempt to master her.

Allen and other Native American women writers have criticized feminism for its failure to acknowledge how different cultural positions affect feminist theorizing: in this case casting the land as female is not inevitably a reinscription of essentialism, nor does essentialism itself necessarily perform the same cultural work of defining women as "other" in Native American literary traditions. Of course, Austin is not Native American nor does she write from within that literary tradition. However, in "Regionalism in American Fiction," Austin does align herself with Native American understandings of the land when she insists that all literature must reflect "in some fashion the essential qualities of the land" (106). Like Allen, Austin believes those essential qualities are linked to a particular definition of femininity that includes activity, intelligence, independence, and mystical power. Here as elsewhere, however, Austin deconstructs her own essentialism with her belief that writers must acknowledge that there is "not one vast, pale figure of America, but several Americas, in many subtle and significant characterizations" (98). *Lost Borders*, then, is Austin's challenge to literary and cultural representations that create "one vast, pale figure of America."

Both the structure and subject of *Lost Borders* enact its title. For instance, the 14 separate stories are unified by a single female narrative voice, eroding the borders between them. Clear demarcations between beginnings and endings of the stories collapse as individual stories may include within them several other stories. While she is neither omniscient nor universalized, the unnamed narrator provides a unifying voice. She acts as a distinctive trail guide through *Lost Borders*, maneuvering the reader through the stories that comprise the desert landscape, privileging her own interpretations, as in "The Fakir," when she begins with her own point of view: "Whenever I come up to judgement, and am hard pushed to make good on my own account (as I expect to be), I shall mention the case of Netta Saybrick, for on the face of it, and by all the traditions in which I was bred, I behaved rather handsomely" (211). Austin's narrator is a witty, bitingly ironic cultural interpreter, a confident trail guide, and a woman compelled to tell the stories of the land: "I had long wished to write a story of Death Valley that should be its final word. It was to be so chosen from the limited sort of incidents that could happen there, so charged with the still ferocity of its moods that I should at last be quit of its obsession, free to concern myself about other affairs" (203). As James Ruppert has pointed out, Austin's understanding of storytelling is influenced by Native American oral poetic traditions ("Discovering America" 256). In *Lost Borders*, the context of the story's telling is emphasized and its origin carefully noted; the reader's participation in determining the story's meaning is valued; and privileged Western ideals such as chronological progression, climax, and resolution are less apparent and dramatic. The collection is structurally calculated to refuse Western models of literature as timeless, self-contained products of individual genius. Instead, Austin's boundary blurring creates indistinct textual divisions and reasserts the importance of context and audience for a story's meaning.

Austin's "Borderers" are Native American women and men, sheepherders, pocket hunters, and the female storyteller patterned after Austin's own biography. Marginalized within the Euro-American culture newly settled in California, these characters safely roam the desert beyond the boundaries of the homesteads and towns that are occupied by these white settlers. In "The Land," their marginal status gives them knowledge that enables them to survive:

> First and last, accept no man's statement that he knows this Country of Lost Borders well. A great number having lost their lives in the process of proving where it is not safe to go, it is now possible to pass through much of the district by guide-posts and well-known water-holes, but the best part of it remains locked, inviolate, or at best known only to some far-straying Indian, sheepherder, or pocket hunter, whose account of it does not get into the reports of the Geological Survey. (159)

The narrator aligns herself with marginal figures whose knowledge of the land surpasses the limits of official knowledge and is a component of their claim to a spiritual authority necessary for survival. Relying on stable boundaries is a dangerous strategy in Austin's desert landscape, where the privilege of masculine entitlement that such boundaries preserve is especially vulnerable: "Out there, then, where the law and the landmarks fail together, the souls of little men fade out at the edges, leak from them as water from wooden pails warped asunder" (156). Although Austin grants her narrator a spiritual authority to speak, she does not privilege her speech as universal. Any pretensions to represent universal truths are deliberately undercut. Elsewhere in "The Land," for example, she responds to a challenge to "find a story" about a piece of pottery with a vow to "make a story," and discovers immediately the impossibility of speaking universally. Stories shift and change to accommodate the needs of their tellers and hearers:

> Next winter . . . a prospector from Panamint-way wanted to know if I had ever heard of the Indian-pot Mine which was lost. . . . I said I had a piece of the pot, which I showed him. Then I wrote the tale for a magazine, . . . and several men were at great pains to explain to me where my version varied from the accepted one of the hills. By this

> time, you understand, I had begun to believe the story myself. . . . Now it only needs that some one should find another shard of the gold-besprinkled pot to fix the tale in the body of desert myths. (158–159)

In this passage, oral and written literature have storytelling in common as their source, and the distinction between them blurs as Austin's narrator relates her story. Moreover, history is revealed as a series of competing interpretations, where gender determines authority. Male knowledge of the story is enough to invest it with the illusion of truth; the male miners display no hesitancy—are "at pains" in fact—to correct the narrator.

"The Land" also contains a macabre warning of the dangers female storytelling can pose to rigid definitions of truth and certainty. The narrator retells a story of settlers who are killed when the salt crust over a lake collapses. She first hears the story from another character, Long Tom Bassit, who heard it from "a man who saw it":

> [The story] was of an immigrant train all out of its reckoning. . . . [N]ear the middle of the lake, the salt crust thinned out abruptly, and, the foreward rank of the party breaking through, the bodies were caught under the saline slabs and not all of them recovered. There was a woman among them, and the Man-who-saw had cared—cared enough to go back years afterward, when . . . long before he reached the point, he saw the gleam of red in the woman's dress, and found her at last, lying on her side, sealed in the crystal, rising as ice rises to the surface of choked streams. (157)

In this, the most ambiguous and disturbing story within a story in the collection, Austin figures the border between safety and death as literally unstable, with a brightly clothed but unnamed woman as a visible marker of instability and border collapse. Silent, this woman entombed in salt is also a symbol of unspeakability, as Austin emphasizes when her narrator attempts to "make a story of it" at dinner:

> I never got through with it. There, about the time the candles began to burn their shades and red track of the light on the wine-glasses barred the cloth, with the white, disdainful shoulders and politely incredulous faces

> leaning through the smoke of cigarettes, it had a garish sound. Afterward I came across the proof of the affair in the records of the emigrant party, but I never tried telling it again. (157)

Race and class determine who may speak and what may be said: White shoulders and the affluence signaled by wine, cigarettes, and leisurely candlelight create a privileged space into which stories about collapsing borders are not allowed to enter. Although the response of an incredulous and disbelieving audience threatens hereafter to silence this storyteller and erase the story, her claim to have "never tried telling it again" is, of course, false. Austin subverts the social constraints on women's speech by having her narrator retell the story within "The Land," and it is retold with each new reader.

The feminized, essentialized landscape of *Lost Borders* is the linchpin of Austin's gender critique. As Annette Kolodny demonstrates in *The Lay of the Land,* feminized landscapes have had a long shelf life in American literature, and in *Lost Borders*, Austin accentuates that tradition by figuring the feminized, eroticized desert as both the testing ground and the hoped-for trophy of many of her white male characters. White women's relationships with the land in *Lost Borders* are sometimes equally troubling in their representation: "Women, unless they have very large and simple souls, need cover; clothes, you know, and furniture, social observances to screen them, conventions to get behind; life when it leaps upon them, large and naked, shocks them into disorder" (165). Yet Austin counters these generalizations with representations of individual women who reject precisely those "social observances" and "conventions."

In "The Walking Woman," Austin presents a particular instance of a marginal character who rejects social observances and challenges conventional demands of femininity: "By no canon could it be considered ladylike to go about on your own feet, with a blanket and a black bag and almost no money in your purse, in and about the haunts of rude and solitary men" (256). Yet even with the Walking Woman, Austin posits an authentic female identity located beneath "the looking and seeming," a phrase that refers to a wide range of incapacitating social behaviors coded feminine: "She had walked off all sense of society-made values, and, knowing the best when the best came to her, was able to take it" (261). Freeing herself from "the looking and seeming" releases the Walking Woman to receive "the best," which in this case means work overseen and valued by men, heterosexual love, and motherhood. Finally, however, ambivalences lodged in "The Walking Woman" undermine these valorized components of institutionalized femininity. The story "The Walking Woman" concludes when the narrator disagrees with the Walking Woman's assertion that freedom from convention requires a woman have work that is valued by men, a heterosexual relationship, and a child, saying, "At least one of us is wrong. To work and to love and to bear children. *That* sounds easy enough. But the way we live establishes so many things of much more importance" (262). The indeterminacy of this passage is characteristic of Austin's skillful ability to undermine the certainty of interpretation. The conclusion refuses final resolution in favor of evocative uncertainty, allowing Austin to privilege the tension between an essential female identity and a socially constructed one.

Austin's inscription onto the landscape of both an essentialized female identity and a spirituality conceived as irreducibly feminine does more than merely invert the historical literary maneuver by which men have celebrated mastery of the female "other" and eroticized their assault on the land. In *Lost Borders*, Austin establishes her alliance with marginalized groups, including women, Native Americans, and the few white men who reject constructions of masculinity that privilege dominance, exploitation, and aggression. For Austin, those who occupy a position of marginality are not situated there exclusively because of their race *or* gender *or* class. Instead, Austin's understanding of marginality as a site of spiritual authority derives largely from individuals' and groups' relationships with the land. Cultural attitudes regarding gender certainly shape the contradicting interpretations the narrator receives of the Walking Woman's potential insanity, but Austin asserts her sanity by presenting her speech as containing "both wisdom and information" (257). More important than the Walking Woman's gender alone, her status as a "Borderer" is established by her relationship with the land. She lives with the land without attempting to master or control it, and therefore has privileged knowledge of it.

By drawing on Native American oral storytelling traditions, Austin is able to challenge boundaries between oral and written literature, and sacred and secular expressions, although she does so at the expense of exoticizing the cultural group to which she is indebted. Nonetheless, I want to suggest that Austin's representation of the desert as female anticipates current feminist debates over the political potential of a "strategic essentialism." For Diana Fuss, deploying essentialism as a method of resistance can grant authority to speak. While Fuss wonders if "calls . . . for a strategic essentialism might be humanism's way of keeping its fundamental tenets in circulation at any cost and under any guise," she points out the need to consider cultural and institutional differences: "The question of permissibility, if you will, of engaging in essentialism is therefore framed and determined by the subject-positions from which one speaks" (86). Austin's insistence on spirituality as enabling female authority allows her to grant agency to the marginalized characters that populate her stories, and her forthright acknowledgment of Native American influence reveals that spirituality is not transcendent, raceless, or universal. Instead, Austin's claims to spiritual authority draw their power to perform cultural critiques from their difference from the universal.

WORKS CITED

Allen, Paula Gunn. "The Feminine Landscape of Leslie Marmon Silko's *Ceremony*." *The Sacred Hoop: Recovering the Feminine in American Indian Traditions*. Boston: Beacon, 1992, pp. 118–126.

Austin, Mary. *Earth Horizon*. Boston: Houghton Mifflin, 1932.

———. *Lost Borders*. New York and London: Harper & Brothers, 1909. Rpt. as *Stories from the Country of Lost Borders*. Ed. Marjorie Pryse. New Brunswick, NJ: Rutgers University Press, 1987.

———. "Regionalism in American Fiction." *The English Journal* (Feb. 1932): 97–107.

———. "Woman Alone." *The Nation* 124 (March 2, 1927): 228–230.

Fuss, Diana. "Reading Like a Feminist." *Differences* 1 (Summer 1989): 77–92.

Kolodny, Annette. *The Lay of the Land: Metaphor as Experience and History in American Life and Letters*. Chapel Hill: University of North Carolina Press, 1975.

Porter, Nancy. Afterword. *A Woman of Genius*. By Mary Austin. Old Westbury, NY: The Feminist Press, 1985, pp. 295–321.

Ruppert, James. "Discovering America: Mary Austin and Imagism." *Studies in American Indian Literature: Critical Essays and Course Designs*. Ed. Paula Gunn Allen. New York: Modern Language Association, 1983, pp. 243–258.

———. "Mary Austin's Landscape Line in Native American Literature." *Southwest Review* 68 (1983): 376–390.

Silko, Leslie Marmon. *Ceremony*. New York: Penguin, 1977.

Ritual and Renewal: Keres Traditions in the Short Fiction of Leslie Silko*

A. LaVonne Brown Ruoff

> At one time, the ceremonies as they had been performed were for the way the world was then. But after the white people came, elements in this world began to shift; and it became necessary to create new ceremonies. I have made changes in the rituals. The people mistrust this greatly, but only this growth keeps the ceremonies strong. . . . That's what the witchery is counting on: that we will cling to the ceremonies the way they were, and then their power will triumph, and the people will be no more.
>
> Betonie in *Ceremony*

For Leslie Marmon Silko (Laguna), the strength of tribal traditions is based not on American Indians' rigid adherence to given ceremonies or customs but rather on their ability to adapt traditions to ever-changing circumstances by incorporating new elements. Although this theme is most fully developed in her novel *Ceremony* (1977), it is also present in her earlier short stories, "The Man to Send Rainclouds," "Tony's Story," "*from* Humaweepi, Warrior Priest," and "Yellow Woman," originally included in *The Man to Send Rainclouds: Contemporary Stories by American Indians,* ed. Kenneth Rosen (1974; page references are to this edition). All but "*from* Humaweepi, Warrior Priest" were republished in *Storyteller* (1981).

The history of Silko's own Laguna Pueblo, influenced by many different cultures, provides insight into why she emphasizes change as a source of strength for tribal traditions.

According to their origin legends, the Laguna tribe (in existence since at least 1300), came southward from the Mesa Verde region. Some versions indicate that after pausing at Zia, they were joined by the head of the Parrot clan, who decided to take his people southward with them. After wandering farther, first southward from the lake at Laguna and then northward back to the lake, they settled Punyana, probably in the late 1300s. After founding Old Laguna (Kawaik) around 1400, they issued invitations to other pueblos to join them. Those that responded were the Parrot clan from Zia, the Sun clan from Hopi, the Road Runner and Badger clans from Zuni, and the Sun clan from Jemez. The tribe occupied the site of what is now called Laguna (New Mexico) by the early 1500s. Additional immigration occurred during the 1690s, when the Lagunas were joined by Indians from the Rio Grande, probably fleeing both drought and the hostility of the Spanish after the Pueblo Rebellion in 1680 and the renewed uprising in 1696. These immigrants came chiefly from Zia, Cochiti, and Domingo, but a few came from Jemez, Zuni, and Hopi. Although some remained to join the Laguna tribe, others returned to their own pueblos when conditions improved. Over the years, a few Navajos intermarried with the tribe, bringing with them the Navajo Sun clan and *kachina* (spirits).[1]

The Spanish first entered the area in 1540, when Francesco de Coronado led an expedition to Zuni and two years later passed through the present site of Laguna on his way back to Mexico. Antonio Espejo, who commanded an expedition to New Mexico in 1582, visited the area in 1583. Between the appointment of Juan de Oñate as New Mexico's first governor in 1595 and the Pueblo Rebellion in 1680, there is little historical data on Laguna. Although the pueblo was not subjected to as many attacks from the Spanish as the Rio Grande pueblos, it was forced to surrender in 1692 after an attack by the troops of Governor Diego de Vargas (Ellis 3; Gunn 22, 35, 47).

Concerning the mixture of people who settled at Laguna, Parsons comments in *Pueblo Indian Religion* that "it is not surprising that Laguna was the first of the pueblos to Americanize, through intermarriage" (888). Around 1860 and 1870, George H. Pradt (or Pratt) and two Marmon brothers

(Walter and Robert) came to the pueblo, married Laguna women, and reared large families. Silko indicates that her great-grandfather Robert and his brother had a government contract to set out the boundary markers for Laguna (Evers and Carr, "Conversation" 29). Walter, appointed government teacher in 1871, married the daughter of the chief of the Kurena-Shikani medicine men. The chief's son later took his place. According to Parsons, this group led the Americanization faction that was opposed by the pueblo hierarchy. The conservatives removed their altars and sacred objects from Laguna and moved to Mesita; around 1880, part of this group resettled in Isleta. While Robert Marmon served as governor, the two *kivas* (underground ceremonial meeting places) of Laguna were torn down by the progressives and what was left of the sacred objects was surrendered. There were no *kachina* dances for some time after the Great Split and the laying of the railroad on the edge of the village. When a demand arose later for the revival of the dances, Zuni influences were introduced into Laguna rituals (Parsons, *Pueblo* 2 888–890; Gunn 96). Parsons closes her description of Laguna with the comment that although the ceremonial disintegration was so marked when she first studied it (around 1920) that it presented an obscure picture of Keresan culture, it later (1939) offered "unrivaled opportunities to study American acculturation and the important role played by miscegenation" (*Pueblo* 890). Silko herself comments on these changes in her description of the impact of mixed-blood families on Laguna clan systems and the varying attitudes toward these families in the stories of that pueblo:

> People in the main part of the village were our clanspeople because the clan system was still maintained although not in the same form it would have been if we were full blood. . . . The way it changed was that there began to be stories about my great-grandfather, positive stories about what he did with the Laguna scouts for the Apaches. But then after World War One it changed. Soon after that there came to be stories about these mixed blood people, half-breeds. Not only Marmons but Gunns [John] and Pratts too. An identity was being made or evolved in the stories that Lagunas told about these people who had gone outside Laguna, but at the same time of the outsiders who

> had come in. Part of it was that the stories were always about the wild, roguish, crazy sorts of things they did (Evers and Carr, "Conversation" 30).

The continuing strength of Laguna traditions and the ability of her people to use alien traditions for their own purposes are strikingly portrayed in Silko's story "The Man to Send Rainclouds." The title alludes to the belief that the dead are associated with cloud beings (storm clouds, or *shiwanna*, in Keres) who bring rain and who live in the six or four regions of the universe (Parsons, *Pueblo* 172). The story deals with an Indian family's observance of Pueblo funeral rituals despite the local priest's attempts to cajole them into observing Catholic ones. Ironically, the young priest is trapped by the Indians into taking part in their ceremony. The importance of ritual in Pueblo Indian life is emphasized at the beginning of the story when Leon and Ken, after finding old Teofilo dead, immediately observe the first stages of the funeral rites. Neglect of burial or death ritual can result in death or sickness because the ghost returns (Parsons, *Pueblo* 69). Before wrapping the body in a blanket, the men tie a gray prayer feather to the old man's long white hair (a custom similar to that of the Zuni) and begin to paint his face with markings so that he will be recognized in the next world—tasks ordinarily performed by a shaman.[2] The face painting is interrupted by an offering of corn meal to the wind and is concluded with the prayer "Send us rain clouds, Grandfather" (Rosen 6).

The pressure on Pueblo Indians to practice Catholicism is introduced when Father Paul stops Leon and Ken on their way home to ask about Teofilo and to urge them all to come to church. Using the age-old Indian technique of telling the non-Indian only what they want him to know, Leon and Ken answer the priest's questions about the old man's welfare ambiguously enough to keep him from learning about Teofilo's death. Only after the Indian funeral rites are almost completed does the family feel the need for the priest's services—to provide plenty of holy water for the grave so that Teofilo's spirit will send plenty of rainfall. Corn meal has been sprinkled around the old man's body to provide food on the journey to the other world.[3] Silko skillfully and humorously characterizes the conflict between the frustrated priest, who is denied the opportunity to provide the last rites and funeral mass, and Leon, who doggedly insists that these are not necessary: "It's O.K. Father, we just want him to have plenty of water" (Rosen 7). Despite his weary protests that he cannot do that without performing the proper Catholic rites, Father Paul finally gives in when Leon starts to leave. Realizing that he has been tricked into participating in their pagan rites and half suspecting that the whole thing may be just a spring fertility ceremony rather than a real funeral, he nevertheless sprinkles the grave with a whole jar of holy water. Leon feels good about the act, which completes the ceremony and ensures that "now the old man could send them big thunderclouds for sure" (Rosen 8). Thus, Silko emphasizes that these Pueblo Indians have not abandoned their old ways for Catholicism; instead, they have taken one part of Catholic ritual compatible with their beliefs and made it an essential part of their own ceremony.

"Tony's Story" deals with the return to Indian ritual as a means of coping with external forces. However, here the ritual concerns the shooting of a state policeman by a traditional Pueblo who becomes convinced that the policeman harassing him and his friend is a witch. Regarding her own views on the presence of witch stories in Laguna oral tradition and on the nature of witchery, Silko says that she never heard such stories until she went to Chinle on the Navajo Reservation. In expressing her agreement with Simon Ortiz, from Acoma Pueblo 20 miles south of Laguna, Silko states that when "everything is in good shape within the pueblo view, then there's not going to be any witchcraft. . . . Witchcraft is happening when the livestock are skinny" (Evers and Carr, 32). Instances are rare; but when they do occur, they are handled by everyone (Evers and Carr, "Killing" 32). The treatment of witchery in this story is especially significant in view of Silko's later treatment of the theme in *Ceremony*.

Parsons defines the Pueblo concept of witchcraft simply as "power used improperly" (*Pueblo* 63). A witch may injure individuals or the entire community: "He may send an epidemic upon the town or he may sicken or kill a person by stealing his heart which is his life or by sending . . . into his body injurious things: insects, a piece of flesh from a corpse or a shred of funeral cloth or a splinter of bone, thorns, cactus spines, glass, anything sharp. . . . He is a potential murderer, a grave-robber, and a perpetual menace" (*Pueblo* 63). She emphasizes that to Pueblo Indians, witchcraft and immorality or crime are almost synonymous and that the witch possesses the traits people consider antisocial: envy, jealousy, revenge, quarrelsomeness, self-assertiveness, uncooperativeness, and unconventionality. Fear of witchcraft affects manners. You offer a visitor food or anything he may admire lest he take offense; you keep your affairs to yourself, do not meddle, and avoid quarrels. Particularly relevant to "Tony's Story" is Parsons's example of the Laguna war captains' shooting a woman thought to be a witch (Parsons, *Pueblo* 65,6).[4] Parsons concludes that at the time she was writing (about 1920), the right of a war captain to perform such an act would not be questioned in most Keresan or Tewan pueblos or in Zuni.[5]

In "Tony's Story," Silko uses the concept of witchcraft as power used improperly. She also uses many of the circumstances associated with witchcraft described above. The all-too-familiar story of the brutal policeman out to harass reservation Indians is made far more complex by Silko's use of the witchcraft theme as well as by her use of irony. Leon, the character beaten and hounded by the policeman without real provocation, is an ex-serviceman whose behavior sets him apart from the others of his pueblo. Although Leon, through his drinking and bold manner, inadvertently triggers the policeman's violence and although he threatens over and over to kill his attacker, he is nevertheless only a passive witness to the final shooting of the policeman. On the other hand, his friend Tony, a traditional Pueblo only wishing to avoid trouble, becomes so convinced that the policeman is a witch that he shoots his adversary and then burns the body by setting fire to the police car. Silko makes clear that the times and the circumstances are such that a young man like Tony could become convinced that witchery is present. The ordinary life of the pueblo has been disrupted by the presence of the returning ex-servicemen, who always seem to cause trouble. Further, there has been a long dry spell—a sure sign in pueblo mythology that something has gone wrong.

The fact that Leon acts differently from Tony and from the others of his tribe indicates how far his experiences outside his pueblo have changed him. As the story opens he is oblivious to the danger of openly drinking in the midst of a festival crowd. Tony's comment that Leon now shakes hands hard like a white man demonstrates that the changes are not merely the result of his drinking. Leon himself admits both his separation from his past and his desire to regain it when he wonders whether he has forgotten what to do during the Corn Dance, in which he plans to participate. Tony's anxiety about Leon's drinking turns to fear when he sees a policeman in the crowd. Without provocation, warning, or explanation, the policeman smashes his fist into Leon's face, knocking him down, cutting his mouth, and breaking some of his teeth. The policeman's sudden violence vividly illustrates the misuse of power associated with witches.

The theme of witchcraft and the identification of the policeman as a witch is explicitly introduced in Tony's dream the night of the attack, when he sees the man point a long bone at him and when the man appears to have not a human face but "only little, round, white-rimmed eyes on a black ceremonial mask" (Rosen 72). Tony's dream serves as a form of clairvoyance, a technique used by many pueblo tribes for detecting witchcraft or witches.[6] As the harassment continues, the difference between the reactions of Leon and Tony becomes increasingly clear: Leon's non-pueblo dependence on verbal bravado and insistence on his legal rights seem to Tony to be dangerous ways to deal with witchery, which can only be overcome by dependence on Pueblo ritual. While Leon threatens to "kill the big bastard if he comes around here again," Tony tries to persuade him to forget the incident (Rosen 72). Leon's subsequent attempt to get redress from the pueblo council results only in an admonishment for drinking on the reservation. As Leon's methods for dealing with the policeman prove ineffective, Tony becomes more and more convinced of the power of witchery. The second confrontation with the policeman takes place after he has forced them off the road. Tony's fear of the policeman's power is so great that he cannot look into the man's eyes—just as, when a child, he was afraid to look into the eyes of the masked dancers lest they grab him. During this episode, the policeman gives his only explanation for tormenting Leon: "They transferred me here because of Indians. They thought there wouldn't be as many for me here. But I find them" (Rosen 74). Still trying to avoid the power of this supernatural force, Tony persuades Leon to go back home and rejects his friend's anger about the violation of his rights, which is not what the policeman was after: "But Leon didn't seem to understand; he couldn't remember the stories that old Teofilo told" (Rosen 74).

In his fear and anguish, Tony becomes increasingly isolated. He does not go to a *shaman* for help nor does he feel he can seek outside help. Old Teofilo, whose knowledge he trusted, is dead, and he is afraid to tell his family for fear he might subject them to harm. In fact, he ignores his father's warning to stay away from Leon, who is regarded as a troublemaker. Tony's attempts to communicate to Leon his perception of the nature of the danger represented by the policeman end in failure. When Tony offers his friend an arrowhead, a Pueblo protection against witchcraft,[7] Leon rejects it, choosing instead to put his faith in his request for help from the pueblo governor and in his own rifle.

The final confrontation takes place when Leon and Tony are driving toward a remote sheep camp. The role reversal, which dominates the final scene, is first indicated by the fact that this time it is Leon who spots the policeman, who is following them in his patrol car. The news interrupts Tony's reverie of what the land was like before the coming of the white man and convinces him that the witch must be destroyed. When the policeman forces them off the road and gets out to beat them with his billy club, he becomes for Tony the witch of his dream and the club, a camouflaged human bone.

Ironically, Tony, who advocated avoidance of trouble and who had objected to Leon's murder threats, shoots the policeman with Leon's gun and then takes charge of burning the police car and body. Tony calmly reassures the panic-filled Leon with the words, "Don't worry, everything is O.K. now, Leon. It's killed. They sometimes take on strange forms" (Rosen 78). As the car burns, rain clouds form, signaling the end of the drought.

At the moment that Tony decides to destroy the witch, he becomes a self-appointed pueblo war captain—a role in which he later involves Leon. The war captains represent the twin heroes Ma'sewi and Uyuyewi, who appear in many Keres stories. The theme of the destruction of a witch by two young men is based on the exploits of these twins, such as their jointly killing two giantesses or as Ma'sewi's single-handedly drowning Pa'cayani, whose tricks brought drought and famine (Boas 13–16, 49–56, 236–237, 249–253; Parsons, *Pueblo* 245; Gunn 110; Lummis 209–212).[8] Although Ma'sewi, the elder twin, appears most frequently in Laguna stories as a monster slayer, here the younger man is given this role. The hero twins in the mythic past would have been praised for their witch killing. The formation of rain clouds immediately after the murder seems to indicate that nature approves of Tony's act, which has rid the pueblo of a menace. Nevertheless, Tony will be judged by neither Keres nor natural law but rather by non-Indian civil law. The conclusion of the story makes clear that the exorcism ritual is complete. What the conclusion leaves unclear are the consequences Tony will suffer for carrying out the ritual.[9]

In "*from* Humaweepi, Warrior Priest," Silko presents the theme of the transmission of Pueblo religion and ritual through oral tradition. Here she focuses on the training given a young Pueblo boy that culminates in his initiation, at age 19, into the priesthood. The significance of the continuum of Pueblo beliefs passed down from one generation to the next is demonstrated through both the description of the boy's years of training by his uncle and his later telling his friend about a lesson taught by his uncle. Most important in this apprenticeship is learning to be part of the land and to express this sense of unity through ritual—to know the ways to live with plant life, animal life, and shelter used by animals, as well as the songs, chants, and prayers for all the seasons. In order to achieve this harmony with nature, Humaweepi must be separated from the pueblo, with its dances and Christian fiestas and its young people who dismiss as "nothing" what the old man taught. Learning to sleep in nests where deer had slept, to eat grass roots and dried wild grapes, and to live on the land during all the seasons is necessary for Humaweepi to reach the point where he is ready to take on animal power. The lesson repeatedly emphasized by the old man is that "human beings are special. . . . [T]hey can do anything"

(Rosen 162). As the years pass, Humaweepi unconsciously learns through observing his uncle's religious rites, listening to his stories, and following his example. As the old man explains, "every day I have been teaching you" (Rosen 164).

When Humaweepi is ready for his initiation, the old man takes him high into the mountains, making him leave his cowboy boots on the way up and making him walk the rest of the way barefoot. After they reach a mountain lake, the old man sings and feeds corn pollen to the mountain wind, his voice becoming like the sound of the night wind in the trees. The scene is beautifully described by Silko: "The songs were snowstorms with sounds as soft and cold as snowflakes; the songs were spring rain and wild ducks returning" (Rosen 165). Humaweepi's moment of initiation comes when the old man shows him the gray bear-shaped boulder, half in the lake and half on the shore. Almost unconsciously, Humaweepi steps into the lake, places his beads on the bear's head, and sings the bear a song asking it to bestow its power on him as a man and warrior priest. All Humaweepi's training has led him to this ritual. By learning to live as animals have lived in nature, he has prepared himself to become a warrior priest who can be transformed into a bear—the special patron of Keresan, Zuni, and Tewan curing societies.[10] In her description of the instruction and of the initiation itself, Silko emphasizes nature and deemphasizes magic, for it is not magic formulas that enable Humaweepi to take on bear power but rather the gradual process of becoming one with nature.

In this story, Silko stresses the importance of the continuum of oral tradition in both religious instruction and in storytelling. Whereas the first part of this tale focuses on the uncle's preparation of Humaweepi for his initiation, the second part focuses on Humaweepi's own storytelling. As his uncle takes him up the mountain to the bear rock, Humaweepi realizes that some day he will be responsible for doing the things his uncle does. In the second part of the tale, Silko indicates that Humaweepi does this by transmitting stories to a friend rather than by transmitting rituals to an apprentice. The particular story told by Humaweepi in Part Two describes the animal power possessed by a holy man after initiation as demonstrated by his uncle's walking barefoot through the mountain snow like a wolf.

The old man, who abandons his yucca sandals partway up the mountain, insists that his feet do not get cold and that people grow to believe they need shoes only because fearful women instill the habit in them as children. "Does the wolf freeze his feet?" he asks (Rosen, 168). When Humaweepi counters that the old man is not a wolf, his uncle reveals the strength of his power by appearing to become transformed: "The old man's eyes opened wide and then looked at me narrowly, sharply, squinting and shining. He gave a long, wailing wolf cry with his head raised toward the winter sky" (Rosen, 168). In the distance, Humaweepi thinks he hears a wailing answer. Animal power, then, is not limited to bear power; although this is the most powerful bear, he can become transformed into other sacred animals as well. In the old uncle's words, "a man can do anything." For Pueblo men to fulfill this potential, the oral tradition must survive. By shifting the focus from ritual in the first part of the narrative to storytelling in the second part, Silko emphasizes that both are important to the continuum of oral traditions—that the traditions and the rituals on which these are based can die out if they become the exclusive property of only a select few who fail to transmit them.

The continuum of the oral tradition and the importance of storytelling are also demonstrated in Silko's "Yellow Woman."[11] Here, however, the emphasis is on personal renewal, derived from experience outside the pueblo, rather than on mastery of religious ritual. Adapting the traditional "yellow woman" abduction tales to contemporary circumstances, Silko vividly illustrates the influence of these stories on the imagination of a modern Pueblo woman and the usefulness of the genre for explaining why this woman, and generations of women before her, would suddenly disappear with a stranger, only to return later with a story about being kidnapped. Many of the traditional tales emphasize the subsequent benefits that came to the pueblo as a result of these liasons, as Silko indicates in her summary of them: "Yellow Woman went away with the spirit from the north and lived with him and his relatives. She was gone for a long time, but then one day she came back and brought twin boys" (Rosen, 355).

Boas summarizes the basic elements of the traditional abduction stories as follows: A woman is usually abducted by a dangerous *kachina*[12] when she goes to draw water. After encountering the abductor, the woman refuses to be taken away because she does not know what to do with her water jar. The abductor then threatens her with death, compels her to place the jar on the ground upside down, and then transports her by various means to his home, where he gives her impossible tasks to perform lest she be killed.[13] In some stories, Yellow Woman is described as the mother of the hero twins Ma'sewi and Uyuyewi, the names given not only to the twin children of the Sun and Yellow Woman but also to all such children of monster *kachinas* and the women they abduct. The children are usually born miraculously and raised after the death of their mothers (Boas 107; Gunn 150). Through bearing twins who subsequently become monster slayers or who simply bring new blood into the pueblo, Yellow Woman becomes a symbol of renewal through a liaison with outside forces. In addition to bringing new life to the pueblo, Yellow Woman renews it in other ways. For example, in the tale of Buffalo Man, Yellow Woman is abducted by him. After she is freed by her husband Arrow Youth, they are pursued by Buffalo Man and his herd. Arrow Youth succeeds in killing the abductor and all the other buffalo. Because Yellow Woman weeps for the death of her buffalo husband, Arrow Youth kills her as well. However, as a result of her abduction and pursuit by Buffalo Man, the pueblo is provided with much-needed meat (Boas 122–127, 261–262; Gunn 184–189).[14]

In general, the abductor is an evil force of great power, frequently associated with mountain spirits. Most common among the abductors in the printed accounts are Fling Wing (who lives on a mountain top), Cliff Dweller (who lives on a high mesa), Whirlwind Man (who may be either an evil *kachina* or who may live among the good *kachinas* at Wenimatse), Whipper, and Buffalo Man (Boas 104–127). Although the abductor in Silko's "Yellow Woman" is the contemporary of all these figures, some of the details in her story more closely resemble the accounts of Cliff Dweller (Ma'ctc' Tcowai) than of other abductors. For example, Cliff Dweller is associated with the north, the direction from which Silko says the abductor *kachina* came. In addition, both Cliff Dweller and the abductor in Silko's story leave their women temporarily to go hunting and bring back meat.[15]

Gunn describes Cliff Dweller as a wayward son who disregarded the teachings and prayers of his mother to become an outlaw and a kidnapper and murderer of women. He never married more than one wife at a time. To get her, he would go into the settlements, marry, and then take his wife to his cliff dwelling; if any refused, he would carry her off by force. When he became dissatisfied with his wife, he would throw her over the cliff and bring home another (Gunn 143).[16] In Boas's version, Yellow Woman goes to draw water but is carried away by Cliff Dweller, who tells her to stand north from him. He rolls the ring (for supporting the water jar on her head) toward her and thus transports her to his house on the cliff (104–105). In the versions given by both Boas and Gunn, Yellow Woman is ordered to grind an enormous amount of corn in a short time or else she will be killed. With the help of Spider Woman, Yellow Woman completes the task in the allotted time. After being given other superhuman tasks (which differ in the versions by Boas, Gunn, and Lummis), she realizes that she is going to be killed whether she completes them or not; consequently, she gets Spider Woman to help her escape by weaving a net to let her down from the cliff. In Boas's version, she escapes briefly, only to be killed by Cliff Dweller. Her sons, the hero twins, are born after her death. In Gunn's version, Yellow Woman survives to bear the twins, and Cliff Dweller himself is killed (Boas 108; Gunn 143–152; Lummis 203–205).

Silko's sources for her "Yellow Woman" story are not the published accounts but rather the oral ones passed on by members of her family. As she makes clear in an interview:

> I figured that anybody could go to the anthropologists' reports and look at them. I have looked at them myself, but I've never sat down with them and said I'm going to make a poem or story out of this. . . . I don't have to because from the time I was little, I heard quite a bit. I heard it in what would have been passed off now as

> rumor or gossip. I could hear through all that. I could hear something else, that there was a kind of continuum. (Evers and Carr 30)

Silko has also indicated elsewhere that one of her sources was her great aunt Alice Little, who used to tell the young Marmon girls stories about Yellow Woman while babysitting them: "It seemed like, though, you keep hearing the same story all the time."[17]

According to Silko, the river in Laguna, where "Yellow Woman" opens, was always associated with stories as places to meet boyfriends and lovers:

> I used to wander around down there and try to imagine walking around the bend and just happening to stumble upon some beautiful man. Later on I realized that these kinds of things that I was doing when I was fifteen are exactly the kinds of things out of which stories like the Yellow Woman story [came], I finally put the two together: the adolescent longings and the old stories, that plus the stories around Laguna at the time about people who did, in fact just in recent times, use the river as a meeting place. (Evers and Carr 29)

She notes that the old adultery stories are better than ever and have become even more intricate, now that indoor plumbing has eliminated some of the excuses for going outside (Evers and Carr 33).

Although Silko's "Yellow Woman" is based on traditional abduction tales, it is more than a modernized version. Silko is less concerned with the events involved in Yellow Woman's abduction and her subsequent return home than with the character's confusion about what is real and what is not. Underlying this is the character's identification with Keres legends and her temporary rejection of the confining monotony of life within the pueblo.

Unlike the recorded traditional abduction tales, Silko's story does not begin with Yellow Woman's initial encounter with her abductor. Instead, it begins when Yellow Woman awakes after spending the night with the stranger she met by the river the previous afternoon. As the story opens, Yellow Woman becomes conscious of various strong physical sensations: the dampness with which her thigh clings to that of her abductor, the sight of the brown water birds, the sound of the water, the appearance of her sleeping lover, and the pangs of her own hunger. Indeed, one of the themes of the story is the power that physical sensations and desire have to blot out thoughts of home, family, and responsibility. Following the river southward to where she met her lover, she tries but fails to catch a glimpse of her pueblo. Her failure is one of the first indications that she has been separated from the world, which no longer seems real to her. Her reality consists of immediate physical sensations combined with vague memory of the legends told by her grandfather, which her own experience now parallels. The interrelationship between the myth of the past and the experience of the present begins when she touches her lover to tell him she is leaving—an unnecessary act if she really meant to leave. The connection between legend and experience is made explicit when he calls her "Yellow Woman," although he stresses that it was she who suggested the parallel the night before. Now, however, her sense of being part of the myth has weakened: she remembers only the touch of his body and the beauty of the moon (the moon is female in Keres mythology). Weakly she insists on her identity and his, separate from the legend. Although the abductor's name is revealed in the story, that of Yellow Woman is not: "I have my own name and I come from the pueblo on the other side of the mesa. Your name is Silva and you are a stranger I met by the river yesterday afternoon" (Rosen 34). That the stranger is the contemporary counterpart of the mythic abductors is underscored by the fact that his name, "Silva," is Spanish for "collection" or "anthology." Despite the young woman's denial that she and Silva are reliving the myth, the mention of it recalls to her the old Yellow Woman stories—not only the abduction tales but also such animal tales as the one about Coyote outsmarting Badger when both animals wanted to sleep with Yellow Woman.[18]

In contrast to the abductors in the recorded traditional stories who relied on threats to get Yellow Woman to go with them, Silva relies instead on his psychological dominance and on her physical desire for him. As Silva touches her and as she moves close to him, she is drawn once more into the world of the legend. Clearly she identifies with Yellow Woman when she wonders whether the legendary Yellow Woman had a life and identity outside the myths as she herself does. Her fear of going away with Silva melted away by her pleasure at the warmth of his body, she dimly perceives why the mythic Yellow Woman would go off so quickly with her abductor: "This is the way it happens in the stories, I was thinking, with no thought beyond the moment she meets the ka'tsina spirit and they go" (Rosen 35). Her resistance to Silva's will that she come with him is limited to her feeble protest that she does not have to go.

Their journey up the mountain intensifies her confusion about what is dream and what is fact. The farther away she goes from home and family, the more powerless she is to prove to herself that she is not Yellow Woman. She hopes to see someone else on the trail so that she can again be certain of her own identity. Although she tries to persuade herself that she cannot be Yellow Woman because the woman of the legend lived in the past and did not experience her modern world, she is nevertheless lured farther and farther into the high country by Silva, who always looks into her eyes and softly sings a mountain song. Only her hunger wrenches her thoughts from him back to her home, where her family would be cooking breakfast and wondering what had happened to her.

The second part of the story takes place high on the mountain where Silva has his home. He does not require her to perform superhuman chores once they arrive, as did the traditional abductors. Instead he sets her the task of frying some potatoes while he continues to watch her closely. As they eat, her thoughts return to the legend, and she asks if he has brought other women here before by telling them also that he was a mountain *kachina*. He does not answer. After showing her his view of the world (the Navajo reservation, the Pueblo boundaries, and cattle country), he arouses her fears when he matter-of-factly informs her that he is a cattle rustler. Although she wonders about this mountain rustler who speaks Pueblo, she convinces herself that he must be a Navajo because Pueblo men do not do things like that—an allusion to the old Navajo practice of raiding Pueblo settlements for food and women. Once again, he overcomes Yellow Woman's fears through seduction, laughing at her for breathing so hard while he caresses her. When she turns away, he pins her down and warns her, "You will do what I want" (Rosen 40). For the first time she realizes that he could destroy her as other abductors destroyed Yellow Woman in the legends. Nevertheless, her fear turns to tenderness as she watches him sleep.

When she awakens the next morning to find him gone, she is overcome by confusion, vainly seeking some evidence of his presence in the house to prove that he will return or even that he exists. Later in the day, after eating and napping, she awakens again to thoughts about her family. That she is going to remain with Silva is evident from her conclusion that her family (including her baby) will get along without her. She feels the only difference her leaving will make is that a story about her disappearance will be created. Like Yellow Woman and her human counterparts, she will become the source for the continuation of the abduction tale in contemporary oral tradition.

Rather than walk home as she set out to do, she returns to Silva's house, where he has brought home a rustled beef carcass instead of the traditional deer meat. Silva tests her loyalty to him by asking whether she intends to come with him to sell the meat. Her questions as to whether anyone has tried to catch him and why he carried a rifle reflect her sense of danger; however, still under his spell, she agrees to accompany him.

Part Three of the story deals with the confrontation between Silva and an unarmed white rancher, an episode comparable to the tests in the traditional tales in which Yellow Woman's life is threatened or in danger; this time, the danger is indirect rather than direct. After the rancher accuses Silva of rustling, the latter orders Yellow Woman to go back up the mountain with the beef, which she starts to do, hearing at least four[19] shots as she rides quickly away. Reaching a ridge, she tries to see where she left Silva but cannot, just as she was unable to see her pueblo at the beginning of the story before she began the journey up the mountain. Her inability to see what she is seeking signals the end of her interlude with Silva. Unconsciously, she has decided to return home—just as her grandfather had said the legendary Yellow Woman usually did before her.

In the concluding section of the story, Yellow Woman makes her way back on foot to the river where she first met Silva. Although she feels sad about leaving him and is disturbed by his strangeness, her desire for him is rekindled when she comes to the spot where the leaves he trimmed from a willow mark their first meeting place. She convinces herself that she cannot return to him because the mountains are too far away but comforts herself with the belief that he will come back again to the riverbank. As she reaches her home, she is brought back to the realities of her own life by the smell of supper cooking and the sight of her mother instructing her grandmother in the white man's art of making Jell-O.

This acculturation explains why the only member of her family for whom she feels an affectionate kinship is her dead grandfather, who loved the Yellow Woman tales that he passed on to his granddaughter. As her link to the mythological and historical past, he would understand that her disappearance was not a police matter because she had only been stolen by a *kachina* mountain spirit. For him, this would have been explanation enough; for her family, however, which no longer possesses this sense of unity with the past, she is forced to create the story of being kidnapped by a Navajo. Thus, the grandfather's belief in the tales in which the lives of the Pueblo people were inextricably intertwined with their gods has been transmitted to his granddaughter, who uses them as an explanation for her temporary escape from routine. Her conviction that her own experiences will serve the pueblo as a new topic for storytelling and that she herself will have to become a storyteller to explain away her absence indicates that the process will continue.

In all four of these stories, Silko emphasizes the need to return to the rituals and oral traditions of the past in order to rediscover the basis for one's cultural identity. Only when this is done is one prepared to deal with the problems of the present. However, Silko advocates a return to the essence rather than to the precise form of these rituals and traditions, which must be adapted continually to meet new challenges. Through her own stories, Silko demonstrates that the Keres rituals and traditions have survived all attempts to eradicate them and that the seeds for the resurgence of their power lie in the memories and creativeness of her people.

Notes

*Originally published in *MELUS* 5.4 (Winter 1978): 2–17. © 1978 *MELUS*. Reprinted with permission.

1. See Ellis, *Pueblo Indians*, Vol. 3, pp. 8–11, and Parsons, *Pueblo Indian Religions*, Vol. 2, pp. 888–890, in "Works Cited" below. I have followed Ellis's account rather than Parsons's, who spent very little time in Laguna. See also Parsons, *Notes on Ceremonialism at Laguna* 9.1, p. 87.

   I have updated this article to incorporate relevant scholarship published after it originally appeared.

2. Turkey feathers are associated with the dead; see Parsons (*Pueblo* 275), and for a discussion of the Pueblo use of prayer feathers, see Parsons (*Pueblo* 285–292). I am unable to identify the face markings described by Silko. They are the closest to the white, green, and blue that Boas says were used by the water clan (295).

3. Corn meal is even more associated with prayer than prayer sticks or feathers (Parsons, *Pueblo* 292). According to Boas's description of a Laguna funeral ritual, both water and food would be placed beside the corpse. After two days, the dead one, who by now has become a vapor, eats for the last time food provided first by a shaman and then sacrificed on the fire by the family (Boas 203–204). Parsons describes the latter sacrifice as occurring on the fourth day (Parsons, *Notes* 128–129).

4. The war captains represent the hero twins Ma'sewi and Uyuyewi. As the "out of town chiefs," they are in charge of all public functions (Boas 286).

5. In addition, witch effigies were "killed" in annual curing ceremonies; townspeople referred to these "witches" as living beings (Parsons, *Pueblo* 84–88).

6. Dreams are frequently but not always bad signs to a Pueblo. Bad dreams are seen as portents of death, and dreams of the dead are considered visitations of the dead (Parsons, *Pueblo* 84–88).

7. Parsons notes that one may use an arrow point or ashes against witchcraft; both are used to separate a person from a dangerous

influence. Arrow points are thought to have power because they have been shot by lightning. The reasons for using ashes remains obscure (Parsons, *Pueblo* 106, 332).

8. Silko retells the story in *Ceremony*.

9. Simon Ortiz's "The Killing of a State Cop" deals with the murder of a policeman on reservation land by a Pueblo Indian. In addition, N. Scott Momaday's *House Made of Dawn* includes an incident in which the central character, Abel, a veteran of World War II, kills an albino tormentor, thinking he is a witch. According to Lawrence Evers, these fictional treatments are based on the murder of Nash Garcia, a Mexican policeman, on Good Friday, 1952, in Grants, New Mexico. See "The Killing of a State Trooper: Ways of Telling an Historical Event."

10. When Keresan, Zuni, and Tewan doctors, called bears, draw on the bear paws, which are the equivalent of a *kachina* mask, they become bears. Doctors and *shamans* have the power literally to turn into bears just as bears may get rid of their skins and become people. Animals are considered the givers of medicinal plants, which are named for them. Because they are considered guardians or protectors, their stone images are primarily displayed on altars and are kept in homes. Keresan and Tewan doctors may give animal images to their patients to protect them against the witches who have made them sick (Parsons, *Pueblo* 188–190).

11. Many of the critical essays in *"Yellow Woman": Leslie Marmon Silko*, ed. Melody Graulich, focus on Silko's storytelling. In "Words Like Bones," Helen Jaskoski examines how *Storyteller* takes its form and theme from the traditional relationship between storyteller and audience.

12. The *kachina* (ka'tsina in Keres) spirits as a class are always kind and helpful; they live in the northwest at Wenimatse, a beautiful mountain region where the spirits gamble, dance, hunt, or farm. The term also refers to spirits who can be impersonated by masks (see Parsons, *Pueblo* 174; Boas 276–277; Purley 31).

13. According to Boas (218–219), "Yellow Woman" is a generic term used to specify heroines in Keres stories. Parsons points out that Kachina Girl or Yellow Woman (Ko'tchina'ko) is paired with the male *kachina* and that this supernatural pair is associated with the colors yellow and turquoise. The practice of pairing, whether of the same or opposite sex, carries an assurance of companionship rather than of number (Parsons, *Pueblo* 101–102).

14. This story is the subject of Silko's poem "Cottonwood, Part Two: Buffalo Story," *Storyteller*, pp. 67–76.

15. Although Flint Wing lives on a northern mountaintop and goes hunting, the tales about his abduction of Yellow Woman are less similar to Silko's story than are those about Cliff Dweller (see Boas 111–118, 258–259; Gunn 122–125).

16. A reference to the Navajo Cliff or Throwing Monster (tse'nenaxli), whose name comes from his habit of catching people in his long sharp claws and throwing them to his children down among the rocks (Reichard 7). When Silva says the Navajo people know him too, he may be alluding either to their knowledge of the abduction stories or to the fact that both Cliff Dweller of the Keres legends and Cliff Monster of the Navajo kill by throwing their victims off cliffs (Boas 108; Gunn 52; Lummis 203–205).

17. See Silko "Poetry and Prose Reading." See also Silko's comments on storytelling in Barnes, pp. 49–52.

18. A reference to the tale recorded by Boas in which Coyote and Badger want to sleep with a brown-haired, light-complexioned Navajo girl, who will permit them to do so only after they bring her rabbits. Each tries to outwit the other (167–169, 271–272). These two animals are very frequently linked in Pueblo stories. See the chapters on "Badger" and "Coyote and Kin" in Tyler.

19. The number four occurs often in Keres tales. However, Parsons notes that among many Indian peoples, it is the favored numeral. It is used so much, especially in folktale and ritual where freedom of repetition is unrestricted, that it frequently means no more than "some" or "several" (Parsons, *Pueblo* 1:100). Boas associates it with the characteristic number in individual Laguna families (8.1: 217).

Works Cited

Barnes, Kim. "A Leslie Marmon Silko Interview." *Journal of Ethnic Studies* 13 (Winter 1986): 83–105.

Boas, Franz. *Keresan Texts.* Publications of the American Ethnological Society. New York: American Ethnological Society, 1928.

Ellis, Florence H. "Anthropology of Laguna Pueblo Land Claims." *Pueblo Indians, American Indian Ethnohistory: Indians of the*

Southwest. Vol. 3. Comp. and Ed. David A. Horr. New York: Garland, 1974, pp. 89–120.

Evers, Lawrence. "The Killing of a New Mexico State Trooper: Ways of Telling an Historical Event." *Critical Essays on Native American Literature*. Ed. Andrew Wiget. Boston: G.K. Hall, 1985, pp. 246–261.

Evers, Lawrence, and Dennis Carr. "A Conversation with Leslie Marmon Silko." *Sun Tracks* 3 (Fall 1976): 28–33.

Graulich, Melody, ed. Introduction, *Yellow Woman*, by Leslie Marmon Silko. New Brunswick, NJ: Rutgers University Press, 1993.

Gunn, John. *Schat-Chen: History and Traditions and Naratives* [sic] *of the Queres Indians of Laguna and Acoma*. Albuquerque, NM: Albright and Anderson, 1917.

Jaskoski, Helen. "Words Like Bones." *Noncanonical American Literature*. Special Issue of the *CEA Critic*. Eds. Bonnie Hoover Braendlin and Fred L. Standley. 55.1 (1992): 70–84.

Lummis, Charles F. *The Man Who Married the Moon and Other Pueblo Indian Folk-Stories*. New York: The Century Co., 1894.

Parsons, Elsie Clews. *Notes on Ceremonialism at Laguna*. Anthropological Papers of the American Museum of Natural History 9.1. New York: Trustees of the AMNH, 1920, pp. 83–131.

———. *Pueblo Indian Religion*. 2 vols. Chicago: University of Chicago Press, 1939.

Purley, Anthony F. "Keres Pueblo Concepts of Deity." *American Indian Culture and Research Journal* I (1974): 29–32.

Reichard, Gladys. *Navaho Religion: A Story of Symbolism*. 2 vols in 1. New York: Pantheon, 1950. 1: 7–4; 2: 420.

Rosen, Kenneth, ed. *The Man to Send Rainclouds: Contemporary Stories by American Indians*. New York: Viking, 1974.

Silko, Leslie Marmon. "Poetry and Prose Reading." MLA-NEH Summer Seminar on Contemporary Native American Literature. Flagstaff, Arizona, June 1977.

———. *Storyteller*. New York: Arcade, 1989.

Tyler, Hamilton A. *Pueblo Animals and Myths*. Norman: University of Oklahoma Press, 1975.

BIBLIOGRAPHY OF COLLECTIONS OF SHORT STORIES BY AMERICAN INDIAN WOMEN

Allen, Paula Gunn (Laguna/Sioux). *Grandmothers of the Light: A Medicine Woman's Sourcebook.* Boston: Beacon, 1991. Allen's recreations of traditional oral stories about women.

———. ed. *Spider Woman's Granddaughters: Traditional Tales and Contemporary Writing by Native American Women.* Boston: Beacon, 1989.

Brant, Beth (Mohawk). *Food & Spirits: Stories by Beth Brant.* Ithaca: Firebrand, 1991. Short fiction.

Cook-Lynn, Elizabeth (Sioux). *The Power of Horses and Other Stories.* New York: Arcade, 1990. Short fiction.

Glancy, Diane (Cherokee). *Fire Sticks: A Collection of Stories.* American Indian Literature and Critical Studies Series, Vol. 5. Norman: University of Oklahoma Press, 1993.

Green, Rayna (Cherokee), ed. *That's What She Said: Contemporary Poetry and Fiction by Native American Women.* Bloomington: Indiana University Press, 1984.

Hogan, Linda (Chicasaw). *Red Clay: Poets and Stories.* Greenfield Center, N.Y.: Greenfield Review Press, 1991.

Johnson, Pauline (Mohawk), ed. *The Moccasin Maker.* 1913. Reprint, with introduction and notes by A. LaVonne Brown Ruoff. Tucson: University of Arizona Press, 1987. Short fiction and one essay.

———. *The Shagganappi.* Introduction by Ernest Thompson Seton. Vancouver: Briggs, 1913. Short Fiction; adventure stories for boys.

Tapahonso, Luci (Navajo). *Sáanii Dahata: Poems and Stories.* Sun Tracks Series, Vol. 23. Tucson: University of Arizona Press, 1993.

Walters, Anna Lee (Pawnee/Otoe/Missouria). *The Sun Is Not Merciful.* Ithaca: Firebrand, 1985. Short fiction.

———. *Talking Indian: Reflections on Survival and Writing.* Ithaca: Firebrand, 1992. Mixed genre: short fiction, autobiography, non-fiction.

Zitkala-Sa [Gertrude Bonnin] (Sioux). *American Indian Stories.* 1921. Introduction by Dexter Fisher. Lincoln: University of Nebraska Press, 1986. Autobiography, fiction, non-fiction.

"A Revolutionary Tale": In Search of African American Women's Short Story Writing

Bill Mullen

> What's the fate of a black story in a white world of white stories?
>
> John Edgar Wideman

In 1950, the first-ever "best" collection of African American short stories was published. *Best Short Stories by Afro-American Writers* featured 40 short stories published in the Baltimore-based *Afro-American* newspaper between 1925 and 1950. In their introduction to the collection, editors Nick Aaron Ford and H.L. Faggett offered that the stories sought to present

> Negro characters outside the familiar stereotypes. They portray them in their normal activities as American citizens, neither as paragons of virtue nor as personifications of ignorance, laziness, stupidity, and vice. They present the darker American laughing, weeping, singing, struggling, achieving, failing, praying, sinning, and dreaming, dreaming of things his whiter brothers [sic] have dared to dream also. (11)

The book included seven stories by the editors and one by a pseudo-anonymous "Ed Lacy," actually a white Jewish ex-Communist named Leonard S. Zinberg,[1] a pulp writer whose black subject matter consistently fooled readers and editors into thinking he was black. Of the remaining 32 stories, 3 were written by African American women—Ruth Johnson, Martha Brown, and Edwina S. Dixon—none of critical reputation. In 1966, John Henrik Clarke published *American Negro Short Stories*, the first representative collection of African American short fiction ever published. Four of its 31 stories were by African American women: "The Gilded Six-Bits," by Zora Neale Hurston, first published in *Story #3* (August 1933); "Solo on the Drums" by Ann Petry; "See How They Run" by Mary Elizabeth Vroman, first published in *Ladies' Home Journal* and later produced by MGM as the film *Bright Road*; and "Reena" by Paule Marshall. In his introduction, Clarke argued that the collection would at last acknowledge the "Negro contribution" to the short story, which, he asserted, did not begin until Charles Chesnutt burst onto the *Atlantic Monthly* scene in 1887 with the stories that would later comprise *The Conjure Woman* (xv).

These two literary anecdotes inadvertently respond to the question raised in the epigraph to this essay, and raise a second. They suggest first that the history of the African American short story unfolds painfully late, inaccurately, and incompletely in the history of African American and American literature. If collections and anthologies may be said to mark "official" self-consciousness not just of quality but of chronology in a literary genre, the appearance of works commemorating African American short fiction as flawed and incomplete as those cited above bespeaks the tardiness and imprecision with which the question of what African American short fiction *is* has been asked. More pointedly, though, these examples underscore the intentional ignorance and inadvertent erasure of more than 140 years of short story writing by African American women.[2] For, in contrast to John Clarke's understanding of the history of the genre, African American short fiction owes its beginnings to a woman.[3,4] According to Ann Allen Shockley's outstanding and reliable *Afro-American Women Writers*,[5] Frances Ellen Watkins Harper's "The Two Offers," published in Thomas Hamilton's *The Anglo-African* in September and October 1859, is the bibliographic and historical starting point for the complex yet heretofore unsketched development of the short story by African American women (58). As with the African American woman herself, the story in its essence is one of "contending forces" between the will of a gifted and persistent community of writers on the cultural margin, and a historically resistant and race-bound force called the literary marketplace upon which the very life of the short story, more than any other genre, absolutely depends. Indeed the fortunes of African American women's short stories, as this essay will show, have historically depended on a series of wars with and accidents around the literary marketplace predicated on the ebb and flow of attitudes toward race and gender among writers and editors both black and white, particularly as these attitudes have influenced and determined black access to publishing (and hence cultural) power. Those attitudes have also reflected the shifting form and content of black women's short fiction, making the genre a remarkably accurate barometer of the gradual emergence of black women's voices in American literature.

> How many African American stories have you ever seen in *The New Yorker*? *The Atlantic Monthly*? *Grand Street*? *Q*? *Redbook*? And even many of the prestigious literary quarterlies?
>
> Terry McMillan

Numerous restrictions in the production and reception of literature by nineteenth-century African Americans made the writing and publishing of black women's short fiction extremely rare. With the notable exception of Harper's "The Two Offers," a convention-bound sentimental story about a white woman who devotes her life to abolition, pre–Civil War black women writers had neither the access to literary forums nor literary models that would have allowed or encouraged short story production. Although Martin E. Dann reports the establishment of *Freedom's Journal* in 1827, edited by John Rasswarm and written by ex- and free black slaves, as the first example of a free black newspaper (17), nineteenth-century magazines, journals, and periodicals were by and large dominated by white publishers and editors. Hamilton's aforementioned *Anglo-African* was the first major and successful exception to this rule; although typical of early black-centered publications, its tenure was short-lived.[6] Dann also notes the temporary flourishing of *Ivy*, a mid-nineteenth-century eight-page journal edited by Mrs. Amelia Johnson, devoted to the publication of "original poems and stories" by black writers (65). Yet for the most part the few white readers and publishers interested in assisting or publishing black writers (Whittier, Garrison, and *The Liberator* being the most famous examples) primarily sought autobiographies or slave narratives that would be useful in promoting abolitionist causes, goals to which the nascent short story genre was ill-suited and inexperienced.

Thus, as several critics have noted, even those nineteenth-century African American women writers who wanted to write were encouraged to produce longer works best suited to mainstream publication primarily for the entertainment of or propagandistic effect on white readers. The postbellum period, for example, saw an outpouring of published work by black women, none of it short fiction: Elizabeth Hobbs Keckley's autobiographical exposé of her years with the Lincolns, *Behind the Scenes; Or, Thirty Years a Slave, and Four Years in the White House* (1868); Frances Ellen Watkins Harper's *Sketches of Southern Life* (1872), containing among other things poems of "wit and irony" (Shockley 191); Clarissa Minnie Thompson's serial romance *Treading the Winepress; Or, A Mountain of Misfortunes* (1885–1886); and Anna Julia Cooper's feminist essays *A Voice from the South: By a Black Woman of the South* (1892).

So aberrant and unlikely was the publication of a "short story" by an African American woman that when one did appear it was mistaken for something else: Victoria Earle Matthews's "Aunt Lindy: A Story Founded on Real Life" was published as a 16-page novel in 1893 (reprinted in its entirety in Ann Allen Shockley's *Afro-American Women Writers: 1746–1933*, pp. 159–164). Matthews's protagonist, the beneficent Aunt Lindy, is an ex-slave and nurse who helps her once cruel master regain his health after he is injured in a fire. Though a reductive and predictable story, "Aunt Lindy" is an important marker in the development of the African American women's short story in several ways. Resembling white abolitionist fiction in its sentimental tone, it also looks back to earlier African American slave narrative incidents and types while remodeling them for the short fiction form. The story also features the first notably stereotypical representation in short fiction of the benevolent maternal black female, a figure of massive embarrassment and contention in twentieth-century black women's writing. Indeed Matthews's story is at bottom an unself-conscious analogue to Chesnutt's contemporary postbellum slave "folktales," thus anticipating the disdainful reaction later Harlem Renaissance fiction writers would have to "naive" nineteenth-century African American literature, and the more overtly negative response of twentieth-century black women writers to portraits of black female submissiveness in the face of white (and patriarchal) domination. Despite its thematic limitations, Matthews's story foreshadowed a flourishing of fiction (and short story) publication by black women writers between 1890 and 1910 when, as Henry Gates has noted, more works of fiction by black women were published than black men had published in a previous half-century (Hull xvi).

In 1895, the 20-year-old Alice Dunbar-Nelson published under her maiden name *Violets and Other Tales*, a collection of sketches, poems, and stories. Dunbar-Nelson's stories radically deviate from Matthews's, introducing both a "modern" racial sensibility and a modernist narrative form into black women's short fiction. Gloria Hull, who has edited the recently republished three-volume series of Dunbar-Nelson's writing, observes that beneath the pleasant surface of Dunbar-Nelson's realist and somewhat naturalistic tales of New Orleans lie "ambivalence about woman's concept of self and proper role in the emerging modern world" (xxxi) and an inclination to "write about difference—for example, Catholic versus Protestant, Anglo versus Creole" (xxxiii). Four years after *Violets*, Dunbar-Nelson continued this exploration of "female confinement and lack of options" (Hull xxxiii) in *The Goodness of St. Rocque*, the first collection of short stories published by a black woman (Shockley 263). The book, published by the respected Dodd, Mead, and Company, reprinted three stories from *Violets* and helped bring the African American woman's short story immediate commercial and literary credibility. Dunbar-Nelson's nuanced observations on black, white, and Creole intermixing; "passing"; and urban adolescent experience not only provided a black female example of the regionalism rage simultaneously sweeping the mainstream literary scene (Howells and Twain, for example) but anticipated the concerns that would dominate

African American women's short story writing in the next century. Finally, and perhaps most importantly, the commercial success of Dunbar's short fiction collection helped set the stage for a revolution in African American publishing closely linked to the literary status of black women's short story writing.

The confluence of literary genius and publishing autonomy that marked the first great period of African American literature and short fiction—the Harlem Renaissance—was first manifest in the dynamic literary career of the African American woman and occasional short story writer Pauline E. Hopkins. In the same year that Hopkins published her monumental novel *Contending Forces* (1900) with the small Colored Co-Operative Publishing Company of Boston, the Co-Operative, led by Walter W. Wallace and a small group of autonomous investors, including the shareholder Hopkins, also brought forth the monthly illustrated magazine *Colored American,* whose inaugural issue featured Hopkins's first short story, "The Mystery Within Us" (Shockley 290). In 1903, Hopkins assumed the literary editorship of *Colored American* and began contributing numerous short stories for publication while publishing the short stories, essays, and journalism of black women writers such as Frances Ellen Watkins Harper, Angelina Grimke, Olivia Ward Bush, Gertrude Mossell, and Gertrude Dorsey Browne, who published numerous stories under a variety of pen names.[7]

Hopkins's successful promotion of unheralded black women writers, providing them a credible, uniquely black-owned literary market, as well as her anti-accommodationist stance as editor of *Colored American*, helped inspire W.E.B. Du Bois to establish the magazine that turned the tide of African American literary production forever to include and celebrate short fiction. The appearance of the first issue of the NAACP *Crisis* under Du Bois's editorship in 1910 provided African American short story writers, including a large number of women, a springboard into the period of hyperactive creative and publishing success in the Harlem Renaissance.[8]

Between 1910 and 1930, the years that most broadly constitute the New Negro movement, *Crisis* published short stories by, among others, Brenda Ray Moryck and Maude Irwin Owens, May Miller, Anita Scott Coleman, Jessie Redmon Fauset, and Effie Lee Newsome. Newsome also provided nature sketches and served as "Little Page" editor for *Crisis*, establishing the first-ever section for children's stories by African American writers (Schockley 452). In 1919, Fauset, still contributing short stories, assumed the literary editorship of *Crisis* and helped inaugurate an annual short story competition, one of many endeavors of its kind that boosted output by black writers during the Renaissance. Indeed *Crisis*'s example under Fauset's literary editorship of commitment to short fiction, particularly by black women, can in retrospect partially alter and challenge Erlene Stetson's appraisal that "if the Renaissance had a gender, it was male" (Shockley 405). Charles Johnson's *Opportunity* magazine, for example, perhaps the second most important journal of the Renaissance, published numerous poems and short stories by African American women in the 1920s alone. These included short stories by Marita Odette Bonner, Eunice Roberta Hunton Carter, Caroline Bond Steward Day, Ottie Beatrice Graham, Florida Ruffin Ridley, Eloise Alberta Veronica Bibb Thompson, as well as Zora Neale Hurston's now-famous second story "Spunk," winner of the magazine's first literary contest for short fiction. In 1926, Dorothy West won second place in *Opportunity*'s contest with "The Typewriter," an ironic race drama about a young female typist and her father in a poor Harlem family. West also published short fiction in the Boston-based Renaissance magazine the *Saturday Evening Quill*, which in addition featured short fiction by African American women writers Gertrude Schalk, Florence Marion Harmon, and Edythe Mae Gordon. Though the *Quill* produced only three "annual" issues in 1928, 1929, and 1930 (Daniel 342), Gordon's story "Subversion," published in its first issue, received an O. Henry Memorial Award Prize in 1928 (Shockley 403). The crowning effort of black women's short fiction during the Renaissance, however, was perhaps the 1926 appearance of the single-issue first black "little magazine" (Daniel 175), *Fire!!*, "midwived" into being partly through the efforts of the then-fledgling short story writers Zora Neale Hurston and Gwendolyn Bennett. Under the editorship of Wallace Thurman, *Fire!!* included two masterpieces of Renaissance short fiction by black women: Bennett's "Wedding Day: A Story," a Stein-esque tale about an American prizefighter, Paul the "black terror," seduced and duped by a young white girl in Paris; and Hurston's classic vernacular "Sweat," a satire on sexual fetish and infidelity notable for its many thematic antecedents to Hurston's breakthrough novel *Their Eyes Were Watching God*.

This record of accomplishment by short story writers during the Harlem Renaissance/New Negro period begs reexamination of Quandra Stadler's 1975 assertion that "during the heyday of the Harlem Movement, black writers had greater difficulty in placing their short stories than in having their novels published" (x). In their recent reference book *Harlem Renaissance and Beyond: Literary Biographies of 100 Black Women Writers*, Lorraine Elena Roses and Ruth Elizabeth Randolph identify 28 black women writers whose short fiction appeared in journals, magazines, and self-published books between 1900 and 1945 alone. While most of their stories were published in *Crisis* and *Opportunity*, Roses and Randolph note the occasional breakthrough of black women writers into other forums such as the 1919 publication of Angelina Weld Grimke's short story "The Closing Door" in Margaret Sanger's *Birth Control Review*. In addition, the book gives supporting evidence of the flourishing cottage industry of self-published books and journals fostered by formal and informal black literary circles that sprang up in and around the period of the Renaissance. Between 1910 and 1935, Howard University's *Stylus*, Philadelphia's *Black Opals*, and Los Angeles's *Ink Slingers* emerged as black-edited periodicals devoted in part to publishing black short fiction. In addition, inspired in part by the successful appearance of short stories by the likes of Dorothy West in the white-owned *Boston Post* and *New York Daily News*, black newspapers like the Baltimore *Afro-American* (cited earlier) began making short fiction a regular feature, providing still more opportunity for black male and female story writers.[9]

More important for this essay, however, is black women's short fiction published during the Renaissance, like the poetry, drama, and novels, that reconstituted the image of African American women. The stories continued to challenge racial taboos like miscegenation as well as racial stereotypes of postbellum black females begun in the turn-of-the-century short fiction of Dunbar-Nelson and Hopkins. They did so by placing black women for the first time in contemporary urban settings, writing explicitly about female sexual attitudes and desire, and by excavating southern black folklore and idiom for inspiration in both subject matter and literary style.

By the 1940s, all of these themes and techniques had reemerged in the published novels of Nella Larsen, Jessie Fauset, Zora Neale Hurston, and Dorothy West, and had begun penetrating the poetry, drama, and short fiction of the likes of Gwendolyn Brooks and Ann Petry, whose fondness for vignettes and short stories helped usher in a continuum of "contemporary" African American women's fiction. Indeed, a key moment in the transition to contemporary African American women's writing and publishing was the bimonthly publication between May 1944 and May 1946 of *Negro Story Magazine*, edited by Alice C. Browning and Fern Gayden and described by Walter Daniel as "a black literary magazine that was almost totally dedicated to publishing the short-story" (288). *Story*'s first issue included one of Brooks' "Chicago Portrait" sketches, and future issues included stories and poetry by Margaret Burroughs, Shirley Graham, and Ralph Ellison (289). The short-lived success of the female-edited *Negro Story* culminated a busy half-century in short story production by black women writers. Indeed, an overview of the contemporary period of black women's short fiction, particularly that produced during the race and gender conscious 1960s, reveals even more clearly how indebted the current second wave Renaissance in black women's fiction is to the gains made in the creation and publishing of short fiction by black women before, during, and after the New Negro movement.

> You see, we were putting out a magazine called *Love Black*. It was a group thing, you know, but it really belonged to all the people. We had learned the secret of why the folks don't read. C'mon, see do you know? You jive, they can too read. But nobody ever writes for them or writes anything they can relate to.
>
> Nikki Giovanni, "A Revolutionary Tale"

Woodie King's 1972 *Black Short Story Anthology* is dedicated to Hoyt W. Fuller, then-editor of *Black World* (until 1970 *Negro*

Digest), the original publisher of many of the stories in King's anthology. In his introduction, King credits Fuller with inspiring him to assemble his book by making him aware that "the National Endowment of the Arts supports short-story anthologies that never include any black authors. The white editors select most of the anthology stories from little magazines that never publish black authors" (vii). King's quasi-militant publishing rhetoric and *Black World*'s own 1970s shift in name and editorial direction from a magazine consisting primarily of reprinted articles to a vanguard black literary journal reflects the concurrent turnabout in the fortunes of black literary channels, African American social standing, and the short story in the contemporary era. The period from the end of the Harlem Renaissance to 1970 saw the coherence of a solid black middle and intellectual reading classes, and the simultaneous emergence of black-targeted journals and magazines like *Phylon*, *Black Fire*, *Ebony*, and *Essence*, each of which had made short fiction a staple of their publication. The black nationalist and black arts movements in African American letters of the 1960s were the radicalized, self-conscious culmination of this slow evolution, prodding a vast reevaluation of both the history and function of African American literary forms. Typical of the era's militant literary reconstructions, King's defiant short story collection, with a politically charged introduction by John O. Killens ("The Smoking Sixties"), was an attempt to recover from a tacitly white-dominated literary history the "secret" history of black short story writing and to balance the scales of racial representation in the genre.

Yet like many other male-dominated revisions of the literary past, King's was shortsighted in its representation of gender. His collection of 28 stories included only 6 by women, 3 of whom, excluding Nikki Giovanni, Alice Walker, and Louise Meriwether, had dubious literary credentials at best. For black female short story writers, this hardly seemed like a breakthrough collection. Those stories that did appear, however, provide in retrospect direct evidence of the groundswell in black women's short story writing that King's collection was perhaps astute in identifying. Meriwether's story, for example, had already appeared in a 1968 volume of the distinguished *Antioch*

Review, and Walker's "Strong Horse Tea" would shortly be collected into her ground-breaking book *In Love and Trouble*. The former fact gave sudden evidence of a "crossover" appeal into the white literary establishment for black short fiction, while the latter, and the book it would become part of, signaled a conscious revolution within the genre. Indeed Walker's astonishing companion story from *In Love and Trouble*, "Really, Doesn't Crime Pay?" reads in retrospect like a fictional manifesto on the emergence of the contemporary black woman's short story. Walker's fledgling black woman writer's knowing, angry response to her husband's attempts to steal her story ideas and then write a book titled "The black Woman's Resistance to Creativity in the Arts" seems to symbolize the emotional and formal energy of a series of stories in her book boldly confronting African American female sexuality, creativity, and political awakening in the contemporary world. Walker's extrapolations on Harlem Renaissance short fiction themes, particularly those of Hurston, now energized by black nationalist and black feminist awareness, heralded the revolutionized nature, form, and function of contemporary black women's short fiction as it suddenly became not a marginal but a central form in African American women's cultural expression.

Yet Walker's road to her "mother's gardens" as well as to crossover commercial and literary success had been well-paved in the period between 1940 and *In Love and Trouble* with the work of numerous other black women. Foremost in importance among them was Ann Petry, whose "Like a Winding Sheet," first published in *Crisis* (1945) was collected in *The Best American Short Stories* of 1946, edited by Martha Foley and dedicated to Petry. Two years before Walker published her own first story, Petry also published "The New Mirror" in the May 29, 1965, *The New Yorker*, one of the first stories published by a black woman in that magazine, later reprinted in her 1971 collection *Miss Muriel and Other Stories*. Petry's collection was also, according to Preston Yancy's bibliography, astonishingly the *first* collection of short stories to be published by an African American woman in the postbellum period (Arthenia Bates did publish *Seeds Beneath the Snow: Vignettes from the South* two years earlier).

Yet Petry's thorough commitment in the short story form to black women's quotidian concerns and inner lives, and her successful publication by a mainstream commercial press (Houghton Mifflin), helped open a floodgate of short fiction collections by black women: Toni Cade Bambara's *Gorilla My Love* (1972) and *The Sea Birds Are Still Alive* (1977); Walker's *In Love and Trouble* (1973) and *You Can't Keep a Good Woman Down* (1981); Gayl Jones's *White Rat* (1977); Ann Allen Shockley's *The Black and White of It* (1980); and Paule Marshall's *Reena and Other Stories* (1983). Of these, Bambara's, Walker's, and Marshall's collections stand out. Bambara's mastery of urban adolescent themes and black colloquial stand her in a tradition of the short "folk" story form, stretching from Hurston to Brooks to Walker. Walker's collections, in addition to announcing aforementioned revolutionary themes in black women's writing, have produced canonical masterpieces like "Everyday Use" and "To Hell with Dying." Yet of all contemporary black female short fiction writers, Paule Marshall perhaps deserves the most careful reconsideration. In addition to producing much-anthologized classics like "Barbados" and "Reena" in *Reena*, Marshall's 1961 *Soul Clap Hands and Sing*, often characterized as four "novellas," in fact may be viewed as thematically interrelated short stories that likely inspired a similar formal experiment in Gloria Naylor's 1982 *The Women of Brewster Place: A Novel in Seven Stories*.[10]

Even more than in earlier periods, this transformation in the standing of short fiction in African American women's literature has been symbiotically linked to the fate of black women in publishing, criticism, and social self-definition. Crucial to this transformation has been the emergence of black feminist and lesbian literary culture. Articulation of "difference" within both black and feminist literary and political discourse has resulted in increasing movement toward autonomy in the literary production of black women's short fiction. Among the important steps in this process have been the appearance of literary collectives, journals, and periodicals dedicated to the publishing of black straight and lesbian fiction, including *Black Light*, *Azalea*, *Salsa Soul Gayzette*, and *Third Woman*. Since the appearance of these journals in the early 1970s, writers such as the late Audre Lorde, Barbara Smith, and Sonia Sanchez have championed the discovery and publication of black feminist and lesbian short fiction, resulting in such important anthologies as *Home Girls: A Black Feminist Anthology* (Kitchen Table Press, 1983). Finally, crucial in the additional gathering of both mainstream and marginal black women's contemporary short fiction is Mary Helen Washington, whose *Black-eyed Susans: Classic Stories by and About Black Women* (1975) became part of the more comprehensive *Midnight Birds: Stories of Contemporary Black American Writers* (1980). Gathering, editing, and introducing stories by already popular writers like Alice Walker and Ntozake Shange, as well as lesser-knowns like Frenchy Hodges and Paulette Childress White, Washington can lay claim to acting as "midwife" to the remarkable second renaissance in black women's short story writing since the 1960s that has extended well into the present moment with collections of short fiction in recent years by Rita Dove (*Fifth Sunday*, 1985) and Wanda Coleman (*A War of Eyes and Other Stories*, 1988).

In her introduction to *Breaking Ice: An Anthology of African American Fiction* (1990), novelist and editor Terry McMillan recalls that in reviewing over 300 submissions for the book, the majority were excerpts from novels. She concludes, lamentingly, that there "apparently aren't as many short story writers as I thought," and speculates that some African American writers have been encouraged to write novels rather than short fiction "if they ever wanted to 'make it' or be taken seriously" (xxii). "It is for this reason," she concludes, "that I think we have more novelists than short story writers" (xxii).

Against the preceding outline of African American women's short story writing, McMillan's lament reduces to what Ralph Ellison might call "a truth and a lie." African American literature, and African American women's literature, is still indisputably dominated by the accomplishments of novelists, poets, and autobiographers. Yet few major African American writers, nor African American women writers, have had a career without publishing an important short story along the way. And virtually no African American writer, male or female, has not published in a black-controlled publication whose very existence depended in part upon the ceaseless proliferation of both writers for and audiences of African American short fiction. Indeed, viewed exclusively from the standpoint of publishing history, it is arguable that some important African American literature would have never been published were it not for the tentative advances toward the commercial sanction of African American literature made at the "grassroots" level, where short stories (and African American culture, in many ways) still make their living in America's broad cultural landscape. For African American women especially, the short story has moved in less than 100 years from the status of marginalized curiosity—"women's work" in literature's gendered hierarchy, where the novel remains patriarch onto others—to the very center of literary self-definition and cultural production. And as in African American literature generally, the liberating story of black women's short fiction has itself become the meaning of its own "revolutionary tale," a long story of struggle toward social and literary autonomy in the primarily "white world" of the short story genre. It is toward a full explication of the roots and meaning of this still unfolding tale that this essay has tried to move.

NOTES

1. For the "secret identity" of Leonard S. Zinberg I am indebted to Alan Wald's essay "The 1930s Left in U.S. Literature Reconsidered," *Re-visiting 30s Culture: New Directions in Scholarship*, ed. Bill Mullen and Sherry Linkon (University of Illinois Press, 1994). Wald notes that Zinberg wrote pseudo-anonymous fiction about black life, including the boxing novel *Walk Hard—Talk Loud* (1940), in part to keep hidden his Communist background.

2. A good example of how criticism has either ignored or distorted the record of black women's achievement in the short story genre is *The Black American Short Story in the 20th Century: A Collection of Critical Essays*, Ed. Peter Bruck (Amsterdam: B.R. Gruner Publishing Co., 1977). While acknowledging in his Preface the general shortage of

critical analysis of black short story writing, Bruck's collection of 13 essays treats short stories by Chesnutt, Dunbar, Toomer, Hughes, Himes, Wright, Ellison, Kelley, Williams, Gaines, Baldwin, and Baraka. None by women.

3. Clarke's recent revised and expanded version of the 1966 book *A Century of the Best Black American Short Stories* (New York: Hill and Wang, 1993) includes many more stories by African American women. In addition to reprinting all of the stories in the original, it adds stories by Maya Angelou, Toni Cade Bambara, Eugenia Collier, Jennifer Jordan, Rosemarie Robatham, and Alice Walker. While these additions make it one of the more inclusive story collections of black male and female writers, it fails to represent black women's short story writing in any but the contemporary period.

4. Only one year after Clarke's anthology appeared, Langston Hughes edited and published *The Best Short Stories by Negro Writers* (New York: Little, Brown, 1967), a much more inclusive collection of black short fiction from 1899 to the present. Included in the collection of 47 stories were those of better-known black women like Zora Neale Hurston, Gwendolyn Brooks, and Paule Marshall as well as lesser-known stories by Alice Childress ("The Pocketbook Game"), Pearl Crayton ("The Day the World Almost Came to an End"), and Kristin Hunter ("An Interesting Social Study"). Hughes's book also included first-time publication of Alice Walker's classic "To Hell with Dying."

5. Because of the dearth of scholarship on the subject of African American women's short story writing, I am particularly indebted in this essay to Shockley's book. It contains reference to numerous obscure African American women writers, many of whose literary careers were limited to short stories published particularly during the Harlem Renaissance.

6. In *The Afro-American Periodical Press: 1838–1909* (Baton Rouge: Louisiana State University Press, 1981), Penelope Bullock notes the 1838 appearance of *Mirror of Liberty* in New York and the *National Reformer* as the "beginning of the black periodicals press in the United States" (1). She also notes that of 97 black periodical titles between 1838 and 1909, 11 were founded in the 25 years preceding or during the Civil War, 85 appeared after Reconstruction (of which 28 appeared in the 1890s and 41 of which appeared between 1900 and 1909). However, none of the black periodicals initiated before the Civil War were in existence after the war, and of those founded between 1880 and 1909, only 23 of 85 lasted longer than 5 years; forty-five, Bullock reports, "apparently folded" in their first or second year (4). Of these nineteenth-century

black periodicals, Bullock reports almost none as publishing short stories.

7. For more information on the career of Gertrude Dorsey Browne, as well as examples of her short fiction, see *Short Fiction by Black Women, 1900–1920,* Ed. Elizabeth Ammons (New York: Oxford University Press, 1991). In addition to stories by Browne, Ammons includes dozens of stories published in *Colored American Magazine* and *Crisis* between 1900 and 1920 and suggests the emergence of various story "types" during the era (e.g., the passing story, the sketch, etc.).

8. My research supports Ammons's contention that *Colored American* and *Crisis* "provided the two largest secular, national outlets for short fiction by black women at the turn of the century" (3).

9. Chester Himes acknowledged the importance of the black popular press in publishing short fiction in his autobiography *The Quality of Hurt*: "My first short stories," he wrote, "were published in weekly newspapers and in magazines published by blacks: the *Atlanta World*, the *Pittsburgh Courier*, the *Afro-American*, the *Bronzeman, Abbot's Monthly* and other similar publications." As quoted in Quandra Prettyman Stadler, ed., *Out of Our Lives: A Collection of Contemporary Black Fiction* (Washington, DC: Howard University Press, 1974), p. xi. Excavation of these periodicals for examples of short stories by black women writers remains to be done.

10. Additional evidence that Marshall's *Soul Clap Hands* "novellas" should be reconsidered as short stories is the republication of "Brooklyn" and "Barbados" from that book in *Reena and Other Stories.*

WORKS CITED

Ammons, Elizabeth, ed. *Short Fiction by Black Women, 1900–1920*. New York: Oxford University Press, 1991.

The Anglo-African Magazine, Vol. 1 (1859). New York: Arno Press and The New York Times, 1968.

Clarke, John Henrik, ed. *American Negro Short Stories.* New York: Hill and Wang, 1966.

Daniel, Walter C. *Black Journals of the United States.* Westport, CT: Greenwood, 1982.

Dann, Martin E., ed. *The Black Press, 1827–1890: The Quest for National Identity*. New York: G.P. Putnam's Sons, 1971.

Dunbar-Nelson, Alice. *The Works of Alice Dunbar-Nelson. Vols. 1–3*. Ed. Gloria T. Hull. New York: Oxford University Press, 1988.

Ford, Nick Aaron, and H.L. Faggett, eds. *Best Short Stories by Afro-American Writers, 1925–1950*. Boston: Meador Publishing Co., 1969.

Hull, Gloria T., ed. Foreword and Introduction. *The Works of Alice Dunbar-Nelson*. Vols. 1–3. By Alice Dunbar-Nelson. New York: Oxford University Press, 1988, pp. vii–xxii, xxix–liv.

Giovanni, Nikki. "A Revolutionary Tale." *Black Short Story Anthology*. Ed. Woodie King. New York: Columbia University Press, 1972, pp. 19–34.

King, Woodie, ed. *Black Short Story Anthology*. New York: Columbia University Press, 1972.

McMillan, Terry, ed. *Breaking Ice: An Anthology of Contemporary African American Fiction*. New York: Penguin, 1990.

Roses, Lorraine Elena, and Ruth Elizabeth Randolph, eds. *Harlem Renaissance and Beyond: Literary Biographies of 100 Black Women Writers, 1900–1945*. Boston: G.K. Hall, 1990.

Shockley, Ann Allen. *Afro-American Women Writers, 1746–1933: An Anthology and Critical Guide*. Boston: G.K. Hall, 1988.

Stadler, Quandra Prettyman, ed. *Out of Our Lives: A Collection of Contemporary Black Fiction*. Washington, DC: Howard University Press, 1975.

Thurman, Wallace, ed. *Fire!! A Quarterly Devoted to the Younger Negro Artists*. 1970. Rpt. Elizabeth, NJ: Fire Press, 1982.

Walker, Alice. *In Love & Trouble: Stories of Black Women*. San Diego: Harcourt Brace Jovanovich, 1973.

Yancy, Preston M., ed. *The Afro-American Short Story: A Comprehensive, Annotated Index with Selected Commentaries*. Westport, CT: Greenwood, 1986.

Society and Self in Alice Walker's *In Love and Trouble**

Dolan Hubbard

Alice Walker's first collection of short stories, *In Love and Trouble* (1973), in retrospect, must be viewed as a lesson in the redemption of black American womanhood. Written at the height of the civil rights movement, Walker moves black women from what one critic describes as being "a vocabulary of objects" in a racist/sexist relationship to individuals in search of self-expression and therefore self-empowerment (Spillers 255).[1] The stories present the self as female and black, as mother, daughter, and grandmother. The typical woman in Walker's fiction tends to be ordinary and dark skinned; she is neither an upper-class matron committed to an ideal of womanhood that few could attain, as in the novels of the Harlem Renaissance, nor a downtrodden victim, totally at the mercy of a hostile society, as in Ann Petry's *The Street* (Christian 238). Within the breaks and interstices in the pattern of woman-making that unfolds in these 13 apprentice stories, more often than not, these women who had once been described as "the mules of the world" are forced to be their own creator.

Walker does not isolate the individual female-centered consciousness from the community; on the contrary, she presents individuals in action in both extra- and intracommunity settings. The former is to be expected while the latter is a surprise as Walker engages imaginatively the patriarchal character of black life and history (Washington 6). In so doing, Walker shows how the lives of black women as social beings are shaped by their historical/empirical need to break free not only from the perpetual present of black people's slave past—abject poverty, spatial restrictions, and the absence of meaningful choices—but also from their abuse at the hands of black men. It is in this sense that we can speak of Walker's use of the title *In Love and Trouble* as referring to the black woman's inward turn to the self that ultimately leads to the deconstruction of an exploitative ideology.

In addition to depicting the destructive pressures that undermine the integrity of the community, Walker explores how the black woman lives in oppression; she focuses on the process itself—how the black woman brings meaning into her life. It is not enough to be *against* (the man or the woman); one must also be *for* "a way of making sense of life lived every day as opposed to life lived in terms of something that's going to happen in the future," which is another way of saying that the black woman must break with the valuational control that the dominant group and black men exercise over the meaning of their own lives (Jones and Hardy 260). The moral vision presented in *In Love and Trouble* is manifested where we can recognize the intersection of the stream of social history and the stream of soul. This intersection gives the stories their dialectical field and provides the source of those generic tensions that make it possible for the black community to see the one face it can never see: its own (Schorer viii–ix).

The stories in *In Love and Trouble* propelled Walker not just onto the nation's literary center stage, but into themes that continue to be developed. Quite simply, Walker's project is to situate the black woman in (her)story—to fill in the missing pages—as she redefines the black woman in relation to community and self. As evident in "To Hell with Dying," "The Child Who Favored Daughter," "Roselily," and "The Revenge of Hannah Kemhuff,"[2] black American literature would never again live by its male-centered orientation because of Walker's treatment of a female self in these stories. Walker presents us with a composite of a multifaceted "I" who is an archetypal "self" demonstrating the trials, rejections, endurance, and triumphs that so many black women share.[3]

Walker's recovery of a female self in these stories entails situating her in history, telling (her)story in a sympathetic though not uncritical voice, and presenting the sex and gender roles that are often used as social governors to prevent her from realizing her fullest potential. The emphasis is on reinserting the woman's voice into a male-dominated discourse. The women in the short fiction of Alice Walker both resist and challenge "the power of social authority and the greedy thoroughness" (Schorer x) of an ideology that strives to erase their personality. Thus they assert their right to be.

"To Hell with Dying" celebrates the very best in the black experience and impresses upon the reader the truism of Nikki Giovanni's observation that "black love is black wealth" (58–59), and which forms the subplot of this moving story. One would be hard-pressed to find the violence and abuse of black women at the hands of black men (which has become a Walker trademark) in this bittersweet story of a girl's coming to grips with death, as will be shown in the discussion that follows. They are overshadowed by love freely given and, equally as important, freely accepted. "To Hell with Dying" is both in time and timeless; it is a delicious conversation that one overhears and does not want to end.

The story is presented as a comic drama with the principal characters being the youthful female narrator and Sweet Little (alias Mr. Sweet), the eternally dying man who somehow defies death. The narrator's family and the sharecropping community that comprise the setting complete the strong supporting cast. She matter-of-factly tells us that her dearly beloved Mr. Sweet is "a diabetic and an alcoholic and a guitar player and lived down the road from us on a neglected cotton farm" (129). In spite of his unrealized dreams—he had wanted to be a doctor or lawyer or sailor (130)—Mr. Sweet, a recognizable figure in the black community, encourages the narrator to dream by reaffirming the infinite possibilities that exist for the dreamer.[4]

It is through the dynamic interplay between the participant-narrator, who never loses her effervescence, and Mr. Sweet, who never loses his capacity to externalize his pain through song (the making of art), that Walker demonstrates her understanding of the complexities of the black experience. In the eyes of a naive girl, Mr. Sweet is a thoughtful playmate (he describes her as his "little princess") who tells funny stories when he is not in a drunken stupor. Through the looking glass of American history Mr. Sweet is a failure, a nonproductive member of society who goes to pieces under the burden of an oppressive society. He is crushed by what Houston Baker Jr. in *Blues, Ideology, and Afro-American Literature* (1984) refers to as "the economics of slavery." In specifically Afro-American terms, Baker continues, the economics of slavery "signifies the social system of the Old South that determined what, how, and for whom goods were produced to satisfy human wants" (26). Despite the abolition of slavery, blacks find it extremely difficult to redefine their historic role as laborers in a culture that is antagonistic to their very being.

Rhetorically, the name "Sweet Little" indicates his reduced stature in this society's exploitative *modus operandi*. "Sweet" connotes a "kept" man, a ladies' man; it resonates with domestic associations. "Little" connotes the erasure of the black man's identity: he is inconsequential in the scheme of things. That black men lead lives in which they have little or no input in the decision making that shapes their own lives as well as the fabric of the entire community borders on the grotesque in Toni Morrison's characterization of the Deweys in *Sula* (1973). Psychologically, they are reduced to being nonproductive members of society consigned to live out their lives in a state of perpetual childhood.

What redeems Mr. Sweet in the eyes of the participant-narrator is her knowledge that though their community was being signified on by the cultural weight of another community, Mr. Sweet did not permit the dominant community's definition of him, as a nonproductive misfit, to define his whole existence; he learned to live with the dominant community's definition of him even as he fashioned a life that permitted him to live with the day-to-day reality of that oppression. It is in this sense that "To Hell with Dying" is also a metaphor for the resiliency and durability of black life—its ability to make something out of nothing, in spite of its awareness that on the empirical/historical level that it is being discriminated against (Jones and Hardy 259). Mr. Sweet's guitar is emblematic of black people's ability to use the gift of song to bring a little joy to an otherwise drab existence. Through his art, Mr. Sweet becomes a vehicle for consciousness. In many respects his blues as a discernible discourse is secondary; the primary element of his message lies in his critique of the continuity in discontinuity and discontinuity in continuity for Americans of African descent—that each generation must confront anew the vestiges of its slave past. He enters into the womb of black America to shape significantly the consciousness of the participant-narrator who is both teller and character in this celebration of the spirit. The reader can see her as storyteller, historian, musician, and, in a limited sense, as priestess. By priestess I mean that the narrator in accepting Mr. Sweet's guitar signifies that she is willing to sing the blues (Beavers 565). Her acceptance of Mr. Sweet's steel guitar upon her return home from her doctoral studies is the external symbol of her bonding to the community. To say that Mr. Sweet is the narrator's first love is to acknowledge that he (and by extension her community) taught her to love herself, the greatest love of all. Walker admits the reader-spectator directly into the life-affirming activities of the integrated consciousness of her ideal woman. In a delightful paradox, Walker's story, which is concerned with the formed individual consciousness, reforms ours. The social sweep of this classic short story about a young girl coming to terms with death is ultimately linked to the well-being of society and self.[5]

Whereas "To Hell with Dying" is an affirmative discourse on the "is-ness" of love, "The Child Who Favored Daughter" is about the death of the spirit. Walker replaces the nurturing family and stable community we see in "To Hell with Dying" with an enraged father who accepts the definition of himself as given by the dominant community. She places in this 12-page story the excesses of the plantation economy. Walker illuminates the relationship between sexism and racism as modes of oppression that restricted the lives of many women and men in this country.

"The Child Who Favored Daughter" traces the bloody history of a man defeated by the economics of slavery. As a boy, the sullen father saw the psychological deterioration of his sister called "Daughter" (38) at the hands of the white man for whom he worked. Tied to her bed, his loved-crazed sister talked him into untying her, whereupon she knocked him to the floor, escaped her prison, and promptly impaled herself "on one of the steel-spike fence posts near the house" (39). Forever scarred by this experience, the sullen man distrusts and hates all the women in his life. The psychological impact of that childhood experience is manifested in the beating of his own wife for "the imaginary overtures of the white landlord" (40). She takes her life, but prior to doing so, she leaves behind "a daughter; a replica of Daughter, his dead sister" (40).

When the daughter (also named Daughter) from this unhappy union enters puberty, the father's repressed rage, as well as his sexual jealousy, once again surfaces. The bloody cycle renews itself in a demonic ritual in which there are no winners, only losers. His daughter falls in love with the son of the plantation owner and still loves him in spite of his marriage to one of his own. Daughter writes him a letter that, perhaps, has been returned by her former lover's doting mother or the bride herself who might have found it among the former's keepsakes or by her former lover himself. At any rate, her hate-filled father intercepts the returned letter.

His interception of the returned letter is his preemptive strike to interrupt Daughter's intercourse with the world beyond their impoverished sharecropper's shack, symbolized by the school bus and mailbox as well as by the church. Perhaps the father, through his domineering presence, has intimidated the black men who would normally make up her social circle.[6]

Godlike, this imposing authoritarian figure straight out of the Old Testament "sits in the cool of the evening reading his Bible" (37). Self-righteous, he does not want his authority (read "word") challenged. His reading of her letter can be equated to the exercise of political power, control, and his determination to make the word mean what he says it means. And it is here that one finds the symbolic import of his wanting Daughter to eat the letter. This import lies not so much in her taking back her words as in his attempt (vain though it is) to force her to accept his significations, the re-placement of (her)story with (his)tory.

The letter may be interpreted as an important paradigmatic statement of the union of subject and object in the act of the mind and the father's interference with his daughter's first signs of expression of the autonomous self (Spivak 3). The running dialogue between the narrator and Mr. Sweet in "To Hell with Dying," the development of a wholly self-sustaining self, is now interrupted in favor of a strict monologue whose sole intent is closure. The sovereign patriarchal subject remains intact, privileged and unchallenged. The father forecloses the possibility of a woman-centered universe.

The center of gravity in this tragic story of misguided love focuses on Daughter's inability to articulate those contending forces that pull her in two directions at the same time. No longer a child and not yet a woman, she is without a language to express her yearnings, as is evident in the observations of the sympathetic narrator:

> Staring often and intently into the ivory hearts of fallen magnolia blossoms she sought the answer to the question that had never really been defined for her, although she was expected to know it, but she only learned from this that it is the fallen flower most earnestly hated, most easily bruised. (43)

The forlorn woman-child symbolizes many of the women in *In Love and Trouble* who have little or no protection. They dream of a better world beyond their reach, yet they have little protection to buffer them from the pain. Like the startling beauty of the unprotected November cotton flower in Jean Toomer's *Cane* (1923), Daughter is struck down before she can live.

Ironically, the father's rage at Daughter's choice of a lover intensifies his sexual jealousy. He feels that he must beat his daughter in order to deny her the pleasures of the body. Crippling Daughter physically or psychologically removes her from being sexually attractive for other men (anyone except himself) and, therefore, places her outside the normal social intercourse for a young woman. It is not just the white man; it is any man who captures his daughter's interest, as is evident from the epigram that introduces this story of unrequited love:

> That my daughter should
> fancy herself in love
> with *any* man!
> How can this be? (35)

In the tension-packed, highly dramatic moment when we find them communicating with each other via body language in a wordless showdown—he on the porch in the chair with letter in one hand and gun in the other and she leaning against one of the posts on the porch—his greatest desire to kill her tends to rival an equally rapacious desire to possess her:

> Without wanting it his eyes travel heavily down the slight, roundly curving body and rest on her offerings to her lover in the letter. [The Father] is a black man but he blushes, the red underneath his skin glowing purple, and the coils of anger around his tongue begin to loosen. (41)

Walker contrasts the images of sexuality—through describing the girl's sensual movement—with the *a*sexual nature of Christianity. "No amount of churchgoing changed her ways. Prayers offered nothing to quench her inner thirst" (43). The enraged father believes her to be spiritually decadent. Warped by his childhood experience, he sees Christianity as a sort of material salvation for his daughter.

With the self-willed blindness that only a fundamentalist can experience, the father interprets his religion narrowly. The female narrator, whose sympathies lie with the defenseless daughter, tells us that "[h]is only guard against the deception he believed life had in store for him [complicated by questions of color and gender] was a knowledge that evil and deception *would come* to him; and a readiness to provide them with a match" (40). For her insolence, he decides that Daughter must die.

If we allegorize the story, we can say that the plight of the child who favored Daughter, this black-eyed Susan, is that of the black woman denied access to her body on the pretext that what is good for the black man is not good for the black woman. The black woman finds herself caught between two worlds that are at once complementary and contradictory. She is not to seek pleasure in the arms of the white man, her former master, nor challenge the hegemony of the black man, her helpmate. These contradictory signals apart, the black woman, more often than not, ends up in the unenviable position of being both provider and protector for her family, as is evident in "Roselily."

In "Roselily," the first story in *In Love and Trouble*, Walker uses a country wedding to illustrate that what is good for the black man is not always good for the black woman, who needs to be freed from an unyielding masculine ideology. Walker provides us with fresh insights about the nature of black womanhood during the civil rights movement of the 1960s and early 1970s as well as the evolution of that self in relation to society. This story assumes the end of one chapter in the development of black women and the beginning of another as Walker writes of "an alternate version of reality seen from the point of view of black female experience" (Braxton 201).

Roselily, whose name suggests a blend of passion and purity comparable to that produced by caresses, perfumes, and scented oils, stands before the altar neither fragrant (redolent of the fragrance of the rose) nor faultless (suggestive of the purity of the lily). Deemphasizing both the passion and purity associated with the compound name Roselily, Walker's world-wise narrator sees the mute bride-to-be as a love-starved lily that is unaware of her own beauty: "Not dead, but exalted on a pedestal, a stalk that has no roots. She wonders how to make new roots" (5–6).

Planted in shallow marital soil, Roselily's marriage will be an empty victory, for it is spiritually deficient in a critical ingredient—a nurturing partner. To sprout new roots, she must learn to draw on her internal resources: patience, prayer, and perseverance. The gross imbalance in the marriage equation in large part explains Roselily's silence as well as her interior monologue, which is emblematic of the divided self.

Structurally, Walker establishes a call (masculine discourse) and response (feminine discourse) pattern between the wedding vows and Roselily's reflections on the decision that leads to her wedding day. An unmarried mother of four with limited education and opportunities, Roselily—a pragmatic woman-child—surrenders her "limited" freedom in order that her three children may know a freedom unknown and perhaps unknowable in the backwoods of Mississippi. Desperately in need of money, Roselily gives her fourth child to his weak-willed Harvard-educated father who spent a summer in Mississippi as a civil rights worker; however, as a prisoner of his double consciousness, he denies his son's (his)tory.

Opportunity arrives in the form of a stern-faced black Muslim from Chicago. That Roselily agrees to marry a man from an alien culture is indicative of a tough-minded resourcefulness in the face of limited options. That her decision to marry the reticent stranger is fraught with paradox does not escape her nimble mind. First, not only are his values the antithesis of her own, but they also lock her into a subservient role rather than into "an escape into freedom" in Chicago, city of possibilities, after a lifetime of black and white lifestyles in a rigidly segregated Mississippi. Second, his adherence "to a stringent code of private and social morality" (Lincoln 80) makes her unacceptable in her eyes. From her perspective, he should be marrying one of her young sisters; they "giggle . . . at the absurdity of the wedding" (6). From his perspective, she is an unfinished sculpture. His expressed intent "to redo her into what he truly wants" (8) does not square with her permissive orientation.

The skeptical narrator tells us that "[Roselily] does not even know if she loves him. . . . His love of her makes her completely conscious of how unloved she was before" (7–8). All of this leaves her spiritually numb. The forced pragmatism of her decision relieves some of her spiritual numbness. She is nevertheless determined that her children shall know a better life, for "in Chicago [they will have] respect, a chance to build. They will have the opportunity to move from "underneath the detrimental wheel [of misfortune]" (4). The intense fire that burns in Roselily's vision enables her to come to terms with what she perceives as a suffocating ideology. On the one hand, Roselily's rational self rebels against racism and sexism, but on the other, her emotional self seeks a way out of what was obviously an untenable situation for her children and herself.

The ponderous wedding vows make little sense when Roselily rethinks her lived experience. A commodity "like cotton to be weighed" (3), she is prized not for her ability to love, but for her ability to produce babies. The discrepancy between her awareness and her husband's lack of passion and tenderness and his inability to see her as a person (rather than as an object) produces the narrative tension. Though unable to articulate this uneasiness that lies in the pit of her soul, she correctly sees herself as a trapped animal: "Something strains upward behind her eyes. She thinks of the something as a rat trapped, cornered, scurrying to and fro in her head, peering through the windows of her eyes. She *desperately* [emphasis added] wants to live for once. But doesn't know quite what that means" (8).

It means that she is dead to life before she knows what it means to live. Metaphorically, her trapped sisters are either naive to the danger that awaits them or are too busy chewing themselves out of their own cages to assist her. Against her better judgment, Roselily, who has known more trouble than love, participates in this masculine-endorsed ritual for the wrong reason. Whereas the Shulamite woman in the Song of Solomon confidently barters her aggressive desire in exchange for boundless love, Roselily barters her one tangible asset, her fine brown body, in exchange for protection and security in order to live in a place in Illinois that she innocently associates with the Great Emancipator.[7]

> Her place will be in the home, he has said, repeatedly, promising her the rest she had prayed for. But now she wonders. When she is rested, what will she do? They will make babies—she thinks practically about her fine brown body, his strong black one. They will be inevitable. Her hands will be full. Full of what? Babies. [*Her head will be full of what? The blues*.] She is not comforted. (7)

Roselily's mechanical repetition of the wedding vows does not still the discomfort that gnaws at her innards and generates the overriding question to which, even as she speaks, she cannot with certainty answer: Is the exchange fair? No longer a girl and not yet a woman, Roselily is between all fixed points of classification. Ostensibly, married life—a liminal stage—should afford her opportunity to reenter the social state at a higher status level (Turner 232). Roselily however, is aware that her material condition will not be significantly altered. What changes, she fervently hopes, will be the opportunities for her children, but on this point, the experienced narrator is not reassuring. The wedding vows, thus, bespeak a romantic tradition that not only is alien to Roselily but is also a luxury that she cannot afford. She brings only two things to what should be a joyous rite of passage: her body, which is looked upon as a prized commodity, and her assumed silence, which is viewed as golden. Her prospective husband brings only his iron-clad authority: "Her husband's hand is like the clasp of an iron gate" (8). This authority serves as an ironic counterpoint to Roselily's association with Lincoln and Illinois. She needs to be emancipated from an unyielding masculine ideology.

Whereas the Song of Solomon depicts marriage as a celebration of the gentleness, the strength, and the delights of human love—as God's ordained purpose for mankind—Walker depicts marriage as an escape into unending drudgery accompanied by an attitude of stoicism. Walker transforms the aggressive desire associated with the Shulamite maiden in the erotic biblical story from the pleasures of loving relationships into a signature for endurance. Whereas the Song of Solomon commodifies the female as the object of desire, Walker commodifies the female as a structurally silent reproductive machine. Her crowning glory is the number of strong, healthy babies she is able to produce. The "hysterical excitability" (Kristeva 10) that leaves both the Shulamite maiden and Roselily's giggling sisters breathless as well as oblivious to reality the day after is replaced with a steely-eyed determination.

Walker replaces the anticipated nuptial bliss we see in the Song of Solomon with an agonizing lament. She creates reader sympathy for the martyred mother, engaged in a ritual of regeneration, who sacrifices herself for the benefit of her children. *Her* agony is *our* agony. At the symbolic level, Walker asserts that the family must go on; at the reality level, she points out the contradiction between men who expect their women to support them in regard to racial solidarity while maintaining gender oppression at home. In short, the cross-cultural marriage provides Walker with the pretext to enter into a larger context—her critique of the male-dominated civil rights movement.[8] In the public sphere, the men preach the rhetoric of inclusion, while in the domestic sphere, they practice the rhetoric of exclusion, which translates into a phallic power that does not recognize women as equal. As Walker sees it, this reactionary discourse means that too many women are excluded both as speaker and as listener. Thus, the black Muslim as metaphor stands as an appropriate reminder of the ways in which racial and sexual oppression influence the appropriation of language. This throws into stark relief the controlling fiction that governs the sacred character of the wedding vows. They may be equally interpreted as a song of love as of lament. Walker thus unveils marriage as ownership and not as the outward manifestation of a mutual agreement between "autonomous, free subjects" (Kristeva 86). Roselily is what happens to the passionate Shulamite maiden when the bud is off the flower.

What the text cannot say is that the male as speaking subject, under the rubric of the marriage vows, situates himself as subject for the speech of his dutifully silent wife (Kristeva 94). He has no need to speak to maintain his sovereignty; she, however, must speak to define herself in opposition to his male-defined sexual mountain. This phallocentric logic asserts arrogantly that I (the male as subject) will render sex unto sex and, yet, I will not render my heart unto your heart. This constitutes the unsaid in Song of Solomon that the breathless female protagonist cannot silence. The subjection forecloses the possibility of reciprocity (expressed in the respective narratives as metaphors of confinement—the enclosed garden in the Song of Solomon and the rat trapped in a cage in "Roselily"). In her move to "depatriarchalize" patriarchal discourse, Walker asserts that "civil rights" begins in the bedroom.

Be that as it may, it would be a mistake to view Roselily as a passive "other"; her stubborn hope foreshadows a generation of black women who came of age during the civil rights movement. They placed themselves at the center of their experience as they moved from beneath the shadow of the male-defined sexual mountain. As a representative of those black women who remain trapped in the shadow of the male-defined sexual mountain, Roselily must break free or spiritually die. To be happy, she must reinvent love, which is to say, she must reconstruct the self.

A Walker character who reinvents love in order to walk freely in the bright sunlight as a socially vibrant self is the indefatigable Hannah Kemhuff. In "The Revenge of Hannah Kemhuff," the paradigmatic story in *In Love and Trouble*, Walker makes a transatlantic pilgrimage and pays her retrospective tribute to Africa and its attendant spiritual presence. Her protagonist stakes a claim to the usable past; that is, she acknowledges the integrity of voodoo to fill the void left by an imperial Christian God who sits high and looks out, but He does not look low. Walker's use of the term *rootworker*, metaphorically speaking, refers to any number of culturally resonant "interchangeable" addresses such as mojo, gri-gri, and conjure. In its strictest sense, rootwork refers to either putting a hex or spell on or removing it from someone (usually in regard to jealous or domestic disputes); in its grandest sense, rootwork is part of that system of belief that Africans brought to the New World known as Hoodoo or Voodoo. It encompasses a set of beliefs that influences how a people think and how individuals perceive themselves in relation to the world they see around them.[9] In "The Revenge of Hannah Kemhuff," Walker mines voodoo, "a suppressed religion" (Hurston 193), for its creative possibility as a mode of resistance against an exploitive ideology. Whereas Roselily's marriage signals her entry into another level of silence, Hannah Kemhuff breaks through her years of enforced silence to redefine her relation to community and self.

This bittersweet narrative about a Mississippi black woman who had it all, lost it all, and recovered her faith interacts with the previously discussed stories in intricate ways that constitute a discourse that has special meaning for the black American woman. Raised in a respectable middle-class home, married with four children, Hannah sinks to the lowest level of society with the onslaught of the Depression. Forced to go on welfare, her family is denied its food rationing by a white woman at the relief station because their clothes indicate that they are prosperous "colored folk." In short order, her husband "with a wandering eye" (61) abandons her; her children starve to death; finally, she snaps, loses her dignity, and becomes a prostitute in order to survive. Her recovery begins when she reaches deep inside herself and discovers something of value; more precisely, she rediscovers her intrinsic worth as a human being. Hannah Lou Kemhuff's visit to the local conjure woman signals the end of her 20-year threnody. She moves from "a theology that denies [her] life" to one that affirms life in all its complexity (Baldwin 23).

At a deeper level, Hannah's visit, in effect, negates the white woman's representational truths in order to represent the undecidability that undermines all acts of understanding. "This epistemological concern," as Ramón Saldívar notes, "becomes a humanistic concern when it is manifested 'allegorically' in narrative as the passions of love, desire, fear, pity, and other emotions" (23–24). The demystification of the white woman's belief system allows a new kind of demystified reading to occur. Hannah Kemhuff, therefore, stands independent not as a reified person, but as a heterogeneous and paradoxical form of forces.

Given the circumstance, it is no wonder that Hannah's visit to the rootworker serves as a real or imaginary vehicle for black American literature. "When the choice is between resignation or faith and humanistic action or reason, literary characters, like their folk counterparts," as Trudier Harris reminds us, "often reject Christianity in favor of a more exacting and humanistic idealism" (52). Hannah rejects the easy way out in favor of more challenging solutions. Harris concludes her trenchant observation by noting that those literary characters who are steeped in Christianity and black folk culture follow a code that

> determines models for love and sacrifices that are willingly made for others. It suggests the mode by which one defines self and the refusal to allow that self to be violated. It determines the line that is drawn between humanness and animality, and it provides a base for the choices the characters make concerning living and dying. They believe in self-determination, and they gladly accept the responsibility for this belief. Instead of an externally imposed God, they look to their secular heritage in folk tradition and to their inner selves for guidance in their actions. (52)

Hannah therefore, as a paradigmatic figure, metaphorically, represents the community as a whole; as the familiar ideal, her(story) speaks to the deepest desire of the black community to free itself from the presence of the other. Her journey to the rootworker (indeed, it is a physical as well as a spiritual journey) rekindles her faith in the moral order. It is in this sense that we can speak of her visit as a homecoming. She taps into the responsive mythology of a usable past.

In order that her spiritual good health be restored, Hannah petitions Tante Rosie to use all of her powers to punish Sarah Marie Sadler, now the socially powerful Mrs. Ben Jonathan Holley. Hannah must be intimately involved in the retribution, a view that flies in the face of the Christian ethos that admonishes the supplicant to pray and wait on the Lord. From Hannah's perspective, the Lord "seemed to have other things on his mind" (66) than answering her prayers. Because she cannot let her children die in vain, she, therefore, is prepared to move heaven and earth to right the gross injustice, as she makes clear in stating the purpose of her visit to Tante Rosie:

> I can survive as long as I need with the bitterness that has laid every day in my soul. But I could die easier if I knew something, after all these years, had been done to the little moppet. God cannot be let to make her happy all these years and me miserable. What kind of justice would that be? It would be monstrous! (67)

After 20 years of being a displaced person, dislocated temporally if not spatially, Hannah must effect closure to this chapter that has defined her life. Tante Rosie is charged with using her magical skills to turn the system back upon itself. The culture authorizes her to critique an exploitative ideology from a point beyond as well as within itself.

With the simultaneously amazed and dumbfounded narrator-apprentice at her side, the conjure woman slowly works herself into a fever pitch as she attempts to provide Hannah with her longed-for desideratum. The narrator, a highly developed intelligence, is smarter than she lets on. She functions as an alter ego for the Zora Neale Hurstons in the black community, women who will not permit a racist/sexist discourse to suppress their artistry. Ostensibly, though her reasons for coming to the rootworker differ from those of Hannah, the narrator-apprentice, too, seeks a safe port in which to anchor her considerable, yet unfocused talent. The unsaid in this story of religion and resistance (which is not apparent to the spunky narrator-apprentice) is her move from a curiosity-seeking dilettante to a committed disciple of voodoo. She emerges with a profound respect for her art.

The eschatological power of the rootworker is made manifest when, as Marie Leveau, "the queen of conjure" (Hurston 200) in New Orleans, sought retribution for those who came to her, Tante Rosie writes the name of "the little moppet" (66) in the Book of Judgment. Together, Hannah and the narrator chant the signature curse-prayer used by voodoo priests and priestesses that Hurston records in *Mules and Men*. Through this chilling conclusion in a series of prayers, Hannah petitions "The Man-God" to bring down his unmitigated vengeance on her enemies, the principal one being the little moppet, who "dragged me in the dust and destroyed my good name [and broke] my heart and caused me to curse the day I was born" (72).

Hannah's clothes symbolize her "unmerited destruction" (72). Her family wore its Sunday best, actually the secondhand clothes given to her sister in Chicago by the rich white folk for whom she worked, to the relief station. A misreading occurs. Whereas the proud Hannah sees the clothes as the outer manifestation of her inner confidence that her family will make it through the Depression, the relief woman reads them as a badge of arrogance. She denies this well-dressed family of black folk their ration of food in order to put them in their place. Twenty years later, on the eve of the civil rights movement, Hannah, her spirit "trampled down" (67), sits before the conjure woman "almost smothered, in a half-dozen skirts and shawls" (60).

I submit that Hannah, smothered under layers of clothing, is emblematic of the thwarted black female. For too long, black women have had to cover up or redirect their artistic ability so as not to draw attention to themselves. This brings into focus Walker's dedication of her story to Zora Neale Hurston, one of the foremothers of twentieth-century black American literature. Walker's intent is to reconfigure the racial mountain that black male writers climb up and define as the black experience. Their experience does not take into consideration how gender may affect one's orientation.[10]

The implicit and explicit references to Hurston's *Mules and Men* is Walker's way of acknowledging that black women writers need to draw upon their literary foremothers—a community in which black women consciously read and relate to each other's work. In addition, Walker's references to Hurston serve to collapse the distinction between her(story) and fiction and to illustrate how the group ethos is shaped by the material conditions. Whether in life or literature, black people, when viewed through the elaborate Manichaean lens of Judeo-Christianity, are viewed as the exotic "other."

Blacks as the exotic "other" dominate the confrontational scene between the signifying narrator and Mrs. Holley, who counted among her hobbies "gossiping with colored women" (73). When the patrician Mrs. Holley learns that the graceful figure in the glowing orange robe works for the renowned Tante Rosie, she at first politely refers to conjure as "colored foolishness" (75); when pressed to prove that she does not believe in conjure, she self-righteously proclaims it to be "nigger magic!" (76). With semantic dexterity, the self-confident narrator surgically isolates the suddenly apprehensive Mrs. Holley from her black domestic with the arresting question: "[W]on't you show us how much you don't have to fear of it [conjure]?" (76).

The epiphanic moment occurs when the narrator informs Mrs. Holley of the judgment that has been brought against her by the victimized Hannah Lou Kemhuff and unemotionally requests specimens so that the punishment may be duly carried out. The rootworker, through her surrogate, "shocks" Mrs. Holley into seeing Hannah as a living, breathing being, which is to say, Mrs. Holley does not recognize black women as wives and mothers with their own responsibilities and as people in their own right (Gwin 143). It is this, more than anything else, the apparent reversibility of Hannah's culturally assigned role, that sends the venerated Mrs. Holley over the edge. Her representational truths are shown to be a fiction. She is dead before she dies.

Whether or not Mrs. Holley dies as a result of Hannah's visit to the conjure woman is debatable. The closed-mouth community of black domestics maintains a conspiracy of silence in regard to voodoo, a subversive religion in the New World. What matters is their belief that Mrs. Holley's death is directly linked to Hannah's visit to a local conjure woman.

Whereas Sadler, who is well versed in the modes of mannerliness associated with the Western concept of womanhood, views Hannah's action as uncivilized mumbo jumbo and therefore monstrous, the closed-mouth community of domestics do not perceive her action as alien. On the most overt plane of self-consciousness, these domestics all participate in an ideology that is commonly known as the black American dream. This takes its dramatic aspect from the invisibility of the black experience, and since the cultural imperative is toward empowerment, Hannah's action is coherent with reality as they know it.

Their reality is expressed in a rebellious spiritual as:

> If I had-a my way,
> I'd tear this building down.
> Great God, then, if I had-a my way
> If I had-a my way, little children,
> If I had-a my way,
> I'd tear this building down . . . (11)

While it may be suicidal for the slave to tear the building down (or for the domestics to burn their brooms), the challenge before the conjure woman as the practitioner of voodoo as one mode of black American religious expression is to channel the community's latent anger into what Charles H. Long refers to as *another* reality. By this, he means that Africans in the New World had to come to terms

> with the opaqueness of their condition and at the same time oppose it. They had to experience the truth of their negativity and at the same time transform and create *another* realty. Given the limitations imposed upon them, they created on the level of the religious consciousness. (177)

Voodoo becomes a weapon to resist "the always already said." This explains why the closed-mouth community of black domestics are not shocked that one of their sisters of the spirit sees fit to call on the rootworker. They see no contradiction between Hannah's practicing Christianity (which daily is profaned in their midst) and using the subversive religion as a mode of resistance against those who hide behind Christianity as they advance their exploitative ideological agenda. It is people like Mrs. Holley who determine not only *where* but also *how* they live. What moves them, albeit silently, to stand against Hannah's bold intrusion into their world is the specter of lost wages and the imminent need to seek employment in a closed community where one is hired by word of mouth. By her bold act, Hannah reclaims this opaque community of women from racist stereotypes.

As a member of the coterie of black women writers that burst upon the American literary landscape in the late 1960s and early 1970s, Alice Walker joins them in the completion of some unfinished business: the redemption of the black woman. Walker's basic themes and metaphors as presented in these stories from *In Love and Trouble* do not so much create meanings as they simply displace significations. They serve to complete our incomplete vision of the whole (Saldívar 19–20). Walker takes the black woman out of the hegemonic shadow of the racial mountain as defined by black men and presents her in a variety of roles as mother, daughter, and grandmother, loved and unloved. Historically cast in the role as "the silent other" in the black community, Walker's female personae, not surprisingly, present the community at its best and worst in "To Hell with Dying" and "The Child Who Favored Daughter," respectively. More often than not, the female narrator, who is usually the voice of experience, recognizes the reality of what it means to be black and female as is evident in "Roselily" and "The Revenge of Hannah Kemhuff." The essential vitality at the center of these stories stems from Walker's ability to make us recognize the problems and social violence that confront a female self in a male-dominated society. Chief among her problems is the society's desire to isolate her as a social being. Cut off from a nurturing discourse, she must turn inward or surrender to psychic suicide. Walker's sympathetic female narrator holds in perspective our sense of fair play and social responsibility, thereby rescuing us from studied indifference, if not outright hostility toward these emergent women. The black woman is under constant pressure to redefine her relation to community and self. Consequently, these four stories interact with each other in complex ways that constitute a discourse that has a special meaning for American women of African descent.

NOTES

*Originally published in *Obsidian* 6.3 (Summer 1991): 50–75. Reprinted with permission.

1. I have taken the concept "the redemption of black American womanhood" from Hortense J. Spillers's perceptive discussion "Cross-Currents, Discontinuities: black Women's Fiction." Spillers reads Walker's first novel, *The Third Life of Grange Copeland* (1970), as "a lesson in the redemption of black American manhood" (255).

2. Subsequent references to these stories from *In Love and Trouble* (1973) will be designated parenthetically.

3. For a reading of how characteristics associated with the emergence of black feminine expression take generic shape, especially as autobiography, see Braxton and O'Neale.

4. "To Hell with Dying," Walker's first published story, appeared as the last story in Langston Hughes's anthology *The Best Short Stories by Negro Writers* (1967). Mr. Sweet may be read as Walker's tribute to Hughes and his celebration of the blues singer. Through his or her music and song, he or she externalizes the community's suffering—the worser the odds, the better the song.

5. Walker treats an extreme example of movement away from community in "The Diary of an African Nun" (113–118). The Ugandan protagonist enters a convent only to discover her "otherness." In his discussion of this story of the diaspora, Chester Fontenot locates it within one of the landmark ideological statements of the century; that is, Du Bois's "double consciousness" (Fontenot 150–156).

6. For a provocative reading of African American fictions of father-daughter incest, including "The Child Who Favored Daughter," see Spillers's "The Permanent Obliquity."

7. One of the more detailed and suggestive studies of the Song of Solomon is Julia Kristeva's "A Holy Madness: She and He" in *Tales of Love* (83–100). Kristeva's project is to unveil those interpreters, usually male, who read the Song of Solomon as a love supreme "assumed by

autonomous, free subjects" (86). Their amatory dialogue masks the underlying reality: "love [is kept] under the husband's rule" (99). In her reading of the Song of Solomon, Francis Landy sees the body as "the focus of metaphor." She notes that the "lovers [who] are two persons, with presumably their own separate biographies . . . search for each other through the world and through language that separates and enfolds them" (305). For a standard background reading, see Blair (143–145).

8. For two views on this controversy between African American men and women that came out of the closet during the turbulent 1960s and early 1970s, see Wallace and Hooks. In what some might regard as "critical cross-dressing," Calvin C. Hernton adds his voice to this controversy as he explores the relations between black female and male writers from a perspective that is a male *womanist* view in *The Sexual Mountain and Black Woman Writers*.

9. For this discussion of voodoo, I draw upon the work of Hurston (193–256); Hemenway (118–123); the essays on Folk Belief in Alan Dundes, ed.; and Mbiti (150–153).

10. In the blending of voices that takes place in "Hannah Kemhuff," coupled with the implicit and explicit references to Hurston, Walker draws the reader's attention to what Deborah E. McDowell refers to as "the theme of the thwarted female artist" (194). This theme informs the narrative discourse of Walker's *Meridian* (1976) as well as Toni Morrison's *The Bluest Eye* (1971) and *Sula* (1974). A classic statement on the subject of the thwarted female artist is, of course, Walker's own essay "In Search of Our Mothers' Gardens" (231–243). For a perceptive analysis of how gender may affect genre, see Keneth Kinnamon (121–134).

11. This spiritual is quoted from Wright (87).

WORKS CITED

Baker, Houston A., Jr. *Blues, Ideology, and Afro-American Literature*. Chicago: University of Chicago Press, 1984.

Baldwin, James. "Everybody's Protest Novel." *Notes of a Native Son*. Boston: Beacon, 1955, pp. 13–23.

Beavers, Herman. "I Yam What You Is and You Is What I Yam: Rhetorical Invisibility in James Alan McPherson's 'The Story of a Dead Man.'" *Callaloo* 9.4 (Fall 1986): 565–577.

Blair, Edward P. *The Abingdon Bible Handbook*. Nashville, TN: Abingdon, 1975.

Braxton, Joanne M. *Black Women Writing Autobiography: A Tradition Within a Tradition*. Philadelphia: Temple University Press, 1989.

Christian, Barbara T. "Trajectories of Self-Definition: Placing Contemporary Afro-American Women's Fiction." *Conjuring: Black Women, Fiction, and Literary Tradition*. Ed. Marjorie Pryse and Hortense J. Spillers. Bloomington: Indiana University Press, 1985, pp. 233–248.

Du Bois, W.E.B. *The Souls of Black Folk: Essays and Sketches*. New York: New American Library, 1969.

Dundes, Alan, ed. *Mother Wit from the Laughing Barrel: Readings in the Interpretation of Afro-American Folklore*. Englewood Cliffs, NJ: Prentice-Hall, 1973.

Fontenot, Chester J. "Alice Walker: 'The Diary of an African Nun' and Du Bois' Double Consciousness." *Sturdy Black Bridges: Visions of Black Women in Literature*. Eds. Roseann P. Bell, Bettye J. Parker, and Beverly Guy-Sheftall. Garden City, NY: Anchor/Doubleday, 1979, pp. 150–156.

Giovanni, Nikki. "Nikki-Rosa." *Black Feeling, Black Talk, Black Judgement*. New York: Morrow, 1970, pp. 58–59.

Gwin, Minrose C. "*Jubilee*: The Black Woman's Celebration of Human Community." *Conjuring: Black Women, Fiction and Literary Tradition*. Ed. Marjorie Pryse and Hortense J. Spillers. Bloomington: Indiana University Press, 1985, pp. 132–150.

Harris, Trudier. "Three Black Women Writers and Humanism: A Folk Perspective." *Black American Literature and Humanism*. Ed. R. Baxter Miller. Lexington: University Press of Kentucky, 1981, pp. 50–74.

Hemenway, Robert E. *Zora Neal Hurston: A Literary Biography*. Urbana: University of Illinois Press, 1977.

Hernton, Calvin C. *The Sexual Mountain and Black Women Writers: Adventure in Sex, Literature and Real Life*. New York: Anchor/Doubleday, 1987.

hooks, bell. *Ain't I a Woman?: Black Women and Feminism*. Boston: South End, 1981.

Hughes, Langston, ed. *The Best Short Stories by Negro Writers*. Boston: Little, Brown, 1967, pp. 490–496.

Hurston, Zora Neale. *Mules and Men*. 1935. Rpt. Bloomington: Indiana University Press, 1978.

Jones, Carolyn M., and Julia M. Hardy. "From Colonialism to Community: Religion and Culture in Charles H. Long's *Significations*." *Callaloo* 11.2 (Spring 1988): 258–271.

Kinnamon, Keneth. "Call and Response: Intertextuality in Two Autobiographical Works by Richard Wright and Maya Angelou." *Studies in Black American Literature, Vol. II: Belief vs. Theory in Black American Literary Criticism*. Eds. Joe Weixlmann and Houston A. Baker. Greenwood, FL: Penkevill, 1985, pp. 121–134.

Kristeva, Julia. *Tales of Love*. Translated by Leon S. Roudiez. New York: Columbia University Press, 1987.

Landy, Francis. "The Song of Songs." *The Literary Guide to the Bible*. Eds. Robert Alter and Frank Kermode. Cambridge, MA: Harvard University Press, 1987, pp. 305–319.

Lincoln, C. Eric. *The Black Muslims in America*. Boston: Beacon, 1961.

Long, Charles H. *Significations: Signs, Symbols, and Images in the Interpretation of Religion*. Philadelphia: Fortress, 1986.

Mbiti, John S. *Introduction to African Religion*. London: Heinemann, 1975.

McDowell, Deborah E. "New Directions for Black Feminist Criticism." *The New Feminist Criticism: Essays on Women, Literature and Theory*. Ed. Elaine Showalter. New York: Pantheon, 1985, pp. 186–199.

O'Neale, Sondra. "Reconstruction of the Composite Self: New Images of Black Women in Maya Angelou's Continuing Autobiography." *Black Women Writers (1950–1980): A Critical Evaluation*. Ed. Mari Evans. Garden City, NY: Anchor/Doubleday, 1984, pp. 25–36.

The Oxford Annotated Bible. New York: Oxford University Press, 1962, p. 815.

Saldívar, Ramón. *Figural Language in the Novel: The Flowers of Speech from Cervantes to Joyce*. Princeton, NJ: Princeton University Press, 1984.

Schorer, Mark. "Foreword." *Society and Self in the Novel*. Ed. Mark Schorer. New York: Columbia University Press, 1956, pp. vii–xvi.

Spillers, Hortense J. "Cross-Currents, Discontinuities: Black Women's Fiction." *Conjuring: Black Women, Fiction and Literary Tradition*. Ed. Marjorie Pryse and Hortense J. Spillers. Bloomington: Indiana University Press, 1985, pp. 249–261.

———. "'The Permanent Obliquity of In(pha)llibly Straight': In the Time of the Daughters and the Fathers." *Changing Our Own Words: Essays on Criticism, Theory, and Writing by Black Women*. Ed. Cheryl A. Wall. New Brunswick, NJ: Rutgers University Press, 1989, pp. 127–149.

Spivak, Gayatri. "The Letter as Cutting Edge." *In Other Worlds: Essays in Cultural Politics*. New York: Methuen, 1987, pp. 3–14.

Turner, Victor. *Dramas, Fields, and Metaphors: Symbolic Action in Human Society*. Ithaca, NY: Cornell University Press, 1974.

Walker, Alice. *In Love and Trouble: Stories of Black Women*. New York: Harcourt Brace Jovanovich, 1973.

———. *In Search of Our Mothers' Gardens*. New York: Harcourt Brace Jovanovich, 1983.

Wallace, Michelle. *Black Macho and the Myth of the Superwoman*. New York: Dial, 1978.

Washington, Mary Helen. "New Lives and New Letters: Black Women Writers at the End of the Seventies." *College English* 43.1 (January 1981): 1–11.

Wright, Richard. "The Literature of the Negro in the United States." *White Man, Listen!* 1957. Rpt. Garden City, NY: Anchor, 1964, pp. 69–105.

Displaced Abjection and States of Grace: Denise Chávez's *The Last of the Menu Girls*

Douglas Anderson

> Naturally I write about what I know, who I am. New Mexico. Texas. Chicanismo. Latinismo. Americanismo. Womanismo. Mujerotismo. Peopleismo. Worldismo. Peaceismo. Loveismo.
>
> Denise Chávez, "Heat and Rain (Testimonio)" (32)

Born in Las Cruces, New Mexico, in 1948, Denise Chávez is the author of a collection of short stories, *The Last of the Menu Girls* (1986); 17 plays produced throughout the United States and at the Edinburgh (Scotland) Festival of the Arts; and a forthcoming novel titled *Face of an Angel*. Chávez's work reflects her Chicano/a heritage, her concerns as a feminist woman writer, and her affection for the arid New Mexican landscape; yet, as her "testimonio" suggests, neither the work nor the writer can be reduced to a single essence or identity. In "Heat and Rain (Testimonio)," Chávez claims multiple allegiances and identities that are neither wholly integrated nor discrete and unrelated. While the terms for what Chávez knows and who she is are inflected by the Spanish-language ending "ismo," suggesting the priority of her Chicano/a heritage, the fact that this suffix is appended to English as well as Spanish words preserves the sense of difference within identity. This difference, in turn, is qualified by an implicit claim of unity or wholeness. Playfully attached to all the words describing Chávez's allegiances and self, the suffix "ismo" suggests exuberant inclusiveness, an identity that is multiple and yet one.

This multiple yet cohesive self Chávez celebrates in her "Testimonio" is also explored in her collection of short stories, *The Last of the Menu Girls*. Set in southern New Mexico and west Texas in the 1950s and 1960s, the book's seven interlocking stories center on the childhood and young adulthood of a Chicana named Rocio Esquibel. Though sometimes described as a coming-of-age narrative, the separate stories of *The Last of the Menu Girls* are not arranged chronologically and do not plot a single, continuous trajectory toward an achieved, unified self. What they do instead is present moments of the protagonist's life, moments of loss, moments of longing, and moments when the multiple self is balanced in what Chávez has called a "state of grace" (Juarez 10). This ephemeral state of grace is opposed to a conception of the self as a permanent essence, a conception that Chávez identifies with the attempt to repudiate the body and project it onto others in a bid for social power. This essay explores the relation between displaced abjection and social hierarchy as it is depicted in the title story of Chávez's collection.

"The Last of the Menu Girls" begins with the categories of a job application. Rocio Esquibel, the story's 17-year-old protagonist and narrator, is applying for a position in the nutrition department of the local hospital. Along with the categories of name, age, and present employment, the application Rocio fills out contains one that is less familiar: "previous experience with the sick and dying" (13). The short answer to the question on the form is the name of Rocio's deceased aunt, Eutilia. The long answer is Chávez's story itself, a narrative that explores her character's desire to construct mortality as something that can be contained in a category and distanced from the self as a discrete "experience."

Set in a hospital, "The Last of the Menu Girls" examines the desire to escape death and, more specifically, the body that dies, the body that grows sick, ages, falls victim to accident, the body that ties us to contingency and humbles the will. Through its biological functions, this body is inseparably linked to what Julia Kristeva calls the abject, the nonobject that is responded to with loathing or disgust because it opens up a void of meaninglessness in which the ego faces annihilation. Rocio makes this connection between the sick and injured body and loathsome or abject substances while insisting on her unwillingness to become a nurse:

> I never wanted to be a nurse, ever. All that gore and blood and grief. I was not squeamish as my sister Mercy, who could not stand to put her hands into a sinkful of dirty dishes filled with floating food—wet bread, stringy vegetables and bits of softened meat. Still, I didn't like the touch, the smells. (13–14)

Because of its connection with abjection, the body is not something to which death simply happens; it is itself the constant presence of death as it threatens those principles or qualities we deem essential to our humanity: will, intellect, order, identity.

A common response to the abject body, "The Last of the Menu Girls" suggests, is flight or denial, the effort to transcend the body and leave it behind. Seeking to elude the body and its humiliation, one imagines oneself as pure will, as that which transcends the physical through its power to judge, impose order, create categories, ascribe meaning. In her roles as official "menu girl" and unofficial and unwilling nurse, Rocio Esquibel illustrates this effort of transcendence both on a personal level and as it defines one society's response to the abject body. As the "menu girl," the person who brings menus to patients' rooms and takes their meal orders, Rocio represents an administrative or institutional response to the body's vulnerability. The hospital is charged with managing illness and with portraying illness as something manageable; the menus Rocio distributes are part of this project. Categorized by day of the week, meal, courses, and selections for each course, the menus structure and mark off the biological process of ingestion that otherwise comes perilously close to processes of elimination that connect the self to decay and death. Sharing a leftover meal in the hospital's laundry room, Rocio and a friend eat fried chicken while "sandwiched between bins of feces and urine stained sheets" (29). Here, the individual is not a self-contained entity but a fragile border between biological processes that threaten to collapse into one another. The menus Rocio distributes, however, are meant to assure sick and, often, dying patients that the process of ingestion is unrelated to other processes linked with death. Eating is a mental or spiritual act, and the patients, at least in this aspect of their experience, are not ailing or afflicted bodies, but represent a disembodied power of choice.

As unofficial nurse, Rocio participates in another kind of official denial of the body and its afflictions. The nurse is, of course, a person charged with the management of illness. Allied with control, she or he is the very antithesis of the patient whose illness represents a falling away from order, requiring management. The nurse's position separate from and above the illness and death she/he treats is consecrated by her/his knowledge of disease and of the cases of individual patients. Thus, the further Rocio is drawn into the role of nurse, the greater are her efforts to acquire this expertise: "Now when I walked into a room I knew the patient's history, the cause of illness. I began to study individual cases with great attention, turning to a copy of *The Family Physician*, which had its place among my father's old books in his abandoned study" (35). Rocio's efforts to master patient histories, causes of illness, and individual cases suggest that the nurse's difference from his or her patient is produced through much the same classifying strategy represented by the hospital menus. Now, however, the object of classification is not food and bodily functions but illness and, at least in part, people who have become ill.

The desire to control and escape the body hidden in Rocio's denied wish to be a nurse is evident when we consider that Rocio does not want to be just any nurse, but the nurse whose painted image adorns one of the hospital walls: Florence Nightingale. In this image, Nightingale looks benevolently down on wounded soldiers so that she is less a body than the power of vision. Struck by the painting, Rocio fantasizes becoming like that nurse of folklore:

> I saw myself in her, helping all of mankind, forgetting and absolving all my sick, my own dying, especially relatives, all of them so far away, removed. I never wanted to be like Great Aunt Eutilia, or Dona Mercedes with the holes in her back, or my mother, her scarred legs, her whitened thighs. (17)

As this passage shows, Rocio's desire to be Florence Nightingale is not motivated only or even primarily by altruism. Her fantasy of becoming the etherealized figure that dispenses benediction to a suffering humanity is a fantasy of being herself immune to or exempt from the afflictions of the body. As a benevolent figure "helping all of mankind," Rocio would have no personal part in the suffering she eased; the sick and dying would remain comfortably "far away, removed."

Rocio's fantasy of becoming Florence Nightingale reveals not only the desire for personal immunity from the body's suffering but something of what that desire means for relations with other people. Casting herself as an ethereal or transcendent figure, Rocio necessarily casts others in the role of the abject body in need of absolution, the abject body she wishes to escape. Her fantasy of transcendence, in other words, is sustained through the projection of the body's suffering onto others and the perception of these others as ineluctably different from the self. Although Rocio is actually a sympathetic character, her need to dissociate herself from the body commits her not only to obsessive judgment of others but to an attitude that denies the humanity of others perceived to participate in the body's abjection. Thus, when Rocio first meets her new employer, Mr. Smith, and finds that he is walleyed and suffers curvature of the spine, her need to create a boundary between herself and his affliction leads her to figure him as something subhuman:

> Was I to work for this gnome? I wanted to rescue souls, not play attendant to this crippled, dried up specimen, this cartilaginous insect with his misshapen head and eyes that peered out to me like the marbled eyes of statues one sees in museums. History preserves its freaks. God, was my job to do the same? No, never! (18)

The sophomoric tone of this internal monologue, the arrogant identification of the self with an abstract history, may allow us to laugh at Rocio's reaction to Mr. Smith, yet the hysteria and, I think, latent violence of her rhetoric are also meant to be taken seriously. The desire for transcendence, Chávez seems to suggest, easily turns aggressive in its effort to figure the other as not like the self. The difference posed between the transcendent self and the abject other consists, ultimately, in a denial of the other's humanity, a figuring of him or her as a nonself.

Though Rocio's youth makes her reaction to bodily suffering particularly intense, that reaction itself, shared with other characters of the story, seems to issue from a culturally determined need to preserve a sense of selfhood or ego identity. Intimations of the body's vulnerability threaten to break down the boundaries that define selves and to reduce the uniqueness of individuals to the terrible undifferentiation of bodies sharing abjection. This power of the body's suffering to dissolve, damage, or diminish identity is suggested most clearly in the way the patients encountered by Rocio respond to their own suffering. A central element in their response is shame or a sense of defilement. The story of Elizabeth Rainey, a young woman admitted to Rocio's hospital for a D and C, for example, suggests how interdependent are our sense of bodily integrity and our sense of a discrete and dignified self. The surgical procedure Elizabeth Rainey is scheduled to undergo is one that transgresses the body's boundaries, threatening the fiction of the body's inviolability and the sense of dignity identified with it. Feeling her identity impugned by the vulnerability of her body, Elizabeth Rainey reacts with "self-loathing" and a desperate attempt to reconstruct on the level of social interaction the transgressed boundaries of the self in the body (27). She tries to keep her suffering "self-contained" and, when Rocio enters her room to take her order, violently tells her to "go away" (27).

This need to reestablish boundaries breached by physical illness or invasive medical procedures is one that Rocio encounters repeatedly in her dealings with sick people:

> How many people yelled to me to go away that summer, have yelled since then, countless people, of all ages, sick people, really sick people, dying people, people who were well and still rudely tied into their needs for privacy and space, affronted by these constant impositions from, of all people, the menu girl! (27)

Rainey's desperate effort to preserve "privacy and space," then, would seem to be a reaction typical of people whose sense of bodily inviolability has been challenged. The body's vulnerability impugns the integrity of the self, and this damage to the self is repaired or disguised through the reinforcement of social barriers. In this project, the ill and the "well" are likely to cooperate, for an individual's un-self-contained suffering threatens not only his or her own identity but that of the "well" person. Thus, Elizabeth Rainey's effort to drive Rocio from her room is complemented by Rocio's frightened withdrawal into herself: "I shrank back into myself and trembled behind the door. I never went back into her room. How could I? It was too terrible a vision, for in her I saw myself, all life, all suffering" (27). The other's abjection, as Rocio here recognizes, touches and claims us despite our efforts to escape because it is, finally, part of "all life." As Elizabeth Rainey's barely suppressed rage suggests, moreover, the social codes dictating the containment of abjection within the person of the sufferer may not always be powerful enough to keep it from overflowing onto others. Nor is the complicity of the sufferer in this containment always to be counted on. A dying patient named Mrs. Daniels, for example, refuses to contain the "outrage and loathing" she feels, letting her "vast torrential feelings of sorrow and hate and fear . . . fall wherever they would, on whomever they might" (30). When the sufferer refuses or is unable to contain abjection, Chávez suggests, the response of the healthy is typically one of determined deafness to the sufferer's calls for empathy:

> Who of us has not heard the angry choked words of crying people, listened, not wanting to hear, then shut our ears, said enough, I don't want to. Who has not seen the fearful tear-streamed faces, known the blank eyes and felt the holding back, and, like smiling thoughtless children, said: "I was in the next room, I couldn't help hearing, I heard, I saw, you didn't know, did you? I know." (30)

Confronting us with abjection, the other's suffering threatens to overwhelm the boundaries of the self and dissolve identity. In response, we may retreat further into the privacy guaranteed by the rules of decorum, the solitary "room" of the individual ego or self.

The threat that the abject body represents to selfhood and the social mechanisms invoked to contain and distance that body might lead us to think that the fear and reaction produced by abjection are universal. Yet Chávez's story makes clear that perceptions of and reactions to the abject are both culturally relative and correlated with social power. Indeed, *The Last of the Menu Girls* suggests that distinctions of social power are derived from and reinforced by a more fundamental or symbolically rich distinction between transcendent selves and abject bodies. As Peter Stallybrass and Allon White suggest in *The Politics and Poetics of Transgression*, the hierarchical order mapped on the body's parts and processes is the privileged model and metaphor for social hierarchy (26, 191). Making a similar point in "The Social Formation of Racist Discourse," David Theo Goldberg argues that "corporeal properties furnish . . . the metaphorical medium for distinguishing the pure from the impure, the diseased from the clean and acceptable" and that these distinctions are the basis of social hierarchy (306).

As a principle underlying social hierarchy, the idea of abjection does not relate to the relative youth, perfection, or health of the body alone but to a variety of social conditions or identities in which disempowerment or marginalization are equated with the abject body's vulnerability or passivity, its lack of will. The "others" figured by our culture as abject, then, are not only the sick, physically handicapped, and dying, but women, ethnic and racial minorities, individuals marginalized for their sexual preferences, and the poor. Chávez's story suggests that women are the group most insistently identified with the abject body and that this identification plays a fundamental role in women's oppression. Mrs. Rainey's operation threatens to damage her selfhood not only because it undermines the fiction of the closed and inviolable self but because it ties her to a feminine identity already figured as vulnerable, damaged, abject. This association of women with their bodies and, hence, with the abject is made especially clear early in the story when Rocio is discussing her inaptitude for nursing. Mentioning her distaste for the touch and smell of leftover food in dishwater, Rocio continues without transition,

> When I touched my mother's feet, I looked away, held my nose with one hand, the other with finger laced along her toes, pulling and popping them into place. "It really helps my arthritis, baby—you don't know. Pull my toes, I'll give you a dollar, find my girdle, and I'll give you two." (14)

As this passage suggests, it is the woman's body, epitomized in the mother's body, which is culturally most closely identified with abjection. Reference to a girdle suggests that cultural prescriptions of proper attire for women are related to the construction of women's bodies as sites of abjection that require control. At the same time, construction of the female body as abject is related to the fetishization of that body:

> "Look at my feet. . . . Aren't they ugly? And up here, look where I had the operations . . . ugly, they stripped them and still they hurt me."
>
> She [Rocio's mother] rubbed her battered flesh wistfully, placed a delicate and lovely hand on her right thigh. Mother said proudly, truthfully, "I still have lovely thighs." (14)

Cultural identification of women with their bodies, Chávez seems to suggest, is also their identification with the abject.

The role that identification with the abject plays in women's oppression is paralleled by the role it plays in the oppression of nonwhite racial or ethnic minorities. In the section titled "Juan Maria/the Nose," Chávez introduces the character of Juan Maria, a poor Mexican man who has entered the United States illegally and, during a drunken brawl, has had his nose bitten off. Defaced, his body's boundaries broken so that he is open to the world, Juan Maria seems to be the archetypal figure of abjection. The loss of Juan Maria's nose metaphorically captures the effect that poverty, displacement from his own culture, and vulnerability to exploitation have on his social identity. His body's boundaries brutally transgressed, Juan Maria has no identity for the nurses who hover around his exhausted figure. For them, he is faceless and nameless, just a "wetback" or "alien" who has no claim on their humanity.

The nurses' efforts to figure Juan Maria as "alien" and "other" are related to their fear that his suffering will touch and include them. Juan Maria's abjection is defined by his loss of personal boundaries, his vulnerability to casual violence, and his nonidentity for an American society that does not recognize him. A "wetback" without boundaries, Juan Maria represents a fluid principle of suffering and abjection that threatens to spill over onto others, and it is to contain a suffering that seems pervasive or contagious that the nurses seek to inscribe him within an abject identity, to define him as nonhuman. As the head nurse, Esperanza Gonzalez, observes, "Some of them, they ain't human" (32).

In figuring Juan Maria as "one of those aliens," an absolute other whose suffering is safely confined to his person, the nurses reconstitute on the level of prejudice or psychology a political or geographical border that has been breached by Juan Maria's illegal entrance into the United States, and suggest something of the meaning of those borders. Stallybrass and White argue in *The Politics and Poetics of Transgression* that

> The high/low opposition in each of . . . four symbolic domains—psychic forms, the human body, geographical space and the social order—is the fundamental basis to mechanisms of ordering and sense making in European cultures. . . . Cultures "think themselves" in the most immediate and affective ways through the combined symbolisms of these four hierarchies. Furthermore, . . . transgressing the rules of hierarchy and order in any one of the domains may have major consequences in the others. (3)

Geographical borders can be analogical to the interpersonal barriers we erect between ourselves and the other defined as abject, and their transgression is attended with some of the fear and loathing that attends transgression of the body's boundaries. Through the transcoding of two symbolisms by which cultures "think themselves," undocumented immigrants like Juan Maria become, as Nurse Gonzalez puts it, an "epidemic" that threatens to infect the geopolitical body with the abjection of poverty (31).

Just as Juan Maria's social marginality or oppression can be represented and rationalized through his identification with the abject body, the social power to impose that marginalization represents itself in images of the body's control and transcendence. Thus, Rocio identifies the hospital's management or control of the body's abjection as a white, and particularly, white male privilege and project: "I never wanted to be a nurse. Never. The smells. The pain. What was I to do then, working in a hospital, in that place of white women, whiter men with square faces?" (17). Rocio's doubts about the nursing profession seem to hinge on her identity as a Chicana, or, rather, on the fact that she is neither white nor male. The privilege of controlling and thereby transcending the body's ills is one that gender and ethnicity bar her from, and, indeed, the hierarchies of gender and ethnicity are conflated. Men are "whiter" than women, and Rocio, neither white nor male, is doubly disqualified, doubly declassed. Nevertheless, Rocio does take a position in the white hospital, which, in fact, seems to be almost entirely staffed by Chicanas like the nurses who symbolically exile Juan Maria. Though controlling or transcending the body is a white male privilege, the sign of this white male power is the ability to absent the self from the unpleasant details of managing the abject body. No white doctors appear in the story, and the task of the body's management appears to have been left to those lower in the social hierarchy. As Esperanza tells her Chicana colleagues, "We're just here to clean up the mess" (32).

As proxies for missing white male doctors, the Chicana nurses are closer to an abject status just by virtue of their proximity to sick bodies and their processes. But if Esperanza and her nursing colleagues occupy a border or liminal position between white male transcendence and the abject bodies of the hospital, it is not only the nature of their work that places them there. As women of color, the nurses are themselves associated with the abject body in need of control, and it is this fact that explains their reaction to Juan Maria. Close to the socially defined abjection of the poor and injured Mexican, vulnerable, like him, to suggestions that they are on the wrong side of a geopolitical border that separates transcendent selves from abject others, the nurses need all the more desperately to figure Juan Maria as an absolute other. The linguistic violence the nurses turn on Maria, consequently, parallels the physical violence with which his nose is cut off. Both acts are intended to deface the other in order to destroy his resemblance to the self.

Though the attempt to figure the other as abject presupposes pure identities and absolute boundaries between conditions, *The Last of the Menu Girls* suggests that both these boundaries and the identities they create are fictions. The irony of Esperanza's effort symbolically to exile Juan Maria is one that accompanies all efforts to project or displace abjection onto the other, the irony that the thing we want to escape by defining it as outside, as not us, already is us. Esperanza is a Chicana whose face and body reveal a despised Amerindian heritage. She is herself a marginalized person in white-dominated American society, and her revulsion for Juan Maria is a revulsion for herself: "Esperanza was dark and squat, pura India, tortured by her very face" (33). The pain caused by displaced abjection, then, is not limited to the depreciated or inferiorized identity imposed upon the other. Since this other is a negative image of the self, displaced abjection also involves self-hatred and self-alienation, enforcing a white system of social classification that depreciates them just as it defaces Juan Maria, Esperanza, and the other Chicana nurses who identify against and misrecognize themselves.

The denial and misrecognition of self produced by social hierarchies based on displaced abjection is made especially clear through the image that tempts Rocio to identify with white power and values. The image of the nurse Rocio encounters on her first visit to the hospital is that of an etherealized Florence Nightingale above and out of reach of the pain she salves. This image of transcendence is a seductive one, and Rocio identifies with it: "I saw myself in her, helping all mankind" (17). The transcendence proposed in the image of Florence Nightingale, however, is not a universal or democratic one. Representing not only the nursing profession, but white and, more specifically, Anglo-Saxon womanhood, the image of Florence Nightingale claims a transcendence of the body that is exclusive to whites or Anglos. As a woman of color, Rocio's position relative to this privilege of transcendence is a necessarily ambiguous one. The illusoriness of white transcendence aside, Rocio can never really be Florence Nightingale because her ethnicity and brown skin identify her with the abject body Nightingale's vision distances and controls. Recognizing herself in Florence Nightingale, Rocio misrecognizes herself.

Though she is seduced by the image of Florence Nightingale, Rocio's marginality within the racial or ethnic hierarchy imposed by white culture and the gender hierarchies of both Anglo-American and Chicano culture ultimately enables her to resist identification with alienating and sterile images of transcendence. In *Chicano Narrative*, Ramón Saldívar argues that the position of Chicanos and Chicanas between Mexican and Anglo-American cultures can be a source of empowerment and liberation. Partaking of both and neither culture, Chicanos/as occupy an extraterritorial space where ideologies may conflict and neutralize each other or perhaps fail to reach altogether. What may look like marginality within both cultures is actually a "precarious utopian margin *between* the two," a space of resistance to or refuge from ideological control and cultural impositions (Saldívar 174). Like Saldívar, Trinh T. Minh-ha suggests that the affirmation of hybrid or multiple identities can disrupt an ideology of unified subjectivity that enforces the oppression of others and the repression of otherness within the self. But she stresses too that ethnic and gender identities are not themselves given or natural essences. Identity must be constructed. And because identity is constructed, it includes difference, and "refers no more to a consistent pattern of sameness than to an inconsequential process of otherness" (Minh-ha 371–372). Resistance to hegemony, Minh-ha suggests in "Not You/Like You: Post-Colonial Women and the Interlocking Questions of Identity and Difference," involves recognizing and re-creating the difference(s) within the self. Because hegemony works by reducing diversity to hierarchized duality, it is opposed when differences are chosen and multiplied: "otherness becomes empowerment, critical difference when it is not given but recreated" (374).

Elaborating a concept of resistance similar to those of Saldívar and Minh-ha, Chávez depicts Rocio's choice of her Chicana identity/difference as a source of empowerment. Rocio eventually rejects both white and patriarchal ideals of transcendence in order to create a Chicano and, more specifically, a Chicana acceptance of the body in its sensuality and vulnerability to abjection. Affirmation of the body and embrace/creation of Chicana identity are interdependent projects for Rocio, and the progress of each is measured largely in terms of her relationship with her Aunt Eutilia. Nevertheless, the Chicana identity Rocio embraces cannot be reduced to the terms of an inherited biological essence. Mediated by dream and memory, Rocio's kinship with Eutilia and the Chicana identity that kinship represents for her are also created and chosen.

Eutilia has been dead for five years by the time Rocio goes to work at the hospital, yet she continues to live on, and die, in her niece's memory. When the reader first encounters her, she is an old woman dying in Rocio's father's abandoned study. In great pain and delirious, her body yielding to disintegration, Eutilia might be seen as the epitome of abjection:

> Great Aunt Eutilia smelled like the mercilessly sick. At first, a vague, softened aroma of tiredness and spilled food. And later, the full-blown emptyings of the dying: gas, putrefaction and fetid lucidity. Her body poured out long, held-back odors. She wet her diapers and sheets and knocked over medicines and glasses of tepid water, leaving in the air an unpleasant smell. (Chávez 14)

Yet Eutilia's abjection is not the static or bounded condition that social hierarchy figures it as. Her body in the process of decay or dissolution, Eutilia represents a process of continual change and transformation that makes it impossible to isolate or partition particular states of being, impossible to distinguish one from another. Conflating the categories of birth and death, Eutilia is both an "old lady" and "a small child" who wears a diaper and wets herself; her deathbed is described as a crib (13). Eutilia's bodily dissolution, likewise, is figured as a kind of production or creation as her body releases discharges, and containers of medicine and water are made to give up their contents. Finally, Eutilia is a figure that combines death and artistic creation. She is identified with dancing (her own and Rocio's), with playing the piano, and with the creation of images from the congealed and sterile walls of the father's study. The fact that the images created by Eutilia ultimately dissolve into "jagged, broken waves" suggests that the creativity she represents is linked to temporality and death (13).

Identified with the abject body, Eutilia represents both the subversion of dichotomies like birth and death, childhood and age, creation and dissolution, and an ongoing transformation in which the self is continually made other or different. Embracing her kinship with Eutilia, Rocio also chooses the abject body and a Chicana "identity" in which the body's difference is accepted.

Rocio takes up this "legacy" from Eutilia through dream and dance, fluid forms that acknowledge the interdependence of body, world, self, and other. Thus, early in the story, Rocio performs a dream dance around the bed of her dying aunt: "Could I have absolved your dying by my life? Could I have lessened your agony with my spirit-filled dance in the deep darkness?" (15). A primitive ritual of redemption in which the aunt's dying is "absolved," the dance Rocio performs seems to enact a sense of her own distinctness from her aunt, her sense that youth empowers her to absolve the shame or guilt of the body's abjection. Similarly, although Rocio chants a song of fleshly identification with her aunt and mother, she is not yet able to acknowledge that this identification binds her to the body's deterioration and death: "I am your flesh and my mother's flesh and you are . . . are . . . Eutilia stared at me" (14).

In a later dream, Rocio again dances for Eutilia, but this time her dance has another meaning:

> Eutilia stirred. She was tired. She did not recognize anyone. I danced around the bed, crossed myself, en el nombre del padre, del hijo y del espiritu santo, crossed forehead, chin and breast, begged for forgiveness even as I danced.
>
> And on waking, I remembered. *Nabos. Turnips.* But of course. (26)

No longer presuming to bring absolution, Rocio needs it for herself. She identifies with the suffering and abjection of her aunt and, in the process, recovers and re-creates a Chicana identity alienated by racism. Recalling the Spanish word for turnip, Rocio affirms the body and Chicana identity together, making "that awesome leap into myself . . . , confronting at every turn, the flesh, its lingering cries" (36). This leap into the self, however, does not inaugurate a fixed, unified, or essentialized identity. Like the other interlocking stories in Chávez's collection, "The Last of the Menu Girls" depicts a moment of balance in ongoing transformation, a fleeting "state of grace."

WORKS CITED

Chávez, Denise. "Heat and Rain (Testimonio)." *Breaking the Boundaries: Latina Writing and Critical Readings*. Eds. Asuncion Horno-Delgado et al. Amherst: University of Massachusetts Press, 1989, pp. 27–32.

———. *The Last of the Menu Girls*. Houston: Arte Publico Press, 1986.

Goldberg, David Theo. "The Social Formation of Racist Discourse." *The Anatomy of Racism*. Ed. David Theo Goldberg. Minneapolis: University of Minnesota Press, 1990, pp. 295–318.

Juarez, Macario. "Performance Writer Previews Upcoming Tour." *New Mexico State University Round Up* 28 (February 1992): 10.

Minh-ha, Trinh T. "Not You/Like You: Post-Colonial Women and the Interlocking Questions of Identity and Difference." *Making Face, Making Soul—Haciendo Caras: Creative and Critical Perspectives by Women of Color*. Ed. Gloria Anzaldua. San Francisco: Aunt Lute Foundation Books, 1990, pp. 371–375.

Saldívar, Ramón. *Chicano Narrative: The Dialectics of Difference*. Madison: University of Wisconsin Press, 1990.

Stallybrass, Peter, and Allon White. *The Politics and Poetics of Transgression*. Ithaca, NY: Cornell University Press, 1986.

Dorothy Parker's Perpetual Motion

Ken Johnson

Somehow it has always been rather easy to dismiss Dorothy Parker and her writing from the collective literary consciousness. After all, she never produced a "big" work such as a novel, and her few plays did not achieve long runs. In addition, she shares the ironic fate of most writers who become identified primarily as humorists working with shorter literary forms: they are not considered "serious." Parker's many celebrated, flip wisecracks (e.g., "One more drink and I'll be under the host.") brought her the kind of notoriety that rarely carves a secure niche for itself in the Westminster Abbey of literary history. And worst of all, for those readers and critics who like to detonate a writer's achievement with unfortunate circumstances from her personal life, Dorothy Parker provides a perfect case of literary self-combustion. Her lack of self-discipline was notorious; her unsuccessful marriages, divorces, abortion, suicide attempts, and alcoholism invite snickering disapproval; and her dwindling output as years passed can reinforce a preconceived idea of marginality.

Yet Dorothy Parker produced a substantial body of work in a range of literary modes, including three volumes of poetry, three plays, several screenplays, a significant number of book and play reviews, and three volumes of short stories, as well as other uncollected stories, poems, and articles. Her career spanned more than four decades, from the late 1910s to the early 1960s, and from the beginning of her popularity until the time of her death, her name carried celebrity status—in other words, once she established herself as a writer and gained an appreciative audience, she never completely faded from the public memory, regardless of her progressively dwindling output. More importantly, in terms of American literary history she was one of the formative voices of the influential *New Yorker* magazine, as well as one of the few women writers of short stories in America during the 1920s and 1930s who put out popularly best-selling collections of stories (*Laments for the Living*, 1930; *After Such Pleasures*, 1933; *Here Lies*, 1939) that have remained in print into the 1990s (in their reincarnation as *The Portable Dorothy Parker* from Viking Press). In contrast, other women fiction writers contemporary to Parker, such as Ruth Suckow, Ellen Glasgow, and Zora Neale Hurston, often saw their works pass out of print, for various reasons, during their lifetimes.

Also, Parker's stories were admired not just by the purchasing reading masses, but by other short story writers acclaimed in their own right both then and now. In 1929, Fitzgerald encouraged Maxwell Perkins at Scribner's to publish Parker (Fitzgerald 25), and in 1938 he commended his daughter for reading (and "liking") Parker's stories (Fitzgerald 215). Parker's short stories, the most substantial portion of her output, display many of the same structural techniques hailed as ground-breaking experiments in the stories of Lardner, Faulkner, and Hemingway: the dramatic monologue, the "dialogue" story, and the juxtaposition of internal and external realities. One of Parker's fortes, the soliloquy story, has no exact precedent in the history of American short stories. Considering all these factors that would suggest the need for a closer study of Parker's work, it is curious indeed that sustained critical attention has rarely been given to her writing.

Four of her stories ("A Telephone Call," "Here We Are," "The Waltz," and "From the Diary of a New York Lady") demonstrate Parker's unique handling of the short story form, and the technical sophistication of stories such as these should secure her a stable position within the canon. What Parker generally brings to the short story form, and to these four in particular, is a unique use of repetition, creating a kind of eternal *perpetuum mobile* that consigns the stories' characters to an endless experiencing of their own superficiality and emptiness. Whether the structural handling of such stories prefigures or even imitates the technical approaches of Hemingway, Lardner, or Faulkner is less important for this essay than how Parker's stories expand on the possibilities of the form in her own way. Before examining Parker's use of repetition, however, a brief consideration of critical responses to her *oeuvre* is necessary in order to appreciate the ironic paradox that the most significant structural and thematic aspect of her fiction—repetition—is also the aspect that has probably contributed most to the frequent dismissal of her work as shallow, usually by male critics. On the other hand, feminist critics have been slow to reevaluate Parker's work for reasons that are not altogether clear.

The typical posthumous critical appraisal of Parker's overall achievement has been neatly, and nattily, summarized by Brendan Gill in his introduction to *The Portable Dorothy Parker*: "The span of her work is narrow, and what it embraces is often slight" (xxvii). Gill's introduction is a study in supreme condescension, which is especially unfortunate since *The Portable Dorothy Parker* is the only collection of Parker's works in print. Gill writes approvingly of other writers from the 1920s and early 1930s, such as Fitzgerald, Lardner, Hemingway, and "the other boys in the back room" (xxii), and then as a sop to the reputation of their erstwhile female companion, he states that it is not "surprising that there should pop up among them, glass in hand, hat askew, her well-bred voice full of soft apologies, the droll, tiny figure of Mrs. Parker" (xxii).

Gill's backhanded dismissal of Parker and her writing differs from other critical judgments only in its extended explicitness. Mordecai Richler, while defending the selections for his anthology *The Best of Modern Humor*, pauses briefly to explain why Parker was not included: in 1980 her style seems, to him, too "brittle." Academic critics have also tended to avoid Parker: she rates only a few references in passing throughout the first two volumes of *No Man's Land*, Gilbert and Gubar's monumental study of twentieth-century American women writers, and no attention at all is given to her in a large-scale reference work such as *American Women Writers: Bibliographical Essays*.

While noting the resurrection by feminist scholars of so many previously forgotten American women writers, one might wonder why Dorothy Parker's works have not been likewise resuscitated during the past two decades. For one thing, the reanimation of literary reputations seems to occur more frequently with nineteenth-century women writers—for example, Elizabeth Drew Stoddard, Rebecca Harding Davis, or Margaret Fuller—in order to demonstrate a number of points: that women were indeed producing substantial writing in an otherwise male-dominated writers' marketplace, that women writers were frequently depicting the unique experiences of female characters from distinctly feminist viewpoints, and that such women writers and their works have been silenced through the hegemony of patriarchal criticism.

Of these concerns, only the last one really applies to Parker's case. Early in her career she cracked the publishing market: *Vanity Fair* began publishing her poetry in 1914, and her first published story appeared in H.L. Mencken and George Nathan's *The Smart Set* in 1922. Once established, Parker was sought after on the basis of her ability and popularity, and she has never been completely swept into the dustbin of literary amnesia, as was the case for many nineteenth- and early twentieth-century women writers. While Parker's fiction is filled with female characters, many of whom dominate the center of their respective stories, her work is generally devoid of the approaches to women's experiences that often appeal first to academic feminist critics: the kind of overt feminist agenda associated with the fiction of numerous later twentieth-century women writers such as Toni Morrison or Alice Walker, or the depiction of a successful (or doomed) awakening of a female protagonist, or a celebration of a community of independent, self-sustaining women. Nonetheless, in her interview for the *Paris Review* in the 1950s, Parker labeled herself a feminist who had been active in the women's movement since the time when New York City "was scarcely safe from buffaloes" (77). But in the same passage she criticizes the lack of artistry in the works of women writers such as Edna Ferber and Kathleen Norris and condemns their proliferation as a result of the very struggle for equality in which she claims to have been a participant. During most of her career she seemed indifferent, even adverse, to placing herself within a tradition of women's writing: in 1929, while working on a novel she would never complete, she wrote in a letter to Alexander Woollcott, "Dear God, please make me stop writing like a woman. For Jesus Christ's sake, amen" (Meade 203). Finally, Parker has probably missed out on a warm embrace from feminist critics in part because, after all, she has been dead only since 1967, and while her reputation has languished, the fact that it has never been firmly established or dismissed places her in a weird nebula where she seems to need neither reevaluation nor rescue—when actually she needs both.

Parker's work has regularly been dismissed, moreover, on the basis of triviality, in content, style, and technique, usually with the implication underlying such a critique that the content, style, and technique of her contemporary male short story writers are hallmarks of substance and depth. Apparently bullfights, African safaris, washed up expatriate writers in France, and ill-starred southern gentry and field hands serve as more suitable subjects for fiction than the lives of middle- and upper-class white urbanites, usually women. Certainly Parker's subject matter does not encompass a wide range of social classes or situations, but the same could be said of Faulkner's subject matter, or Fitzgerald's, or just about any writer's, depending on the slant from which it is described. Instead of merely cataloguing the number of different topics an author chooses to deal with, a better way to consider an author's subject matter might be to study the methods in which it is presented. Parker's female characters rarely lead lives beyond the role defined by patriarchy (mother, wife, mistress, housekeeper, secretary), and their abiding concerns often revolve around the status of a relationship with a man. These women are frequently the victims of the roles created for them by society, but Parker's stories do not deal solely with the oppression of women: Parker's male characters are no less victims of their own circumstances. More importantly, all of Parker's characters, male or female, usually create their predicaments in the same degree to which other forces contribute to those predicaments.

However, Parker usually portrays her characters within only a brief time frame (the consequences of which will be discussed shortly), frequently avoids giving them distinguishing idiosyncratic characteristics, and often uses the speaking passages of a central character to reveal characterization. Indeed, Parker develops many of her typical female characters through their speech rather than through narrative exposition—reflecting Rosalind Coward's assertion that in the twentieth century "above all, the female protagonist has become the speaking sex" (39)—and in all of Parker's stories mentioned earlier (except "Here We Are"), the speech or writing of the female protagonist *is* the story. Parker clearly intends to work with surfaces, an intention that is neither accidental nor a botched attempt to analyze the motivation of her characters. Paula Treichler has observed that a "language-centered analysis" of Parker's stories is crucial due to their stylistic intricacy (46–47). Unfortunately, a result of Parker's constant stylistic repetition of action and language, coupled with the naturally repetitive cadences of a character's pervasive speaking voice, has often been the critical charge of shallowness. The point of so many Parker stories, however, is to portray *shallowness itself* as it occurs in the lives of her characters. In fact, Parker's technique of repeating action and repeating language creates an innovative fictional effect of perpetual motion in many of her stories that would seem to extend the lives of her characters beyond the beginning and ending boundary of each story.

Much of this sense of perpetual shallowness is achieved through the time frame established in Parker's stories. Arthur Kinney has described her fiction as "radically condensed" (143), and it is especially in her more original short stories (such as those mentioned earlier) that the shortened time frame contributes to the thematic effect of superficiality. Indeed, Jean Pickering has suggested that all the elements of a short story, including "structure, theme, characterisation, language . . . are influenced by [their] particular relation to time" (53). The dancer in "The Waltz" thinks her poisonous thoughts only throughout the duration of a single waltz; the voice of the soliloquizer in "A Telephone Call" speaks as long as it takes to mull through six pages of stream-of-consciousness thinking; and the newlyweds in "Here We Are" converse for about half an hour while their train approaches New York City. "From the Diary of a New York

Lady" follows, obviously, an altogether different structure with its five-paragraph daily entries and therefore a different kind of time frame, yet the tone of each entry gives the sense of hasty composition, in part through the capsule references to repeated and similar activities. In each case the time frame of action is severely limited, and consequently all aspects of the respective stories are affected, the most significant being characterization. None of the characters in these stories achieves the kind of full development that critics, and readers, often seek. As a matter of fact, none of the characters in these four particular stories is even given a name.

But Parker is not attempting to dissect the psyches of these characters; her intent seems closer to that of Poe with his nameless, deranged characters in their dramatic monologues, such as "The Tell-Tale Heart" or "The Cask of Amontillado," in which the speakers relate their involvement in gruesome murders, often detailing physical action with sordid precision, but rarely pausing to examine the motivation behind their actions or their confession. The tales horrify as much because of their gruesome content as because of the superficially conceived tone of the narrators' voices. Parker's stories do not rely on Gothic horror to draw out the psychological shallowness of her characters, but her characters in these four stories do share with Poe's characters that anonymity, in both name and personality, which heightens the sense of the characters' superficiality and reinforces what is surely one of the author's thematic concerns about the horror of shallow self-understanding.

The short time frame in each of Parker's stories does not allow for complex psychological development of the characters. Even though, in the case of three of these stories, the central character does all the speaking, how much depth can a character believably reveal within one fifteen-minute speech, especially when the speech is permeated with a single, obsessive concern? Valerie Shaw has warned about the problem of character free will, and consequently of characterization itself, inherent to the "tightly controlled quality" of the short story form:

> [it reduces] the possibility of showing characters making free, let alone complicated choices. Willpower often seems to have become the privilege of the author alone: para-

> doxically, [her] desire to give a story inevitability may have the effect of depriving [her] characters of any self-determining power, making them appear to be locked in a structure which has been specially designed to fate them to passivity and sameness. (208)

For authors who intend to portray highly developed, individual characters (and for the readers who expect to read about them), Shaw's caveat certainly carries weight, but a conception of the importance of this kind of character development excludes the uses (the necessity, even) of other types of characterization. In fact, Shaw's statement implies that an author has some sort of responsibility for creating characters with absolute free will. (Here, one might remember that when questioned whether his characters take on independent realities of their own during the process of creation, Vladimir Nabokov snorted in negation and referred to his characters as "galley slaves.") What about an author who wants to make a deterministic point about "passivity and sameness"?

While Parker's characters are not necessarily at the mercy of overwhelmingly deterministic forces and consequently do not come across as helpless pawns in some inscrutable chess game, her characters do often seem limited in their choices. But such limitations come about through an inability to rise above or see beyond obsession and pettiness. The soliloquizer in "A Telephone Call" could attempt to move on with her life by simply moving beyond the range of her telephone. The dancer in "The Waltz" could decline another dance. The newlyweds in "Here We Are" could go to bed and get past the initial trauma of sexuality. The socialite in "From the Diary of a New York Lady" could surely look beyond the color of her fingernail polish.

Of course, it is Parker herself who does not allow these characters to make such substantial changes in their actions and personalities: superficiality is the aim of these Parker stories, but superficiality for a purpose. Not only are the characters illustrative targets of a satiric ideal of shallowness, but they also give the impression of eternal sameness, and in this way, Parker's stories are often every bit as horrifying as Poe's stories because they imply an everlasting repetition of superficiality and emptiness; in a Poe story the gory action has already occurred in the past and is being remembered, or even confessed, for unexplained reasons by one of the nameless participants, whereas Parker's stories imply ongoing action (indeed, the events of "The Waltz" and "A Telephone Call" unfold in the present tense while the first-person narrators speak) that will continue forever. In other words, these four Parker stories resist closure. Of course, open-ended fiction is hardly a revolutionary construction, but the open-endedness of Parker's stories results not so much from a range of ambivalent interpretations—Parker's satiric intentions are not so subtle as to be inscrutable; rather, the open-endedness of her stories comes about through the implication of continuing, repetitive action.

Parker achieves this implication through both the content of the stories and the stylistic device of repetition. In "Here We Are," the greatest portion of Parker's satire is given over to the unstated anticipation of the sexual consummation of the honeymoon night, with the husband barely concealing his squirming expectation with the verbal tic "I mean—I mean" whenever his statements veer too closely to references about the approaching night. Parker also takes aim at petty marital discord—in this case, taken to the extreme since the couple has been married for only a few hours. Their entire conversation is a study in vacuity: they discuss how the bridesmaids looked, they discuss the wife's new hat, they discuss the millions of marriages that must have occurred concurrently with theirs, they discuss how quickly the day has passed. And they quarrel. The wife accuses the husband of disliking her family, disliking her new hat, making eyes at one of the bridesmaids; the husband accuses the wife of wanting to marry an old boyfriend, misunderstanding him. Does this unlikable couple suffer merely from a case of honeymoon jitters? Hardly, since readers discover from the wife seven pages into the bickering, after the husband exclaims, "Hell, honey lamb, this is our honeymoon. What's the matter?" that "[they] used to squabble a lot when [they] were going together and then engaged and everything, but [she] thought everything would be so different as soon as [they] were married" (131). Clearly this couple has been quarreling since they met; Parker shows them at a brief, key point in time in their relationship—during the honeymoon, the official beginning of the new life together—still quarreling. At the end of the story, the husband's mind is still focused on the approaching sexual activity, and Parker concludes with a final repetition of the husband's verbal tic as well as another more subtle repetition in the closing words of both characters:

> "Pretty soon we'll be regular old married people. I mean. I mean, in a few minutes we'll be getting in to New York, and then we'll be going to the hotel, and then everything will be all right. I mean—well, look at us! Here we are married! Here we are!"
>
> "Yes, here we are," she said. "Aren't we?" (134)

The final line of the story would seem to freeze the action of these two characters as well as of the entire story, in part because it is the final line, but also because the words refer to a specific juncture in time and space, both literal and figurative: end of train journey/beginning of wedded life; train compartment/ temple of marriage. Yet Parker's construction of the story, with its repetition of content and speaking style in this couple's dialogue, implies continued and continuing motion, so that the final printed statements of the husband and wife, spoken by each ("Here we are"), are really just another step in the series of actions and speeches that Parker has constructed for this pair to send them into their fictional eternity—especially since the concluding statements also serve as the very first words that Parker allows these characters to speak in the opening of the story.

Parker's characters never become aware that they are doomed to a fictional infinity of superficiality; the newlyweds in "Here We Are" might delude themselves momentarily into expecting a peaceful future, but readers know better from Parker's depiction of them. The socialite whose diary is reproduced in "From the Diary of a New York Lady" has no power of self-criticism whatsoever, and it is especially in this highly stylized story that Parker uses repetition of content to underscore both a projection into eternity for this character and a damnation of her shallowness. This story shares a structural similarity with Charlotte Perkins Gilman's "The Yellow Wallpaper" in its use of diary entries of a nameless female protagonist who has lost control of her life. Gilman's protagonist is fully aware of her powerlessness while consigned by her doctor-husband to a "rest" therapy in the country; the grim irony of the story asserts itself at the end when the diarist, confident that she has regained control of her sanity, has actually lost it.

In contrast, Parker's protagonist never seems aware that she lacks control of her life: the emptiness of her daily life is a secret shared by Parker and her readers. During five consecutive nights she cannot decide which dress to wear to the opening night of five new plays with titles like *Never Say Good Mornin*, *Everybody Up*, and *Run Like a Rabbit* (even these titles imply continuing movement), and then flits off to parties (always escorted by some flunky named Ollie Martin, after failing to land one of her "new cute numbers") at which the same Hungarian musicians in green coats perform, and where the same cutup named Stewie Hunter always vies for attention by leading the band with a lamp or a fork or some other outrageous pseudo-baton. Each morning she recovers from a hangover, sends messages to unreceptive "new numbers," and worries about the condition of her fingernails. The story has no conclusion in any traditional sense: the entries merely stop after the fifth day, having presented a sequence of actions that is a representative slice of a much longer sequence of the same actions. The interest in such a story lies not in finding out what ultimately happens to the diarist because there is never any sense of "ultimateness" or climax, as in the more traditionally plotted "The Yellow Wallpaper," where a climax occurs when the diarist finally disintegrates psychologically. Rather, the interest in Parker's story lies in discerning the pattern of the diarist's life and realizing that the pattern never changes in substance or direction, only in detail and sequence (e.g., What new calamity will befall the diarist's fingernails? When will the diarist again damn Miss Rose, her manicurist?). Parker has set this woman into a literal perpetual motion, like a top, consigned night after night to spinning through the emptiest of lives with the most vacuous of companions.

Parker's masterful use of repetition and variation distinguishes a story like "From the Diary of a New York Lady," but it also serves to propel the perpetually repeating superficiality beyond the final line of the story. Parker uses the same technique in her best soliloquy, "A Telephone Call," in which a female speaker agonizes while waiting for a male acquaintance to call. She begins countless sentences with the word "maybe," as she runs through every conceivable possibility for why he has not called. She carries on a one-sided dialogue with God, asking, begging, pleading, threatening—working through every rhetorical device available in order to arrive at an understanding about the man's apparent rejection of her. And she counts. In the second paragraph of the story she decides that the phone might ring by the time she has counted to five hundred by fives; she makes it to fifty before reverting to her stream-of-consciousness meanderings. Nearly halfway through the story she decides to count again to prove that a supplication to God will bring about results by the time she reaches five hundred by fives; she makes it to fifty-five. At the very end of the story she decides to count a third time, and the soliloquizer is last heard at the number thirty-five followed by an ellipsis. That she would reach five hundred is doubtful considering her previous attempts, and the ellipsis is certainly Parker's way of dooming this anonymous, speaking neurotic to endless repetitions of the same cycle.

Because of its content (as indicated by the title), "The Waltz" best illustrates Parker's use of structural repetition in conjunction with a story's content to fling a character into everlasting motion. In "The Waltz" a female character traps herself into dancing with a man: she warmly accepts the dance invitation (the words of which Parker represents in italics) and then launches into an interior diatribe against her partner and his dancing ability. This woman has the opportunity, in the first place, to decline the dance invitation, but she only exacerbates her unhappiness when she coyly blames herself (in the words she speaks to her partner) after he stomps on her feet, inwardly cursing him. To herself she claims the dance has lasted "thirty-five years" and envisions being trapped with her partner "throughout eternity" (50). Yet she agrees to dance throughout the band's encore, and in the story's final paragraph, Parker leaves the woman speaking to her partner:

> Oh, they've stopped, the mean things. They're not going to play any more. Oh, darn. Oh, do you think they would? Do you really think so, if you gave them twenty dollars?

> Oh, that would be lovely. And look, do tell them to play this same thing. I'd simply adore to go on waltzing. (51)

Despite nearly five pages of inward griping, the speaker has consigned herself to another waltz, one of which has already dissolved the boundary of her perception of time. When she falsely declares that she would "simply adore to go on waltzing" it is clear that Parker has granted that wish in terms of the structure of the story: As the story concludes, the speaker will be seen whirling off into her fictional eternity on a dance floor with a klutz, sharing the fate of perpetual, superficial motion that Parker visits upon her other characters.

Each of these stories exhibits Parker's skillful ability to use the structural device of repetition in a unique way, producing stories that embody endless motion through an overall structuring uncommon to most American short stories. While this aspect of her stories represents one contribution to the short story form, it also indicates a useful approach to her work for feminist scholars: despite Parker's own prayer that she not "write like a woman," the lack of climax in many of her stories, her abiding use of stylistic repetition, and the open-ended nature of the action of her stories all point to what some critics view as a distinctive women's way of writing. This assessment complements the arguments of Kathryn Allen Rabuzzi, who maintains that the repetitive nature of the traditional domestic existence of women has influenced the way women writers structure their work: the progressiveness of the Aristotelian plot is replaced by a structure favoring stasis and cyclicity (163–167). With the structural spin that she initiates for most of her characters, Parker may have been writing "like a woman" whether she wanted to or not.

In any case, Parker rarely seems to have much sympathy for her characters, male or female; certainly they do not seem to realize that their personalities have trapped them in an eternal spin. Of course, it is Parker herself who orchestrates the action of each story and creates the participating personalities, and it is she who does not allow her characters to realize what has happened to them. The fate that Parker devises for her characters might be expressed in the same words that congressional clergyman and theologian Jonathan Edwards used to warn his congregation of everlasting damnation: "There will be no end to this exquisite horrible misery. When you look forward, you shall see a long forever, a boundless duration before you, which will swallow up your thoughts, and amaze your soul; and you will absolutely despair of ever having any deliverance, any end, any mitigation, any rest at all." Unlike Edwards's God, however, Parker gives her characters no warning, no chance for repentance and redemption. Instead, she has created the particular situations with her own distinctive fictional technique of repetition, demonstrating Nancy Walker's assertion that American female humorists create "forms suited to their own lives and needs" (12), to satirize superficiality in a number of its manifestations, and to condemn such superficiality to eternal, repeating perpetual motion.

WORKS CITED

Coward, Rosalind. "The True Story of How I Became My Own Person." *The Feminist Reader: Essays in Gender & the Politics of Literary Criticism*. Eds. Catherine Belsey and Jane Moore. Cambridge, MA: Blackwell, 1989, pp. 35–47.

Fitzgerald, F. Scott. *The Letters of F. Scott Fitzgerald*. Ed. Andrew Turnbull. New York: Scribner's, 1963.

Gill, Brendan. Introduction. *The Portable Dorothy Parker*. New York: Viking, 1973.

Kinney, Arthur F. *Dorothy Parker*. Boston: Twayne, 1978.

Meade, Marion. *Dorothy Parker: What Fresh Hell Is This?* New York: Penguin, 1989.

Parker, Dorothy. Interview. *Writers at Work: The* Paris Review *Interviews*. Ed. Malcolm Cowley. New York: Viking, 1958.

———. *The Portable Dorothy Parker*. New York: Viking, 1973.

Pickering, Jean. "Time and the Short Story." *Rereading the Short Story*. Ed. Clare Hanson. New York: St. Martin's, 1989, pp. 45–54.

Rabuzzi, Kathryn Allen. *The Sacred and the Feminine: Toward a Theology of Housework*. New York: Seabury, 1982.

Richler, Mordecai, ed. Introduction. *The Best of Modern Humor*. New York: Knopf, 1983.

Shaw, Valerie. *The Short Story: A Critical Introduction*. London: Longman, 1983.

Treichler, Paula A. "Verbal Subversions in Dorothy Parker: 'Trapped Like a Trap in a Trap.'" *Language and Style* 13.4 (Fall 1980): 46–61.

Walker, Nancy A. *A Very Serious Thing: Women's Humor and American Culture*. Minneapolis: University of Minnesota Press, 1988.

The "Feminine" Short Story in America: Historicizing Epiphanies[1]

Mary Burgan

Under the fixating strobe light of recent theorizing—especially the theorizing based upon the continental break with phenomenology—the dimension of time implicit in narrative tends to be hypostatized into spatial figures in a way that emphasizes conceptual structure over the dynamics of chronicity. Working as figures themselves in a diagram in which the text provides but one of the points of reference, critics "situate" themselves, "locate" the text within some context, identify "margins" and "centers," and "colonize" this or that "sphere." Locutions like "site" and "scene" may help to describe the rhetorical architecture of stories, but they also obscure the temporal preoccupations of narrative. Thus in a critical environment that is suspicious of formalism, the vocabulary of spatial ordering seems as insistent now as it was in the heyday of New Criticism.[2]

Such spatial terminology may point to the wariness that poststructuralist theory harbors about the metaphysical danger of becoming preoccupied with the representation of time at all. J. Hillis Miller's attack on Paul Ricoeur's exhaustive study of time and narrative may suggest why; the phenomenological heritage of temporal preoccupation has a tendency eventually to engage conceptions of causality through the emphasis on the sequence of memory and expectation, and such interests may move the critic to celebrations of myth, symbol, transcendence, presence.[3]

If some current theorizing suspects the representation of the moment for its nostalgic invocation of phenomenological metaphysics, there are feminist theoretical positions that embrace the representation of temporality as a gendered modality of the feminine imagination. I am thinking here of Hélène Cixous and Catherine Clèment's evocation of a flowing, "feminine" writing that counters the static forms of masculine inscription with an ongoingness that resists the interruption of symbolic abstraction:

> [H]er writing also can only go on and on, without ever inscribing or distinguishing contours, daring these dizzying passages in other, fleeting and passionate dwellings within him, within the hims and hers whom she inhabits just long enough to watch them, as close as possible to the unconscious from the moment they arise. (88)

Such a description accents the unboundedness of women's time even as it risks advocating formlessness as a marker of feminine writing. The short story, so bounded by its own brevity, would seem a contradiction in form to such a definition of *écriture feminine*, but I want to suggest that an attunement to the "just long enough" describes the concerns of women who have chosen the short story as a genre that might permit the representation of passing time in moments that are significant, but that refuse rhetorical gestures toward enclosed meaning.

Although the definition of the epiphany as a focus of modernist narrative originates with James Joyce's discussion in *Stephen Hero*, the evolution of the epiphany in short stories by women owes greatly to the narrative experiments of writers like Virginia Woolf and Katherine Mansfield, with whom Woolf conferred extensively on their writing between 1918 and 1922 (McLaughlin). Woolf understood the presiding motive of the modernist turn as an attempt to represent slight incidents of implication within the structure of an intensively managed fictional form. The very titles of such stories as her own "The Moment" or Katherine Mansfield's "Prelude" suggest the generative power of a conception of the short story as a genre that organizes the flow of time into a narrative configuration that can then be held by the atemporal fixity of the writer's (and reader's) attention, while honoring the essential resistance of the flow of perception to the confinement of language.

Woolf elaborated the originating set of assumptions in a number of famous texts. I quote a less well-known formulation from her review of a slight book of short aperçus by Logan Pearsal Smith (1918); here she sets up the boundaries of her own project as a connoisseur of the moment in her fiction:

> If we are not mistaken, it is his purpose to catch and enclose certain moments which break off from the mass, in which without bidding things come together in a combination of inexplicable significance, to arrest those thoughts which suddenly, to the thinker at least, are almost menacing with meaning. Such moments of vision are of an unaccountable nature; leave them alone and they persist for years; try to explain them and they disappear; write them down and they die beneath the pen. (75)

The history of the modernist short story thus evolved under the conditions of the writer's attempt to make a "sudden arrest" of the moment and thus to keep in suspension the incipient meaning that activated its encirclement. The intuition of transcendence in this encircling, the "menace of meaning," is kept at bay and resists articulation. As Katherine Mansfield wrote to Virginia Woolf in 1919, referring to Chekhov, "What the writer does is not so much to *solve* the question but to *put* the question" (204). Thus Woolf and Mansfield invoked the moment as espistemologically innocent—inexplicable, unaccountable, but persistent.

The impulse behind temporal experimentation in the formative short stories of modernist women writers like Woolf and Mansfield was unassuming; it was not the imperial project of capturing time—authorized by a philosophical conviction that temporal flow is merely an epistemological structuration that can be mastered by language. It was, rather, a strenuous effort to intuit (in the fashion of some versions of phenomenology) the punctuation of duration by consciousness. While the approaches of Woolf and Mansfield were anti-foundationalist in their acceptance of the subjective basis of representation; however, they nevertheless attempted to intensify the signifying moment by structuring it within networks of "women's" time—especially time in the context of collective, familial memory. Thus Mansfield's stories of the Burnell family in "Prelude" and "At the Bay" attempt to reconstruct the young Kezia Burnell's development of a moral sense through the accretions of her epiphanies over time; the episodic elements of these stories set the most critical revelations within vagrant memories of the protagonist's childhood. Woolf's short stories, by contrast, might seem but brief exercises in stream-of-consciousness technique; they are less imbued with personal memory than Mansfield's. Woolf seeks to represent the moment as more instantaneous, more attuned to the flash of the present as it impersonally passes in nature. In "Kew Gardens," for example, Woolf plots through imagery, posing the epiphany as a subjective defense against the blindness of Darwinian evolution to the fleeting aspirations of its human context. Further, Woolf's narrative experiment with time in *Between the Acts* locates epiphanal time not only within the "deep time" of evolution but also within the framework of a local pageant chronicling English history organized by an aging woman in implied resistance to the threat of German air raids at the beginning of World War II.

The narrative practices of Mansfield and Woolf suggest, then, that although the free-floating moment resided at the center of the modernist short story in its origins, it resided within a continuum of personalized temporal progressions. The effort to enlarge the implications of the moment in the short fiction of the founding mothers thus provided a variety of possibilities for their successors. Mansfield sought to understand identity as the gathering of instants of revelation into a provisional self. Woolf (a much more historically oriented writer than we usually notice) sought to incorporate the understanding of history as made up of lived inspirations within the scattered subjectivities that finally constitute a collective community—a family, a place, a culture. Under such practice, duration could be represented in a developmental or historical dynamic without positing the universal truths implicated in that length that implies a web of causalities in the conventional novel.[4]

In suggesting that a woman's tradition in the short story derived from such temporal elaborations, I do not want to replicate the theoretical discussions of the nature of the genre that has marked much of the recent thinking about short stories; the best of such discussions work empirically, in any case.[5] Instead, I want to look at the American women's tradition in the short story as building on the British experiments. Thus in the transportation of the Woolf/Mansfield model to America, we may observe that founding mothers of the American modernist short story Katherine Anne Porter and Eudora Welty thought about the short story in dialogue with Woolf's and Mansfield's practice.[6]

The redefinition of the moment in the woman's tradition of the short story in America extends Mansfield's and Woolf's explorations in women's time by generating specifically American narratives of "developmental" and "historical" memory. This extension was rooted in the local situations of American writers, for I believe that the complicated narrative maneuvers of Porter and Welty derived from their situation not only as women writers but as women writers from the American South. Thus although their stories center upon the epiphanic moment, the moment is not sufficient in and of itself to gather the implications in the experience of their characters as marginal subjects in a marginal culture. The stories of Porter and Welty search for ways to represent the moment of insight into a feminine network of sensation and recollection that is immersed in growing up in Texas or Louisiana or Mississippi, but they also represent these moments as independent from tight narrative definition. In arguing this case, I disagree with Thomas Leitch's notion that the American short story debunks "conventional assumptions about personal identity" in a preview of postmodernist decentering that parallels the discourses of contemporary theory (Lohafer 147).[7] On the contrary, I see the women's tradition in American story writing as seeking ways to recover some kind of personal identity for characters whose rearing in the narrow, despised "poor white" South has forced them to dismantle the past and then challenged them to put it back together again in a revisionary way that would permit them to survive its racist and sexist myths.

Porter's Miranda stories in "Old Mortality" and "The Old Order" and the novella "Pale Horse, Pale Rider" seem especially relevant in this American elaboration of the epiphanic model, suggesting an intertextual link with Mansfield's Burnell family stories. Like the Burnell family in "Prelude" and "At the Bay," the family of Miranda is presided over by a wise grandmother. The young girl's perceptions are guided by her sense of the grandmother's framing force of character: the stories weave a history of the grandmother's life through Miranda's overhearings and glimpses. In the most typically Mansfieldian of these stories, "The Circus," Miranda has a sudden vision of the terror implicit in the trickery of circus clowns and tightrope walkers and has to be taken home as a "crybaby" by the long-suffering black nursemaid, Dicey. Only the grandmother understands the import of the child's anguish, and she pronounces a judgment on the relations between childhood moments and mature character that is a kind of motto for Miranda's whole development: "The fruits of their present are in a future so far off," she tells Miranda's father, ". . . neither of us may live to know whether harm has been done or not. That is the trouble" (347).

If Porter's Miranda resembles Mansfield's Kezia in being the repository of a future whose potentiality resides in fleeting moments of vision, she also contrasts. Her crossing over from the bewildered amazement of childhood to the willed confusions of maturity is portrayed as a rejection of the kind of nostalgia that can encase the past in false innocence. In "Part III" of "Old Mortality," Miranda returns home to a funeral from a northern city to which she has eloped to escape her family. On the train she learns the truth about her Aunt Amy—a legendary New Orleans belle, said to have died in youth and sanctified in family myth for her beauty, spirit, and pathos. As they travel home together, an elderly suffragist cousin tells Miranda that Amy had been a sex-starved flirt who died a messy death. The myth of family solidarity and feminine gentility through which Miranda had built her sense of self collapses in her recognition of how little she has ever understood about the past. She resolves to cut all her ties with this web of illusions, and in musing over this incipient escape, she addresses the question of the "truth" in any perception:

> What is the truth, she asked herself as intently as if the question had never been asked, the truth, even the smal-

> lest, the least important of all the things I must find out? and where shall I begin to look for it? Her mind closed stubbornly against remembering, not the past but the legend of the past, other people's memory of the past, at which she had spent her life peering in wonder like a child at a magic-lantern show. (221)

In the last line of the story, however, Porter emphasizes the arrogance of Miranda's resolve to find her own separate truth: "At least I can know the truth about what happens to me, she assured herself silently, making a promise to herself, in her hopefulness, her ignorance" (221). But as Porter notes the futility of attempts to disentangle truth from memory, she also sponsors the necessity to try.

For Porter, then, the self, made continuous through the aggregations of flashes in time, must resist regression—a resistance she did not always find in Mansfield's lapses into sentimentality. Miranda must not engage in the delusion of willing herself back, even though the freshness and constancy of her childhood is always somehow available. Thus, for example, "The Grave" dramatizes a sharp memory of a day in the woods with her brother when she was nine years old. They had shot a pregnant rabbit on that day, and conspired together to forget the mysterious revelation of the tiny creatures in its womb. Finding a ring and a dove in an old grave in the same adventure, they have sealed their knowledge of birth and death through an exchange of its objects. Now that moment floods Miranda's consciousness as an unexpected gift in the squalid surroundings of her adult wanderings in a Third World country:

> One day she was picking her path among the puddles and crushed refuse of a market street in a strange city of a strange country, when without warning, plain and clear in its true colors as if she looked through a frame upon a scene that had not stirred nor changed since the moment it happened, the episode of that far-off day leaped from its burial place before her mind's eye. (367)

The frame of this epiphanic memory cannot obliterate the repellent present, where "the smell in the market, with its piles of raw flesh and wilting flowers was like the mingled sweetness and corruption she had smelled that other day" (367).

Nevertheless, the memory enables the mature imagination to respond with a sense of the continuing relevance of "even the smallest, the least important of all the things I must find out."

Thus Porter creates the family chronicle in episodes that at once foster and critique her protagonist's development through glimpses that are "plain and clear"—acknowledging their feminine sources in the mysterious prebirth of the unborn animals. In the context of the southern celebration of feminine sensibility, which too easily erases the perceptions of slaves, servants, and the poor, such memories can only frame the structures of power, as imaged, for example, in Miranda's brother's act of killing the rabbit. But the silence of Dicey—and the retreat of the grandmother's servant and former slave, Nannie, away from the white family's appropriation of her subjectivity in "The Last Leaf"—signals Porter's critique of the "out-of-date sentimental way of thinking" that "had always complacently believed that Nannie was a real member of the family, perfectly happy with them" (349). Thus Porter's short stories discern the privilege of a reliance on private revelations that make no reference to the historical realities of servitude and slavery.

Eudora Welty was also aware of the privilege of the personal epiphany within the context of a culture that can be murderously blind to its historical determinants and its victims. In her most considered evocation of the epiphany, she renders the revelation of the moment within the ambitions of the male to control time by killing its feminine embodiment, even as Miranda's brother kills the mother rabbit in "The Grave." In "A Still Moment," Lorenzo Dow, a circuit-riding Calvinist preacher; James Murrell, an outlaw horse thief; and Audubon, the scientist and artist, meet by chance in the middle of the Old Trace just at sunset and just in time to view a snowy heron feeding. These figures are driven by the abstractions of salvation, rebellion, and art, respectively, and each represents the ruination of the moment under the grip of such abstractions. Welty describes the exquisite modesty of the bird as they perceive her, in a shyness and brightness of being that is later gendered female. In the vulnerability of its moment the bird offers freedom from obsession: "Take my flight" (196). But the masculine response is one of control:

> What each of them had wanted was simply *all*. To save all souls, to destroy all men, to see and to record all life that filled this world—all, all—but now a single frail yearning seemed to go out of the three of them for a moment and to stretch toward this one snowy, shy bird in the marshes. It was as if three whirlwinds had drawn together at some center, to find there feeding in peace a snowy heron. Its own slow spiral of flight could take it away in its own time, but for a little it held them still, it laid quiet over them, and they stood for a moment unburdened. (196)

The moment cannot outlast the apocalyptic, end-of-time imperatives driving each observer as he seeks his total mastery of those whom the preacher addresses as the "Inhabitants of Time" (191). It is Audubon who shoots the bird so that he can take it home and paint it; Murrell moves on toward the night in which he will murder the innocent; and Lorenzo rides slowly away, meditating on separateness and love, God and time:

> Perhaps it was that God never counted the moments of Time, Lorenzo did that, among his tasks of love. Time did not occur to God. Therefore—did He even know of it? How to explain Time and Separateness back to God, Who had never thought of them, Who could let the whole world come to grief in a scattering moment? (198)

This question besets the understanding of the preacher, and he casts aside the beauty of the heron with the word "Tempter!" (199), riding on to meet a congregation to which he will preach on the text, "in that day when all hearts will be disclosed" (199).

In the magnificent narration of "A Still Moment," Welty mourns the masculine responses to the epiphany in the pre–Civil War South, rejecting even the artist's disruption of it to serve his ambition to know and record. Audubon, carrying the body of the bird away to study and draw, "knew that the best he could make would be, after it was apart from his hand, a dead thing and not a live thing, never the essence, only a sum of parts." (198). And so Welty implicitly rejects the spatial art of the painter for the temporal art of a narrative that represents the moment without capturing, confining, or killing it. And thus her stories resist closure, even as they represent the epiphany in language of great visual clarity that recalls Woolf's placement of it within the deep time of evolutionary inevitability; her description of Woolf seems a self-description, "the imprisonment of life in the word was as much a matter of the senses with her as it was a concern of the intellect" ("Reading and Writing" 172).

Many of Eudora Welty's other stories work different changes upon epiphanic moments, placing them within the less aggressive, more richly sensory experience of her women characters. In "A Curtain of Green," for example, Welty reworks the imagery plotting of a story like "Kew Gardens" by placing the revelation within the impersonal plenitude of nature. In the crisis of coping with the death of her husband, who was killed by a falling tree, Mrs. Larkin has turned obsessively to her garden, frantically enmeshing herself with its implacable fullness: "To a certain extent, she seemed not to seek for order, but to allow an over-flowering, as if she consciously ventured forever a little farther, a little deeper, into her life in the garden" (108). But as her obsession increases, Mrs. Larkin experiences the urge to control by striking the young black boy who works with her as he dreams over his chores, oblivious to her temptation to destroy his own still moment. Standing above him, with full knowledge of her power to harm, she asks, "Was it not possible to compensate? to punish? to protest?" But her revelation is interrupted by a sudden shower, which converts her epiphany of alienation into one of solidarity: "In the light from the rain, different from sunlight, everything appeared to gleam unreflecting from within itself in its quiet arcade of identity" (111). Accepting her powerlessness before nature, the woman sinks into the ground and lets the rain incorporate her into the heedless garden, even as the boy wakes from his own vision to look in amazement and terror on her sleeping form. Rejecting the right to command through violence, Mrs. Larkin rejoins boundless woman's time in which personal subjective claims do not edge out the claims of other identities. Thus while Welty's "A Still Moment" places the epiphany within the historical setting of men's depredations in the Old South, "A Curtain of Green" places it within the inevitability of evolutionary growth that cannot be gardened into human order.

Despite the profound engagement of writers like Woolf, Mansfield, Porter, and Welty in wrestling with the nature of time, their efforts have come to be discounted as "feminine" because of their focus on the moment. For example, Doris Lessing rejected the narrative of the moment in reaction against the temptation to an evanescent, "feminine" writing crippled by the effort to stay within the moment, politically inert because of the modesty of its mimetic aspirations. Writing in the early 1960s about the formal choices open to her as a short story writer, Lessing testified to the writer's need to contest the modernist tradition in an age of ideological consciousness. In the preface to a collection of her African stories, she points to a very early piece of her own and rejects it, noting that it was "intense, careful, self-conscious, mannered—[and] could have led to a kind of writing usually described as 'feminine.'" She wanted to choose instead a method that is "straight, broad, direct" and "has the freedom to develop " (*African Stories* 9). I have suggested elsewhere that Lessing ventured into a flat realism, structured by a Laurentian directness of statement, but that she also returned to the epiphany in a story like "Dialogue."[8]

Lessing's description of the "feminine" short story suggests the American model of *New Yorker* fiction. The *New Yorker* story is perhaps best embodied in the stories of J.D. Salinger, whose establishment of the vagrantly innocent susceptibility of girls as an ethical gauge of almost mystical surety both elevated and trivialized the epiphany as an organizing narrative principle. In such a version of the moment of insight, its femininity becomes an attitude, a style, rather than the founding mothers' philosophically contemplated engagement with the difficulty of finding a ground of meaning within the flow of experience. In fact, one of the limitations in contemporary minimalist stories, edited to the bone, is that their understated representations do not grapple with the moment so much as make a gesture at its flight through the portentous fractures of decentered plotting, the easy ironies of banal, name-brand realism, or the heartbreaking wisecrack. It seems to me that such southern writers as Ellen Gilchrist and Bobbie Ann Mason run this risk under cover of the southern aura in their writing. But the appeal of southern stories is one that Dorothy

Allison describes in the preface to *Trash*, when she sees her own writing as having to refuse the exotic flavor of the southern in their struggle to bring the harsh truths of survival to words, the shattered identity together over time: "The decision to live when everything inside and out shouts death is not a matter of moments but of years, and no one has ever told me how you know when it is accomplished" (11).

In making similar moves away from easy epiphanies, a number of women writers in North America have ventured into science fiction, allegory, and a blend of the apocalyptic with the quotidian. I am thinking here of writers like Joyce Carol Oates, Margaret Atwood, and Ursula Le Guin, for whom the gender and ecological crises of the present require the fabular tradition of such other American forerunners in the short story as Charlotte Perkins Gilman and Kate Chopin.

Despite the suspicion of the epiphanic story, however, the American woman's tradition has drawn a main strand of its practice from the historicizing of the moment by Katherine Ann Porter and Eudora Welty. And this turn of women writers to the moment as a generic focus for the short story suggests a formal alternative to the plenitude, and obscurity, of "feminine" writing generated by such explorers of narrative as Cixous, Monique Wittig, and those other feminists influenced by the French school, who seem to take recourse in the fallacy of imitative form to represent the durational imperative in women's writing. American modernists like Katherine Anne Porter and Eudora Welty were indeed formalists; their *écriture feminine* privileged compression over expansion. They perceived that it was in their power to manipulate the signifying moment in narrative structures of their own devising so as to represent the rhythms of feminine understanding in a tour de force of language. It was in this realization that the structure of temporality contained within the epiphanic short story could be their achievement, that they mastered the paradox of brevity in the service of women's time—its access to the material facticity of sensation, change, and process as well as its full knowledge of the terror of history.

NOTES

1. Parts of the argument in this essay will appear in "The 'Feminine' Short Story: Recuperating the Moment" in *Style* (Fall 1993).

2. John Carlos Rowe remarks on this phenomenon in his entry under "Structure" in *Critical Terms for Literary Study* (Lentriccia & McLaughlin 23).

3. Miller accuses Ricoeur, among other things, of flattening temporal dimensions in the texts he analyzes by the overuse of spatial metaphors (1104).

4. Elizabeth Bowen has remarked that "narrative of any length involves continuity, sometimes a forced continuity: it is here that the novel too often becomes invalid" (152).

5. Lohafer's anthology presents an excellent sample of these theories.

6. Both Porter and Welty mention Mansfield and Woolf in their various reviews of the short story writer's art. Porter wrote one of the earliest American tributes to Mansfield in a review in the early 1930s (as did Willa Cather).

7. Leitch overlooks women's contributions to the American short story, giving only Flannery O'Connor extended space in his survey.

8. See "The 'Feminine' Short Story" (Spilka 218–240). Mark Spilka has given a full account of Lessing's affinities with Lawrence.

WORKS CITED

Allison, Dorothy. *Trash*. Ithaca, NY: Firebrand, 1988.

Bowen, Elizabeth. "Introduction to the Faber Book of Modern Short Stories." *Short Story Theories*. Ed. Charles E. May. Athens: Ohio University Press, 1976, pp. 152–158.

Cixous, Hélène, and Catherine Clèment. *The Newly Born Woman*. Translated by Betsy Wing. Minneapolis: University of Minnesota Press, 1986.

Leitch, Thomas. "Debunking in the American Short Story." *Short Story Theory at a Crossroads*. Eds. Susan Lohafer and Jo E. Clarey. Baton Rouge: Louisiana State University Press, 1989, pp. 130–147.

Lentriccia, Frank, and Thomas McLaughlin, eds. *Critical Terms for Literary Study*. Chicago: University of Chicago Press, 1990.

Lessing, Doris. *African Stories*. London: Michael Joseph, 1964.

———. *Stories*. New York: Vintage, 1980.

Lohafer, Susan, and Jo E. Clarey, eds. *Short Story Theory at a Crossroads*. Baton Rouge: Louisiana State University Press, 1989.

May, Charles E., ed. *Short Story Theories*. Athens: Ohio University Press, 1976.

Miller, J. Hillis. "But Are Things as We Think They Are?" *Times Literary Supplement* Oct. 9–15, 1987: 1104–1105.

McLaughlin, Ann L. "The Same Job: The Shared Writing Aims of Katherine Mansfield and Virginia Woolf." *Modern Fiction Studies* 24.3 (Autumn 1978): 369–382.

Mansfield, Katherine. *The Letters of Katherine Mansfield*. Ed. J. Middleton Murry. New York: Knopf, 1932.

Porter, Katherine Anne. "The Art of Katherine Mansfield." *The Nation* (Oct. 23, 1937): 435–36.

———. *The Collected Stories of Katherine Anne Porter.* New York: Harcourt Brace Jovanovich, 1979.

Spilka, Mark. "Lessing and Lawrence: The Battle of the Sexes." *Contemporary Literature* 16.2 (Spring 1975): 218–240.

Welty, Eudora. *The Collected Stories of Eudora Welty*. New York: Harcourt Brace Jovanovich, 1980.

———. "The Reading and Writing of Short Stories." *Short Story Theories.* Ed. Charles E. May. Athens: Ohio University Press, 1976, pp. 159–177.

Woolf, Virginia. "Moments of Vision: Review of *Trivia*, by Logan Pearsal Smith. (23 May 1918)." *Contemporary Writers*. Ed. Jean Guiguet. London: Hogarth, 1965, pp. 74–76.

Joyce Carol Oates: Reimagining the Masters, Or, A Woman's Place Is in Her Own Fiction

Margaret Rozga

Novelist, poet, playwright, and critic, as well as short story writer, Joyce Carol Oates achieved mastery of the short story at an early age. Born in Millersport, New York, on June 16, 1938, educated at Syracuse University (B.A., 1960) and the University of Wisconsin (M.A., 1961), Oates published her first two volumes of short stories, *By the North Gate* (1963) and *Upon the Sweeping Flood* (1966), before she was age 30. Shortly thereafter, she received a special award from the O. Henry Short Stories Award Committee for continuing achievement (1970). Since then, Oates has more than justified the judgment of the committee, publishing "literally hundreds of short stories of considerable formal and thematic range" (Bender vii).

Critic Greg Johnson singles out the stories in two collections, *The Wheel of Love* (1970) and *Marriages and Infidelities* (1972), as being those that "established her as one of America's preeminent masters of the short story" (5). Two of these stories, "The Lady with the Pet Dog" and "The Dead," are particularly important in demonstrating what Eileen Teper Bender calls the central concern of the whole body of Oates's work; it is "essentially revisionary" (viii). Bender reviews the often contradictory assessments of Oates to conclude that her "criticism and her imaginative literary expression reflect a curious sense of transition and expansion, the 'blur' of genres caused by the interpenetration of old pieties and new visions" (9). Concentrating on Oates's novels, Bender sees that they "test and rediscover values of the literary and cultural past" and, at the same time, yield "statements peculiarly her own" (9).

In her revisions of well-known stories by Anton Chekhov and James Joyce, "The Lady with the Pet Dog" and "The Dead," Oates has the same kind of twofold purpose Bender finds in the "revisionary" novels. She expresses admiration for the earlier writers as she expands the range of their concerns to embrace new visions, especially a new vision of women characters, whom she sees not as passive beings to be provided for, but as more active shapers of their own plots.

Oates's admiration for Chekhov and Joyce is well documented. In an interview with Joe David Bellamy, for example, just after she had written "The Dead" and "The Lady with the Pet Dog," Oates said, "These stories are meant to be autonomous stories, yet they are also testaments of my love and extreme devotion to these other writers" (Milazzo 19). Oates's devotion, however, is not merely of the cheerleading variety. If she imagines, as she told Bellamy, "a kind of spiritual 'marriage'" between herself and these other writers, it is a marriage in which two voices are heard. There is the echo of Chekhov or James, but there also resonates a voice concerned with how the visions of these earlier writers apply to the lives of late twentieth-century women.

As Joyce Carol Oates reimagines "The Lady with the Pet Dog" and "The Dead," then, she accomplishes at least two goals. First, she pays homage to these earlier writers whom she admires for their sensitivity to women's issues and for their vivid dramatic scenes. Secondly, she brings the woman's point of view to the foreground and thereby offers a critique not only of the social world of the earlier stories but also of the contemporary social world. She would not have the male character always the focus, always the guide to what we see and how we see it. The change in point of view results in an important reversal of focus; instead of stories of pompous, self-important male characters who are brought to a more humble sense of self, we have stories of uncertain and undervalued women characters who nonetheless find the strength to influence the shape of their destiny.

All of the central female characters in these four stories are at odds with the roles assigned them, but Oates's characters seem more so than Chekhov's or Joyce's. Chekhov's Anna is bored in her marriage to a "flunky"; Oates's Anna, unable to find a sense of herself in her marriage, is suicidal. Joyce's Gretta still longs, we find out at the story's denouement, for her youthful lover; Oates's Ilena is disillusioned with both husband and lovers much earlier in the story than Joyce's Gretta.

In the resolutions of the stories as well, Oates's characters find themselves further from traditional choices. Chekhov's Anna trusts that Gurov will find a way to create a place for them, and Joyce's Gretta sleeps. In contrast, Oates's Anna balks at the idea that love is the answer, and her Ilena sleeps only with the aid of drugs. But Oates's Anna is also able to resist suicide, and Ilena thinks her way through the drugged consciousness. Their early disenchantment with traditional social roles allows the major concern of their stories to be not the process of their disillusionment but the process by which new insights propel the characters to new conclusions.

In the stories by Chekhov and Joyce, contact with the natural environment offers a new perspective on life. In Oates, the perspective offered by the natural world is more ambiguous. Oates's characters retreat from large open spaces to smaller spaces, bathrooms or cars, as if the confinement and/or reduction of space would simplify the world, make it proportionately more manageable, or lock out the troubling elements. But that reduction is also dysfunctional and, in fact, deadly; a new sense of space is needed, and it is toward this we see the characters struggle.

In her story "The Lady with the Pet Dog," Oates stays closer to the Chekhov counterpart in character and plot so that the points of contrast more clearly stand out. Points of contrast in presentation of place especially stand out. In the original Chekhov story, the action takes place in three different settings: Yalta, Moscow, and the provincial city of S____, each place clearly distinguished by some feature of its physical geography and social climate.

Despite the differences in the settings, Anna never takes possession of more than the limited space of a hotel room. Gurov, on the other hand, is seen outdoors in all three places, in contact with nature and in control of himself. The denouement occurs when the self-concept he has outdoors is challenged by a vision he has when he is indoors, within the hotel room with Anna. In the most famous scene in Chekhov's story, Gurov sees himself in the mirror as a man who is aging and losing his attractiveness. "Now at last, when his hair was turning gray, he had fallen in love—real love—for the first time in his life" (302). With this vision he is more kindly to Anna, attempting now to comfort her as she cries, whereas in a similar scene earlier, he simply ate watermelon. He tells Anna that they will talk and think of some answer to their predicament, but he cannot answer his own question, "How?"

The story, then, ends with their perception that "the hardest and most difficult part was only beginning" (303). Gurov has transcended the rigid social structure that assigned everyone a place and assigned him to a loveless marriage. He is inspired both by the mountains and sea at Yalta, and by Anna, who is presented mostly as a factor in his life, rather than as her own person, who begins with no illusions that she is in control, and who lets Gurov have the last word.

In her story "The Lady with the Pet Dog," Oates acknowledges a debt to Chekhov by keeping the basic love triangle plot, by naming her character Anna, and by building upon the idea that place is as much a matter of social relations as it is a matter of geography. But she updates the story, setting it in twentieth-century America, and she brings the point of view of the woman character to the foreground.

As a counterpart to Yalta, where Chekhov's lovers meet, Oates gives us Nantucket. Her Anna had come to be alone in the house of her family. But even the memory of their presence still affects her sense of place, in the sense of social role: "It was a two-story house, large and ungainly weathered. It was mixed up in her mind with her family, her own childhood, and she glanced up from her book perplexed, as if waiting for one of her parents or her sister to come up to her" (337). Even when she looks back at the book she has selected, she feels the presence of her father in the passages that he has underlined. She does not, however, get much sense of herself in this "large, drafty house" (338).

She does not fare much better when she goes out to a restaurant with the man who will become her lover. She arranges "her own face" to match the expression on the drawing he had done of her. She wonders, "Did he see me like that, then?—girlish and withdrawn? She felt the weight of his interest in her, a force that fell upon her like a blow, a repeated blow" (337–338).

Nor does she find solace in nature. The natural world emerges here almost as another imposition upon the character. Nantucket has no quiet sea as did Yalta: "On the beach everything had been noisy with sunlight and gulls and waves" (339). Even at the start, Oates's Anna finds that social relations outweigh geography as the most distinctive feature of a place.

In place of Gurov's home in Moscow, Oates gives us her lovers on the road as they drive Anna to her sister's home in Albany, New York. In the new setting, Anna feels that "she did not know [her lover] at all" (339). The change of scene is a time of questioning, as was the case in Chekhov's Moscow, a time to ask if the relationship has any permanent meaning. Oates's Anna asks herself: "What did it mean to enter into a bond with another person?" (329). She comes to a conclusion: "No, she did not really trust him; she did not really trust men" (329). Her distrust of men initially emerges the night they first make love. She sends her lover from her house and thinks, "He was a man who drew everything up into himself, like all men, walking away, free to have his own thoughts, free to envision her body, all the secrets of her body" (339). At this point, his independence seems a threat to her.

On the road these doubts reassert themselves, overshadowing the memories of the talk and the laughter on the beach. As if to protect herself from such thoughts, Anna retreats to a smaller space. "At a gas station she splashed her face with cold water. Alone in the grubby little rest room, shaky and very much alone. In such places are women totally alone with their bodies. The body grows heavier, more evil, in such silence" (339). Being alone and being in a small space may provide a respite, but it does not provide a healthy sense of self.

Unsettled by the experience in these two places, Oates's Anna returns home to Ohio, her counterpart to Chekhov's provincial S____. Though it is less oppressive in appearance than is the home and home town of Chekhov's Anna, it is a place characterized only by her husband's concerns: "his own loneliness, his worries about his business, his health, his mother" (330). As a result, Anna can achieve no sense of herself there: "Her spirit detached itself from her and drifted about the room of the large house she lived in with her husband, a shadow-woman delicate and imprecise. There was no boundary to her, no edge" (330).

Again Anna retreats to the bathroom, as if the smaller space would give her a sense of self. The small space is, as before, temporarily comforting. She relishes long hot baths, but even this refuge has a dysfunctional aspect. Anna finds herself acting suicidally: "One day in January she drew a razor blade lightly across the inside of her arm, near the elbow, to see what would happen" (331). Her flirtation with suicide shows that the comfort of the smaller space does not solve the problem of finding her identity. Insofar as she makes herself comfortable despite the fact that she has "no edge," that is, no self-definition, she drifts further toward boundlessness, or nonbeing. To have a sense of identity is to have boundaries—an ability to be this but not that. To give up one's life is, in this case at least, to give up the attempt to draw personal boundaries. The blood flowing from Anna's arm is an effusion, a physical dispersal that matches her self-abnegating, rather than self-assertive, psychological state.

After her lover comes to her in Ohio, the pressure to make choices, to define herself, increases. Once again she seeks the refuge of a small space, but she now finds she has outgrown the image she finds there. In her closet, she finds the drawing her lover had done of her in Nantucket. Now she views it critically: "The dog in her lap hardly more than a few snarls, a few coarse soft lines of charcoal, . . . her dress smeared, her arms oddly limp, . . . her hands not well drawn at all" (340). The image that she has of herself, an image she got from him, is now less satisfying, but she is able to define her own feelings. Whenever her lover comes to visit, she has two men, two claims upon her, and two contradictory feelings about the one man: "Ah, what despair!—what bitter hatred she felt!—she needed this man for her salvation, he was all she had to live for, and yet she could not believe in him" (341).

She takes the next step, to a vision beyond this tangled knot of old roles and new desires, when she gets a sense of perspective from the depth that a mirror gives to a small space. In a scene that echoes and yet innovates on the mirror scene with Chekhov's Gurov, Oates's Anna sees in the mirror not herself but her lover as he is preparing to leave the hotel room. The image of his independence is no longer threatening. Quite the contrary, it is now liberating for her: "The image of her lover fell free of her, breaking from her . . . and she realized that he existed in a dimension quite apart from her, a mysterious being. And suddenly, joyfully, she felt a miraculous calm" (343).

With this insight, Anna suddenly gains the ability to determine her own relation to places and to the people that define those places: "This man was her husband, truly—they were truly married, here in this room—they had been married haphazardly and accidentally for a long time. In another part of the city she had another husband, a 'husband,' but she had not betrayed that man, not really" (343). It is a difficult, apparently contradictory, passage, but it makes sense if seen as evidence of Anna's ability to define for herself her place and her relationships to others.

She has decided in favor of her new desire rather than her old role. She appropriates the language of the old relationship and applies it to the new one. For her, her lover, not the man to whom she is married, is her "husband." The quotation marks around the word "husband" in Oates's text are significant. The word has, as it is ordinarily used, a set meaning. Anna upsets that meaning. Her use of the term outside its conventional meaning indicates that she now actively defines meaning for herself.

The experiences she had in Nantucket and on the way to Albany unsettled her and forced her to face difficult questions about her own life until she was able to come to a new vision, one that could sustain her. The effectiveness of her new vision is such that her lover is startled. Their roles seem to have been reversed; now he feels threatened by her independence: "She felt the abrupt concentration in him, the focusing of his vision on her, almost a bitterness in his face, as if he feared her" (343–344). Thus Oates's Anna has a more powerful effect on the conclusion than did Chekhov's Anna. Oates's couple may not settle themselves into marriage either, but the story ends with a sense that whatever agreement has taken shape between them, the conditions of their relationship at least partially on Anna's terms and with Anna's affirmation.

Oates, then, pays tribute to powerful scenes in Chekhov's story by making parallel contemporary scenes come to life. But her vision adds a dimension to Chekhov's. Like Chekhov, she sympathizes with the plight of those confined to unfulfilling social roles. Unlike Chekhov, however, Oates focuses on the female character as decision maker. Her Anna is not waiting, like Chekhov's, for a lover to find a path for her. Instead, Oates has her character redefine the terms of her relationships and set the tone both for herself and for her lover. Her story ends with the lover beginning a question and Anna cutting him off with her affirmative response. In other words, she is no longer retreating into the privacy of her mind, her closet, or her bathroom, where she grappled with these intensely vital questions. That struggle is over. She has arrived at her definitions. She is not passively awaiting his answer, awaiting to see what he can arrange for them. As Anna articulates her own answer, Oates gives us a much more assertive view of a woman's role.

In "The Dead," Oates departs more radically from the original story by Joyce. Characters' names and circumstances, as well as particulars of the plot, are just different enough to confound attempts to draw easy comparisons. Once again, Oates's protagonist is a woman, and therefore, she is the counterpart of two different characters in Joyce's story. Oates's Ilena is the protagonist as was Joyce's Gabriel, and like Gabriel, Ilena is the guest of honor at a party. Alternately, she has qualities or actions reminiscent of Joyce's Gretta.

Gabriel's story is summarized well by Lucy Maddox. She writes, "The evening at his aunts' party has made him aware of his inadequacies as intellectual, Irishman, husband, son, father, even nephew; what remained was his anticipated success as a lover" (276). We know, of course, that he fails as lover as well, learning that his wife has, since their youth, carried in her heart the image of another man. As a result, a "radically revised image of himself" is "forced upon him" (276). That is, Gabriel gives up his patronizing posture and sees himself in more modest terms.

Oates's Ilena, on the other hand, for most of the story, is clearly undervalued by others, and as a result, her own sense of self suffers. At the Detroit university where she had taught, she was "disappointed by the low salary and the bad schedule" (385). When she begins to have some success as a writer, a psychiatrist friend tells her that her husband is jealous and advises her to "fail at something yourself" (384). When she moves to Buffalo, New York, with greater success as a novelist behind her, colleagues "cautioned her against believing the praise that was being heaped upon her, that she would destroy her small but unique talent if she took all this seriously" (395). Even when she returns to Detroit and is guest of honor at a reception for the "most esteemed ex-staff member" (402), Ilena senses in the attitude of the department chair, Father Hoffman, "a barely disguised contempt for her—for all women" (402). Clearly, then, Ilena moves through most of her story from a position on the opposite end of the spectrum from Gabriel's. Her literary accomplishments and profound political sense contrast Gabriel's pretensions. While Gabriel luxuriates in an exaggerated estimation of his own value, Ilena struggles to maintain any sense of self-worth.

Her struggle comes to a head when Ilena returns to Detroit. She attends a reception hosted by the university where she had taught. From her new vantage point as outsider, however, she can now see exactly what is happening. The social group at the university functions as a defense mechanism for the faculty there. The words of their conversations do not so much deal with the harsh realities that seem to be the subject matter as much as they act as a shield against those realities. Ilena sees "these people talking so casually of Vietnam, of drugs, of the death of little Emmett Norlan—these people—the very words they used turning flat and banal and safe in their mouths" (405).

Ilena herself, for much of the story, would like to hide behind a defensive wall. The wall she chooses, however, is one of narcotics, not words. She ponders the label on the pill bottle with its caution against use where "complete mental alertness" is required. She questions what the words mean and thinks "it wisest to avoid complete mental alertness. That was an overrated American virtue" (380). She takes the pills as a defensive measure. She retreats from the university party at its worst to the comforting, enclosed space of the bathroom, where she takes whatever pills are available. To the end, however, she nevertheless keeps herself attuned to what she values: academic integrity, belief in marriage as a sacred "plunging into another's soul" (398), and, most of all, belief in her own worth as a writer and as a thinking human being.

In some of these values, Oates's Ilena is more a counterpart to Joyce's Gretta than a parallel to Gabriel. She has loved and has found that, though the power of her love is not enough to give or to sustain life, love does have powerful and enduring effects. In Oates's story, the portrayal of that love, its insufficiencies and results, is more direct and central.

Detroit is a place where love dies. Though Ilena believes that "marriage was the deepest, most mysterious, most profound exploration" (397), Detroit is the place where her marriage dies. She and Bryan had fallen in love "years ago in Madison, Wisconsin" (403), for Ilena a place like Gretta's western Ireland, where love could blossom. But transplanted to the "cataclysmic flowering" (383) of hatred in Detroit, the love is too fragile to survive.

Ilena's student, Emmett Norlan, for whom Detroit is literal death, is an echo of Gretta's love, Michael Furey. Emmett is young and intense, and after Ilena has left for Buffalo, he confesses that he was in love with her. Like Michael Furey, Emmett is kept from following through on his love. He dies, partially because of a police beating, partially because of his own drug use.

Death and destruction characterize Detroit on many other levels. It is also a place where values die. Father Hoffman, head of the English department at the small Catholic university where Ilena taught, is "a little corrupt in his academic standards: The Harvard years had been eclipsed long ago by the stern realities of Detroit" (392). Hoffman's corruption costs Ilena her job there.

She resigns quickly rather than risk being fired for refusing to agree to grant a degree to Brother Ronald, a master's candidate, when she realizes during his master's exam that his command of literature is almost nonexistent; in fact, he cannot even name any poem at all. Ilena's sense of value leaves her "astonished" that "anyone would allow him to teach English anywhere" (393). Her academic integrity, her taking on the brotherhood, the male hierarchy that dominates the university, costs her a job and plunges her into a new search for life outside the negative atmosphere of Detroit.

Freed from her attachment to Detroit, she can begin to see it for what it is, a place where larger external pressures have become for her intertwined with personal issues. At one point Ilena had even seen the Detroit riots as an outgrowth of the decay of her relationship with Bryan. She needs to gain the perspective of distance from this place, both artistically and geographically. She moves on to teach at Buffalo and completes the novel that brings her success. The places to which she journeys may not be much better, but being away from Detroit allows her some respite and a chance to see how fragile anyone might be facing the pressures that had come together for her in Detroit. Not the love of husband and wife, nor the love of lovers, nor the love of student and teacher for each other can withstand these greater forces—war, rioting, collapse of educational standards.

Gretta retained an image of youthful romantic love that apparently sustained her when her lover died and life became less romantic. But we do not know exactly how she fared on a daily basis. On the other hand, Ilena's losses and her reactions are seen in detail. Her days are frantic, her nights sleepless or nightmarish. The loss of romance, the traditional female catastrophe, is only partially the cause. More important is the refusal of those around her to take her and their own careers seriously. Whereas the Joyce story shows us a character who finally sees through the delusions of his place in his aunts' household and in Dublin society, the Oates story shows a character whose values are affirmed by the writer and reader, if not by the other characters. Ilena demonstrates not only the strength to maintain any sense of value, despite the overwhelming odds presented by Detroit and, in fact, all of America but also the strength to act on that sense of value.

In the end we see Ilena in a position beyond the questions that have troubled her, with focus on the simple drawing of her breath. She finally eases up on herself, and instead of trying to account for the whole past, she focuses on the present life, the breathing of her lover in congruence with the rhythm of the snow, another image transposed from the James Joyce story: "Her brain seemed to swoon backward in an elation of fatigue, and she heard beyond this man's hoarse, strained breathing the gentle breathing of the snow, falling shapelessly upon them all" (409). The snow does not obliterate everything that has happened. Ilena is aware, this seems to say, of the particulars of her life in perspective, in relation to life itself. In contrast, moreover, to Joyce's Gretta, at the end of her story, Ilena is awake.

Ilena's wakefulness by itself is significant. Though she had disavowed the benefit of "complete mental alertness," neither does she want to drift into unconsciousness, hard as she has struggled to maintain a sense of herself. The sleeping beauty of Gretta is no longer the ideal.

Nor is Ilena's wakefulness the nightmarish insomnia that plagued her earlier, when she feared dreams of "the assassination of Kennedy," rerunning "in her brain like old newsreels" and bringing "him back to her not as a man: as a corpse" (384). Instead, Ilena's state now has a modified tone; it resembles the Chagall lithograph Ilena had studied as her lover approached her at the party: two "lovers embraced, in repose; yet a nightmarish dream blossomed out of their heads, an intricate maze of dark depthless foliage, a light window, faces ghastly-white and perhaps a little grotesque" (405). This image is similar to what we see after Gordon drives them to her hotel. "They were suddenly very comfortable together, sadly comfortable" (406). The sadness continues, but the comfort is the first Ilena has felt in a long time, and their time in her room is spent "gently." Like Joyce's couple, they do not make love; Ilena frightens Gordon off as she stifles a scream thinking of Emmett Norlan. Ilena remembers her husband Bryan, as well as her dead student. She is brought back, however, not to a corpse, but to Gordon's breathing and the sense of life it represents.

Such details contrast both Ilena's own state at the beginning of this story and Gretta's greater unconsciousness at the end of the Joyce story. Unable to shake the nightmare completely even in repose, Ilena has nevertheless proven herself a survivor. Her story, in fact, suggests such survival is no mean feat. Even though her colleagues, especially those who are male, may deny a woman's talents and pressure her to succumb to whatever may be the exigencies of her "Detroit," a path through that world can be forged. Though it has taken most of her strength, this Ilena has done.

Both Ilena in Oates's "The Dead" and Anna in her "The Lady with the Pet Dog" are frustrated with the roles assigned them by their time and place. Their pain and anguish is vividly depicted. Because of this pain they seek, in one way or another, an escape from those places. Their means of escape—love affairs, taking drugs, retreating to smaller places—may include self-destructive elements. But by breaking out of the routine, the role or the place that had earlier confined them, they are thrown into a new realm where there is more potential for them to define themselves. The degree of success that they have in achieving self-definition may be ambiguous, but the comparison to the female characters in the Chekhov and Joyce stories shows them clearly to be women of the late twentieth century. They have more of the initiative of the male protagonists in the Chekhov and Joyce stories while they retain the perseverance of the women for whom they are counterparts.

Thus a close reading of these stories substantiates Elaine Showalter's general assessment in "My Friend, Joyce Carol Oates: An Intimate Portrait." Within these stories there certainly are "transforming revisions of perspective that come from female experience" (Milazzo 131). Oates's protagonists speak to the issues Oates admires Chekhov and Joyce for raising. Like these "masters," Oates sees women yearning for a more meaningful social role or greater affirmation of their points of view. Denied that, their frustration causes pain both for themselves and for others. Oates's fiction then takes another step, transforming that grief into a vision of a place of one's own making.

WORKS CITED

Bender, Eileen Teper. *Joyce Carol Oates, Artist in Residence*. Bloomington: Indiana University Press, 1987.

Chekhov, Anton. "The Lady with the Pet Dog." *The Image of Chekhov: Forty Stories in the Order in Which They Were Written*. Ed. Robert Payne. New York: Knopf, 1963, pp. 284–303.

Johnson, Greg. *Understanding Joyce Carol Oates*. Columbia: University of South Carolina Press, 1987.

Joyce, James. "The Dead." *Dubliners*. New York: Modern Library, 1954, pp. 224–288.

Maddox, Lucy B. "Gabriel and Othello: Opera in 'The Dead.'" *Studies in Short Fiction*. 24 (Summer 1987): 271–277.

Milazzo, Lee, ed. *Conversations with Joyce Carol Oates*. Jackson: University Press of Mississippi, 1989.

Oates, Joyce Carol. "The Dead." *Marriages and Infidelities*. Greenwich, CT: Fawcett, 1973, pp. 380–409.

———. "The Lady with the Pet Dog." *Marriages and Infidelities*. Greenwich, CT: Fawcett, 1973, pp. 327–344.

———. *The Wheel of Love and Other Stories*. New York: Vanguard Press, 1970.

Gender and Genre: The Case of the Novel-in-Stories

Margot Kelley

> Each epoch has its own system of genres, which stands in some relation to the dominant ideology, and so on. Like any other institution, genres bring to light the constitutive features of the society to which they belong. (Todorov 19)

Roberta Fernández's *Intaglio: A Novel in Six Stories*, which received a Multicultural Publishers Award in 1991, is composed of stories about women finding ways to "express themselves creatively in a preliterate society" (Interview). In it, Fernández wanted not only to present several women in relation to distinct art forms but also to convey a sense that creative energies are transmitted from the women of one generation to those of the next. To communicate this combination of distinctness and continuity, she composed a series of stories that worked together to form a novel, much like Gloria Naylor's *The Women of Brewster Place*. Indeed, Fernández said that when she first read *Brewster Place*, her reaction was a sense of legitimation because "someone else [was] doing this. And so it gave me validity" (Interview).

Fernández and Naylor are far from alone in creating books that work as what I call *novels-in-stories*; to the contrary, this genre, which merges elements of the short story with those of the novel, is among the most widely explored recent developments in North American fiction. The novel-in-stories has precursors among the framed tales that "date back at least as far as the *Panchatantra* (compiled before A.D. 500) and Ovid's *Meta-*

morphosis," as well as among short story cycles, which Susan Garland Mann notes have become especially popular during the twentieth century in the United States (7). Sherwood Anderson's *Winesburg, Ohio* and William Faulkner's *Go Down, Moses* are permutations of the short story cycle that can be read well as novels, and they are among the works that spring to mind as possible early instances of (or at least precursors to) the contemporary novel-in-stories. While these two works were written before 1980, this intergenre has become widely employed only by writers earning popular and/or academic acclaim during the last decade. Further, about 75 percent of the current writers are women, often women who live in positions of double marginality as members of visible minorities or as lesbians. This link between authorial identity and genre development merits exploration. In the pages that follow, I will offer a working definition of the novel-in-stories, offer a rationale for why they are becoming important at this historical moment, and indicate some reasons why this form is especially appealing to female authors.

Offering a structure-oriented definition (and calling it a *rovelle*), Dallas M. Lemmon situated the novel-in-stories on a continuum ranging from the short story collection to various forms of framed tales to the short story cycle to the rovelle to the novel (20, 23). Lemmon said that "in an ideal rovelle, each story, if plucked from the whole, would be able to stand alone and complete, yet the whole would be weakened by the loss of one of its parts—each story, when in its place in the overall sequence, would enrich and be enriched by the stories around it" (1). Having offered this definition, he also asserts that as of 1970, "no example [had achieved] this ideal" (1–2), explaining that either the short stories could not be "plucked" readily from the whole or they did not all "enrich" the novel. Today, in contrast, one can find many texts that achieve his ideal. Beginning, as Fernández aptly noted, with the arrival of Gloria Naylor's *The Women of Brewster Place* in 1980, bookstores of the last decade have carried a variety of novels-in-short-stories that have earned national attention. Louise Erdrich's *Love Medicine* (1985), *The Beet Queen* (1986), and *Tracks* (1989), all novels-in-stories, established her as a best-selling and widely taught contemporary writer. Amy

Tan's *The Joy Luck Club* (1989) spent months on the *New York Times* Bestseller List, while Jewelle Gomez's *The Gilda Stories: A Novel* (1991) has been similarly successful in feminist and gay/lesbian bookstores. (See bibliography for more novels-in-stories.)

Lemmon's description of the form as a combination of mutually enriching stories is an excellent preliminary definition; to it, we need to add some specific textual criteria, and should take into account the way in which the reader's interaction with the text differs in novels-in-stories from her interactions with a more conventional novel or a short story collection. In novels-in-stories, we find the following seven attributes:

1. Characters recur. In short story cycles, unity is often based on spatial and temporal proximity, or on thematic continuity. While such unities are also evident in novels-in-stories, the novel-in-stories must also have some characters who are present—or whose existence is implied—in all of the stories. Thus, while James Joyce's *Dubliners* is often cited as a short story cycle, it cannot be discussed usefully as a novel-in-stories. In contrast, Cornelia Nixon's work *Now You See It* can be considered a novel-in-stories, even though no single character is present in every story, because all of the stories concern Edward Hooper's family. The lives of the various family members are so interwoven that stories about one person presume the existence of, and inevitably provide resonances for stories about, the other family members.

2. Distinction between major and minor characters is blurred. Different characters function as protagonist in different stories. Further, the figures who would be minor characters in a novel, like neighbors, often assume more prominent positions—sometimes even narrating a story or two. In Rand Richard Cooper's *The Last to Go*, a neighbor whose significance has been minimal throughout the first 14 stories is central to the penultimate story.

3. Point of view and/or narrator vary. Just as the protagonists vary among stories, so do the narrators. And

(albeit less often) point of view may shift, either in fairly subtle ways related to the degree of omniscience or more explicitly between first and third person. When multiple narrators are used, the same event or moment is frequently described in different stories from shifting subject positions. For example, in Louise Erdrich's *Love Medicine*, the second and third stories ("Saint Marie" and "Wild Geese") both concern the day that Marie Lazarre and Nector Kashpaw encounter one another on the hill near the convent, and this incident is rendered in quite different terms by the two protagonists. This practice seems similar to William Faulkner's use of multiple perspectives; however, whereas we cannot satisfactorily read Darl's or Vardaman's or Cash's chapters independently in *As I Lay Dying*, Erdrich's stories can make sense alone.

4. Characters evolve. In short stories, we frequently see epiphanic moments, but not the follow-up to them; in novels-in-stories, we see that the characters have become different by the close of the entire text. In Gloria Naylor's *The Women of Brewster Place*, for example, the women are able to unite in "The Block Party" (if only in Mattie's dream) because of insights they have gained in the preceding stories.

5. Important events occur off-stage. One of the consequences of this inversion between what is emphasized and what is implied is a refocusing of our attention. In a sense, the spaces between stories operate the way bracketing does in Virginia Woolf's *To the Lighthouse*, where significant events, like family members dying, are presented in parentheses. If an author implies the occurrence of certain events in the gaps between stories, and does not assert them in parenthetical remarks (as Woolf did), she can markedly shift our perceptions. We see this method used well in Ruthann Robson's *Cecile*; between the consecutive stories "Home(less)" and "East of New York" the narrator is offered and accepts a job. Situating this seemingly major event in the gap indicates

that the moment of the job offer matters less than the effect it has on life afterward. Further, having events occur in the spaces between chapters suggests that the reader's interventions are going to be of particular importance in making meaning.

6. Each story has a climax, and these climaxes build upon each other. Consequently, the short stories each have epiphanic moments, and the action of the larger narrative follows a "rising sawtooth" pattern, creating a sense of development that is not shaped by teleology or by traditional notions of progress. This pattern resembles one described by French feminists Hélène Cixous and Luce Irigaray as an element of a viable *écriture feminine*. For example, in Roberta Fernández's *Intaglio*, the same narrator tells each story; however, the stories overlap temporally and therefore we do not get a feeling of linear development. But because the narrator describes more and more obviously momentous situations, their increased significance and the accretion of stories combine to create a sense of heightened climaxes later in the narrative.

7. Framing devices are minimal. For example, the brief "Dawn" and "Dusk" sections of *The Women of Brewster Place* provide the outer parameters for the amount of framing material appropriate to a novel-in-stories.

Of these features, only the sixth seems closely aligned with a gendered narrative property, so this list does not make it entirely clear why female authors in particular are the ones merging the short story with the novel. I suggest that the other traits, although not inevitably gendered, can be best understood in connection with theories about how identity is differently constructed along gender lines. Further, many of these traits seem logical extensions of postmodern techniques, a connection that suggests another reason this form is being explored now.

But perhaps the most often suggested explanation for merging the two forms is that short story writers realize that novels sell better than do story collections, and this new form allows them to break into the literary market more quickly.

Certainly, this is a plausible reason; first novels do sell better than first collections of short stories. Indeed, Cooper proffered this rationale when explaining why the hardcover version of his novel-in-stories, *The Last to Go*, was marketed as "a book of stories," while the paperback (over which he had less input) was marketed as "a novel." However, individual short stories have an even greater chance of being disseminated than either novels or collections. In fact, Cornelia Nixon said she wanted to write short stories precisely for their marketability. She explained that she wrote *Now You See It* in part because she decided not to write a conventional novel; after having written several novels that have not been published, she decided that writing short stories was "something [she] needed to do," both in order to continue writing and to earn some public recognition (Interview). Noting that her husband, poet Dean Young, is able to publish frequently and thereby earn immediate recognition for his work, Nixon said,

> He's constantly publishing in magazines. So he gets all this sense of accomplishment from that and he can be a poet even before he had a book published. And so, I don't know if he actually said it to me, but I figured out by watching him that it was something that I needed to do, to try and write stories. Plus, I had never written stories, and I think it's a completely different genre from the novel, and very exciting. Intellectually very exciting. You have to do something significant and satisfying in a very short space. (Interview)

She went on to say that "after I finished one of these short stories and I started on the second one, I just naturally started thinking of the same characters" (Interview). She also indicated that the multiperspectival *Alexandria Quartet* (1957), by Lawrence Durrell, and the near-novel-in-stories *Machine Dreams* (1984), by Jayne Anne Phillips, were among her aesthetic influences for *Now You See It*. Thus, while market pressures are important, they cannot decisively explain the emergence of this form.

From an authorial standpoint, another reason for the merger of forms may be that authors recognize something in short stories that they can use to stave off the impending exhaustion of the novel as a genre in postmodern America

(Barth). Indeed, as Ruthann Robson explained when discussing her novel-in-stories, *Cecile,* the novel per se was not a viable form for the story she wanted to tell because "form is a political thing, you know, [and the form of the novel is tied to] nineteenth century notions of progress," notions that did not seem appropriate to conveying the exigencies of contemporary life in general and to her chronicling of a lesbian couple's daily life in particular (Interview). Similarly, Jewelle Gomez explained that *The Gilda Stories* began as a series of related stories, and that when her publisher urged her to make it more novel-like, she was adamant that "it still be called 'The Gilda Stories'." She said, "I felt that's the way I needed to skip through history. And while I agreed that creating a narrative storyline would be valuable, I didn't want to give up the episodic sense of it" (Interview). Robson and Gomez do not simply reject the short story and the novel; they revise these two preexisting literary forms to do various things that seemed impossible within the confines of either. In doing so, they illustrate Tzvetan Todorov's claim that new genres come "quite simply from other genres. A new genre is always the transformation of an earlier one, or of several" (15). Further, they demonstrate the soundness of Hans Robert Jauss's assertion that a "new form . . . does not appear just 'in order to relieve the old form that already is no longer artistic.' It also can make possible a new perception of things by preforming the content of a new experience" (41). The novel-in-stories form certainly makes possible new perceptions and new perspectives, for both reader and writer. And these new perspectives are not confined to the literary, but are linked inextricably to new perceptions in the cultural sphere as well. More broadly speaking, a reciprocal relationship between cultural change (new cultural perspectives) and literary change exists and is contributing to the present proliferation of novels-in-stories. Furthermore, while the definition offered above focuses upon narratological matters, it is also true that the content of novels-in-stories reflects a changed sensibility: Many of these works concern new family structures, like the lesbian couple and their son in Robson's book, and many provide new slants on traditional literary topics.

Hayden White discusses this sort of link between literary form and culture in "The Problem of Change in Literary History":

> Writers may experiment with different genres, with different messages, even with different systems of encodation and decodation. But a given product of such experimentation will find an audience "programmed" to receive innovative messages and contacts only if the sociocultural context is such as to sustain an audience whose experience of that context corresponds to the *modes of message formulation and conveyance* adopted by a given writer. (107–108)

Following his cue, we can say that writers are producing novels-in-stories now not only because the market will bear them, and because writers see the narrative possibilities as intriguing, but also because members of the general audience are ready (or "programmed") to receive such texts. White explains that we have become ready for works like these because we, members of the "potential audience," have been "so constituted as to render unintelligible or banal both the messages and the modes of contact that prevailed in some preceding era" (108). When we consider Jauss once again, our "horizon of expectations" has been altered, in part by "the everyday experience of life" (41)—so much that the new form seems not merely acceptable, but rather desirable, for it seems to "solve formal and moral problems left behind by" past works (32).

One element of our everyday lives that may be particularly relevant is television. In "Television and Recent American Fiction," Cecelia Tichi considers how the ideas of media critic Raymond Williams and the broadcast analyst John Ellis might apply to "TV-age fiction." Williams has noted that broadcast has changed our perceptual processes: Instead of thinking about discrete entities, we are now attuned to thinking of "sequence as *flow*" (Tichi 118). Ellis modifies this claim, suggesting that within the flow are "'segments,' all demanding 'short bursts of attention.' In this sense, [Tichi points out that] 'flow' is really segmentation without closure, something like an endless string of bright beads" (119). Like television series, novels-in-stories are characterized by "segmented flow," although the literary works have more readily apparent closure than do television series. (Erdrich's *Love Medicine* is the exception; in 1992, she discovered several stories in her notebooks that she felt belonged in the novel, and in 1993 a new edition of the book was published.)

Thanks to our new horizon, we are prepared to accept new forms and to see the "notion of progress" implicit to the classic realist text, for example, as problematic. And sensing that, we can recognize that ideological commitments are embedded not only in the content but also in the form of a narrative. Fredric Jameson argues persuasively that the ideological component of a text is especially clear "in the area of literary genre," because "genre is essentially a socio-symbolic message, or in other terms, . . . form is immanently and intrinsically an ideology in its own right" (99).

Without the (ad)vantage of spatial or temporal distance, one can comment only in a limited way upon the ideology of a contemporary genre; nonetheless, two features of the novel-in-stories that differ from earlier forms and that are likely important are the interconnections among the stories and the conspicuously constructed nature of the characters. Through these two elements, authors of novels-in-stories are able to assent to postmodern fragmentation and dissociation and still offer modes of being and knowing that allow their characters—and potentially their readers—to move beyond the paralysis implicit to many postmodern visions. And it is in terms of this renewed hope generally, and its mode of representation specifically, that we can understand why women (particularly Chicanas, African American women, and lesbians) find this form conducive to their needs.

In "The Short Story: The Long and the Short of It," Mary Louise Pratt offers eight distinctions between novels and short stories. The first is that "the novel tells a life, the short story tells a fragment of a life" (182). Most often, she says, this "fragment of a life" is a "moment-of-truth" from which one can "deduce things about the whole life"; when this occurs, the short story is "more novel-like, . . . more complete" (183). In other words, she suggests that good "moment-of-truth" short stories are like miniature novels; that is, the distinction between the two forms is a matter of scale. In a novel-in-stories, then, we would say that the whole is an accretion of self-similar scalar parts. This understanding raises a concern about how these stories fit together, for a series of short stories does not inevitably form a novel-in-stories any more than a cluster of branches does a tree. Quoting literary critic Forrest Ingram on a closely related form, the short story cycle, Susan Garland Mann points out that one of the ways that the stories fit together is by establishing a governing "tension between the one and the many, . . . asserting the individuality of its components on the one hand and of highlighting, on the other, the bonds of unity which make the many into a single whole" (18). Like the relational models for female psychological development put forward by theorists Nancy Chodorow, Carol Gilligan, and others, this genre model suggests that a coherent or unified identity requires both autonomy and connectivity. Therefore, it comes as little surprise that many of the recent novels-in-stories are not only woman-authored but are explorations of family life with a focus on mother-daughter relationships, a topic that emphasizes this tension (see *Intaglio, The Joy Luck Club, Monkeys*, and others).

Describing a closely related form, J. Gerald Kennedy suggests that the way this tension is manipulated is in the arrangement of the stories—"three strategies of arrangement seem most clearly related to the production of signification: progression, combination, and juxtaposition" (15). He goes on to note that "between any two adjacent stories in a collection lies a node of signification which may be more or less suggestive, depending upon the connections and oppositions between the specific tales" (17). Like ellipses in fiction, the gaps between the stories are a space where the reader is especially responsible for generating significance. Shari Benstock argues in *Textualizing the Feminine* that such spaces exceed conventional representation practices; accordingly, they are sites that correspond "textually to the traversable inner limit between Kristeva's symbolic and semiotic: . . . the vanishing point of rational meaning and the entrance to unconscious structures of representation" (139). In short, they are a space where the "feminine" can be registered textually without being (re)contained.

Both the dynamic of the overall structure and the uses to which the individual gaps between stories are put can be understood using feminist psychoanalytic models. These two narrative elements offer writers alternatives that help them to circumvent the ideological assumptions about a coherent subject that are implicit to both the conventional short story and the novel, while not miring them in the uncertainties of postmodern forms. Furthermore, as we begin considering the novel-in-stories through such a lens, we realize that the characters themselves are frequently doing analogous work to shore up their own fragmented identities. And, it is only through the accretion of stories into a novel that relatively coherent images of/for the characters emerge. By foregrounding the constructedness of the characters' identities, and by recapitulating the formal discontinuities at the level of characterization, novel-in-stories writers prompt us to think about the characters (and, by extension, the subjects more generally) as multiply identified, as entities for whom identity is relational and, equally significant, negotiated.

Such a subject is precisely the kind contemporary feminists have been trying to describe. Indeed, as Paul Smith points out in *Discerning the Subject*, the "properly feminist agent" or "subject" is one who exists "at the interstices between a humanistically identified 'subject' and some more radical or utopian and dispersed 'subject,' [where] both notions operate in a mutually enabling dialectic, bound together by their very contradictions or by the negativity that underpins their heterogeneity" (150). Such a subject is not a unified, coherent, fixed subject, nor is it a decentered, fragmented, poststructuralist one; such a subject manifests "a recognition of both the specificity of any 'subject's' history and also of the necessary negotiations with other 'subjects'" (158). Negotiating between coherence and fragmentation, as well as between autonomy and interactivity, this subject is aware of its multiple, ideologically interpollated subject-positions and, in fact, consequently is able to act subversively. Smith notes that "what binds subject-positions together is precisely their difference. That is, the contradictions between them are a product of the negativity which enjoins the 'subject' to construct, recognize, and exploit difference. It is negativity which also and simultaneously produces the human agent" (150).

This feminist subject is a useful model for understanding the characters in novels-in-stories, whose multiple identities are presented in sundry stories; in a novel-in-stories, the reader presumes a coherence among all the characters who bear the same name (in Nixon's *Now You See It*, for example, the Edward Hooper who appears in the opening story, "Alf's Garage," is the "same" Edward Hooper who dies in the closing story, "Now You See It"). Yet, the reader also knows, through the focus on individual moments, that identity is constituted through relations with other subjects, and is continually negotiated and renegotiated, making identity itself a somewhat evanescent phenomenon.

One can see the significance that such a subject and structure will have to the kind of story that can be told by considering Amy Tan's first book, *The Joy Luck Club*, and her description of it. Composed in four sections of four stories each, the book alternates between stories narrated by the Chinese mothers and others told by their first-generation American daughters. Because Suyuan Woo has died, her daughter Jing-mei narrates the sections that would, according to the book's structure, have been Suyuan's. The structure nicely evinces not only the varied perspectives the women have regarding similar events but also the tenuous balance between separation and connection that many psychoanalytic theorists argue is a key to understanding mother-daughter relationships. Tan maintains that she "wasn't as clever as most people make [her] out to be," regarding the form of *Joy Luck*. At first, she said that she "did not have in mind structuring them so tightly, although they were four sections. I always had four sections, an intro piece to each one that was based more on emotional content that was linked. . . . [But] it was always four mothers and four daughters" (Interview).

Despite the tightness and aptness of the structure, Tan did not regard the book as a novel, and said that she was initially "very suspicious" about her publisher's desire to label it as one. Her editor agreed to call it a short story collection and "the galley copies say 'stories' very clearly on the title page"; nevertheless, the "early advance reviews, from Alice Walker and Louise Erdrich, all called it a novel. . . . So we compromised. In the jacket it says 'A first work of fiction'. . . . And most of the reviews called it a novel" (Interview). Now, Tan assents that *The Joy Luck Club* is like:

> Louise Erdrich's sense of the novel. That it is a novel of a community, and that it is linked emotionally and through interconnections of those people. It does not follow a traditional plot line, a traditional narrative line that you can follow in the same sense (although I think it is very structured in terms of the emotional flow). That the beginning is about loss and a sense of a lack of connection, and the end is a movement toward that connection, that feeling that there is some reconciliation, that there is some way to still find the connection even after death. (Interview)

The final paragraph of Tan's novel-in-stories conveys Jing-mei's success in reconnecting with her female relatives, while also maintaining the tension between separateness and connection. Standing in an airport with the two half-sisters whom she has just met, Jing-mei is watching a photograph of the three of them develop:

> The gray-green surface changes to the bright colors of our three images, sharpening and deepening all at once. And although we don't speak, I know we all see it: Together we look like our mother. Her same eyes, her same mouth, open in surprise to see, at last, her long-cherished wish. (332)

Distinct though the three women remain, they are connected through the facial features they share with each other and with their mother.

Just as the narratological features described above are especially appropriate for evading patriarchal formulations of identity, then, the subject/agent constituted within novels-in-stories is uniquely suitable for writers who wish to explore feminist modes of being in the wake of poststructuralism. As neither short story nor novel (but both), populated with characters who are neither fragmented nor coherent (but both), valorizing neither complete autonomy nor total unity (but both), the novel-in-stories provides writers who exist in various liminal cultural positions an ideologically appropriate genre with which to enter the literary economy. It also provides a form consistent with the experiences and desires of not only members of visible or sexual minorities but of an ever-increasing percentage of the population seeking ways to move beyond postmodernism.

WORKS CITED

Barth, John. "The Literature of Exhaustion." *Atlantic Monthly* (August 1967): 29–34.

Benstock, Shari. *Textualizing the Feminine: On the Limits of Genre*. Norman: University of Oklahoma Press, 1991.

Cooper, Rand Richard. Personal Interview. June 16, 1992.

Fernández, Roberta. Telephone Interview. August 1, 1992.

Gomez, Jewelle. Personal Interview. June 12, 1992.

Jameson, Fredric. *The Political Unconscious: Narrative as a Socially Symbolic Act*. Ithaca, NY: Cornell University Press, 1981.

Jauss, Hans Robert. *Toward an Aesthetic of Reception*. Translation by Timothy Bahti. Introduction by Paul de Man. Minneapolis: University of Minnesota Press, 1982.

Kennedy, J. Gerald. "Toward a Poetics of the Short Story Cycle." *Les Cahiers de la Novelle/Journal of the Short Story in English* 11 (Autumn 1988): 9–25.

Lemmon, Dallas M., Jr. "The Rovelle, or The Novel of Interrelated Stories: M. Lermontov, G. Keller, S. Anderson." Diss. Indiana University, 1970.

Mann, Susan Garland. *The Short Story Cycle: A Genre Companion and Reference Guide*. Westport, CT: Greenwood, 1988.

Nixon, Cornelia. Personal Interview. April 11, 1992.

Pratt, Mary Louise. "The Short Story: The Long and the Short of It." *Poetics*. 10 (February 1981): 175–194.

Robson, Ruthann. Personal Interview. June 30, 1992.

Smith, Paul. *Discerning the Subject*. Minneapolis: University of Minnesota Press, 1988.

Tan, Amy. *The Joy Luck Club*. New York: Ivy Books, 1989.

———. Personal Interview. May 19, 1992.

Tichi, Cecelia. "Television and Recent American Fiction." *American Literary History* 1.1 (Spring 1988): 110–130.

Todorov, Tzvetan. *Genres of Discourse*. Translated by Catherine Porter. Cambridge, UK: Cambridge University Press, 1990.

White, Hayden. "The Problem of Change in Literary History." *New Literary History* 7.1 (Autumn 1975): 97–111.

NOVELS-IN-STORIES*

*In further refining the category "novel-in-stories," one might decide that some of these texts no longer "fit." This is a working list.

Alvarez, Julia. *How the Garcia Girls Lost Their Accents*. New York: Plume, 1992.

Ascher, Straus. *Red Moon/Red Lake*. New York: McPherson, 1988.

Barth, John. *Lost in the Funhouse*. New York: Bantam Books, 1969.

Birdsell, Sandra. *Agassiz: A Novel in Six Stories*. Minneapolis, MN: Milkweed, 1991.

Brown, Rosellen. *Street Games: A Neighborhood*. Minneapolis, MN: Milkweed, 1991.

Busch, Frederick. *Domestic Particulars: A Chronicle*. New York: New Directions, 1976.

Chappell, Fred. *I Am One of You Forever*. Baton Rouge: Louisiana State University Press, 1985.

Chávez, Denise. *The Last of the Menu Girls*. Houston: Arte Publico Press, 1986.

Cisneros, Sandra. *The House on Mango Street*. Houston: Arte Publico Press, 1989.

Cooper, Rand Richard. *The Last to Go*. New York: Avon Books, 1988.

Doerr, Harriet. *Stones for Ibarra*. New York: Viking, 1978.

Donnelly, Nisa. *The Bar Stories: A Novel After All*. New York: St. Martin's, 1989.

Erdrich, Louise. *The Beet Queen*. New York: Holt, 1986.

———. *Love Medicine*. New York: Bantam Books, 1985. Rpt. New York: HarperCollins, 1993.

———. *Tracks*. New York: Harper & Row, 1989.

Faulkner, William. *Go Down, Moses*. 1942. Rpt. New York: Random House, 1991.

Fernández, Roberta. *Intaglio: A Novel in Six Stories*. Houston: Arte Publico Press, 1990.

Gomez, Jewelle. *The Gilda Stories: A Novel*. Ithaca, NY: Firebrand, 1991.

Laurence, Margaret. *A Bird in the House*. Toronto: McClelland and Stewart, Ltd., 1974.

McNally, T.M. *Low Flying Aircraft: Stories by T.M. McNally*. Atlanta: University of Georgia Press, 1991.

Minot, Susan. *Monkeys*. New York: Washington Square Press, 1986.

Munro, Alice. *Lives of Girls and Women*. New York: Plume Fiction, 1971.

Naylor, Gloria. *The Women of Brewster Place: A Novel in Seven Stories*. New York: Penguin, 1980.

Nixon, Cornelia. *Now You See It*. Boston: Little, Brown, 1991.

O'Brien, Tim. *The Things They Carried*. New York: Penguin, 1990.

Phillips, Jayne Anne. *Machine Dreams*. New York: Pocket Books, 1984.

Porter, Connie. *All-Bright Court*. New York: HarperCollins, 1991.

Rivera, Tómas. *. . . Y No Se lo Trago la Tierra/ . . . And the Earth Did Not Devour Him*. Translated by Evangelina Vigil-Piñón. Houston: Arte Publico Press, 1992.

Robson, Ruthann. *Cecile*. Ithaca, NY: Firebrand, 1991.

Shapiro, Jane. *After Moondog*. New York: Harcourt Brace Jovanovich, 1992.

Straight, Susan. *Aquaboogie: A Novel in Stories*. Minneapolis: Milkweed, 1990.

Tan, Amy. *The Joy Luck Club*. New York: Ivy Books, 1989.

Tyler, Anne. *Dinner at the Homesick Restaurant*. New York: Knopf, 1982.

Updike, John. *Too Far to Go: The Maples Stories*. New York: Fawcett Crest, 1979.

Welty, Eudora. *The Golden Apples*. San Diego: Harcourt Brace Jovanovich, 1949.

The Great Ventriloquist Act: Gender and Voice in the Fiction Workshop*

Julie Brown

1. Six men get together for a hunting trip. They drink beer and shoot animals, but the real party begins when a truck full of "babes" pulls up.
2. A male prison guard develops a friendship with a male prisoner and eventually learns that their lives have been similar—both are "trapped" by society.
3. Two men in a bar get drunk together, share their fantasies about ideal women, and become friends.
4. A man strives for spiritual enlightenment, and is later visited by God himself—disguised as a poor, innocent boy.
5. A house catches on fire. The owner saves his daughter, but must forever live with the guilty knowledge that he could not rescue his wife.

You might not be surprised if I told you the stories summarized above were written by undergraduate students in an introduction to a fiction writing course. But would you be surprised if I told you the stories above—and many others like them—were written by *female* students? For several years, I have been studying stories by my female undergraduate creative writing students and have observed that the students are, with alarming frequency, finding male voices preferable to their own. It was a male colleague of mine, Robert Brown, who first brought this issue to my attention; although I am committed to feminism and teach courses in the Women's Studies Department at Youngstown State University, I failed to notice that a large percentage of my female students write stories that privilege the male gender at the cost of their own. The students themselves, unfortunately, usually fail to notice this as well.

Many female student writers appropriate a male persona to serve as narrator for their stories. More than half of my female students in a given quarter used male narrators to tell at least one of their stories. There was Virginia's story, for example, about a man who hates his boss and hates his job. After he finds a new job, he returns to murder his old boss. Or there was Jennifer's story, about a death-obsessed man who plays chess with a new friend. When the chess game ends, the friend dies.

The choice of narrator does not seem to be dictated by the subject matter. In these two stories, as well as the five above, a female narrator would have worked just as well and might have been more original or more interesting. Curious, I asked these authors why they decided to use male narrators. Virginia said, "It was more challenging this way." Jennifer answered, "It was easier to do it like this." They were both right, but I suspected there was more to it than that.

If the story is told in third person, female authors will often choose a male character to be the protagonist. The protagonist is unlike the author in that he is male, but he often resembles the author in other areas: race, age, class, education, and family situation. One student, a shy, older, single woman, wrote a story called "The Loner," about a man who is shy, older, and single. When I asked her why she chose a male protagonist, she said it was because she wrote the story as an imitation of Donald Barthelme's "The Genius," an option that I had given them. I wondered why she had chosen a male-authored story to imitate.

Like a female impersonator who fools an unsuspecting audience, these women often develop their male characters in such a convincing manner that the reader is completely taken in. When we workshop the stories anonymously, the other students assume the author is male. They rarely question the authenticity of the voice, or ask, "Would a man *really* say this?"

They especially don't question the author's gender when the narrator or protagonist is clearly misogynist. I read four or five short stories last winter that shocked me with the horrifying manner in which the male characters treated the female characters. One woman wrote about a man who beats up his mother in a rage because she has ruined his favorite book. Another wrote about a man who beats his daughters mercilessly after their mother dies of illness. In both cases the motivation for the male's anger was provided in order to make the reader sympathize with the protagonist, rather than with the victim. If male students had written these stories I would have been angry. Somehow, these stories made me feel sad—not for the fictional victims, but for the authors who created them.

When I ask these women why they use male narrators and protagonists, they are often unable—or unwilling—to discuss the thought process behind their writing. They sense that Feminism (with a capital F) is once again challenging the decisions they have made and, by extension, who they are. When I push for answers, I often get quick responses like Virginia's or Jennifer's—that using a male point of view is either more challenging or easier than using a female point of view. But if this were true, it would seem likely that as many male students would use the female point of view in their stories. Of course, male students do occasionally use female narrators (I still remember a brilliant male-authored story about a woman's decision to have an abortion), but these instances are rare; I would guess that fewer than one in ten has tried using a female voice.

In *The Anxiety of Influence*, Harold Bloom theorizes that the text an author writes is actually a revision of the text(s) she has read. It makes sense, then, to see these female authors writing in response to the male-authored texts they have been reading. When I survey my students about what literature they read in high school, they still respond with canonical favorites: *Huckleberry Finn*, *The Old Man and the Sea*, *The Great Gatsby*, and so on. They may wish, then, to revise the themes of the "American tradition," to write stories about friendship, about courage, or about shattered dreams. Since they do not read works that show female protagonists in these roles, it must indeed be easier, as Jennifer said, for these authors to use male heroes. This tendency is tellingly dramatized by one female student's detective story: the fictional detective is a young man whose favorite author is Poe.

It is certainly true that more women are writing than ever before and that their works are being published with greater frequency. One might even argue that women have an easier time being published than men do in literary journals that are consciously trying to recognize marginalized groups. But somehow, this new sensitivity to gender has not trickled down to my working-class, nontraditional, first-generation students yet. Their literary role models are still largely limited to the dead white Western males they read in their public school anthologies. When I ask them to name female authors who have influenced them, Emily Dickinson is one of the few "literary" female authors they can name. And she did not write short fiction.

It may be that the female appropriation of the male voices has less to do with influence than with acceptance. Joanna Russ has suggested that because our culture is dominated by the male perspective, our cultural myths and literature are too (4). Russ believes that women writers who wish to gain recognition in a male-dominant literary world have historically had two options available. One option is to write about the adventures of men; the other is to write about the women who love them.

And this is what beginning female students write about—men. Perhaps they are already sensitive to society's double standard that writing about women is "women's writing," while writing about men is "writing." Are they afraid that stories about women's experiences will not be taken seriously? Can it be that these women are writing about male adventures in an attempt to please the audience they are writing for? In a workshop situation, is it their male peers whose approval they value most? How far are they willing to go in order to gain that approval? Are they willing to swallow their own voices?

The writing workshop, like any other group, develops a dynamic that is partly based on the gender of its members. It has been my observation that when a male student or two begins to dominate the discussion, the females say less and less. It only takes one such remark as "I can't stand stories about girls getting their period" or "Who cares about this character's sewing project" to convince young authors that they had better find new subject matter—if they want their work to be accepted by "the group."

Writing about male experience through the gendered lens of a male perspective is indeed challenging for women authors, as Virginia explained. It is also costly. As Russ points out, when the female author ignores female culture, the female physiological experience, and her own female history, she places herself in a position of falsification:

> She is an artist creating a world in which persons of her kind cannot be artists, a conciousness central to itself creating a world in which women have no consciousness, a successful person creating a world in which persons like herself cannot be successes. She is a self trying to pretend that she is a different Self, one for whom her own self is Other. (10)

I remember the very first short story I wrote as an undergraduate for a creative writing class twelve years ago. It was about a young man who was a writer and a painter who used both media to create the essence of a perfect woman. Against his will, the love object begins to determine her own fate, both in the story and in the portrait. Eventually, she erases herself from his typewritten pages and from his canvas. Naive, I admit. Derivative, I confess. But why did I use a *male* protagonist for this story? Why did I relegate the female character to the position of object? And a self-destructive one at that? I suspect I may have had ambivalent feelings about my "right" to see myself as an author.

Russ maintains that only one other option has been historically available to women authors who wish to gain literary acceptance. That is to invent female characters who fit into the traditional heroine pattern—The Woman Who Fell in Love—including such variations as "How She Got Married. How She Did Not Get Married (always tragic). How She Fell in Love and Committed Adultery. How She Saved Her Marriage but Just Barely. How She Loved a Vile Seducer and Eloped. How She Loved a Vile Seducer, Eloped, and Died in Childbirth" (9).

Thus, when a female student does create a female protagonist, the character is often developed in relation to the male characters of the story; she is the wife, daughter, or mother of an important man, and this is how her characterization unfolds. Younger authors are especially prone to this. When I examined several dozen short stories written by local high school girls, I found that nearly every female character was somebody's girlfriend. Her identity is so intertwined with her boyfriend's that her very survival sometimes depends upon his existence. In "Mercy," for example, a young girl mediates on an earlier breakup with her boyfriend. At the story's close, she commits suicide. Has this young author been reading Flaubert? Tolstoy? What message has she learned from these literary giants about the options of fictional heroines?

While many terrific stories and novels have been written about women and the human relationships they are involved in, I believe it is also important for women to read and write works in which women have careers, goals, and dreams that do not revolve around the business of being someone else's caretaker or appendage.

Finally, it may be that the young woman who sits down to write her first story writes about the experience of a man because the society she lives in valorizes male experience over female, and she herself has internalized this value system. When she hears men discussed on the evening news, sees men on the cover of *Time* magazine, and reads about men in her history books, she receives a message—that only men and their exploits are worth writing about. She may feel that her own experience is trivial, not worth recording or sharing. Josephine Donovan discusses this concept in terms of "the masculinization of women's minds" that occurs when "men hold power and define women in relation to themselves" (98). Thus it is not usually a conscious decision to use a male hero in her story. The author is merely reduplicating the larger text of her culture.

I am reminded here of a well-known psychological study that tested a roomful of children by offering them two dolls to play with: one was black, the other white. Not surprisingly, the white children all chose the white doll to play with. The majority of black children, however, preferred the white doll as well. The message of this study is chilling—that minority children who grow up surrounded by the media and culture of a dominant group will, for a time at least, perceive images of that group as desirable, even preferable to their own. And so it is with female authors who find themselves surrounded by androcentric media and culture: they speak through the internalized voice of the dominant group, leading to what Donovan calls "psychic alienation that is fundamentally schizophrenic" (100). This alienation is further revealed by stories in which the male hero turns against the females in the story; the author identifies more strongly with her oppressors than with her fellow oppressed.

After my "male author" story, I went on to write a series of love stories. It was not until *Cream City Review*'s editor, Val Ross, pointed out to me that my stories always depicted women in relation to men that I became conscious of what I was doing. Her comment awakened in me a new sensitivity to fiction by and about women. It also challenged me to begin searching for other kinds of stories to write—stories about women who work, buy houses, travel, and develop friendships with other women. I like to offer my female students a similar challenge.

For when they toss away the ventriloquist's dummies and begin to search for their own voices, exciting things happen in their writing. They remember what they surely must have known all along—that their own gendered experience, rooted in female physiology, culture, and history, does indeed provide a richly varied and interesting subject matter worth writing about. They learn that a female voice can enable them to sing, to mourn, to express what they could not express with a male voice. They also gain a sense of community with other women writers and with women who might someday read their works.

Gaining a sense of community is a vital step toward reclaiming the female voice in student writing. Donovan theorizes that banding together is an important step for any oppressed group that seeks to free itself from oppression:

> For the silenced Other to begin to speak, to create art, she must be in communication with others of her group in order that a collective "social construction of reality" be articulated. Other social witnesses from the oppressed

> group express their views, to validate one's own truth, that one may name it. (101)

This is one reason why I like to give creative writing assignments in my women's studies literature courses. In a class that is usually most if not all female, women have an easier time writing about female issues without fearing the groans or rolling eyes of male students.

One summer I taught a course called "Reading and Writing Women's Short Stories." The quarter was broken into three components. We spent roughly half the time reading and enjoying and discussing short stories by U.S. women authors including Sarah Jewett, Willa Cather, Zora Hurston, Amy Tan, Ann Beattie, Bobbie Ann Mason, Alice Walker, Louise Erdrich, Joyce Carol Oates, and others. We read entire collections by some authors and individual stories by others.

We then spent about a fourth of the time studying the critical questions pertaining to women's short story writing: What is women's literature? What is *écriture feminine*? Why is the short story genre appealing to women writers? To women readers? What is the relationship between women's short stories and the magazines in which they appear? What differences appear in the way women of different groups use the short story form? What contributions have U.S. women made to the short story genre? Why have short stories by women received so little critical attention? We began by reading Ruth Sherry's excellent *Studying Women's Writing: An Introduction* (which, incidentally, covers only novels, poems, and plays by women—no short stories), then read various articles that addressed the above questions. I also had the students work in the library in small groups to see what they could find out about the questions our literature discussion had raised.

In the final few weeks, the students themselves wrote short stories. After they studied women writers, they *became* women writers (there were 12 women and 2 men in the class). Since many of them had never written a short story before, this was an exciting first for them. They had the option to rewrite a fairy tale into a modern setting, to rewrite (from a different point of view) a story we had all read, to write a fictionalized version of an experience that had happened to them, or to write a purely fictional story. This turned out to be the students' favorite part of the course; they all enjoyed writing short stories and reading them out loud to the group. I asked them what they learned from the assignment. One woman said she was surprised that her story showed "women's circular time" in the way it was structured. One woman remarked that she never realized how hard it was to write realistic dialogue. Another said she used a male protagonist for her story "without really thinking about it," and we discussed the possible reasons for her decision. I was so encouraged by what the students learned that I have decided to use creative writing assignments in all women's literature classes.

While we become sensitive to the fact that young women are swallowing their voices as they write fiction, we should remember that other identity traits are often erased as well. One spring term, for example, a student named Carolyn turned in several apparently nonsexual stories. On the last day, she shyly handed me a story, telling me "this is what I *really* want to write." It was a lesbian love story. At that point, I realized that I had not included any lesbians on the reading list. I immediately gave her a bibliography so she could at least read some lesbian stories on her own. I also thanked her for sharing her work with me. In a similar situation, a black woman named Vicky wrote a series of children's stories in which her characters' physical traits were not described. When I asked her why, she said she wanted the others in the class (all white) to see her not as a "Black author," but as an "author." I was not sure what to say, other than to note that I thought African American children would be thrilled to read a book about children who looked like them. I told her I hoped that one day she would be comfortable enough to celebrate her heritage in her writing.

I believe we have a responsibility to foster a learning environment in which all students feel comfortable writing about and sharing their own gendered experience. It is not an easy task, and there is no guarantees our efforts will uncover the next Charlotte Gilman or Zora Hurston. Still, there are a few steps we might consider taking that would enable all of our students—male and female—to recognize the role that socially constructed gender plays in the production and reception of literature. The following suggestions pertain mostly to creative writing courses, but other courses might incorporate them as well.

1. Assign a good deal of fiction reading to the students, especially works by female authors.
2. Share essays with students about the challenges of writing, including essays about struggles that female authors face.
3. Give an assignment that asks students to write a fictional account of an experience that happened to them, using a narrator of the same gender. Then, ask all of the students to rewrite their stories from the opposite gender's point of view. Discuss the difference in the writing process for each version.
4. Encourage female authors to write about their own gender, and let them know that their own experiences are valuable and worth sharing.
5. English departments should make sure there are women in the department who can teach creative writing, and should bring in female guest readers to serve as role models.

Recognize that beginning writers often search for an authentic voice by first "trying on" and discarding a multitude of voices. Eventually, the writers who stay with it will find a voice that has a greater measure of authenticity—one that comes from the self.

NOTE

*This article first appeared in *AWP Chronicle* 26.1 (Sept. 1993): 7–9. Reprinted with permission.

WORKS CITED

Donovan, Josephine. "Toward a Women's Poetics." *Feminist Issues in Literary Scholarship.* Ed. Shari Benstock. Bloomington: Indiana University Press, 1987, pp. 98–107.

Russ, Joanna. "What Can a Heroine Do? Or, Why Women Can't Write." *Images of Women in Fiction.* Ed. Susan Koppelman Cornillon. Bowling Green, OH: Bowling Green University Press, 1972, pp. 3–19.

Sherry, Ruth. *Studying Women's Writing: An Introduction.* London: Edward Arnold, 1989.

Bibliography of Primary Sources

Susan Koppelman

Selected Bibliography of U.S. Women's Short Story Collections

Alcott, Louisa May (1832–1888)

Flower Fables or Fairy Tales (1855)

Hospital Sketches; and Camp and Fireside Stories (1863–1869)

Silver Pitchers (1876)

Glimpses of Louisa: A Centennial Sampling of the Best Short Stories (Ed. Cornelia Meigs. New York: Little, Brown, 1968)

A Double Life: Newly Discovered Thrillers of Louisa May Alcott (New York: Little, Brown, 1988)

Alternative Alcott (Ed. Elaine Showalter. New Brunswick, NJ: Rutgers University Press, 1988)

Louisa May Alcott: Selected Fiction (Ed. Daniel Shealy, Madeleine B. Stern, and Joel Myerson. New York: Little, Brown, 1990)

Austin, Mary Hunter (1868–1934)

Lost Borders (New York: Harper, 1909)

One-Smoke Stories (New York: Houghton, 1934)

Western Trails: A Collection of Short Stories by Mary Austin (Ed. Melody Graulich. Reno: University of Nevada Press, 1987)

Bambara, Toni Cade (1939–)

Gorilla, My Love (New York: Random House, 1972)
The Sea Birds Are Still Alive (New York: Random House, 1977)

Beattie, Ann (1947–)

Distortions (New York: Doubleday, 1976)
Secrets and Surprises (New York: Random House, 1978)
What Was Mine (New York: Random House, 1991)

Boyle, Kay (1902–)

Wedding Day and Other Stories (New York: Smith, 1930)
The First Lover and Other Stories (New York: Random House, 1933)
The White Horses of Vienna and Other Stories (New York: Harcourt Brace Jovanovich, 1936)
Thirty Stories (New York: Simon & Schuster, 1946)
Smoking Mountains: Stories of Post-War Germany (New York: McGraw-Hill, 1951)
Nothing Ever Breaks Except the Heart (New York: Doubleday, 1966)
Fifty Stories (New York: New Directions, 1992)

Brown, Alice (1856–1948)

Meadow-Grass: Tales of New England Life (1895)
Tiverton Tales (1899)
High Noon (New York: Houghton Mifflin, 1904)
Country Neighbors (New York: Houghton Mifflin, 1906)
The Country Road (New York: Houghton Mifflin, 1906)
The One-Footed Fairy and Other Stories (New York: Houghton Mifflin, 1911)
Vanishing Points (New York: Macmillan, 1913)
The Flying Teuton and Other Stories (New York: Macmillan, 1918)
Homespun and Gold (New York: Macmillan, 1920)

Cary, Alice (1820–1871)

Clovernook Papers, Or, Recollections of Our Neighborhood in the West (New York: Redfield, 1852)

Clovernook Papers, Or, Recollections of Our Neighborhood in the West, Second Series (New York: Redfield, 1853)

Clovernook Children (New York: Lovell, 1854)

The Adopted Daughter by Alice Cary and Other Tales (New York: Evans, 1859)

Pictures of Country Life (New York: Derby & Jackson, 1859)

Cather, Willa (1873–1947)

The Troll Garden (New York: McClure, 1905)

Youth and the Bright Medusa (New York: Knopf, 1920)

Obscure Destinies (New York: Knopf, 1932)

Old Beauty, and Others (New York: Knopf, 1948)

Five Stories (New York: Vintage, 1956)

Early Stories of Willa Cather (Ed. Mildred R. Bennett. New York: Dodd, 1957)

Willa Cather's Selected Short Fiction (Lincoln: University of Nebraska Press, 1965)

Uncle Valentine and Other Stories: Willa Cather's Uncollected Short Fiction, 1915–1929 (Lincoln: University of Nebraska Press, 1973)

Chávez, Denise (1948–)

The Last of the Menu Girls (Houston: Arte Publico Press, 1986)

Child, Lydia Maria Francis (1802–1880)

Evenings in New England (Boston: Cummings, Hilliard and Co., 1824)

The Coronal: A Collection of Miscellaneous Pieces, Written at Various Times (Boston: Carter and Hendee, 1831)

Flowers for Children, First and Second Series (New York: C.S. Francis and Co., 1844)

Fact and Fiction: A Collection of Stories (New York: C.S. Francis and Co., 1846)

Flowers for Children, Third Series (New York: C.S. Francis and Co., 1846)

Autumnal Leaves: Tales and Sketches in Prose and Rhyme (New York: C.S. Francis and Co., 1857)

Hobomok & Other Writings on Indians (Ed. Carolyn L. Karcher. New Brunswick, NJ: Rutgers University Press, 1986)

Cisneros, Sandra (1954–)

The House on Mango Street (Houston: Arte Publico Press, 1985)

Woman Hollering Creek and Other Stories (New York: Vintage, 1992)

Cooke, Rose Terry (1827–1892)

Somebody's Neighbors (1881)

Root-Bound (1885)

The Sphynx's Children (1886)

Huckleberries: Gathered from New England Hills (1891)

How Celia Changed Her Mind & Selected Stories (Ed. Elizabeth Ammons. New Brunswick, NJ: Rutgers University Press, 1986)

Davis, Rebecca Blaine Harding (1831–1910)

Silhouettes of American Life (New York: Scribner's, 1892)

Dove, Rita (1952–)

Fifth Sunday: Stories (Lexington: Callaloo Fiction Series, 1985)

Ferber, Edna (1887–1968)

Buttered Side Down (New York: Doubleday, 1912)

Personality Plus: Some Experiences of Emma McChesney and Her Son, Jock (New York: Stokes, 1914)

Roast Beef, Medium: The Business Adventures of Emma McChesney and Her Son, Jock (New York: Stokes, 1914)

Emma McChesney & Co. (New York: Stokes, 1915)

Cheerful, by Request (New York: Doubleday, 1918)

Half Portions (New York: Doubleday, 1920)

Gigolo (New York: Doubleday, 1922)

Mother Knows Best (New York: Doubleday, 1927)

They Brought Their Women: A Book of Short Stories (New York: Doubleday, 1933)

Your Town: Stories: Buttered Side Down; Cheerful, by Request; Gigolo (Stamford, CT: World, 1948)

One Basket: Thirty-One Short Stories (New York: Doubleday, 1957)

Freeman, Mary Eleanor Wilkins (1852–1930)

A Humble Romance and Other Stories (New York: Harper and Row, 1887)

A New England Nun and Other Stories (New York: Harper and Row, 1891)

Pot of Gold and Other Stories (New York: Lothrop, 1892)

Young Lucretia and Other Stories (New York: Harper and Row, 1892)

People of Our Neighborhood (New York: Doubleday, 1898)

Silence and Other Stories (New York: Harper and Row, 1898)

The Love of Parson Lord and Other Stories (New York: Harper and Row, 1900)

Understudies (New York: Harper and Row, 1901)

Six Trees: Short Stories (New York: Harper and Row, 1903)

The Wind in the Rose Bush and Other Stories of the Supernatural (New York: Doubleday, 1903)

The Givers: Short Stories (New York: Harper and Row, 1904)

The Winning Lady and Others (New York: Harper and Row, 1909)

The Copy-Cat and Other Stories (New York: Harper and Row, 1914)

Edgewater People (New York: Harper and Row, 1918)

The Best Stories of Mary E. Wilkins (Ed. Henry Wysham Lanier. New York: Harper and Row, 1927)

Selected Stories of Mary E. Wilkins Freeman (Ed. Marjorie Pryse. New York: Norton, 1983)

The Uncollected Stories of Mary Wilkins Freeman (Ed. Mary R. Reichardt. Jackson: University Press of Mississippi, 1992)

Gilchrist, Ellen (1935–)

In the Land of Dreamy Dreams (New York: Little, Brown, 1981)

Victory over Japan (New York: Little, Brown, 1984)

Drunk with Love (New York: Little, Brown 1986)

Glasgow, Ellen Anderson Gholson (1873–1945)

The Shadowy Third and Other Stories (New York: Doubleday, 1923)

The Collected Stories of Ellen Glasgow (Ed. Richard K. Meeker. Baton Rouge: Louisiana State University Press, 1988)

Hurst, Fannie (1889–1968)

Just Around the Corner: Romance en Casserole (New York: Harper and Row, 1914)

Every Soul Hath Its Song (New York: Harper and Row, 1916)

Gaslight Sonata (New York: Harper and Row, 1918)

Humoresque: A Laugh on Life with a Tear Behind It (New York: Harper and Row, 1919)

The Vertical City (New York: Harper and Row, 1922)

Song of Life (New York: Knopf, 1927)

Procession (New York: Harper and Row, 1929)

We Are Ten (New York: Harper and Row, 1937)

Hurston, Zora Neale (1903–1960)

Spunk: The Selected Stories of Zora Neale Hurston (Philadelphia: Turtle Isle, 1985)

Jewett, Sarah Orne (1849–1909)

Deephaven (1877)
Play Days: A Book of Stories for Children (1878)
Old Friends and New (1879)
Country By-Ways (1881)
The Mate of the Daylight and Friends Ashore (1884)
A White Heron and Other Stories (1886)
The King of Folly Island and Other People (1888)
Strangers and Wayfarers (1890)
Tales of New England (1890)
A Native of Winby and Other Tales (1893)
The Life of Nancy (1895)
The Queen's Twin and Other Stories (1899)
Best Stories (Ed. Willa Cather. New York: Houghton Mifflin, 1925)
Deephaven and Other Stories (Ed. Richard Cary. Albany, NY: College and University Press, 1966)
The Country of the Pointed Firs and Other Stories (New York: Norton, 1968)
The Uncollected Stories of Sarah Orne Jewett (Ed. Richard Cary. Colby, ME: Colby College Press, 1971)

Leguin, Ursula (1929–)

The Wind's Twelve Quarters (New York: Harper and Row, 1975)

Mason, Bobbie Ann (1940–)

Shiloh and Other Stories (New York: HarperCollins, 1990)

Naylor, Gloria (1950–)

The Women of Brewster Place (New York: Viking, 1982)

Oates, Joyce Carol (1938–)

By the North Gate (New York: Vanguard, 1963)

Upon the Sweeping Flood and Other Stories (New York: Vanguard, 1966)

The Wheel of Love and Other Stories (New York: Vanguard, 1970)

Marriages and Infidelities: Short Stories (New York: Vanguard, 1972)

All the Good People I've Left Behind (Santa Barbara, CA: Black Sparrow Press, 1979)

A Sentimental Education: Stories (New York: Dutton, 1981)

Last Days: Stories (New York: Dutton, 1984)

Raven's Wing (New York: Dutton, 1986)

Heat and Other Stories (New York: Dutton, 1991)

Where Are You Going, Where Have You Been?: Selected Early Stories by Joyce Carol Oates (Princeton, NJ: Ontario Review Press, 1993)

O'Connor, Flannery (1925–1964)

A Good Man Is Hard to Find and Other Stories (New York: Harcourt Brace Jovanovich, 1955)

Everything That Rises Must Converge (New York: Farrar, 1965)

The Complete Stories (New York: Farrar, 1971)

Olsen, Tillie (1912–)

Tell Me a Riddle (New York: Lippincott, 1961)

Parker, Dorothy (1893–1967)

Laments for the Living (New York: Viking, 1930)

After Such Pleasures (New York: Viking, 1933)

Here Lies: The Collected Stories of Dorothy Parker (New York: Viking, 1939)

Collected Stories (New York: Modern Library, 1942)

The Portable Dorothy Parker (New York: Viking, 1944)

The Portable Dorothy Parker (Revised. Ed. Brendan Gill. New York: Viking, 1973)

Dorothy Parker Stories (New York: Outlet, 1992)

Phelps, Elizabeth Wooster Stuart (1815–1852)

The Angel Over the Right Shoulder, Or, The Beginning of the New Year (1852)

The Last Leaf from Sunnyside (1853)

The Tell-Tale, Or, Home Secrets Told by Old Travelers (1853)

Silko, Leslie Marmon (1948–)

Storyteller (New York: Seaver Books, 1981)

Slesinger, Tess (1905–1945)

On Being Told That Her Second Husband Has Taken His First Lover and Other Stories (New York: Elephant, 1990)

Stein, Gertrude (1874–1946)

Three Lives (New York: Vintage, 1936)

Mrs. Reynolds and Five Earlier Novelettes (New Haven, CT: Yale University Press, 1952)

Fernhurst, Q.E.D., and Other Early Writings (New York: Liveright, 1971)

Matisse, Picasso, and Gertrude Stein: With Two Shorter Stories (Millerton, NY: Something Else Press, 1972)

Stoddard, Elizabeth (1823–1902)

The Morgesons and Other Writings, Published and Unpublished (Ed. Lawrence Buell and Sandra A. Zagarelli. Philadelphia: University of Pennsylvania Press, 1984)

Stowe, Harriet Beecher (1811–1896)

The Mayflower and Miscellaneous Writings (1843)

Sam Lawson's Oldtown Fireside Stories (1871)

Betty's Bright Idea . . . (1876)

Stories, Sketches and Studies (1896)

Tan, Amy (1951–)

The Joy Luck Club (New York: Putnam, 1989)

Walker, Alice (1944–)

In Love and Trouble: Stories of Black Women (New York: Harcourt Brace Jovanovich, 1973)

You Can't Keep a Good Woman Down: Stories (New York: Harcourt Brace Jovanovich, 1981)

Ward (Phelps), Elizabeth Stuart (1844–1911)

Men, Women, and Ghosts (1869)

Sealed Orders (1879)

Fourteen to One (1891)

The Oath of Allegiance and Other Stories (New York: Houghton Mifflin, 1909)

The Empty House and Other Stories (New York: Houghton Mifflin, 1910)

Welty, Eudora (1909–)

A Curtain of Green (New York: Doubleday, 1941)

The Wide Net and Other Stories (New York: Modern Library, 1943)

Golden Apples (New York: Harcourt Brace Jovanovich, 1949)

Selected Stories: Containing All of a Curtain of Green, and Other Stories, and The Wide Net, and Other Stories (New York: Modern Library, 1954)

Bride of Innisfallen and Other Stories (New York: Harcourt Brace Jovanovich, 1955)

Selected Stories (New York: Modern Library, 1971)

The Collected Stories of Eudora Welty (New York: Harcourt Brace Jovanovich, 1980)

Wharton, Edith Newbold Jones (1862–1937)

The Greater Inclination (New York: Scribner's, 1899)

Crucial Instances (New York: Scribner's, 1901)

The Descent of Man and Other Stories (New York: Scribner's, 1904)

Hermit and the Wild Woman, and Other Stories (New York: Scribner's, 1908)

Madame de Treymes (New York: Scribner's, 1907. Rpt. 1970)

Tales of Men and Ghosts (New York: Scribner's, 1910)

Xingu and Other Stories (New York: Scribner's, 1916)

Here and Beyond (New York: Appleton, 1926)

Certain People (New York: Appleton, 1930)

Human Nature (New York: Appleton, 1933)

World Over (New York: Appleton, 1936)

Ghosts (New York: Appleton, 1937)

An Edith Wharton Treasury (Ed. Arthur Hobson Quinn. New York: Appleton, 1950)

Best Short Stories of Edith Wharton (Ed. Wayne Andrews. New York: Scribner's, 1958)

Old New York (New York: Scribner's, 1964)

Roman Fever and Other Stories (New York: Scribner's, 1964)

The Collected Short Stories of Edith Wharton (Ed. R.W.B. Lewis. New York: Scribner's, 1968)

The Ghost Stories of Edith Wharton (New York: Scribner's, 1973)

Ethan Frome, and Other Short Fiction (New York: Bantam, 1987)

Wolfenstein, Martha (1869–1906)

Idyls of the Gass (Philadelphia: Jewish Publication Society, 1901)

The Renegade and Other Stories (Philadelphia: Jewish Publication Society, 1905)

Yezierska, Anzia (1885–1970)

Hungry Hearts (New York: Houghton Mifflin, 1922)

Children of Loneliness: Stories of Immigrant Life in America (New York: Funk, 1923)

The Open Cage: An Anzia Yezierska Collection (Ed. Alice Kessler Harris. New York: Persea, 1979)

II. Selected Bibliography of American Women's Short Story Anthologies*

Allen, Paula Gunn, ed. *Spider Woman's Granddaughters: Traditional Tales and Contemporary Writings by Native American Women.* Boston: Beacon, 1989.

Ammons, Elizabeth, ed. *Conflicting Stories: American Women Writers at the Turn of the Twentieth Century.* New York: Oxford University Press, 1991.

Antler, Joyce, ed. *America and I: Short Stories by American Jewish Women Writers.* Boston: Beacon, 1990.

Aswell, Marie Louise, ed. *It's a Woman's World: A Collection of Stories from Harper's Bazaar.* New York: McGraw-Hill, 1944.

Barbach, Lonnie, ed. *Erotic Interludes: Tales Told by Women.* New York: Doubleday, 1986.

———. *Pleasures: Women Write Erotica.* New York: Harper and Row, 1984.

Barber, Karen, ed. *Bushfire: Stories of Lesbian Desire.* Boston: Lace, 1991.

Barolini, Helen, ed. *The Dream Book: An Anthology of Writings by Italian American Women*. New York: Schocken Books, 1985.

Barreca, Regina, ed. *Women of the Century: Thirty Modern Short Stories.* New York: St. Martin's, 1993.

Bell-Scott, Patricia, et al., eds. *Double-Stitch: Black Women Write About Mothers and Daughters.* Boston: Beacon, 1991.

Bendixen, Alfred, ed. *Haunted Women: The Best Supernatural Tales by American Women Writers.* New York: Ungar, 1985.

*By Susan Koppelman with assistance from Julie Brown, Meg Schoerke, and Ellen K. Reid

Bernadette, Jane, and Phyllis Moe, eds. *Companions of Our Youth: Stories by Women for Young People's Magazines, 1865–1900*. New York: Ungar, 1980.

Bulkin, Elly, ed. *Lesbian Fiction: An Anthology*. Watertown, MA: Persephone Press, 1981.

Cahill, Susan, ed. *Among Sisters: Short Stories by Women Writers*. New York: New American Library, 1989.

———. *Growing Up Female: Stories by Women Writers from the American Mosaic*. New York: Mentor, 1993.

———. Motherhood: *A Reader for Men and Women*. New York: Avon, 1982.

———. *New Women and New Fiction: Short Stories Since the Sixties*. New York: New American Library, 1986.

———. *Women and Fiction: Short Stories by and about Women*. New York: New American Library, 1975.

Conlon, Faith, Rachel de Silva, and Barbara Wilson, eds. *The Things That Divide Us: Stories by Women*. Seattle: Seal Press, 1985.

Fetterley, Judith, ed. *Provisions: A Reader from 19th-Century American Women*. Bloomington: Indiana University Press, 1985.

Gibson, Mary Ellis, *Homeplaces: Stories of the South by Women Writers*. Columbia: University of South Carolina Press, 1991.

———. *New Short Stories by Southern Women*. Columbia: University of South Carolina Press, 1989.

Grahn, Judy, ed. *True to Life Adventure Stories, Vol. 1*. Oakland, CA: Diana, 1978.

———. *True to Life Adventure Stories, Vol. 2*. Trumansberg, NY: Crossing Press, 1983.

Green, Jen, ed. *Reader, I Murdered Him: Original Crime Stories by Women*. New York: St. Martin's, 1989.

Haining, Peter, ed. *The Gentlewomen of Evil: An Anthology of Rare Supernatural Stories from the Pens of Victorian Ladies*. New York: Taplinger, 1967.

Hamalian, Linda, and Leo Hamalian, eds. *Solo: Women on Women Alone*. New York: Delacorte Press, 1977.

Hoffman, Nancy, and Florence Howe, eds. *Women Working: An Anthology of Stories and Poems*. Old Westbury, NY: The Feminist Press, 1979.

Holoch, Nancy, and Joan Nestle, eds. *Women on Women: An Anthology of American Lesbian Short Fiction.* New York: Plume, 1993.

———. *Women on Women 2: An Anthology of American Lesbian Short Fiction*. New York: Plume, 1993.

Honey, Maureen, ed. *Breaking the Ties That Bind: Popular Stories of the New Woman, 1915–1930.* Norman: University of Oklahoma Press, 1992.

Kanwar, Asha, ed. *The Unforgetting Heart: An Anthology of Short Stories by African American Women (1859–1993).* San Francisco: Aunt Lute Books, 1993.

Kessler, Carol, ed. *Daring to Dream: Utopian Stories by United States Women: 1836–1919.* Boston: Pandora, 1984.

Knopf, Marcy, ed. *The Sleeper Awakes: Harlem Renaissance Stories by Women.* New Brunswick, NJ: Rutgers University Press, 1993.

Kono, Juliet S., and Cathy Song, eds. *Sister Stew: Fiction and Poetry by Women.* Honolulu: Bamboo Ridge Press, 1991.

Koppelman, Susan, ed. *Between Mothers and Daughters: Stories Across a Generation*. Old Westbury, New York: The Feminist Press, 1985.

———. *"May Your Days Be Merry and Bright" and Other Christmas Stories by U.S. Women Writers: 1856–1986.* Detroit: Wayne State University Press, 1988.

———. *Old Maids: Short Stories by Nineteenth Century U.S. Women Writers.* Boston: Pandora, 1984.

———. *The Other Woman: Stories of Two Women and a Man.* Old Westbury, New York: The Feminist Press, 1984.

———. *"Two Friends" and Other 19th Century U.S. Lesbian Stories.* New York: Meridian, 1994.

———. *Women's Friendships: A Collection of Short Stories.* Norman: University of Oklahoma Press, 1991.

Larson, Ann E., and Carole A. Carr, eds. *Crossing the Mainstream: New Fiction by Women Writers.* Seattle: Silverleaf Press, 1987.

McIntyre, Vonda N., and Susan Janice Anderson. *Aurora: Beyond Equality—Amazing Tales of the Ultimate Sexual Revolution.* New York: Random House, 1974.

McSherry, Frank Jr., Charles G. Waugh, and Martin Greenberg, eds. *Civil War Women: American Women Shaped by Conflict in Stories by Alcott, Chopin, Welty, and Others.* Little Rock, AR: August House, 1988.

Martin, Wendy, ed. *We Are the Stories We Tell: The Best Short Stories by North American Women Since 1945.* New York: Pantheon, 1990.

Martz, Sandra, ed. *When I Am an Old Woman I Shall Wear Purple: An Anthology of Short Stories and Poetry.* Manhattan Beach, CA: Papier Mache Press, 1987.

Mazow, Julia Wolf, ed. *The Woman Who Lost Her Names: Selected Writing of American Jewish Women.* New York: Harper and Row, 1980.

Muller, Marcia, and Bill Pronzini, eds. *She Won the West: An Anthology of Western and Frontier Stories by Women.* New York: Morrow, 1985.

———. *Witches Brew: Horror and Supernatural Stories by Women.* New York: Macmillan, 1984.

Nejola, Charlotte, and Paula Rabinowitz, eds. *Writing Red: An Anthology of American Women Writers, 1930–1940.* Old Westbury, NY: The Feminist Press, 1987.

Paretsky, Sara, ed. *A Woman's Eye: New Stories Featuring the Finest Female Detectives by the Best Women Crime Writers Ever.* New York: Delacorte Press, 1991.

Park, Christine, and Caroline Heaton, eds. *Close Company: Stories of Mothers and Daughters.* New York: Ticknor and Fields, 1989.

Piekarski, Vicki, ed. *Westward the Women: An Anthology of Western Stories by Women.* New York: Doubleday, 1984.

Rafkin, Louise, ed. *Unholy Alliances: New Women's Fiction.* Pittsburgh: Cleis Press, 1988.

Reed, Helen, ed. *About Women: A Collection of Short Stories.* New York: World, 1943.

Robinson, Lou, and Camille Norton, eds. *Resurgent: New Writing by Women.* Chicago: University of Illinois Press, 1992.

Rotter, Pat, ed. *Bitches and Sad Ladies.* New York: Harper's Magazine Press, 1975.

Ryan, Alan. *Haunting Women.* New York: Avon, 1988.

Salmonson, Jessica Amanda. *"What Did Miss Darrington See?"* and Other Supernatural Stories by Women. Old Westbury, NY: The Feminist Press, 1989.

Sargent, Pamela, ed. *More Women of Wonder: Science Fiction Stories by Women about Women.* New York: Vintage, 1976.

———. *The New Women of Wonder: Recent Science Fiction Stories by Women about Women.* New York: Vintage, 1978.

———. *Women of Wonder: Science Fiction Stories by Women about Women.* New York: Vintage, 1974.

Scheffler, Judith A., ed. *Wall Tappings: An Anthology of Writings by Women Prisoners.* Boston: Northeastern University Press, 1986.

Smith, Marie, ed. *Ms. Murder, Vol. 1: The Best Mysteries Featuring Women Detectives by the Best Women Writers.* New York: Citadel, 1989.

Solomon, Barbara H., ed. *American Wives: Thirty Short Stories by Women.* New York: New American Library, 1986.

———. *The Experience of the American Woman: Thirty Stories. New York:* New American Library, 1978.

———, ed. *Short Fiction of Sarah Orne Jewett and Mary Wilkins Freeman, Including "The Country of the Pointed Firs."* New York: New American Library, 1979.

Spinner, Stephanie, ed. *Feminine Plural: Stories About Growing Up.* New York: Macmillan, 1972.

———. *Motherlove: Stories by Women About Motherhood.* New York: Dell, 1978.

Stones, Rosemary, ed. *More to Life Than Mr. Right: Stories for Young Feminists.* New York: Holt, 1989.

Sturgis, Susanna J., ed. *Tales of Magic Realism by Women: Dreams in a Minor Key.* Freedom, CA: Crossing Press, 1991.

———. *Women Who Walk Through Fire: Women, Fantasy, and Science Fiction.* Freedom, CA: Crossing Press, 1990.

Sullivan, Ruth, ed. *Fine Lines: The Best of Ms. Fiction.* New York: Scribner's, 1981.

Swansea, Charleen, and Barbara Campbell, eds. *Love Stories by New Women.* Charlotte, NC: Red Clay Books, 1978.

Velez, Diana, ed. and trans. *Reclaiming Medusa: Short Stories by Contemporary Puerto Rican Women.* San Francisco: Spinsters/Aunt Lute, 1988.

Walker, Nancy, and Zita Dresner, eds. *Redressing the Balance: American Women's Literary Humor from Colonial Times to the 1980s.* Jackson: University Press of Mississippi, 1988.

Walker, Scott, ed. *The Graywolf Annual II: Short Stories by Women.* St. Paul, MN: Graywolf Press, 1988.

Wallace, Marilyn, ed. *Sisters in Crime.* New York: Berkley, 1989.

Washington, Mary Helen, ed. *Black-Eyed Susans.* New York: Anchor Press, 1975.

———. *Midnight Birds: Stories by Contemporary Black Women.* New York: Anchor Press, 1980.

Wolff, Cynthia Griffin. *Four Stories by American Women.* New York: Penguin, 1990.

Zahava, Irene, ed. *The Fourth Womansleuth Anthology.* Freedom, CA: Crossing Press, 1991.

———. *Hear the Silence: Stories by Women of Myth, Magic, and Renewal.* Freedom, CA: Crossing Press, 1986.

———. *Lesbian Love Stories* (2 Vols.) Freedom, CA: Crossing Press, 1989.

———. *Love, Struggle, and Change: Stories by Women.* Freedom, CA: Crossing Press, 1988.

———. *My Father's Daughter: Stories by Women.* Freedom, CA: Crossing Press, 1990.

———. *My Mother's Daughter: Stories by Women.* Freedom, CA: Crossing Press, 1991.

———. *Speaking for Ourselves: Short Stories by Jewish Lesbians.* Freedom, CA: Crossing Press, 1990.

———. *Through Other Eyes: Animal Stories by Women.* Freedom, CA: Crossing Press, 1988.

———. *The Womansleuth Anthology: Contemporary Mystery Stories by Women*. Freedom, CA: The Crossing Press, 1990.

———. *Word of Mouth.* Freedom, CA: Crossing Press, 1990.

Zipes, Jack, ed. *Don't Bet on the Prince: Contemporary Feminist Fairy Tales in North America and England*. New York: Methuen, 1986.

Bibliography of Secondary Sources

Amy Shoenberger

Bibliographical Works

Deodene, Frank. *Black American Fiction Since 1952: A Preliminary Checklist*. Chatham, NJ: The Chatham Bookseller, 1970.

Duke, Maurice, Jackson R. Bryer, and M. Thomas Inge, eds. *American Women Writers: Bibliographic Essays*. Westport, CT: Greenwood, 1983.

Farmer, David. *Flannery O'Connor: A Descriptive Bibliography*. New York: Garland, 1981.

Garrison, Stephen. *Edith Wharton, a Descriptive Bibliography*. Pittsburgh: University of Pittsburgh Press, 1990.

Kelly, William W. *Ellen Glasgow, a Bibliography*. Charlottesville: University Press of Virginia, 1964.

Kimbel, Bobbie Ellen, ed. *American Short Story Writers—Before 1880*. Detroit: Gale, 1988.

———. *American Short Story Writers, 1880–1910*. Detroit: Gale, 1989.

———. *American Short Story Writers, 1910–1945*. Detroit: Gale, 1989.

Kinnard, Cynthia D. *Antifeminism in American Thought: An Annotated Bibliography*. Boston: Hall, 1986.

Lauer, Kristen O. *Edith Wharton: An Annotated Bibliography*. New York: Garland, 1990.

Lercangee, Francine. *Joyce Carol Oates: An Annotated Bibliography*. New York: Garland, 1986.

Lohafer, Susan, and Jo Ellyn Cleary, eds. *Short Story Theory at a Crossroads*. Baton Rouge: Louisiana State University Press, 1989. Appendix B: 328–336.

May, Charles E., ed. *Short Story Theories*. Athens: Ohio University Press, 1976. Bibliography: 226–251.

Newson, Adele S. *Zora Neale Hurston: A Reference Guide*. Boston: G.K. Hall, 1987.

Pratt, Louise H. *Alice Malsenior Walker: An Annotated Bibliography*. Westport, CT: Meckler, 1988.

Ragen, Abel Brian. "Grace and Grotesques: Recent Books on Flannery O'Connor." *PLL: Papers on Language and Literature* 27 (Summer 1991): 386–399.

Shaw, Valerie. *The Short Story: A Critical Introduction*. New York: Longman, 1983. Bibliography: 270–284.

Showalter, Elaine, ed. *The New Feminist Criticism: Essays on Women, Literature, and Theory*. New York: Pantheon, 1985. Bibliography: 379–400.

Springer, Marlene. *Edith Wharton and Kate Chopin: A Reference Guide*. Boston: G.K. Hall, 1976.

Swearingen, Bethany C. *Eudora Welty: A Critical Bibliography*. Jackson: University Press of Mississippi, 1984.

Thompson, Victor H. *Eudora Welty: A Reference Guide*. Boston: G.K. Hall, 1976.

Yancy, Preston, ed. *The Afro-American Short Story: A Comprehensive and Annotated Index with Selected Commentaries*. Westport, CT: Greenwood, 1986.

Biographical Studies

Ammons, Elizabeth. *Edith Wharton's Argument with America*. Athens: University of Georgia Press, 1990.

Baer, Helene. *The Heart Is Like Heaven: The Life of Louisa May Alcott*. Philadelphia: University of Pennsylvania Press, 1964.

Carabi, Angels. "Belles Lettres Interview: Gloria Naylor." *Belles Lettres: A Review of Books by Women* 7 (Spring 1992): 36–43.

Downey, Jean. "A Biographical and Critical Study of Rose Terry Cooke." Diss. University of Ottawa, 1956.

Erlich, Gloria C. *The Sexual Education of Edith Wharton.* Berkeley: University of California Press, 1992.

Fink, Augusta. *I-Mary, A Biography of Mary Austin.* Tucson: University of Arizona Press, 1983.

Gelfant, Blanche H. *Women Writing in America: Voices in Collage.* Hanover, NH: University Press of New England, 1984.

Gobold, E. Stanley. *Ellen Glasgow and the Woman Within*. Baton Rouge: Louisiana State University Press, 1972.

Hemenway, Robert E. *Zora Neale Hurston: A Literary Biography*. Urbana: University of Illinois Press, 1977.

Lyday, Jo W. *Mary Austin; the Southwest Works.* Austin, TX: Steck-Vaughn, 1968.

Lyons, Bonnie, and Bill Olliver. "An Interview with Bobbie Ann Mason." *Contemporary Literature* 32 (Winter 1991): 449–441.

MacDonald, Ruth. *Louisa May Alcott.* Boston: Twayne, 1983.

McLaughlin, Ann L. "The Same Job: The Shared Writing Aims of Katherine Mansfield and Virginia Woolf." *Modern Fiction Studies* 24 (Autumn 1978): 369–382.

McQuade, Molly. "Joy Williams; a Gum-Chewing Puritan, She Writes 'Teeming, Chaotic' Fiction About 'The Ever-Approaching Nothing.'" *Publishers Weekly* 26 (Jan. 1990): 400–402.

Materassi, Mario. "Imaginations Unbound: An Interview with Cynthia Ozick." *Salmagundi* (Spring–Summer 1992): 85–114.

Meade, Marion. *Dorothy Parker: What Fresh Hell Is This?* New York: Villard, 1988.

Meigs, Cornelia Lynde. *The Story of the Author of* Little Women*: Invincible Louisa.* Boston: Little, Brown, 1933.

Merina, Anita. "Joy, Luck, and Literature: An Interview with Amy Tan." *NEA Today* 10 (Oct. 1991): 9–10.

Milazzo, Lee, ed. *Conversations with Joyce Carol Oates*. Jackson: University Press of Mississippi, 1989.

Osborne, William S. *Lydia Maria Child.* Boston: Twayne, 1980.

Payne, Alma J. *Louisa May Alcott, a Reference Guide*. Boston: G.K. Hall, 1980.

Raper, Julius Rowan. *From the Sunken Garden: The Fiction of Ellen Glasgow.* Baton Rouge: Louisiana State University Press, 1988.

Rouse, Blair. *Ellen Glasgow*. New York: Twayne, 1962.

Smith, Wendy. "Ellen Gilchrist: The Prize-Winning Short Story Writer Now Finds Novels Better Serve Her Vision." *Publishers Weekly* 2 (March 1992): 46–48.

Somogyi, Barbara, and David Stanton. "Amy Tan: An Interview by Barbara Somogyi and David Stanton." *Poets & Writers* 19 (Sept.–Oct. 1991): 23–32.

Stern, Madeleine B. *Louisa May Alcott.* Norman: University of Oklahoma Press, 1950.

Stineman, Esther. *Mary Austin: Song of a Maverick.* New Haven: Yale University Press, 1989.

Welty, Eudora. *One Writer's Beginnings*. Cambridge, MA: Harvard University Press, 1984.

Related Critical Studies and Feminist Theory

Allen, Paula Gunn. *The Sacred Hoop: Recovering the Feminine in American Indian Traditions.* Boston: Beacon, 1986.

Ammons, Elizabeth. *Conflicting Stories: American Women Writers at the Turn of the Twentieth Century.* New York: Oxford University Press, 1991.

Asals, Frederick. *Flannery O'Connor: The Imagination of Extremity.* Athens: University of Georgia Press, 1982.

Bastian, Katherine. *Joyce Carol Oates's Short Stories: Between Tradition and Innovation*. Frankfurt am Main: Peter Lang, 1983.

Bauer, Margaret D. "Alice Walker: Another Southern Writer Criticizing Codes Not Put into 'Everyday Use.'" *Studies in Short Fiction* 29 (Spring 1992): 143–152.

———. "The Evolution of Caddy: An Intertextual Reading of *The Sound and the Fury* and Ellen Gilchrist's 'The Annunciation.'" *Southern Literary Journal* 25 (Fall 1992): 40–52.

Baym, Nina. "Onward Christian Women: Sarah J. Hale's History of the World." *New England Quarterly* 63 (June 1990): 249–271.

Bell, R.P., B.J. Parker, and B. Grey-Sheftall, eds. *Sturdy Black Bridges: Visions of Black Women in Literature*. Garden City, NY: Anchor/ Doubleday, 1979.

Bender, Eileen Teper. *Joyce Carol Oates, Artist in Residence*. Bloomington: Indiana University Press, 1987.

Bendixen, Alfred, and Annette Zilversmit, eds. *Edith Wharton: New Critical Essays*. New York: Garland, 1992.

Benstock, Shari. *Textualizing the Feminine: On the Limits of Genre*. Norman: University of Oklahoma Press, 1991.

Bevilacqua, Winifred Farrant, ed. *Fiction by American Women: Recent Views*. Port Washington, NY: Associated Faculty, 1983.

Birkett, Jennifer, and Elizabeth Harvey. *Determined Women: Studies in the Construction of the Female Subject, 1900–1990*. Savage, MD: Barnes & Noble, 1991.

Bloom, Harold, ed. *Joyce Carol Oates*. New York: Chelsea House, 1987.

———. *Zora Neale Hurston*. New York: Chelsea House, 1986.

Bone, Robert A. *Down Home: A History of Afro-American Short Fiction from Its Beginnings to the End of the Harlem Renaissance*. New York: Putnam, 1975.

Bonheim, Helmut. *The Narrative Modes: Techniques of the Short Story*. Cambridge, U.K.: D.S. Brewer, 1982.

Booth, David. "Sam's Quest, Emmet's Wound: Grail Motifs in Bobbie Ann Mason's Portrait of America After Vietnam." *Southern Literary Journal* 23 (Spring 1992): 98–110.

Braxton, J.M., and A.N. McLaughlin, eds. *Wild Women in the Whirlwind: Afro-American Culture and the Contemporary Literary Renaissance*. New Brunswick, NJ: Rutgers University Press, 1990.

Brinkmeyer, Robert H. *The Art and Vision of Flannery O'Connor*. Baton Rouge: Louisiana State University Press, 1989.

Caputi, Jane. "'Specifying' Fannie Hurst: Langston Hughes's 'Limitations of Life,' Zora Neale Hurston's *Their Eyes Were Watching God*, and Toni Morrison's *The Bluest Eye*, as 'Answers' to Hurst's 'Imitation of Life.'" *Black American Literature Forum* 24 (Winter 1990): 697–717.

Castillo, Susan Perez. "Postmodernism, Native American Literature and the Real: The Silko-Erdrich Controversy." *Massachusetts Review* 32 (Summer 1991): 285–295.

Clark, Michael. "Flannery O'Connor's 'A Good Man Is Hard to Find': The Moment of Grace." *English Language Notes* 29 (Dec. 1991): 66–69.

Cogan, Frances B. *All-American Girls: The Ideal of Real Womanhood in Mid-Nineteenth Century America*. Athens: University of Georgia Press, 1989.

Cohen, Sarah Blacher. "The Fiction Writer as Essayist: Ozick's 'Metaphor & Memory.'" *Judaism: A Quarterly Journal* 155 (Summer 1990): 276–282.

Cohn, Jan. *Romance and the Erotics of Property*. Durham, NC: Duke University Press, 1989.

Conrad, Susan Phinney. *Perish the Thought: Intellectual Women in Romantic America, 1830–1860*. New York: Oxford University Press, 1976.

Current-Garcia, Eugene. *What Is the Short Story?* Chicago: Scott, 1961.

Davies, Kathleen. "Zora Neale Hurston's Poetics of Embalment: Articulating the Rage of Black Women and Narrative Self-Defense." *African American Review* 26 (Spring 1992): 147–160.

DeKoven, Marianne. *Rich and Strange: Gender, History, Modernism*. Princeton, NJ: Princeton University Press, 1991.

Donawerth, Jane. "Teaching Science Fiction by Women." *English Journal* 79 (March 1990): 39–47.

Donovan, Josephine. *After the Fall: The Demeter-Persephone Myth in Wharton, Cather, and Glasgow*. University Park: Penn State University Press, 1988.

———. *New England Local Color Literature: A Woman's Tradition*. New York: Ungar, 1983.

———, ed. *Feminist Literary Criticism: Explorations in Theory*. Lexington: University Press of Kentucky, 1975.

Douglas, Ann. *The Feminization of American Culture*. New York: Anchor, 1988.

Downey, Jean. "A Biographical and Critical Study of Rose Terry Cooke." Diss. University of Ottawa, 1956.

Earnest, Ernest. *The American Eve in Fact and Fiction, 1775–1914*. Urbana: University of Illinois Press, 1974.

Easterly, Joan. "The Shadow of a Satyr in Oates's 'Where Are You Going, Where Have You Been?'" *Studies in Short Fiction* 27 (Fall 1990): 537–543.

Elbert, Sarah. *A Hunger for Home: Louisa May Alcott's Place in American Culture*. New Brunswick, NJ: Rutgers University Press, 1987.

Evans, Elizabeth. *Eudora Welty*. New York: Ungar, 1981.

Feldman, Gayle. "Spring's Five Fictional Encounters of the Chinese American Kind." *Publishers Weekly* 8 (Feb. 1991): 25–28.

Fetterley, Judith. *The Resisting Reader: A Feminist Approach to American Fiction*. Bloomington: Indiana University Press, 1978.

Findlan, Barbara. "Bold Types." *Ms.* 2 (July–Aug. 1991): 87–88. [On Jewelle Gomez.]

Friedman, Ellen G., and Miriam Fuchs, eds. *Breaking the Sequence: Women's Experimental Fiction*. Princeton, NJ: Princeton University Press, 1989.

Friedman, Melvin, and Beverly Lyon Clark, eds. *Critical Essays on Flannery O'Connor*. Boston: G.K. Hall, 1985.

Fryer, Judith. *Felicitous Space: The Imaginative Structures of Edith Wharton and Willa Cather*. Chapel Hill: University of North Carolina Press, 1986.

Fuss, Diana. "Reading Like a Feminist." *Differences* 1 (Summer 1989): 77–92.

Goodman, Susan. *Edith Wharton's Women: Friends and Rivals*. Hanover, NH: University Press of New England, 1990.

Habegger, Alfred. *Gender, Fantasy and Realism in American Literature*. New York: Columbia United, 1982.

Hardwick, Elizabeth. *Seduction and Betrayal; Women and Literature*. New York: Random House, 1974.

Hedrick, Joan D. "Parlor Literature: Harriet Beecher Stowe and the Question of 'Great Women Artists.'" *Signs* 17 (Winter 1992): 275–303.

Herndl, D.P., and Warhol, R.R., eds. *Feminisms: An Anthology of Literary Theory and Criticism*. New Brunswick, NJ: Rutgers University Press, 1991.

Hinze, Diana. "Texas and Berlin: Images of Germany in Katherine Anne Porter's Prose." *Southern Literary Journal* 24 (Fall 1991): 77–88.

Hume, Beverly A. "Gilman's 'Interminable Grotesque': The Narrator of 'The Yellow Wallpaper.'" *Studies in Short Fiction* 28 (Fall 1991): 477–485.

Jacobus, Mary, ed. *Women Writing and Writing About Men*. New York: Barnes & Noble, 1979.

Johnson, Greg. "Some Recent Herstories." *Georgia Review* 44 (Spring–Summer 1990): 278–289.

Johnston, Georgia. "Exploring the Lack and Absence in the Body/Text: Charlotte Perkins Gilman Prewriting Irigaray." *Women's Studies* 21 (April 1992): 75–87.

Jones, Anne Goodwyn. *Tomorrow Is Another Day: The Woman Writer in the South*. Baton Rouge: Louisiana State University Press, 1981.

Kennedy, J. Gerald. "Toward a Poetics of the Short Story Cycle." *Les Cahiers de la Novelle/Journal of the Short Story in English* 11 (Autumn 1988): 9–25.

Koppelman, Susan, ed. *Images of Women in Fiction: Feminist Perspectives.* Bowling Green, OH: Bowling Green University Press, 1972.

Kornfeld, Eve. "Reconstructing American Law: The Politics of Narrative and Eudora Welty's Empathic Vision." *Journal of American Studies* 26 (April 1992): 23–40.

Kowalelski, Michael. "On Flannery O'Connor." *Raritan: A Quarterly Review* 10 (Winter 1991): 85–105.

Kreyling, Michael. *Eudora Welty's Achievement of Order*. Baton Rouge: Louisiana State University Press, 1980.

Langlois, Karen S. "Mary Austin's 'A Woman of Genius': The Text, the Novel and the Problem of Male Publishers and Critics and Female Authors." *Journal of American Culture* 15 (Summer 1992): 79–87.

Leary, William. "Jean Stafford: The Wound and the Bow." *The Sewanee Review* 98 (Summer 1990): 333–350.

Lee, A. Robert, ed. *The Nineteenth-Century American Short Story*. Totowa, NJ: Barnes & Noble, 1985.

Levy, Andrew. *The Culture and Commerce of the American Short Story: America's Workshop.* New York: Cambridge University Press, 1993.

Lewellyn, Kurtis L. "Structure and Theme in Katherine Anne Porter's 'Magic.'" *Studies in Short Fiction* 27 (Winter 1990): 104–106.

Lindberg-Seyersted, Brita. "The Color Black: Skin Color as Social, Ethical, and Esthetic Sign in Writings by Black American Women." *English Studies* 73 (Feb. 1992): 51–68.

Little, Howard. *Zora Neale Hurston*. Boston: Twayne, 1980.

MacKethan, Lucinda H. *Daughters of Time: Creating Woman's Voice in Southern Society*. Athens: University of Georgia Press, 1990.

Marsella, Joy A. *The Promise of Destiny: Children and Women in the Stories of Louisa May Alcott*. Westport, CT: Greenwood, 1983.

Martin, Carter. *The True Country; Themes in the Fiction of Flannery O'Connor.* Nashville: Vanderbilt University Press, 1969.

May, Charles E., ed. *Short Story Theories*. Athens: Ohio University Press, 1976.

Moi, Toril. *Sexual/Textual Politics: Feminist Literary Theory*. New York: Methuen, 1985.

Monteith, Moira, ed. *Women's Writing: A Challenge to Theory*. New York: St. Martin's, 1986.

Nudd, Donna Marie. "Establishing the Balance: Re-examining Students' Androcentric Readings of Katherine Anne Porter's 'Rope.'" *Communication Education* 40 (Jan. 1991): 49–60.

Oschorn, Kathleen G. "A Cloak of Grace: Contradictions in 'A Good Man Is Hard to Find.'" *Studies in American Fiction* 18 (Spring 1990): 113–118.

Piwinski, David J. "Oates's 'Where Are You Going, Where Have You Been?'" *Explicator* 49 (Spring 1991): 195–197.

Pratt, Mary Louise. "The Short Story: The Long and the Short of It." *Poetics* 10 (June 1981): 175–194.

Prenshaw, Peggy Whitman. *Eudora Welty: Critical Essays*. Jackson: University Press of Mississippi, 1979.

Pryse, Marjorie, and Hortense J. Spillers, eds. *Conjuring: Black Women, Fiction, and Literary Tradition*. Bloomington: Indiana University Press, 1985.

Radford, Jean, ed. *The Progress of Romance: The Politics of Popular Fiction*. New York: Routledge & Kegan Paul, 1986.

Rainwater, Catherine. "Reading Between Worlds: Narrativity in the Fiction of Louise Erdrich." *American Literature* 62 (Sept. 1990): 405–423.

Randisi, Jennifer Lynn. *A Tissue of Lies: Eudora Welty and the Southern Romance*. Lanham, MD: University Press of America, 1982.

Raper, Julius Rowan. *From the Sunken Garden: The Fiction of Ellen Glasgow*. Baton Rouge: Louisiana State University Press, 1988.

Robinson, Lillian S. "Killing Patriarchy: Charlotte Perkins Gilman, the Murder Mystery, and Post-Feminist Propaganda." *Tulsa Studies in Women's Literature* 10 (Fall 1991): 273–286.

Rosenfeld, Natania. "Artists and Daughters in Louisa May Alcott's 'Diana and Persis.'" *New England Quarterly* 64 (March 1991): 3–22.

Ruppert, James. "Discovering America: Mary Austin and Imagism." *Studies in American Indian Literature: Critical Essays and Course Designs*. Ed. Paula Gunn Allen. New York: MLA, 1983, pp. 243–258.

Russ, Joanna. *How to Suppress a Woman's Writing*. Austin: University of Texas Press, 1983.

Ryan, Barbara T. "Decentered Authority in Bobbie Ann Mason's 'In Country'" *Critique: Study in Contemporary Fiction* 31 (Spring 1990): 99–112.

Saldívár, Ramón. *Chicano Narrative: The Dialectics of Difference*. Madison: University of Wisconsin Press, 1990.

Sanderson, Rena. "'A Modern Mephistopheles': Louisa May Alcott's Exorcism of Patriarchy." *American Transcendental Quarterly* 5 (March 1991): 41–56.

Saxton, Martha. "The Secret Imaginings of Louisa May Alcott." *Critical Essays on Louisa May Alcott*. Ed. Madeleine B. Stern. Boston: G.K. Hall, 1984, pp. 259–260.

Schmidt, Peter. *The Heart of the Story: Eudora Welty's Short Fiction*. Jackson: University Press of Mississippi, 1991.

Schultz, Lydia A. "Fragments and Ojibwe Stories: Narrative Strategies in Louise Erdrich's *Love Medicine*." *College Literature* 18 (Oct. 1991): 80–96.

Shear, Walter. "Generational Differences and the Diaspora in *The Joy Luck Club*." *Critique: Studies in Contemporary Fiction* 34 (Spring 1993): 193–200.

Shockley, Ann Allen. *Afro-American Writers, 1746–1933: An Anthology and Critical Guide*. Boston: G.K. Hall, 1988.

Showalter, Elaine, ed. *The New Feminist Criticism: Essays on Women, Literature, and Theory*. New York: Pantheon, 1985.

———. *Sister's Choice: Tradition and Change in American Women's Writing*. Oxford, U.K.: Clarendon, 1991.

Smiley, Pamela. "Incest, Roman Catholicism, and Joyce Carol Oates." *College Literature* 18 (Feb. 1991): 38–50.

Story, Kenneth E. "Throwing a Spotlight on the Past: Narrative Method in Ann Beattie's 'Jacklighting.'" *Studies in Short Fiction* 27 (Winter 1990): 106–110.

Stout, Janis P. *Strategies of Reticence: Silence and Meaning in the Works of Jane Austen, Willa Cather, Katherine Anne Porter, and Joan Didion*. Charlottesville: University Press of Virginia, 1990.

Summers, Claude J. "'A Losing Game in the End': Aesthetics and Homosexuality in Cather's 'Paul's Case.'" *Modern Fiction Studies* 36 (Spring 1990): 103–120.

Tanner, Laura E. "Reading Rape: *Sanctuary* and *The Women of Brewster Place*." *American Literature* 62 (Dec. 1990): 559–583.

Thiebaux, Marcelle. *Ellen Glasgow*. New York: Ungar, 1982.

Tracy, Laura. *"Catching the Drift": Authority, Gender, and Narrative Strategy in Fiction*. New Brunswick, NJ: Rutgers University Press, 1988.

Trensky, Anne. "The Unnatural Silences of Tillie Olsen." *Studies in Short Fiction* 27 (Fall 1990): 509–517.

Turner, W. Craig, and Lee Emling Harding, eds. *Critical Essays on Eudora Welty*. Boston: Hall, 1989.

Vande Keift, Ruth M. *Eudora Welty*. New York: Ungar, 1981.

———. "Eudora Welty and the Right to Privacy." *Mississippi Quarterly: Journal of Southern Culture* 43 (Fall 1990): 475–485.

Vickers, Joanne F. "Woolson's Response to James: The Vindication of the American Heroine." *Women's Studies* 18 (Sept. 1990): 287–295.

Walton, Geoffrey. *Edith Wharton: A Critical Interpretation*. Rutherford, NJ: Fairleigh Dickinson University Press, 1971.

Washington, Mary Helen, ed. *Invented Lives: Narratives of Black Women, 1860–1960*. Garden City, NY: Anchor, 1987.

Wesley, Marilyn C. "Father-Daughter Incest as Social Transgression: A Feminist Reading of Joyce Carol Oates." *Women's Studies* 21 (June 1992): 251–264.

———. "New Lives and New Letters: Black Women Writers at the End of the Seventies." *College English* 43 (Jan. 1981): 1–11.

———. "The Simultaneous Universe: The Politics of Jamesian Conversion in Joyce Carol Oates's Fiction." *Essays in Literature* 18 (Fall 1991): 269–276.

———. "The Transgressive Other of Joyce Carol Oates's Recent Fiction." *Critique: Studies in Contemporary Fiction* 33 (Summer 1992): 255–263.

Westling, Louise Hutchings. *Sacred Groves and Ravaged Gardens: The Fiction of Eudora Welty, Carson McCullers, and Flannery O'Connor*. Athens: University of Georgia Press, 1985.

Widdicombe, Toby. "Wharton's 'The Angel at the Grave' and the Glories of Transcendentalism: Deciduous or Evergreen?" *American Transcendental Quarterly* 6 (March 1992): 47–58.

Wilson, Robley. "The Feminizing of the Short Story." *American Notes and Queries* 5 (Oct. 1992): 258–260.

Winchell, Donna Haisty. *Alice Walker*. New York: Twayne, 1992.

Winn, Harbour. "Echoes of Literary Sisterhood: Louisa May Alcott and Kate Chopin." *Studies in American Fiction* 20 (Autumn 1992): 205–208.

Wolff, Cynthia Griffin. *Classic American Women Writers: Sarah Orne Jewett, Kate Chopin, Edith Wharton, and Willa Cather*. New York: Harper & Row, 1980.

Zandy, Janet, ed. *Calling Home: Working-Class Women's Writings*. New Brunswick, NJ: Rutgers University Press, 1990.

Zeidenstein, Sondra. *A Wider Giving: Women Writing After a Long Silence*. Goshen, CT: Chicory Blue, 1988.

Contributors

Douglas Anderson is a graduate student in English at the University of Iowa. His research focuses on the social construction and performance of gender, ethnic/racial, and class identities in twentieth-century American fiction.

Stephanie Branson is assistant professor of English and director of Women's Studies at the University of Wisconsin–Platteville. She was a featured speaker at the 2nd International Conference on the Short Story in English held in Iowa in 1992. Branson is the author of "'Experience Illuminated': Veristic Representation in Ellen Glasgow's Short Stories," an article to appear in *Ellen Glasgow: Feminist Perspectives* from the University of Tennessee Press.

Julie Brown is associate professor of English at Youngstown State University, where she teaches American literature, women's literature, and creative writing. In addition to publishing articles on feminist criticism and writing pedagogy, she has also published over a dozen short stories in journals such as *The Southern Review, Indiana Review, Michigan Quarterly Review, Greensboro Review*, and other places. Her stories have won various awards including an Ohio Arts Council Grant, the Lawrence Foundation Award, the Chris O'Malley award, a YSU Research professorship, and a Pushcart Prize nomination. She is the author of 15 children's books.

Mary Burgan, professor and former chair of English at Indiana University–Bloomington, has published articles on Victorian and Modernist fiction and academic administration. Her book *Illness,*

Gender, and Writing: The Case of Katherine Mansfield is forthcoming from Johns Hopkins University Press. She is currently working on a study of Southern American women short story writers.

Lillian Faderman is the author of *Odd Girls and Twilight Lovers: A History of Lesbian Life in Twentieth-Century America* and the award-winning *Surpassing the Love of Men: Romantic Friendship and Love Between Women from the Renaissance to the Present* as well as *Scotch Verdict*, a historical recreation of the trial on which *The Children's Hour* was based. She has edited several anthologies of ethnic minority and lesbian literature and has published numerous articles on lesbian life and literature. She teaches at California State University–Fresno.

Ellen Gruber Garvey teaches American studies at Temple University. Her book, *Reading Consumer Culture: Gender, Fiction, and Advertising in American Magazines, 1880s–1910s,* is forthcoming from Oxford University Press. She is currently researching the movement of brand names and advertising characters into ordinary speech and writing.

Dolan Hubbard is an associate professor of English at the University of Georgia with a joint appointment from the Institute of African American Studies. His *The Sermon in the Making of Black American Literary Imagination: Voices and Visions* is due in 1994 from the University of Missouri Press.

Ken Johnson is assistant professor of English at Upper Iowa University in Fayette. His research interests include *The New Yorker* humorists, Willa Cather, and prose style.

Linda K. Karell is a graduate student in English literature at the University of Rochester and works as the director of the Syracuse Academic Improvement Program in Syracuse, New York. She is completing her dissertation, entitled "Literary Borderlands and Unsettling Stories: American Women's Writing Between the Renaissances." This is her first publication.

Margot Kelley is an assistant professor at Ursinus College in Pennsylvania, where her teaching emphasis is recent American literature and literary theory. She is currently exploring ways in which contemporary science, new narrative genres, and multiethnic U.S. literature can be considered together. She is especially interested in ideas of complexity in feminist theory and in both literature and science.

Susan Koppelman has worked since 1972 as an historian/archeologist/theoretician of short stories by American women writers. She has edited several anthologies, including *Between Mothers and Daughters: Stories Across a Generation; Women's Friendships: A Collection of Short Stories; Signet Classic Book of Southern Short Stories;* and *"Two Friends" and Other Nineteenth-Century Lesbian Short Stories by U.S. Women Writers.* Two books on Fannie Hurst will be out in 1995. She is currently at work on *The History of the Short Story in the United States: 1826–Present* and *One Hundred Seventy Years of American Women's Stories: 1826–1996: An Historical Anthology.*

Sherry Lee Linkon is associate professor of English at Youngstown State University, where she teaches women's studies, American literature, and professional writing. She has published articles on feminist pedagogy and women writers, as well as poetry and book reviews.

Bruce Mills received his Ph.D. from the University of Iowa and is currently assistant professor of English at Kalamazoo College. His book, *Cultural Reformations: Lydia Maria Child and the Literature of Reform*, will be published by the University of Georgia Press in 1994.

Timothy Morris teaches American poetry and American women writers at the University of Texas at Arlington, where he is assistant professor of English. His articles have appeared in *Studies in American Fiction, Studies in the Novel,* and *American Literature.* He is the author of *Becoming Canonical in American Poetry* (forthcoming) published by the University of Illinois Press.

Bill Mullen is associate professor of English at Youngstown State University where he teaches twentieth-century American literature, African American literature, and courses in American literature of the 1930s. His essays, notes, and reviews have appeared in *Partisan Review, The Longman Anthology of World Literature by Women,* and *The Philadelphia Inquirer.* He is co-editor with Sherry Linkon of *Re-visioning Thirties Culture: New Directions in Scholarship,* forthcoming from the University of Illinois Press.

Barbara Patrick received her Ph.D. from the University of North Carolina at Chapel Hill in 1991. She has published on the dramatic poetry of W.H. Auden and on collaborative writing in the classroom. She is currently compiling an anthology of ghost stories by American women. She now teaches American literature at Rowan College in New Jersey.

Margaret Rozga is an associate professor of English at the University of Wisconsin Center-Waukesha County, where she teaches composition and contemporary literature. Her poems have appeared in many journals.

A. LaVonne Brown Ruoff is professor of English at the University of Illinois at Chicago. Her publications include *American Indian Literatures* and *Redefining American Literary History,* edited with Jerry W. Ward, Jr., both published by the Modern Language Association. Ruoff directed NEH Summer Seminars for College Teachers on American Indian Literatures in 1994, 1989, 1983, and 1979; she received an NEH fellowship in 1993 and a research grant in 1981.

Amy Shoenberger is an undergraduate English major at Youngstown State University. She is currently editor in chief of YSU's student literary publication, *The Penguin Review.* She plans to pursue an M.F.A. in creative writing and a Ph.D. in English. This is her first scholarly publication.

Barbara Shollar is author and editor of several books on education, collaborative learning, and the teaching of writing and academic literacy, as well as of *The Longman Anthology of World Literature by Women, 1875–1975.* Forthcoming publications include her book *Writing Ethnicity/Writing Modernity: The Autobiographies of American Jewish Women* and an introduction to the reprint of Pauline Leader's *And No Birds Sing*. She currently teaches at Queens College and serves as a consultant to the New York City Board of Education and other non-profit agencies.

Gail K. Smith is assistant professor of English at Marquette University, where she teaches American literature. She is completing a book on Harriet Beecher Stowe and beginning a study of the image of the epidemic in nineteenth-century American literature and religion.

Index